C000221827

ON THE ROAD
WITH U'S AND BLUES

ON THE ROAD
WITH U'S AND BLUES

CARL MARSTON

With photographs by Warren Page

A regional reporter's
rip-roaring tour of 124
Football League and
Premier League press
boxes over 30 years,
following the fortunes
of Colchester United
and Ipswich Town

DB
PUBLISHING

Front page images: Main, Layer Road, the former home of Colchester United; Top inset, the author Carl Marston, working at the Ricoh Arena; Bottom inset, former Ipswich Town manager Roy Keane. All pics: (WP)

First published 2021 by DB Publishing, an imprint of JMD Media Ltd, Nottingham, United Kingdom.

Copyright © Carl Marston

Picture credits: (WP) - Warren Page. (CM) - Carl Marston

All Rights Reserved. No part of this publication may be reproduced, stored in a retrieval system, or transmitted in any form, or by any means, electronic, mechanical, photocopying, recording or otherwise without the prior permission in writing of the copyright holders, nor be otherwise circulated in any form or binding or cover other than in which it is published and without a similar condition being imposed on the subsequent publisher.

ISBN 9781780916224

Printed in the UK

CONTENTS

ACKNOWLEDGEMENTS

I AM deeply indebted to my good friend – and fine photographer – Warren Page for the bulk of the images in this book. I have yet to come across a better snapper in all my years as a football journalist. Looking back, I have probably spent more hours with Warren on each Saturday, on average, than with my own wife. It was appropriate, then, that Warren should take the pictures at our wedding, just a few weeks after Colchester United had won promotion to the Championship in 2006.

In the various press boxes, up and down the land, I have sat alongside several scribes from the *Colchester (Daily) Gazette*, including Francis Ponder in the early years, John Pakey in the middle years, and Jon Waldron in the later years, with occasional guest appearances from the likes of Matt Plummer and Simon Spurgeon. And I have been treated to the dulcet tones of radio gurus Glenn Speller and Neil Kelly, from BBC Essex, for most of the last 30 years. Glenn's habit of producing chocolate bars of bewildering variety during the half-time interval has always been welcome. From my own publication, the *East Anglian Daily Times*, I had the good fortune to follow in the footsteps of Neal Manning as Colchester United reporter from 1992, with colleagues such as Mike Bacon, Chris Brammer and Dave Vincent stepping in occasionally as deputies, while my trips with Ipswich Town have been all the richer in the company of such doyens of the trade as Tony Garnett, Dave Allard and Elvin King, all from an age when newspapers ruled the roost. In later years, Dave Gooderham, Stuart Watson and Andy Warren have all reported on Town for the newspaper.

At Layer Road, old-timers Bernie Webber and Hal Mason sat at either end of the press box during my formative years, an inspiration to us all. Matt Hudson and David Gregory at Colchester, and Steve Pearce at Ipswich, have always been very helpful in their press officer roles, under various job titles. Others I have had the pleasure of brushing shoulders with over the last three decades, in various capacities, include Ben Fryer, Robin Chipperfield, Jonathan Overend, Steve Houghton, Georgie Bingham, Kelly McCormack, Steve Waller, Richard Blaxall, Bryan Knights, Brenner Woolley, Dave Buckingham, Steve Mellon, Derek Davis, Peter Harlow, Donovan Blake, Tom Williams, Dave Cockburn, Mel Henderson, Nick Garnham, Huw Tubervill, Robin Scott-Elliot, Jim French, Victoria

Polley, Ross Halls, Mark Heath, Ronnie Smyth, Roger Hebert, Chris Liddamore, Robert Hadgraft, Tony Kinsella, Mick Mills; the list is seemingly endless.

Finally, I thank my mum and dad, Coral and Eric, for nurturing my love for sport and writing, and my wife Helen plus step-sons Jack and Harry for putting up with my often colourful language when the Wi-Fi has failed or stories have been lost somewhere in outer space. Also my nephew Matt Le Poidevin, a Colchester supporter with a soft spot for the giant hot dog, a delicacy of the Colchester Community Stadium, and a fellow fan of the 1970s hairstyle.

INTRODUCTION –
PRINT THE TRUTH

A PRE-MATCH pie in the press box and a post-match interview in the press lounge, sandwiching a frantic 90 minutes or so of grappling with the identity of goalscorers, weak phone connections and unreliable Wi-Fi. Such has been the life of the much-travelled regional football reporter over the last 30-odd years, at least in my case.

Plenty of perks, but plenty of misery as well. Complimentary press passes do come at a cost, often in the form of missed newspaper deadlines, or angry managers, usually baying for your blood after an ill-judged headline (that you haven't even written!). I guess what I'm saying is that it's not all about the free food, or the chance to pass the time of day with a Roy Keane or a Kevin Keegan. There are days when the sausage rolls have all been eaten, and when a manager has slipped away without comment.

I have certainly not had the privilege of wolfing down never-ending hot dinners in the vast majority of press lounges up and down the land. There are a few notable exceptions, courtesy of the odd sortie to the Emirates, Stamford Bridge or Old Trafford. But a complimentary hot dinner, or warm lunch, is not why you spend a few wistful hours in the comfort of the press havens at Spotland, Priestfield, the Crown Ground or Field Mill. If it was then you would be a sorely disappointed and very hungry hack.

The quality of a hot dog, the price of a pint and the strength of the tea/coffee/Bovril/hot chocolate/dubious vegetable soup can rank very highly on a football fans' list of priorities when travelling the length and breadth of the country in pursuit of happiness (or more likely misery).

More often than not, as the stats prove in the away columns of football league tables at every level of the pyramid, you are more likely to see your team lose than win while on the road.

But that's not really the point.

The result might be all-important at the time, even all-consuming, but those initial feelings of utter despair mellow with age as each season drifts by.

What you are left with are mostly happy memories of visits to far-flung football stadia; the sights, sounds, smells. Sure, the results remain a constant. They will never change, but perversely there is often more to be gained in the long-term from witnessing your team slither to a demoralising defeat at Huish Park, the home of Yeovil, than basking in the glory of a cup success at Anfield. Well, perhaps not. But the winning isn't everything, just as the availability of a roast in the press lounge is not crucial. A cold cuppa at Brunton Park can be more welcome than a hot cut of meat at Wembley, and more prized in my eyes at least.

What follows is my own journey as a local press hound to all corners of England and Wales, scaling dicey steps, squatting in cramped, sweaty boxes perched somewhere in the main stand, often peering through filthy glass and usually with a pillar or a column or a stubborn home supporter standing in the way of one of the goals.

As one desperate Colchester United fan told me in no uncertain terms on recognising my wily figure and scruffy beard in a nondescript motorway services station, I think somewhere up the M6, 'Print the truth, print the truth!' Though this is easier said than done when you've just spent a Saturday afternoon blessed with a view that only extends to one of the two penalty areas. That's when a slice of poetic license can come in handy. 'Print the truth' as much as you can, but sometimes you have to embellish just a little bit, especially when the away manager and his players are reluctant to spill the beans on how the hosts' sixth goal went in during the post-match press conference taking place in light drizzle beside a muddy dugout, with a couple of lawnmowers droning as they are pushed up and down the pitch by energetic members of the ground staff. That's when the identity of the deliverer of the cross for that sixth goal, before the internet took hold and social networking was born, might be a bit hazy. An educated guess, assuming the right-winger crossed from the right flank, was not always the right one.

Still, with regards all that follows here, I will endeavour to 'print the truth'.

I became a sports writer for my local newspaper, the *East Anglian Daily Times*, an Ipswich-based regional daily with two sister papers, the *Evening Star* and the *Green 'Un* football paper for good measure, back in 1989.

And there I have remained for the next 30-odd years, spilling across four decades. That's not actually strictly true, seeing as though the offices did physically move, although only by a matter of a few hundred metres to sit in the shadow of Portman Road, the home of Ipswich Town FC.

A walk of a few feet took me from the Archant sports desk to the football stadium.

My football reporting career has never reached any great heights, but I have had the good fortune to visit more than 120 different Football League grounds over the last 31 years. I cut my teeth, and craned my neck, plotting Cambridge United's dramatic rise from fourth-tier minnows to Premier League hopefuls, competing for a place in the inaugural Premier League of 1992 by dint of the play-offs where they lost to Leicester City in the semi-finals, thanks to manager John Beck's infamous route-one football (a harsh description, I always felt, for a team that utilised wingers and good old-fashioned hard graft). Granted, it was not very pretty, but it was very, very effective.

Cambridge's brush with the Premier League over, I found more solid ground following the fortunes of Colchester United from 1992 for more than a quarter-of-a-century.

My love affair with the Essex-based U's blossomed, initially with Roy McDonough, one of football's bad boys pulling the strings at an old and dilapidated Layer Road, which has long since been bulldozed to become part of a housing estate. McDonough, the former centre-forward, picked up 22 red cards during his professional career, an impressive collection.

After McDonough there was George Burley for six months, before he committed the cardinal sin, in U's fans' eyes, of becoming the Ipswich manager, Scouser Steve Wignall with two Wembley outings, Mick Wadsworth with a brief tenure in 1999, and a trio of long-term bosses in Steve Whitton (1999–2003), Phil Parkinson (2003–'06) and Geraint Williams (2006–'08).

These were heady times at Colchester, the best of times, with two years in the Championship topped by an FA Cup trip to José Mourinho's Chelsea. It has been back to the real world since 2008, however, with a return to the third tier and then the fourth under a succession of managers – big names Paul Lambert and Aidy Boothroyd, an elder statesman in John Ward, followed by some appointments from within via the Academy in Joe Dunne, Tony Humes, John McGreal, Steve Ball and Wayne Brown, a trend briefly abandoned in favour of an unsuccessful but mercifully short stint under West Ham stalwart Kevin Keen, and more recently Hayden Mullins.

Over the years there have been two promotions, two relegations, two Wembley appearances and an unprecedented tenth-placed finish in the Championship, encompassing more than 1,100 games, several laptops, a few mobile phones, hundreds of pens and pads, pairs of spectacles getting stronger by the year, and more miles on the road than I care to mention.

Exactly 16 miles down the road, more specifically 16 miles in a north-easterly direction along the A12, over the River Stour (the county boundary) and into Suffolk, I have also been a regular at the aforementioned Portman Road on and off since the 1970s.

Initially as a young supporter, basking in the glory of those golden days under Sir Bobby Robson, and then as an occasional Town reporter (the equivalent of a supply teacher, I suppose) during the 1990s, I temporarily switched allegiance from Colchester to Ipswich for two hectic seasons in 2009/10 and 2010/11, which included the whole of Roy Keane's fateful stay on the Portman Road hot-seat. There was never a dull moment covering Keane's Town, especially in the press lounge frequenting each and every one of the Irishman's lengthy press conferences, which often had more in common with a trip to the theatre than a mundane series of football interviews, due to the sheer size of the press gatherings. The newspaper reporters, radio reps and TV interviewers came up from London, and even across from Dublin, to take note of (or pay homage to) Keane's musings. The Portman Road press lounge was often full to the rafters. The sleepy Suffolk club had never seen anything like it before, even during the Sir Alf Ramsey and Sir Bobby Robson eras, and nor had I. Every Keane conference was an event in its own right.

But the closest I have actually come to being squeezed out of a press conference was at a makeshift press venue at Layer Road (the bar area) when ex-England and Tottenham talisman Teddy Sheringham was unveiled as Colchester's new striker, at the ripe age of 41, back in the summer of 2007, having been released by West Ham. The U's were relegated that season, Sheringham having scored just three goals and having made just three appearances since the turn of the year. He could take solace from the fact that he was the oldest player in the top four divisions that season, and he did get to play in the U's final match at Layer Road as a 62nd-minute substitute in a 1-0 defeat to Stoke City, for whom Richard Cresswell became the last player to score a league goal at the Us old ground.

It was the U's first relegation in 18 years, since they disappeared out of the Football League for a couple of seasons in 1990. Sheringham therefore retired on a low note, and the U's began life back in the third tier at their new ground, within a stone's throw of the A12, the same road which took Sheringham back home to London.

As a footnote to the Keane reign at Ipswich, so rudely interrupted by that Sheringham aside, and by contrast to the lively press gatherings in the lounge upstairs, I have to report that, alas, there was more than a dull moment or two in the actual press box, watching Keane's team fail dismally on the pitch most Saturday afternoons and on the occasional Tuesday evening.

On the road, I'd like to say that everything has always run smoothly with regards delivering clean, prompt copy to the newspaper, but there have been many hiccups and minor disasters scattered over the various decades.

For instance, there was the occasion of me being left behind by the team coach after a Third Division fixture down in Devon at Plainmoor, the home of Torquay United. The year was 1994 and George Burley was the Colchester manager. In those days, I used to travel on the team coach, on occasions sitting near the front of the bus behind the management team, with the players spread behind, usually a couple of card schools on the go, the usual footy set-up. But this was no ordinary afternoon. Paul Trollope had given Torquay an early lead, an advantage they held until after the hour before five goals crammed into 26 minutes left the final honours even at 3-3. Three times the U's fell behind, and three times they equalised, forcing me to hastily rewrite my introduction more than once to meet the tight deadline for the Saturday night *Green 'Un*. Home striker Duane Darby put the Gulls 3-2 up on 88 minutes; visiting midfielder Tony Dennis equalised a mere 60 seconds later. You couldn't even afford to blink. The deadline was met, just, but when I finally emerged from the main entrance of Plainmoor to find the team coach, there were no signs of life. The coach had gone, the U's contingent obviously keen to escape the English Riviera after such an energy-sapping afternoon of high drama.

I eventually tracked down a loitering steward who suggested that the team had perhaps stopped off at the local chippy to collect a massive order of fish and chips (in the region of 20 portions – those were the days of just three substitutes, and a bare minimum number of backroom staff, not seven subs and an assortment of coaches). This prompted me to run down the road with my laptop case flying off my shoulder, like a charging bull, in search of the chippy and hopefully a coach, decked in blue and white, pulled up outside. No such luck.

I trudged back to Plainmoor and sat down on a wall to count my cash. Enough money to perhaps book into a seedy bed and breakfast but not enough to get home on the train the following day. I had no bank cards, no cheque book, no ticket home, no hope. Just when I was on the point of leaving the home of Torquay United to find the cheapest, dingiest B&B in town, something wonderful happened. The coach suddenly came into view, around a corner, and pulled up in front of me in an otherwise deserted car park. Apparently, Burley himself, or perhaps his physio/right-hand man Brian Owen, had spotted my absence several miles out of town, and so the coach had turned around and returned to pick me up – me! A still wet-behind-the-ears, insignificant local reporter. I have rarely felt relief like it, saved from a fate worse than a night at Fawlty Towers. To top it all, they had saved me a portion of fish and chips as well.

Since then, I have never had a bad thing to say about Colchester United, or George Burley!

Also, since that incident I have mostly travelled to away games in the car. Not necessarily more reliable, but at least it cuts out the danger of being left behind 'at the end of the day' (I couldn't write a football-related book without including that irritatingly popular phrase).

Other mishaps have befallen me.

My laptop crackled, blinked and briefly took on the appearance of a kaleidoscope before dying a death during a match at Colchester's new Community Stadium. This was due to heavy, driving rain sweeping through the open press section, situated low down to the left of the players' tunnel. The computer of a fellow U's hack, Jonathan Waldron of the *Colchester Gazette*, suffered the same fate. Let down by our drowned machinery, we were both late with our reports for our respective websites that evening.

Newspaper deadlines have also been severely tested by pitch invasions, an infrequent but frustrating aspect of the game. Two spring to mind in particular, at Doncaster Rovers' tumbledown former home at Belle Vue, and at Leyton Orient's Brisbane Road. On both occasions, Colchester were the visitors, hence my presence in the press boxes, and on both occasions the respective hosts, Rovers in 1998 and the O's in 2017, were about to be relegated out of the Football League. I had sympathy for both clubs' causes. I never like to see clubs steeped in tradition disappear through the Football League trapdoor and land on the non-league stage with a bump, but when their organised pitch invasions cause me to miss a deadline, well, that's enough to test my patience. Fortunately, Doncaster returned to the Football League after five years, while it took the O's just one season to return to the dizzy heights of the fourth tier.

Naturally, there have also been struggles to make kick-off times due to the perils of motorway travel.

On my way to Sunderland on a 505-mile round trip, we travelling press corps suffered a puncture just two miles into our journey, just past a church in the tiny village of Westley, on the outskirts of Bury St Edmunds. We ground to a halt just off the slip road leading to the A14 and fitted a temporary spare tyre before retracing our steps back to my home driveway to change cars. John Pakey, another of the *Colchester Gazette* sports gurus, had ironically offered to drive that day, a rare treat, and it was his pool car that had failed to get us more than two miles down the road towards our Wearside destination. I had been looking forward to a day of non-driving but instead I had to take to the wheel of my own vehicle and set off, for a second time, for Sunderland, 90 minutes after the scheduled departure.

We still made it to the Stadium of Light on a trip devoid of comfort breaks (or garage pasties/pies), before the official team sheets landed in the press lounge, always a good sign, but there have been other times when I have arrived well after the line-ups have been distributed to the gaggle of reporters. For a visit to Bristol City's Ashton Gate, I had insisted on watching the televised 100m final from the Sydney Olympics of 2000 before heading off in the direction of the M4 and the West Country. Hampered by heavy traffic, and no reservation slot in the official car park, I eventually took my seat in the heavily occupied press box at 2.59pm, just in time to see the teams kick off. A minor triumph, although I guess it was sod's law that Colchester should score inside the first two minutes, and that I should miss it due to someone walking past my line of vision at just the moment when striker Tony Lock, enjoying a rare start, slotted home. Lock did not score that many goals, a mere 13 in 105 league appearances (60 of which were substitute outings), so it was galling to miss one of his finest moments.

I have only ever missed the start of one match. That was on a Friday night, the worst time to travel, when all the press reps from Essex arrived en masse (ie. in the same car) at the Racecourse Ground, the home of Wrexham FC, 20 minutes after the advertised kick-off time of 7.45pm, on the last day of October 2003. The score was goalless when we caused a mini stir by bursting into the Wrexham press box like a bunch of gatecrashers at a party. The local press guys all agreed that we had missed absolutely nothing, just 20 minutes of a nondescript third-tier clash, though we only have their word for it to this day. The match ended in a 1-0 victory for Colchester courtesy of a 35th-minute winner from Wayne Andrews – I know this, because no one walked in front of me for that goal.

The technology has changed over the years. When I first started out, I would leave the house with a 'mobile' telephone almost the size of my car (and it wasn't a small Reliant Robin). My huge Motorola of the late 1980s had a massive battery, as big as a picnic hamper, which I took to every football ground in order to convey my words of wisdom down the line to a copy-taker, usually Pam (a formidable lady) or Midge (a scary lady), who were seated back at base camp, namely the office. I would ring over several instalments during the course of the 90 minutes, which all fitted seamlessly into a full match report, topped by a scoreline and an intro sent at the full-time whistle. I remember these days clearly, not least because whenever I tapped in the numbers to dial up Pam or Midge, the whole press box and immediate surrounding area, especially in the cramped quarters of the Abbey Stadium, the home of Cambridge United, would reverberate to the sound of the pressed digits. I always felt like a few thousand fans were then primed to listen to my poorly constructed few paragraphs of copy.

Then of course the mobile phones started to slim down to below suitcase size, the laptops became widespread, newspaper websites emerged and then came the joys of e-mail, social networking sites, tweets, live blogs, vlogs, podcasts and alike. I love my iPhone but I do miss my old Motorola and the accompanying shoulder ache that came with carrying it from the car to the stadium.

I have spent many, many hours in the car with Warren Page, a work colleague and photographer who has seen just as many matches as me over the years, though often while sitting in the rain by a corner flag, sheltering from the sleet down a touchline, or squinting into a low sun by the dugouts. In the early days, before the digital age, I would sometimes have to drive Warren (or give him my car keys) to the nearest newspaper office so that he could get his negatives developed and photographs processed, such as a visit to Wigan Athletic's old Springfield Park stadium, and the nearby *Wigan Post*. You had to adapt in those days. Now, one click of the iPhone and I can upload my own grainy picture to a tweet or a story. More speed, greater quantity, shame about the quality.

Fortunately, a wide selection of Warren's stunning action shots comfortably outnumber my own miserable iPhone offerings across the pages of this book.

I could ramble on, and on. Frozen pitches, dressing room lock-ins, snowdrifts, colleagues being locked in toilets, dodgy press pies, stubborn stewards, frosty post-match interviews, the fierce glare of a manager (usually Roy Keane), the angry phone calls of a manager (never Roy Keane), leaking pens, dodgy Wi-Fi, flat car batteries, flat laptop batteries, mistaken identities (usually goalscorers), irate players (usually due to receiving a poor rating out of ten), unhappy player relatives (again usually due to a below-average rating for their precious son or nephew), happy fans and unhappy fans.

But now it's time for a spot of ground-hopping, big-style. And I will try to 'always print the truth'.

SECTION ONE –
THE EARLY 1990s

1 ABBEY STADIUM

Club: Cambridge United
Founded: 1912 (as Abbey United)
Ground: Abbey Stadium (since 1932)
First visit: 26 January 1991; Cambridge 2 Middlesbrough 0

This was home-from-home, rather than an 'away' ground, during the early 1990s when I had the good fortune to witness a good portion of the John Beck era at Cambridge United.

Not that the brand of football was particularly pleasing to the eye, with Beck being an exponent of the merits of the long ball, but because, a bit like Roy Keane's ill-fated time further eastwards along the A14 at Ipswich Town, there was always something going on behind the scenes.

Unlike the Keane era, which brought little more than misery and certainly little in the way of footballing success to Portman Road – with the exception of a League Cup run all the way to the semi-finals, and a two-legged tussle with Arsenal – the Beck days at the Abbey are regarded as the most successful chapter in Cambridge United's history. Successive promotions from the fourth tier to the second tier were followed by a remarkable season in the old Second Division which almost culminated in promotion to the new Premier League.

There are many legendary tales surrounding these colourful years under Beck's stewardship. As a former regular visitor to the Abbey Stadium press box, perched to the rear of the Main Stand on the east side of the ground, closer to the Allotments End, I was aware of many of Beck's pranks/tactics unfolding on the pitch; but keeping my ear to the ground, I was also aware of a few more goings-on inside the dressing rooms.

The obvious included leaving the grass long near the corner flags, to halt the ball and so facilitate Cambridge's direct, long-ball approach. Humping the ball up long and high gave wingers of the calibre of Lee Philpott and Michael Cheetham something to chase. The not-quite-so-obvious, but much-discussed, was the lack of hot water in the away dressing room, plus the heaters being turned up full blast to leave the visitors a little jaded. As for the home players, their senses were sharpened by buckets of cold water being chucked over them before kick-off, and were constantly being instructed not to take more than one touch of the ball, and to favour the long pass over the short pass.

The press box, stuffy and compact, with too many journalists and too little air, was a reality check for all the national hacks who descended from London during the glory years. It had been built in 1970, following the club's successful election to the Football League. There was a press overspill in front of the box, basically a small row of seats in the Main Stand, which had the advantage of fresh air, but the box was where it all happened and where, in those early days, the all-important telephone landlines were shared out, usually just a few minutes before kick-off.

The pitch at the Abbey Stadium was a leveller – just how Beck liked it – and had in fact been out of bounds for the fortnight leading up to my first press trip, an FA Cup fourth round tie against Middlesbrough in January of 1991, due to drainage problems. And in the week before the visit of Sheffield Wednesday, for the next round of the cup, 350 tons of snow had been removed from the pitch on the Tuesday, and a further 500 tons on the Thursday. Cambridge won that one 4-0.

Back to the Boro visit and my huge old 'portable' phone, with the massive battery, took up the whole of my portion of the long press table. No room for anything else.

The view from the press box at the Abbey Stadium, complete with the all-important kettle. (CM)

John Taylor, a 26-year-old striker recruited from non-league Sudbury Town (later amalgamated with Sudbury Wanderers to form AFC Sudbury) for a mere £1,000, scored both goals in a 2-0 win. The Abbey Stadium was rocking that afternoon, though not in the jam-packed press box, where elbow room was in short supply. Taylor, in his third season with the U's, headed home the opener from Dion Dublin's 67th-minute cross, and then beat keeper Kevin Poole again ten minutes later after latching on to Philpott's inch-perfect through ball.

Second Division Middlesbrough, who had ex-Ipswich stalwarts John Wark and Trevor Putney in their ranks, were well beaten in front of a near-capacity crowd of 9,531.

After the match, a wily Beck told me, in one of my first post-match interviews, 'There was a lot of door slamming and a lot of shouting going on at half-time, because we weren't playing our usual game. Overall, we probably didn't deserve the win.' Match-winner Taylor was more philosophical, 'If we can beat a Second Division team without playing our best, then we are not doing badly.'

That was the first of many, many visits to the Abbey Stadium, a footballing home that has never looked very appealing from the adjacent Newmarket Road. It's a collection of small club offices and ticket booths, several big advertising boards with giant lettering, and a snug car park which always reminded me of Arthur Daley's rather shady car lot in the TV series *Minder*. It may have been short on good looks, and still is, with an access route rather worryingly known as 'Cut Throat Lane', but it retains a homely feel.

Clambering up the long staircase at the back of the two-tiered Main Stand (built in 1967) has always been a good gauge of my current fitness, and I always enjoyed the view from the press box to the south, with local residents working on their allotments, oblivious to the match, just behind the away fans standing on the former uncovered terrace at the Allotments End. That open terrace was replaced by a new 1,500-seater South Stand in 2001, after permission had been granted to build on some of the land owned by the Whitehill Allotment Society.

My first appearance with Ipswich Town had been 14 months after the aforementioned Middlesbrough clash, on 21 March 1992, when Town and Cambridge were fierce rivals for promotion to the new Premier League. Town were destined to be champions, but they had to dig deep to a secure a 1-1 draw at the Abbey, a result which suited them far more than it did Beck's troops. Simon Milton drilled the visitors into a 53rd-minute lead, only for the hosts to net a controversial equaliser just three minutes later – defender Mick Heathcote appeared to foul Town keeper Craig Forrest before back-heeling the loose ball into the net.

Boss Beck, who had earlier made a strange decision to substitute striker Steve Claridge after just 22 minutes – Claridge walked straight to the dressing room with his head bowed – was his usual mischievous self during the post-match press gathering. Referring to Heathcote's controversial goal, Beck said, 'I thought Mick's contribution was marvellous.'

Priceless.

As for Colchester United, despite a number of high-scoring encounters and rip-roaring league showdowns, the one visit that has always stuck out was a low-key Auto Windscreens

Shield southern section first round tie on 10 December 1996, played on a Tuesday night in front of a meagre crowd of 1,108. The match was dire, and everyone was gearing up for a long night, spilling over into sudden death extra time and the prospect of a penalty shoot-out, when Steve Whitton somehow squeezed home a low shot past Cambridge custodian Scott Barrett, the former Colchester keeper, to snatch a 1-0 away win in the 89th minute. A surprise end to a dull evening, with the dubious reward of another midweek trek for a second round tie.

So why so memorable? Well, despite assistant manager Whitton's late intervention saving me a mad scramble to meet newspaper deadlines, it was also the first tentative step on a journey all the way to the Football League Trophy Final, and a first visit to Wembley Stadium. True, Wembley still seemed a long, long way off after that sting in the tail at the Abbey Stadium that cold December night, but from small beginnings come great things.

Which is why I have always liked the Abbey.

2 HIGHBURY

Club: Arsenal
Founded: 1886 (as Dial Square)
Ground: Highbury (from 1913 to 2006)
First visit: 9 March 1991; Arsenal 2 Cambridge 1

An FA Cup quarter-final at Highbury, the home of the club with the longest continuous stay in the top flight – running since 1919 – was an unnaturally high benchmark start to my away days as a rookie reporter, in the spring of 1991. It can be strongly argued that it has been downhill from thereon in.

John Beck's unfashionable Cambridge side had already left a scene of destruction behind them in previous rounds, as I had witnessed myself at the Abbey, with Wolves, Middlesbrough and Sheffield Wednesday all booted out of the competition.

As with most first visitors to Highbury, I was overwhelmed by the whole experience, right from the moment I emerged from the Arsenal underground station in north London, the only such station to be named after a football club.

There were the crowds of people walking up Gillespie Road, Avenell Road and the surrounding lanes, with all the various Arsenal-related shops and restaurants en route, from the Gunners Pub on Blackstock Road (A1201) to the Arsenal Fish Bar just down the road. Everywhere was a riot of red and white, and then there was the noise – a hum of expectation, excited voices at every street corner, followed later by the deafening roar inside the stadium.

The ground itself looked so beguiling from the outside, especially when approaching the glorious Grade II-listed East Stand with its off-white exterior and 'Arsenal Stadium' in bold red lettering, together with the distinctive single horizontal canon of the club crest, sitting proudly high above the main entrance.

With a small-ish pitch (100 metres long, 67 metres wide), tightly surrounded by four main stands, the famous North Bank and Clock End (South Stand) at both ends, and the Art Deco East and West Stands down either side, everything was set up for a cracking atmosphere. My first visit was just before the stadium was upgraded to meet the recommendations of the Taylor Report in the wake of the Hillsborough Stadium disaster of 1989. The huge open terracing at the Clock End, with its famous circular clock – this used to be positioned at the North Bank (formerly known as the Laundry End) until the latter became covered in 1935 – had been upgraded with its own roof and 48 executive boxes in 1989. The North Bank terrace, meanwhile, was destined to be demolished at the end of the following 1991/92 season.

The match was an FA Cup classic; top-flight leaders Arsenal at full strength with David Seaman in goal, Tony Adams and Steve Bould in the heart of defence, and Paul Merson, Alan Smith and Kevin Campbell among the attacking outlets.

Campbell headed home Nigel Winterburn's cross to give the Gunners a half-time lead, only for Dion Dublin to equalise in spectacular fashion by diverting home Michael Cheetham's cross. Adams scrambled home a close-range winner on the hour for George Graham's men. Try as they might, Cambridge could not respond, Dublin having a goalbound shot blocked by Adams, but I do recall the underdogs being given a warm ovation by the appreciative crowd of 42,960 at the final whistle.

Cup football at its best.

Arsenal lost 3-1 in the semis to arch rivals Tottenham, who had been near-neighbours since the Gunners moved from their former home on the south bank of the River Thames in 1913, but Graham's side did go on to win the league, ahead of closest rivals Liverpool and Crystal Palace.

Ten years later and I was back at an almost deserted Highbury, much older and much wiser, to report on an FA Youth Cup third round tie on the night of Wednesday, 14 November 2001.

The U's suffered a 2-0 defeat in the FA Youth Cup at Highbury in December 2002, a year after losing 5-0 at the same ground. Here U's keeper Dean Gerken can only watch the ball fly into his net. (WP)

Arsenal, under Don Howe, predictably cruised to victory against visiting Colchester United with striker David Bentley scoring a first-half hat-trick in a 5-0 win for the holders. The likes of Justin Hoyte (68 senior games for Arsenal, and later 162 for Middlesbrough), John Spicer (Burnley and Doncaster) and Nicky Nicolau (Southend and Barnet) were also in the Arsenal team that night.

Micky Cook, the U's director of youth football, admitted, 'It was men versus boys, really. Perhaps they were a bit overawed by the stadium and the occasion. The lads would have loved to have had another go.'

Still, many of the young U's team that night went on to have good careers in the professional game, including keeper Dean Gerken, the versatile Greg Halford, striker Dean Morgan and defender John White. As for young Gunners hat-trick hero Bentley, he made the grade at Blackburn and Tottenham, but retired in 2014 at the age of 29, citing that he had fallen out of love with football.

However, that November night, as a 17-year-old back in 2001, Bentley was very much in love with the game. Just as I, as a 25-year-old back in 1991, was briefly in love with Highbury.

3 ROOTS HALL

Club: Southend United
Founded: 1906
Ground: Roots Hall (from 1955)
First visit: 4 April 1991; Southend 0 Cambridge 0

Whenever I think about the Roots Hall press box, which I confess is not very often, my back begins to ache. The visiting scribes tend to be allocated seats at the back of the small box, which has a sloping wall that encourages you to lean forward for 90 minutes, hence the back pain going into injury time. The home regulars tend to inhabit the more comfortable front row.

Some of my early visits to Roots Hall, the home of Southend United since 1955, were during the dynamic season of 1991/92, when the East Anglian duo of Ipswich and Cambridge were vying for promotion to the upcoming new Premier League, and the Shrimpers were intent on derailing their respective bandwagons. I went down to the Essex side of the Thames estuary to report on the fortunes of both Town and Cambridge that season, an earlier trip at the back end of the previous Second Division campaign ending in a goalless draw between the two soon-to-be promoted clubs, Southend and Cambridge. Visiting keeper John Vaughan pulled off several spellbinding saves that evening.

They were heady times, crazy times, exciting times, successful times, in an era before the onset of regular football club websites, Twitter (founded in 2006) and YouTube (founded in 2005). I phoned my long-winded but lovingly-composed match reports through to the copy-takers back in the office during those days, rather than grapple with a laptop.

Jamie Cureton celebrates scoring the second of his hat-trick of goals in the U's 3-0 win at Roots Hall in 2007. (WP)

That previous season, both Cambridge (champions) and Southend (runners-up) had been promoted from the old Third Division, so joining a Town side who had finished a disappointing 14th in the second-tier table.

The 1991/92 season was a thriller, and remains one of the best campaigns I have ever followed. Town were crowned champions thanks mainly to a superb home record – 16 wins from 23 at Portman Road – with Middlesbrough in the second automatic promotion slot. Cambridge eventually drifted to fifth, and were beaten by Leicester City in the play-off semi-finals, although it was Kenny Dalglish's Blackburn Rovers who joined Town and Boro in the newly established Premier League. Town doubled Southend, which helped them to the title; by contrast, Cambridge took just one point from six against their old foe, via a 1-1 draw at Roots Hall in December.

Town's visit to Southend, on 4 April 1992, had a sensational ending, Neil Thompson netting a last-gasp wonder goal to rubber-stamp their title credentials. Centre-half Phil Whelan had marked his Town debut with the opening goal. Whelan scored in his next appearance as well, a win over Wolves three days later, but ironically never scored again in a Town shirt. Spencer Prior equalised for David Webb's hosts, but left-back Thompson's stunning long-range shot from wide out on the left, into the top corner, won it.

The away following, housed in the North Stand with its low, barrel-shaped roof improving acoustics – although the many pillars could obstruct the view – went wild. The crowd was 10,003 that day.

Almost exactly 15 years later, on a spanking hot Good Friday early afternoon on 6 February 2007, the away fans in the North Stand were again in terrific voice, although this time they were Colchester United supporters celebrating a 3-0 win over their Essex rivals in the Championship. Jamie Cureton was the man of the moment, clutching on to the match ball while addressing the media after plundering a hat-trick. The stadium had undergone several changes since my early visits, the previous 72-stepped terrace on the South Bank having been mostly sold off in 1988, and eventually replaced with a small two-tiered stand, opened six years later. Blocks of flats overlook this end, to the left of the press box (with its sloping back wall), which is situated in the main East Stand, although the West Stand on the opposite of the pitch is the largest in the ground.

An on-song Cureton, rightly chuffed with his hat-trick, gave interviews in the car park behind the East Stand after the match, which had been beamed across the land, or at least to subscribers of Sky Sports. The evergreen 31-year-old, having broken the deadlock within 38 seconds, scored two more crackers on 63 and 79 minutes to become only the 12th Colchester United player to reach the magic 20-goal target for a Football League campaign. 'I think I'm playing the best football of my career,' announced a sun-kissed Cureton, who had put rival striker Freddy Eastwood in the shade with his performance. 'I've put my head down and got on with it. It's been a great day for me, and the club.' The U's went on to finish tenth in the Championship; the Shrimpers were relegated.

No visit to Roots Hall would be complete without a walk along the seafront, and its impossibly long pier, the longest leisure pier in the world. By coincidence, Southend was to be voted Pier of the Year for 2007, later that year, by the National Piers Society. But by the time I had finished typing up all of Cureton's quotes, for Saturday's newspaper, it was too late to amble along the 1.34 miles of the soon-to-be award-winning pier, especially with a sore back. So I made do with fish and chips instead.

I blamed Jamie Cureton.

4 VICARAGE ROAD

Club: Watford
Founded: 1881 (as Watford Rovers)
Ground: Vicarage Road (from 1922)
First visit: 31 August 1991; Watford 1 Cambridge 3

The only football ground where I used to park at a hospital, the nearby Watford General Hospital (no longer parking for football fans on site), Vicarage Road has undergone a major face-lift in recent years.

Manager Roy Keane pleads with the referee during Town's 2-1 defeat at Watford in 2010. (WP)

My first visit was at the end of August 1991, seven years after Watford's 2-0 defeat in the FA Cup Final to Everton in 1984. Newly promoted Cambridge made it five wins in a row to extend their 100 per cent start to life in the Second Division. Cambridge had not even scored in their previous six visits to Vicarage Road, but goals from Lee Philpott, Steve Claridge and Michael Cheetham steered John Beck's side to a 3-1 win, and second place in the table behind Ipswich. Luther Blissett netted a consolation for the battered hosts, one of 186 goals (148 in the league) he bagged in a record-breaking 503 first-team outings for the club.

Much of the ground was given to open terracing, with fans exposed to the elements. The Vicarage Road End, which was just an earthen bank in the early days, and then an uncovered terrace, was reinvented as a £2.3m all-seater just two years later, for away fans, while the Rookery End was also transformed from a terrace to a seated stand during 1994/95.

However, the stadium was in a transition period when I returned with Ipswich Town, 19 years after my first trip, in March 2010. The old main stand (East Stand), built back in 1922 following the Hertfordshire club's move from Cassio Road, was a virtual no-go area, having been closed for a few years due to safety reasons, although there was still a small section open where the press sat, all on their own, like a colony of lepers. But it wasn't so bad. There was no need for a safety helmet, and tea was served from a temporary building in a corner behind the condemned stand. Managers were interviewed by standing at the entrance to the makeshift tunnel after the match.

It was a Tuesday night fixture so newspaper deadlines were tight, and a misfiring Wi-Fi had put me well behind schedule after the final whistle had sounded on Watford's 2-1 home win. It was a miserable evening for Ipswich, and manager Roy Keane in particular, and it turned into a miserable one for me as well. Championship strugglers Town were awful in the first half and were lucky to only be trailing to a seventh-minute free kick by Arsenal loanee Henri Lansbury at half-time. The Hornets struck the woodwork twice, and although Jack Colback threatened to rescue a point for the visitors with a 68th-minute equaliser, striker Will Hoskins lashed home the winner with 13 minutes remaining.

Keane locked the dressing room for an hour, after the final whistle – or at least the door never opened – leaving me to consider tearing out my hair, waiting for some back-page quotes. He finally emerged, a little before 11pm, still seething.

'We were shocking, and I'd have taken four or five players off, if the rules had allowed. It was rubbish, to start playing an hour late,' blasted Keane. He might have been late himself, addressing the small huddle of press still inside the ground, but as usual his words did not disappoint; more than enough to fill that gaping hole on the back page. Gathering momentum, he continued, 'There'll be changes for Saturday, you can bet on that. It just shows what a big, big job I have ahead of me. Watford wanted to win more than us, and that's very difficult for me to swallow. I'm not happy.'

I had become used to Keane spending extra time with his players in the dressing room. It comes with the territory. It had happened at Crystal Palace following a 3-1 loss the previous Boxing Day, and also at Peterborough's London Road and Blackpool's Bloomfield Road following more recent defeats, but the Irishman set a new record at Vicarage Road for the longest gap between the final whistle and his appearance for the press conference. Some things are worth waiting for – just not on a midweek night with deadlines looming!

The backdrop of a dilapidated main stand was quite poignant that night, matching Town's sombre mood. These days, that old stand has been replaced by the impressive Sir Elton John Stand, down the east side of the ground. Opened at the end of 2014, with lifelong fan Sir Elton, former owner and chairman, attending the opening ceremony, it features a central bank of red seats, flanked by a section of yellow seats. A splash of bright colour and comfort, unrecognisable from the condemned stand that hosted Keane's blast of a few years earlier.

On the subject of 'colour', not many clubs have dabbled in such a bewildering array of colour schemes, in terms of their kit, than Watford. Red, green and yellow were prevalent during the early seasons, including a hooped pattern featuring all three colours. A more sedate black and white was introduced in 1909, superseded by an all-royal blue strip in the 1920s and then gold and black from 1959, at which point the club embraced the Hornets nickname. This lasted until the 1970s, when red was introduced and the gold was replaced by yellow.

Sunglasses are advised, to soften the glare.

Former hospital parking, condemned grandstands, the theme tune to nostalgic TV police drama series *Z-Cars* to greet the teams, ever-changing garish colours and a tendency to frustrate Roy Keane – Watford has never been a club to conform.

That was never more evident than during the mid-1970s to the early 1980s, when the Hornets rose from the Football League basement to the top of the First Division (92nd to first) in a seven-year period from 1975, mostly under manager Graham Taylor. Not bad for a club that began life in the early 1880s with a small group of boys kicking a ball around Cassiobury Park, an estate owned by the Earl of Essex, under the name of Watford Rovers.

Expect the unexpected at Vicarage Road.

5 THE DEN

Club: Millwall
Founded: 1885 (as Millwall Rovers)
Ground: The Den (1910 to 1993)
First visit: 7 September 1991; Millwall 1 Cambridge 2

'No one likes us, we don't care.' So sing the Millwall faithful, and that was certainly the case at their infamous old home.

Hostile, dark, dank, intimidating, edgy. The Den had a bad reputation, and it was well-earned. I was not disappointed when I paid my first visit, for a Second Division clash again featuring John Beck's upwardly mobile Cambridge United, in the autumn

Flashback: the author's match report of Cambridge's surprise 2-1 win at Millwall in 1991.

Cambridge silence The Den

By Carl Marston

Millwall 1, Cambridge Utd 2

BATTLING Cambridge, ravaged by injury and trailing to a fifth minute penalty, staged a thrilling comeback to leave the home Lions licking their wounds after a memorable Second Division clash at the Den on Saturday.

Not many teams claw back a deficit at he home of Millwall, a daunting arena with impassioned home supporters surrounding the pitch on all sides, but newly-promoted Cambridge stunned he locals with a gutsy recovery culminating in a fairytale winner for 7-year-old Gary Rowett.

That was the best performance I've een from a Cambridge side since I've een involved with the club," enthused nited manager John Beck after a nailting finale. Bury St. Edmunds referee elvin Morton kept the nerve-ends tining by adding on six minutes of injury-ne.

"It was a victory against all the odds. I ve an injury list as long as my arm with ly 13 fit players on the staff at the ment, and I thought that we had no nce after falling behind in the first minutes," added Beck.

Michael Cheetham had an outstand- game, both on the right flank and up nt, and it was his equalising goal that un substitute Rowett with the chance

ing, while central defender Phil Chapple was not fully fit.

And there was misery for the visitors when Millwall were awarded a penalty in their very first attack. United keeper John Vaughan was adjudged to have felled Chris Armstrong, and up stepped Paul Kerr to convert the spot kick.

Encroachment

There was a momentary reprieve for Cambridge when referee Morton spotted an encroachment into the area before Kerr's conversion, but the Millwall midfielder again beat Vaughan with the re-take, slotting the ball low into the right-hand corner.

There was a real danger that shell-shocked Cambridge would be blown aside by the rampaging Lions in this fiery opening, and new signing Armstrong, bought from Fourth Division Wrexham for just £75,000 in the close-season, gave Gary Clayton a testing time with his elusive running.

And the home side were appealing for a second penalty just a minute after the goal. Armstrong's electric speed and precise cross saw John Colquhoun, the former Hearts favourite, fall in the six-yard box while trying to convert the chance.

John Taylor walked sadly off the pitch with a head injury.

This meant a reshuffle with Cheetham joining Steve Claridge up front and young Rowett, making his first senior appearance, patrolling the right wing.

The tide turned in dramatic fashion in the 32nd minute. A long free-kick from left-back Alan Kimble caught the Millwall defence napping, and Cheetham rifled a ten-yard effort into the roof of the net.

It was a shock equaliser, but there was more joy for Cambridge when, after soaking up intense pressure, they stole the points with a "Roy of the Rovers" goal from Rowett.

Lee Philpott provided the perfect cross for Rowett, from 15 yards out, to rise high and send a glorious header past keeper Aidan Davison, the ball ending up wedged in a stanchion of the Millwall goal.

A product of the YTS scheme, Rowett will remember his first senior goal forever, and Cambridge survived some tense final moments with Clayton clearing one effort off the goal-line to register their fourth league win of the season.

MILLWALL: Davison, Wood, Cooper Bogie, Thompson (sub. Cunningham in 50t of 1991. From the moment that I parked the car (it felt like I had abandoned it), near a railway embankment in New Cross, to the short walk to the ground, and the afternoon spent in the press box surrounded by home fans spitting venom, and hurling abuse at the opposition and the officials, I was immersed in the unique Millwall experience.

The stadium had seen better days, not surprising with the move to a new ground less than two years down the road. Plenty of cold, concrete terracing, with away fans stuck in a corner behind a giant floodlight pylon. This was proper home advantage. No wonder most away fans, and no doubt the press, put The Den on top of their list of the most feared grounds in England. It is also perhaps no surprise that Millwall, taking advantage of their many overawed, intimidated visitors, have held the record for scoring the most home league goals in a season for nearly 100 years, a landmark achieved back in 1927/28 when they plundered 87 at The Den during their Third Division South campaign.

Millwall had moved south of the river for the first time, from their former Isle of Dogs base, to take up residency at their fifth ground in 1910, in New Cross. The Den was a magnet for Surrey Dockers, although fans from their early days in the East End of London continued to support them by walking through the Greenwich Foot Tunnel under the Thames. The ground was sparse, made up of three huge terraces with just one area for seating in the Main Stand, built in 1948 after the old one had been burnt down during the Second World War. The North Terrace was also extensively bombed during the Blitz, forcing the Lions to play elsewhere in London for a few months.

The stadium did undergo a refurbishment during the 1980s, just before my visit, although it made little difference to the general impression. It was merely 'touched up'

Mick McCarthy, a future Ipswich manager, who was the Millwall boss during their defeat to Cambridge in 1991. (WP)

with new seats, new toilets, new turnstiles and alike. Otherwise, the old terraces with their yellow crash barriers were the same, only partially covered to the rear by shrunken, narrow roofs, while the surrounding area was just as squalid and sinister as always, a sprawl of scrap yards, railroads, dark tunnels and hole-ridden car parks. The walk along the narrow cobbled Cold Blow Lane, or the approach to the Ilderton Road End, was not for the faint-hearted on a Tuesday night.

I expected Cambridge to put up a good fight, they always did, but I didn't think they would have the audacity to beat their hosts and slip quietly away, under the River Thames via the Rotherhithe Tunnel, with all three points. To rub salt into the wounds, Mick McCarthy's Millwall were downed by a rookie, Gary Rowett, who marked his senior debut with the winning goal in a 2-1 success. Ironically, 28 years later Rowett was appointed the manager of Millwall.

The Lions were licking their wounds after this defeat, especially having taken a fifth-minute lead through Paul Kerr's penalty. Keeper John Vaughan upended summer signing Chris Armstrong, a £75,000 buy from Wrexham, and Kerr then beat Vaughan twice from the spot, his first having been ruled out for encroachment. Cambridge could have gone under. Already weakened by the absence of star striker Dion Dublin, skipper Danny O'Shea and key midfielder Richard Wilkins, striker John Taylor also only lasted 20 minutes due to a head injury.

But the tide turned in front of a disbelieving 8,000 Millwall fans. Michael Cheetham rifled home a 32nd-minute equaliser from Alan Kimble's deep free kick, before 17-year-old substitute Rowett, a product of Cambridge's youth team, rose high to head home a 72nd-minute winner past keeper Aidan Davison.

In true John Beck fashion, Rowett was later substituted after missing a tackle in the middle of the park, and duly got an ear-bashing for his troubles in the dressing room.

'That was the best performance I've seen from a Cambridge side since I've been involved with the club,' insisted Beck. 'It was a victory against all the odds. I thought we had no chance after falling behind in the first few minutes.'

Personally, I was just happy to find my car still in one piece that evening.

As a footnote, a few months later I returned for Millwall versus Ipswich Town on 1 February 1992, this time in the back seat of a company car – long-time journalists and Town scribes Tony Garnett and Dave Allard were in the front, so I knew my place – for another second-tier clash. Town won 3-2 with goals from Jason Dozzell, Neil Thompson and Chris Kiwomya, but I remember the trip mostly for a pre-match visit to a nearby public house. The place was virtually empty, and when we asked why, the landlord calmly explained that there had been an 'altercation' the night before, and that someone had died. There was no outline of a body chalked on the floor of the bar, but it was still a bit disconcerting.

We didn't ask any more questions, we just drank up and left. I was already pining for sleepy Suffolk, and we hadn't even got to The Den yet!

6 OLD TRAFFORD

Club: Manchester United
Founded: 1878 (as Newton Heath LYR)
Ground: Old Trafford (since 1910)
First visit: 25 September 1991; Manchester United 3 Cambridge 0

There was a 28-year interlude between my two visits to the famous home of Manchester United, both for League Cup ties, the first against Cambridge United in September of 1991 and the second against Colchester United in December of 2019.

And much had changed during the intervening years.

Just over 30,000 were inside The Theatre of Dreams for the Rumbelows Cup second round first leg on a Wednesday evening for the visit of Cambridge. In the pre-match build-up, Cambridge winger Michael Cheetham admitted, 'Not many of us have ever even been to Old Trafford,' but his hopes of keeping the tie alive were scuppered by a 3-0 defeat.

Alex Ferguson selected a strong squad – they were the European Cup Winners' Cup holders – albeit with the absence of Peter Schmeichel, that most reliable of keepers. Schmeichel was on duty with the Danish team in a European Championship qualifier

The busy press lounge at Old Trafford, including the author's curry and rice, before kick-off against the U's in 2019. (CM)

against the Faroe Islands. His deputy Gary Walsh, making his first appearance of the season, probably had less to do than Schmeichel did against the Faroe Islands that night. Cambridge did weather the United storm for 44 minutes, before Ryan Giggs and Brian McClair scored either side of half-time, and centre-half Steve Bruce netted the third with a trademark firm header from Denis Irwin's corner.

During the early 1990s, around the time of my first visit, the capacity at Old Trafford had shrunk to around 44,000 due to the phasing out of terracing, and the lack of development. But success on the pitch, under Ferguson (he won 38 trophies between 1986 and 2013) helped to engineer dramatic facelifts to all four stands, boosting the capacity to nearly 75,000, making it the largest club football stadium in the UK.

Sited close to the Bridgewater Canal, just off the north end of the Warwick Road in Old Trafford, a suburb of Stretford, Manchester United have been playing their home games there since 1910, with the exception of a lengthy spell during the 1940s when the effects of bombing during the Second World War saw them ground-share with Manchester City at Maine Road. United had already tasted success before their move to Old Trafford, having lifted the First Division title for the first time in 1908, and then winning the FA Cup the following year by beating Bristol City 1-0 in the final at Crystal Palace.

The stadium was a formidable place, even before the dramatic transformation of the 1990s. A roof around the circumference of the ground had been completed by 1973 to create a bowl shape, although the famous Stretford End, which could once house up to 20,000 fans, was still an all-terraced stand when I visited with Cambridge in the autumn of 1991. It was reconstructed the following season.

The press box, in the Sir Bobby Charlton Stand, formerly the South Stand, boasts one of the best views in the country. Okay, so the Wi-Fi has been hit-and-miss over the years, but the media are very well looked after in the middle of the upper section. Extra tiers have been added to the North, West and East Stands, boosting the capacity to just under 75,000. Both ends, the Stretford End and Scoreboard (East) End, look very similar with their larger lower tiers, although the Sir Alex Ferguson (North) Stand is huge with its three-tiered bank of red and white seats. Its sheer bulk is mesmerising.

On my return visit, 28 years later, I filled my boots, or rather stomach, with two helpings of excellent curry in the press lounge, followed by chips at half-time, reported on the rather predictable 3-0 defeat suffered by Colchester United in the EFL League Cup, kick-started by Marcus Rashford's 51st-minute opener, and then enjoyed the relaxed experience of manager Ole Gunnar Solskjaer's post-match interview in the auditorium, a cross between a lecture hall and a theatre. No need to huddle outside a players' tunnel or shiver by a dugout to get the quotes.

That was the nuts-and-bolts account of it, although that visit of 18 December 2019 deserves some meat on the bones because the U's, under John McGreal, did keep mighty Manchester United at bay for the first 50 minutes of a special evening. Backed by 5,000 travelling supporters, the fourth-tier U's defended like their lives depended on it during

A view from the press box at Old Trafford, with United manager Ole Gunnar Solskjaer on the mini TV screen. (CM)

a superb backs-to-the-wall performance in the first half, on what was the Essex club's first visit to Old Trafford.

However, their dreams of causing a hat-trick of big upsets, after knocking out Premier League opponents Crystal Palace and Tottenham via penalty shoot-outs in earlier rounds to reach the quarter-final stage, were dashed by three quickfire goals. Rashford chased on to Nemanja Matic's excellent through ball to break the deadlock and open the floodgates. Solskjaer's men doubled their lead in the 56th minute, U's right-back Ryan Jackson diverting home Mason Greenwood's dangerous cross from inside the six-yard box, while under heavy pressure from Rashford, for an own goal. Anthony Martial added a third on 61 minutes, poking home Rashford's accurate low cross from a matter of a few feet out. The tie was over in a flash.

And so to the auditorium to await a smiling Solskjaer. 'We dominated, created chances, but you are never sure until you get the first goal. Colchester are a hard team to break down,' admitted Solskjaer. U's boss McGreal, more accustomed to talking to two or three rather than 40 or 50 journalists, then took to the stage. 'It was a brilliant journey for the club,' insisted McGreal, referring to his side's proud progress through to the last eight of the competition, not the previous day's trip up the M6.

Old Trafford. What's not to like? The only downers were the traditional pre-match Manchester downpour, which soaked me to the skin between the car park and the media entrance in the South Stand, plus the endless security checks focused on my battered laptop bag, which only contained a laptop, notepad and a bruised banana.

Otherwise, it was five-star treatment, all the way. But did I prefer it to the more down-to-earth (in more ways than one), press experience at near-neighbours Salford City, Rochdale or Oldham? That's a tough one to answer. But the curry was nice.

7 UPTON PARK

Club: West Ham United
Founded: 1895 (as Thames Ironworks, from 1900 as West Ham United)
Ground: Upton Park (1904–2016)
First visit: 22 October 1991; West Ham 2 Cambridge 1

In the days when it was sometimes possible to sneak a press pass for a friend, who had no official press credentials, I drove down to east London with a pal, Neil Carter, who worked nights at the post office in Bury St Edmunds and was an ardent West Ham fan, in October 1991. He also happened to play in the same pool team as me, at our local pub (The Ipswich Arms in Bury St Edmunds), albeit in the 'B' team. I intended to put him to work, gathering a few quotes, to ease the pressures of a midweek deadline.

But Neil actually turned out to be more of a liability than an asset at this Zenith Data Systems Cup (Full Members' Cup) second round tie on a mild Tuesday evening. This was a short-lived competition, from 1985 to 1992, created after English clubs were banned from European competition following the Heysel Stadium disaster.

West Ham, with Billy Bonds on the manager's hot-seat, beat John Beck's Cambridge United 2-1, thanks to a winner from poacher Frank McAvennie, who scrambled home a low cross by Mike Small on the hour, although Small did appear to be in an offside position. Earlier, a delightful chip by powerhouse George Parris had put the hosts 1-0 up just after the half-hour, with young Gary Rowett heading home a 50th-minute equaliser from Lee Philpott's corner past Czech international keeper Ludek Miklosko.

Unfortunately, my mate Neil failed dismally in his role as a post-match interviewer. When Bonds asked the group of journalists whether there were any more questions, at a rather informal, all-standing, post-match gathering, Neil said, 'Yes, can I have your autograph?'

At the time, Upton Park (my preferred title, named after the area and the nearby tube station, as opposed to the Boleyn Ground), still had terracing at both ends, on the North Bank and South Bank, with the 'new' Chicken Run along the east side, which had replaced the famous old Chicken Run (the old wooden stand was topped by a sloping roof and surrounded by wire that made it resemble a chicken run) at the end of the 1960s. The ground felt very tight and compact, dark and enclosed, with players often having to lean back towards the fans standing in the East Stand before launching a long throw into

Upton Park, otherwise know as the Boleyn Ground, the former home of West Ham.

the danger area. No wonder many visiting players found it an intimidating experience, especially if you happened to be a winger or full-back hugging the touchline down that side.

Ironically, although the stadium, on Green Street, was hemmed in by residential roads, it had a very spacious beginning as a bare field, owned by a Roman Catholic School, occasionally used for growing cabbages or potatoes. This led to the pitch being affectionately referred to as the 'Cabbage Patch' or the 'Potato Field' during its formative years. There was no sign of a cabbage, or potato (apart from the chips on sale) during either of my two visits – I did return within a month, again with Cambridge United, although this time Charlton Athletic rather than West Ham were the hosts, for a Second Division clash on 23 November 1991.

Charlton were tenants at Upton Park for one full season, 1991/92, plus part of the following term. They had ground-shared with Crystal Palace at Selhurst Park for the previous six years, until Wimbledon had moved into the Eagles' home as tenants. Understandably, crowds were not big for Charlton home games in this corner of east London, although on balance most Addicks fans preferred it to Selhurst. Cambridge certainly loved it on this particular occasion, goals from the strike force duo of John Taylor and Dion Dublin securing a 2-1 away win in front of a crowd of 6,350.

I remember it as a thunderous encounter, as well as an opportunity for Beck to again cause a stir with his team selection. He dropped leading scorer Steve Claridge for Taylor, who promptly broke the deadlock with a typical Cambridge goal, heading home after a long throw by Richard Wilkins had caused mayhem in the box. Taylor then teed up

Dublin for the second in the 38th minute, much to the delight of the travelling fans on the South Bank terrace. Paul Gorman ensured a nervous finale by heading a late consolation.

'Cambridge deserved to win. They do a job and they are good at it. We are certainly not going to knock Cambridge's style of play, they are a hard side to play against,' admitted Charlton's joint manager Alan Curbishley, who shared the top job with Steve Gritt. Beck confirmed, provocatively, as was his habit, 'Steve Claridge wasn't injured, he was dropped. He didn't play for the good of the team last week against Brighton.'

The Addicks, who narrowly missed out on the play-offs in seventh spot, finally returned to The Valley in December 1992, leaving the Hammers to get on with updating their ground to an all-seater. All four sides of the ground were redeveloped from the mid-1990s onwards, with new stands built at both ends of the ground, and major refurbishments on the east and west sides. I guess it no longer felt so intimidating, though I never did have the chance of a third visit. If I had, I would have kept it quiet and left Neil Carter in the pub!

8 HIGHFIELD ROAD

Club: Coventry City
Founded: 1883 (as Singers FC, 1898 as Coventry City)
Ground: Highfield Road (1899–2005)
First visit: 4 January 1992; Coventry 1 Cambridge 1

Once upon a time, Coventry City were a settled club with a settled home. Highfield Road was their happy abode for more than a century, a traditional venue close to the city centre in the Hillfields district, boasting a close affinity with its fanbase, albeit for the odd fall-out, like the early all-seater experiment of the early 1980s. Sure, parking the car could prove a challenge in the surrounding residential streets – most of them red-bricked terraces – but the atmosphere within the stadium was often electric, the pitch was one of the largest and best in the country, and the team played in the top flight for 34 consecutive seasons until 2001.

Many of the fans used to walk from the city centre, along crowded streets and past full and noisy pubs; others used to cycle, and leave their bikes near Primrose Hill Park. There was always a buzz of expectation, a sense of occasion. Above all, there was a sense of community.

But those days are over, and have been for a while.

Since leaving Highfield Road after a 106-year stay in 2005, the Sky Blues have led an uncertain life, often on the road. They played at the newly built Ricoh Arena from 2005 until 2013, when a row over rent saw them move to Northampton Town's Sixfields, a 70-mile round trip. After a year at Sixfields, the Sky Blues triumphantly returned to the Ricoh in 2014, although this second stay only lasted for five years, leading to another ground-share, this time a shorter 42-mile round trip to and from Birmingham City.

Coventry City fans on the pitch on the occasion of the club's last-ever match at Highfield Road in 2005. (Coventry Evening Telegraph)

I had the good fortune to visit the Highfield Road press box on several occasions to report on Cambridge, Colchester and Ipswich, the first in early January 1992. Former England and Town centre-half Terry Butcher was the Sky Blues' manager at the time, one of my boyhood heroes, but Cambridge's visit for an FA Cup third round tie was to be his last in the hot-seat. John Beck's Cambridge were good value for a 1-1 draw, helped by Dion Dublin's first-half opener, and that was to prove the final nail in 33-year-old Butcher's managerial coffin – he was sacked two days later.

Two memories stick out: interviewing a subdued Butcher after the match, and the problem I had parking the car down any available side street.

Cambridge won the replay 1-0 in dramatic fashion back at the Abbey Stadium. Dublin's injury-time penalty was saved by Coventry keeper Steve Ogrizovic – who went on to become the club's record appearance-maker with 601 first-team outings – although in the mad scramble that followed, the rebound was knocked in by Lee Hurst for an own goal. It was not a great way for Don Howe to make a mark as the new interim boss, but he did manage to keep Coventry in the top flight by one place and two points at the end of the season, to become founder members of the Premier League.

Highfield Road still had terracing on my first visit, despite becoming the first all-seater stadium in England under chairman Jimmy Hill's watch, in 1981. That experiment lasted just four years, before some seats were removed and it was possible to stand on a partially rebuilt Kop again. Just over a year after my visit with Cambridge, the terracing was finally replaced for good by the new East Stand, at a cost of £4.3m. Yet the venue still retained its old-fashioned look, with four separate stands.

Coventry were on the slide when I accompanied Colchester United for an FA Cup fourth round tie in January 2004 and witnessed a pulsating 1-1 draw. They had been relegated back to the second tier, and in truth the orange-shirted third-tier U's swarmed all over their hosts during a one-sided first half at an expectant Highfield Road, much to the delight of 2,000 travelling fans. An own goal by Dele Adebola, who headed Joe Keith's free kick past keeper Darren Ward, put the U's deservedly ahead, although Coventry equalised just three minutes later in fortuitous fashion, defender Liam Chilvers's attempted clearance ricocheting off Julian Joachim and ballooning over keeper Richard McKinney into the roof of the net. Coventry, with Eric Black as manager, were just relieved to get a replay, especially as visiting striker Scott McGleish had rattled a post late on.

'Coventry might not fancy the replay at our place,' insisted McGleish, after the dust had settled at Highfield Road and most of the home fans had strolled back towards the city centre, perhaps via a pub or two. He was proved right. A hat-trick from Rowan Vine blew the Sky Blues away in the Layer Road replay, propelling Phil Parkinson's men into the last 16 of the FA Cup.

My last visit, later that year, was while tracking Joe Royle's Ipswich. It was the Suffolk club's final trip to the old ground on a Sunday, 3 October 2004, with Coventry set to leave their long-term home the following year. Dean Bowditch, aged 18 and sporting a new-look close-cropped hairstyle, drilled home the opener in a 2-1 win. Speed on 16 years and I found myself reporting on another Bowditch goal, this time for ninth-tier club Stowmarket Town, of the Eastern Counties League, during the aborted 2019/20 season. He has aged well.

But I digress. Back to Ipswich's last win at Highfield Road, and a match that was also noted for a fine penalty save by Town keeper Lewis Price, who kept out Stern John's spot-kick. John went on to play seven games on loan for Ipswich towards the end of his career, under Roy Keane in 2009/10. It was not a particularly successful stay, with just one goal scored, although ironically it was against his old club Coventry in a rare Town victory (3-2). Cameroon striker Patrick Suffo's 77th-minute equaliser for City in 2004 was cancelled out by Town's late winner, an 87th-minute own goal by home defender Matt Mills, a cruel moment for the 18-year-old.

City's last game at Highfield Road ended in a 6-2 win over Derby County, a fitting end to a wonderful legacy. Ironically Dele Adebola, who had scored an own goal on my visit with Colchester, and Stern John, who had missed a penalty on my return with Ipswich, were both on the score sheet on that tearful afternoon.

Some clubs have flourished on their moves away from long-standing, antiquated old grounds in the city or town centre. Alas, Coventry, FA Cup winners in 1987, have not been one of them. They have floated between the second and third tiers, so no wonder many of their older fans still pine for Highfield Road.

Even I do.

9 OAKWELL

Club: Barnsley
Founded: 1887
Ground: Oakwell (since 1888)
First visit: 8 February 1992; Barnsley 0 Cambridge 0

For me, a visit to Oakwell is never complete without my laptop flipping off a flexible desk in the press box, sipping on a cup of the milkiest tea at half-time in the press lounge, and perhaps having a leak in the open-roofed male urinals behind the West Stand, alongside former cricket umpire Dickie Bird.

I do like Oakwell.

The two-tiered West Stand, with many of its seats still being the originals from the early 1900s, houses the press box, which was expanded behind the visiting directors' box to accommodate life in the media glare of the Premier League (Barnsley have spent just one season there, 1997/98). I have had many an afternoon at Oakwell trying to keep my laptop upright on the individual little desks, which have a tendency to flip up at any moment. It's a bit like going back into the classroom. I have had to pick up my computer off the floor on nearly every visit, and retrieve notepads and pens, the scene complicated further by a network of wires to recharge various electronic gadgets. The press lounge, which used to be the size of a cupboard, was relocated to an old office block in a corner behind the West Stand, where I have sipped that milky tea, poured from a giant pot, and attended post-match press conferences. The outdoor urinals, close-by, is where I once had a slash at the same time as lifelong Tykes supporter Dickie Bird (or a very good Dickie Bird look-a-like).

On the pitch, I have once again reported on the delights of Cambridge, Colchester and Ipswich over the last three decades, most of these matches ending in home wins for a proud South Yorkshire club who started out life as a church team. Reverend Tiverton Preedy, a Church of England clergyman who liked to utilise sport as a way of helping the poor, founded an association football club, Barnsley St Peters, in 1887, after losing patience with the rugby club for insisting on playing a match on Good Friday.

I don't know whether Reverend Preedy can still exercise a degree of divine intervention at Oakwell, but there has been a suspiciously high number of last-gasp injury-time goals scored by the Tykes during my travels up here to the former coal mining town.

My most infamous visit to Oakwell ended with one TV reporter perhaps hoping for some sort of divine intervention after asking Roy Keane whether he would be reconsidering his role as Ipswich Town manager after the late heartache of a 2-1 defeat, on 3 October 2009. I was standing next to the reporter and Keane in the Oakwell tunnel, and you could have cut the atmosphere with a knife. Keane didn't reply straight away, hardly surprising, especially as the stare did all the talking for him. That stare seemed to go on forever. I could hear my watch ticking. I doubt whether even Reverend Preedy could have saved him, even if he was present. The TV reporter never did get his answer, in words, but he got the message. It was then my turn to ask a few questions, although I didn't mention his job, a possible resignation or probable sacking. Self-preservation was my priority that evening at Oakwell.

As for the game, 'disbelief' was the word I used in the following Monday morning's newspaper report to describe the emotions of Town's players and supporters. Rock bottom of the Championship table, with no wins from their first ten matches of the season, Town at least seemed to be heading for a point at 1-1 going into stoppage time. It was at this point, in the sixth minute of added-on time, that Tommy Smith conceded a free kick for a needless foul, and former Town loanee striker Jon Macken drilled home from the set-piece to seal a 2-1 home win.

I remember Town's players being reluctant to leave the pitch after referee Phil Gibbs had blown his final whistle just seconds later. It was as if they couldn't comprehend what had just happened, especially as a similar kick in the teeth had befallen them just four days earlier, also in South Yorkshire, when Sheffield United skipper Chris Morgan had poked home a 92nd-minute equaliser in a 3-3 draw.

No wonder Keane wasn't enamoured by any post-match questions about his own managerial future.

The following season, the Oakwell curse struck again. I was again a witness from the press box, although this time Paul Jewell was the unfortunate Ipswich manager. Jason Scotland's eighth goal of the season, netted in the 83rd minute, looked enough to bag the visitors all three points on 12 February 2011, until Jacob Mellis's 93rd-minute shot rolled over the goal line to salvage a 1-1 draw for Barnsley.

Town players are left stunned after Jon Macken's injury-time winner for Barnsley at Oakwell in 2009. (WP)

And yet despite these late setbacks, I do love going back there.

Oakwell retains a charm, the scent of steaming Bovril in the air, mainly due to the classic-looking West Stand and its old corrugated roof, which only covers the rear of the stand (fortunately the press box is under the roof). Much of the ground has altered, and dramatically improved, since I first visited for a goalless draw with Cambridge United in February 1992. The impressive East Stand opposite, with its 7,000-plus red seats, was opened the following year, while the Pontefract Road End (Ponty End) to the south, in front of the main car park with all the club offices behind, was revamped two years later. The away fans also had cause to celebrate when the former open bank of terracing on the North Stand was replaced by a big single tier of covered seating in 1999. That has, I presume, cut down on the number of visiting supporters suffering from the flu after a visit to Oakwell and a long afternoon spent at the mercy of the Yorkshire weather.

Add to this the backdrop of rolling hills, for inspiration, and a visit to the nearby fish and chip shop for sustenance, and you have the perfect day out.

Just avoid the Roy Keane stare.

10 FILBERT STREET

Club: Leicester City
Founded: 1884 (as Leicester Fosse)
Ground: Filbert Street (1891 to 2002)
First visit: 13 May 1992; Leicester 5 Cambridge 0

An assortment of stands, surrounded by a warren of terraced streets, Leicester City's long-term home was a great place to be on a big night of football, and that was my impression on my visit for a winner-takes-all Second Division play-off semi-final second leg on 13 May 1992. Fans streamed to the ground, along the busy narrow streets towards Burnmoor Street and Raw Dykes, not far from the River Soar, the ground hemmed in by terraced housing and small back yards, and the away end accessed behind a myriad of Victorian houses.

It was a world away from the future rise of the new stadia, with their big, sprawling concourses, surrounding car parks (like moats), vast media suites, generous leg room for every seat within the all-seater complexes, and the smell of a thousand roast dinners.

The main stand at Filbert Street was still standing, just, when John Beck's Cambridge United rolled into town for the play-off semi-final showdown, although it was to be demolished that summer, to be replaced by the new Carling Stand in December 1993. The old two-tiered main stand, with its many supporting pillars and its media gantry perched precariously on top of the roof, had its origins in the early 1920s although it was rebuilt following damage during the Second World War. Ironically, the impressive Carling Stand, sporting 9,500 seats, 28 executive boxes and built at a cost of £6m, only lasted nine

Beck's gamble ends in disaster

By Carl Marston

CAMBRIDGE United's dreams of securing promotion for a record breaking third successive season were shattered by rampant Leicester City in a packed Filbert Street last night.

Starting the game on level terms following Sunday's 1-1 draw at the Abbey, John Beck's side was thrown away in the second leg of the Division Two play-off semi-final.

Trailing by two goals at the break through Tommy Wright and Steve Thompson, Beck gambled by replacing skipper and centre half Danny O'Shea with striker Michael Norbury four minutes into the second-half.

It was a brave move, but one that back fired as Leicester gorged themselves of three goals in five minutes through Kevin Russell, Man of the Match Wright and Alan Ormondroyd.

United's battle weary troops had no answer to the slick moves through the centre and down both flanks, most of them instigated by livewire Wright.

Having crashed 5-1 at the Abbey in a league encounter back in September, last night's goal feast was sweet revenge for Leicester's jubilant side who now go forward to contest the play-off final against Blackburn Rovers on May 25.

Leicester City 5
Cambridge United 0
(aggregate 6-1)

For Cambridge, a season that promised so much has ended in bitter disappointment. After promotion via the playoffs in 1990 and last season's Third Division championship exploits, a promotion treble was up for grabs.

United striker Dion Dubbin, playing probably his final game for Cambridge, received a stormy reception by the Leicester faithful who had not taken kindly to remarks aimed at City defender Steve Walsh after the first leg. Walsh had allegedly elbowed Dublin in the face towards the end of the Abbey confrontation but the United striker silenced the home crowd with a couple of useful headers and a dangerous break forward.

Micky Heathcote lofted a high ball over the City defence and Dublin raced clear, pulling back a low cross which keeper Carl Muggleton did well to gather before Steve Claridge could pounce with the vital touch.

Only woodwork denied Cambridge an opening goal in the 18th minute, a strike that could well have altered the whole course of the game.

Lee Philpott swung over a looping corner and Heathcote rose high to send a crisp header thudding back of the underside of the bar. The rebound almost dropped in via keeper Muggleton, but City somehow managed to scramble the ball to safety.

Leicester having weathered the early storm, broke the deadlock in the 29th minute. A corner from Mike Whitlow was missed by United midfielder Richard Wilkins and Wright scooped the ball into the top of net from just one yard out.

Cambridge conceded a second seven minutes later, Simon Grayson sliced through the United defence, and although John Vaughan blocked the initial shot, Thompson was on hand to drive the rebound into the empty net.

The visitors threw everything at Leicester in the first 14 minutes of the second-half, before Leicester killed the game with three classic breakaway goals.

Beck's final gamble of the season to play just three at the back for the bulk of the second-half cost his side dear.

Beck said: "I'm disappointed most of all that we failed to take our chances in the first 20 minutes. "Once we were two behind we had something and we put five at the front but d the break."

The big Premier League clubs may celebrating the fact that Cambridge's style has failed to get them through to the but Beck said: "The Premier League is feeding the fat cats and we've done our share over the years. "Maybe we'll be fat cats one day if we can hang on to our financial hold of the quality players we have at the

Jubilant Leicester manager Brian mented: "Cambridge played three against the back in the second-half and we took of this. But I can understand John Beck He had done it several times this season worked for him in the past.

"Throughout this season we have able to bounce back, and after our last ing defeats at the end of the League have done it again."

The teams

LEICESTER CITY: Muggleton, N Oldfield 82 mins), Hill, Walsh, Grayson, Wright, Ormondroyd and Ru
CAMBRIDGE UTD: Vaughan, Dennis, Chapple, O'Shea (sub Cheetham, Wilkins, Dublin, Claridge.
Referee: M. Bodenham (Cornwall).
Attendance: 21,024.

Ragout: Cambridge's 5-0 defeat at Filbert Street, as reported in the East Anglian Daily Times in 1991.

years before it was demolished following the club's move to their new home at the Walkers Stadium.

The crowd was more than 21,000, so Filbert Street was an intimidating place that night. The Kop (South Stand), known as the 'double decker stand', still had a bank of terracing in front, while the opposite Filbert Street End looked rather odd and ugly with a row of 20 executive boxes on top, above a bank of red-orange seats. The Popular East Side (Cattle Shed), with its blue seats and corrugated roof, completed a rather jumbled feel to the stadium, looking uncoordinated and patched up. The pitch was never great, often more bog than grass, mainly due to the 'double decker' Kop blocking out much of the sun.

But to Leicester City fans, it was home.

The two sides had drawn 1-1 in the first leg at the Abbey Stadium, and everyone anticipated a thunderous second leg, albeit a very nerve-wracking affair. However, it actually turned out to be a woefully one-sided encounter. Leicester scored twice in the first half, through Tommy Wright and Steve Thompson, and Cambridge boss Beck reacted by going for broke, replacing his skipper and centre-half, Danny O'Shea with striker Mick Norbury just four minutes into the second half. The all-out attack ploy never worked and classy Leicester struck three times on the break with Kevin Russell, man-of-the-match Wright (his second) and Ian Ormondroyd all scoring. There was no need for a re-write that evening – the report was effectively done long before the final whistle sounded.

It was a humbling experience, although I do remember a key moment when the second leg was still goalless, defender Micky Heathcote rattling the underside of the bar with a header from Lee Philpott's corner and the ball almost ricocheting in off keeper Carl Muggleton. If that had gone in, perhaps Cambridge would have achieved the feat of three successive promotions to reach the new Premier League.

Leicester boss Brian Little had sympathy for Beck's tactics, 'Cambridge played three against three at the back, and we took advantage of this. But I can understand his [Beck's] position because it had worked for him in the past this season.' The Foxes lost to Blackburn in the final, and lost in the play-offs again the following year, but it was third time lucky in 1994.

And that was my one and only taste of Filbert Street, the 111-year middle chunk of Leicester's rich history. A club that started out as a group of former pupils from Wyggeston School meeting for matches behind Fosse Road, playing under the name of Leicester Fosse, eventually became the club that shocked the world by winning the Premier League title in 2015/16 as 5,000/1 rank outsiders. By then, of course, Filbert Street was long gone.

11 CITY GROUND

Club: Nottingham Forest
Founded: 1865
Ground: City Ground (since 1898)
First visit: 31 October 1992; Nottingham Forest 0 Ipswich 1

Although Cambridge missed out on being founder members of the Premier League, I did find my way into a few top-flight press boxes in that inaugural 1992/93 season with Ipswich Town.

Whenever senior writers Tony Garnett or Dave Allard, of the *East Anglian Daily Times* and *Evening Star*, were on holiday or otherwise unavailable, I would step in as a wholly inadequate understudy, hence a trip to City Ground, the home of Nottingham Forest, in the late autumn of 1992.

That meant catching the back end of Brian Clough's successful 18-year reign as Forest boss, which had included back-to-back European Cup triumphs in 1979 and 1980. Forest were a pale shadow of that side from more than a decade earlier, and Clough too had lost most of his powers, and most of his mystique. He retired at the end of this 1992/93 season, ironically after a 2-1 defeat at Portman Road in the return match. His son Nigel scored that day, and shortly afterwards star player Roy Keane left to join Manchester United for £3.75m, setting a British transfer record at the time.

I remember parking up, in the shadow of the Trent Bridge cricket ground, by miracle of a car park press pass, and going for a walk along the banks of the River Trent with a spring in my step. Forest may have been on the wane, not helped by Teddy Sheringham's move to Tottenham at the end of August, just a week after scoring the club's first Premier League goal, against Liverpool, but they still had some decent players. Mark Crossley was in goal, Stuart Pearce at left-back, and of course Keane in central midfield.

The City Ground always looks a picture from the Trent, an appealing splash of red, and back in the early 1990s the ground was dominated by the mighty Executive Stand (later

The City Ground, pictured from the north bank of the River Trent. (CM)

renamed the Brian Clough Stand), built in the 1980s. It dwarfed the old Trent End, while the Bridgford Stand had just been rebuilt with Town fans seated at this end, blessed with a bird's eye view of what proved to be the only goal of the afternoon.

Forest first moved there in 1898, 33 years after their formation. In fact, with neighbours Notts County's drop into the National League in 2019, Forest took on the mantle of being the oldest Football League club in England. The press area was in the oldest, smallest and lowest stand, the Main Stand (renamed the Peter Taylor Stand in 2015), built in the mid-1960s just off Pavilion Road. The spacious press lounge was downstairs, beyond a brick wall not far from the players' entrance, and the press box was at the top of the stand. All very impressive to a still dewy-eyed young reporter but, as I said at the time, the club was on a downward spiral, at least in terms of success on the pitch.

As for the game, midfield maestro Jason Dozzell put Town 1-0 up inside six minutes with the sweetest of headers at the aforementioned Bridgford Stand end, and John Lyall's men held that lead to win 1-0 in front of a modest crowd of 21,411 on 31 October 1992. Town's five-man defence easily coped with Forest's huff-and-puff approach to leave the hosts rock bottom of the new Premier League. A tongue-tied Clough slipped away from the City Ground in a haunted mood, as befitting a Halloween night, while Town first team coach Mick McGiven admitted that his team had been under the cosh, 'We were hanging on at the end. It was a bit of an onslaught in the second half as they really bombarded us.'

U's centre-half Wayne Brown is left floored by Forest's lucky winner, his attempted clearance ricocheting into the net off James Perch, in 2006. (WP)

The new back-pass rule had recently been implemented, which led to one moment of controversy when Town's Mick Stockwell was penalised with an indirect free kick for passing back to keeper Clive Baker. 'We have had all the tapes about the new back-pass rule, and so have the referees,' explained coach McGiven. 'But players and managers are nonplussed at the moment. I thought that Micky's pass was accidental and not deliberate. There are too many inconsistencies.' For the record, Pearce ended up cracking a ferocious left-footed drive straight into the defensive wall from the close-range free kick, with all 11 Town players lined up in front of goal. No one was hurt.

Forest ended up rock bottom that season, and were the first club to be relegated from the Premier League, but Town, with John Lyall by now the director of football and McGiven in management control, finished in 16th spot, three points above the drop zone, helped by that league double over Forest.

I returned to the City Ground with Colchester United during the U's League One promotion-winning campaign of 2005/06, when a freakish goal by James Perch earned a 1-0 home win for caretaker boss Ian McParland's side in front of a crowd of more than 22,000, on 8 April 2006. The goal was a fluke. Defender Wayne Brown slipped while trying to clear Nathan Tyson's low cross, and his scuffed clearance hit team-mate Karl Duguid and flew off the onrushing Perch, the ball looping into the net. A comedy of errors. Fortunately, the defeat did not ultimately ruin the U's promotion bid.

As for the City Ground, it looked better than ever, boosted by the construction of the new Trent End in the mid-1990s since my earlier visit with Town. It almost hovers over the river, such is its bulk and beauty, housing more than 7,300 red and white seats inside. A far cry from a 100 or so years ago, when fans used to be at the mercy of the elements on three open sides.

I guess Perch scoring beside the River Trent should have inspired a fish-linked headline, for my match report, along the line of 'Perch finds net to catch out U's'.

Alas, that ship has sailed.

12 LAYER ROAD

Club: Colchester United
Founded: 1937
Ground: Layer Road (1937-2008, formerly the home of Colchester Town from 1910)
First visit: 21 November 1992; Colchester 4 Rochdale 4

I have a confession to make – I used to have a second home.

I'm not rich. My second home was not a cottage in the Cotswolds, or an apartment in the Canaries. It wasn't even a beach hut in Clacton. No, my second home was better than all of these. It had windows and a door, a line of rickety chairs and a long table. It also had a set of coat hooks. And best of all – it had the best views in Essex. I went back there, every alternate weekend and also the odd weekday evening, for the next 16 years.

I am of course referring to the press box at Layer Road, the old home of Colchester United, a timeless place jam-packed with memories. On the outside, it looked exceedingly small and, unlike Dr Who's Tardis, it was quite cramped on the inside as well. The windows steamed up, a few posts and pillars obscured the view at the far end of the pitch, and after one particular summer I returned to my second home only to find that it had shrunk by about a third, the police having commandeered it and filled the space with CCTV cameras.

Yet I didn't care. It still felt like home to me.

In fact, I loved it so much that I hardly missed a Colchester home game between November 1992, and May 2008. I have close to 500 matches to choose from to settle on my 'featured visit', not least some big scalps in the Championship, headed by Sunderland, Derby, Leeds, Stoke City, Southampton, Wolves and East Anglian neighbours Ipswich and Norwich, who were all defeated on north-east Essex soil during 2006/07.

Yet it's impossible to pick just one from an impressive array, so why not settle on my first visit to the Layer Road press box for an extraordinary fourth-tier encounter against Rochdale, in November 1992? On the face of it, just a run-of-the-mill Third Division fixture between two unfashionable clubs. But first appearances can be deceptive.

The dug-outs at Layer Road, with visiting (Sunderland) manager Roy Keane and home boss Geraint Williams, in 2007. (WP)

In the cramped press box, with its grubby window which kept steaming up through condensation, I was flanked by two doyens of the Colchester United press, Bernie Webber and Hal Mason. They sat at each end of the box, Bernie on the far left in charge of the telephones and Hal on the far right nearest the corner flag, in control of the communal boiled sweets. They were both in the twilight of their careers, having covered U's home matches since the 1950s, but they were still earning their crust, phoning over copy to any newspaper that showed a glimmer of interest and sending out regular updates to local radio stations. They were short on poetry but heavy on detail. Needless to say, I was in awe of them both.

Hal and Bernie, partners in crime, gave the impression that they had been sitting in these same seats for 200 years. Their knowledge of Colchester United was second to none and their foreheads almost bulged with a lifetime of hoarding memories of their beloved U's. They had long since retired from full-time employment but they continued to do a brisk trade in the world of freelance journalism. No job was too small or too big for them. They wrote stories for the nationals, and waffled long reports for local weeklies. Bernie would often be on two phones at the same time, usually forgetting who he was talking to, or who had scored the winning goal. But he would always muddle through. Hal was just as busy. He alternated between regurgitating managers' quotes and munching on those boiled mint sweets.

Hal and Bernie both passed away long before the U's finally left Layer Road for good in 2008. They lost count of the number of times that a possible move to a new stadium was discussed during their lifetimes, but deep down both knew that Layer Road would finally be deserted for something newer, plusher and grander.

However, like me, they loved every minute of every visit to the tiny, airless, Layer Road press box, sited in the old 1930s Main Stand. It was a second home to us all.

There was no press lounge, although in later years it was possible to get a cup of tea in the maintenance room under the Main Stand, where the washing machines were always in action. The capacity was about four; a tea lady and three journalists at a time.

And as for that first press box appearance, against Rochdale, it was a rude awakening. No goalless draw or regulation 1-0 home win to bed me in. Instead it was a rip-roaring, what-the-hell-is-happening 4-4 thriller. I didn't know which way to turn. Eight goals and three penalties, one of which was missed. Even Bernie and Hal struggled to keep up with the action, or update the scores to the various media outlets in Rochdale and the larger Greater Manchester area. I remember the day clearly, especially Colchester keeper Ron Green, who endured a calamitous home league debut. A balding Green, who was not really match fit, conceded two penalties, the first being the result of a dreadful clearance which saw him bring down Andy Flounders for 1-0 and the second for racing off his line to upend Steve Whitehall to make it 3-3.

Player-manager Roy McDonough, who had a penalty saved earlier in the second half, did put the U's 4-3 up with a stunning chip from the edge of the box, but Flounders rescued a point with a looping header that dropped in off the underside of the bar, much to the dismay of the more vocal home fans standing on the Barside Popular Terrace.

McDonough, never afraid to speak his mind, told me after the match, 'Ron [Green] should really have been sent off for that first challenge. Things then tended to pile up against him.'

One match and four long hours into my career as a U's scribe, and I was already needing a holiday. Sixteen years later, having covered the club's last competitive match at Layer Road, a 1-0 home defeat to Stoke City, I left the press box for the last time, but not without accidentally snagging my sweater on a protruding nail.

As always, Layer Road had the last laugh.

In all, I reported on two U's promotions, one relegation, several great cup runs, a few pitch inspections, some dodgy referees, a streaker, the occasional crowd protest, and one footballing magician (African striker Lomana LuaLua, the darling of Layer Road at the turn of the 21st century). But for me, the biggest pleasure was sharing my 'second home' with the fans on the small terraces, the players on the tight pitch, the management in the cosy dugouts, and of course Hal and Bernie in the snug press box.

I like the Cotswolds, a beach hut in sunny Clacton would have been most welcome, and I wouldn't have minded an apartment in Tenerife. But I wouldn't have swapped the Layer Road press box for any of them.

13 EDGAR STREET

Club: Hereford United
Founded: 1924 (until dissolved in 2014, replaced by phoenix club Hereford FC)
Ground: Edgar Street (since 1924)
First visit: 28 November 1992; Hereford 3 Colchester 1

I have yet another confession to make – Edgar Street is perhaps my favourite of all the Football League away grounds I have visited.

I know, an unusual choice, but it was the scene of my first away game as a Colchester United reporter, back in late November 1992. It was love at first sight, the ground squatting beside the old cattle market (now a shopping centre) on the edge of the city, with the public lavatories near the ticket office providing a distinctive whiff before admission to the stadium. Inside, the press box was homely, and the tea was served with china cups, accompanied by a slice of fruit cake on a china plate. Those were the days!

I have visited Hereford on many occasions, whether in search of the Mappa Mundi, a medieval map of the world housed in the splendid Cathedral, or in search of a pint at the Green Dragon Hotel, but Edgar Street has always been my main port of call, the name of the ground inspired by the same name of the street behind it, which doubles as the A49.

There was, and indeed is, nothing quite like Edgar Street, especially in the days when the old livestock market was just next door, a stone's throw from the city centre, and when the original club was plying its trade in the Football League. The farmyard smells

Happiness at Edgar Street as the U's celebrate Mark Yeates' goal, in 2009. (WP)

and sounds of that market were a joy to the senses, wafting over the football ground, and in truth the market did well to last so long at this central location. In fact, it was the last surviving inner-city cattle market up until its eventual closure and move outside the city in 2011. Inside the ground, the press box is in the main Merton Stand, built in 1968 and extended the length of the pitch when the club secured promotion to the Football League in 1972. Before, the stand had been flanked by two small terraces, aptly called 'cowsheds'. The tour of the ground is completed by the Len Weston Stand opposite, a curious-looking, ungainly two-tiered structure with a small overhanging upper tier of seats above a terrace, equipped with several chunky white pillars, an unusually semi-circular shaped terrace at the Meadow Lane End to the north, and the condemned Blackfriars Street End, also curved in shape, with the cathedral spire poking above its roof to the south.

It's not particularly comfortable, pretty or clean. But it's still a delight.

Edgar Street's finest hour was the FA Cup third round replay victory over Newcastle United in 1972 when a long-range thunderbolt by Ronnie Radford, which prompted a pitch invasion, and an injury-time winner from substitute Ricky George secured a memorable 2-1 win. Helped by the publicity from this cup run, Hereford won election to the Football League at the end of that 1971/72 season, despite only finishing second to champions Chelmsford City in the Southern League Premier Division, with Barrow voted out of the Fourth Division.

The white-and-black-decked Bulls were too strong for Roy McDonough's Colchester side on my inaugural visit, on 28 November 1992. U's player-boss McDonough would no doubt have smashed a few of the press box china cups if he had got his hands on them following a 3-1 defeat at the hands of Greg Downs's men.

It was a game where a dismal first 20 minutes cost the U's dear. An early goal by leading scorer Owen Pickard and an own goal by right-back Warren Donald put Hereford 2-0 up, before the visitors' pair of Steve Ball (destined to be appointed U's manager in 2020) and Peter Cawley were both carried off injured. Richard Jones added a lucky third on the stroke of half-time via a heavily deflected free kick, with substitute Darren Oxbrow netting a second-half consolation.

'We got away with murder,' admitted Bulls boss Downs, the former Norwich City left-back. His opposite number McDonough was not a happy man. 'I'm fuming. I don't know which way to turn after a display like that. We had a blinding season last season, but this year has been a comedy of errors,' blasted McDonough, with reference to the U's Conference/FA Trophy double success of 1991/92.

Instead, though, I would prefer to dwell on my second visit to Edgar Street a year later, not that it got any better for Colchester. In fact, it was far, far worse, in what turned out to be one of the more remarkable games of football. Hereford romped to a 5-0 win, but that told only half the story. The U's finished with nine men, having had two keepers sent off, with home striker Chris Pike enjoying the rare feat of scoring a hat-trick of goals, each of them netted against a different keeper.

The headline which topped my match report, in Monday's *East Anglian Daily Times*, declared, 'A nightmare on Edgar Street.' That just about summed it up. Pike had already netted the opener with a header past John Keeley, then the latter was then sent off for bringing down Hereford winger Chris Fry (he was later to sign for Colchester). Player-manager McDonough temporarily went in goal but could not keep out Pike's ensuing penalty. Substitute keeper Nathan Munson appeared for the second half but he too was beaten by Pike for the hat-trick goal, before being shown a red card for charging out of his area to bring down Derek Hall.

McDonough was not amused, but channelled most of his criticism towards referee Ron Groves. 'We now have to fork out wages to get a keeper on loan for a month,' rued McDonough. 'I will definitely be reporting him [the referee] to the FA. I don't want him refereeing another Colchester match, if I can help it.'

I was still a fresh-faced reporter, not yet bearded and beleaguered, but I aged dramatically that October afternoon in Herefordshire, in 1993.

14 PRIESTFIELD

Club: Gillingham
Founded: 1893 (as New Brompton)
Ground: Priestfield (from 1893)
First visit: 5 December 1992; Gillingham 1 Colchester 1

I have been to Priestfield on many occasions without ever being quite sure how to judge the journey time due to the unpredictable perils of the Thames crossing. In fact, everything about Priestfield has been unpredictable. I have encountered huge traffic jams, attended failed pitch inspections and lost my car for the best part of an evening within a maze of streets. They are the negatives.

On the plus side, it is only a short drive from Colchester or indeed Ipswich (a mere 86 miles from Suffolk's county town to the Medway), the press box is well positioned at the back of the main stand, and these days there's a warm, spacious press lounge, following the construction of the imposing Medway Stand at the turn of the century.

But back to those negatives.

Especially on a midweek night, or on a busy Saturday in August, the Dartford crossing can create problems for the unwary journalist when the Queen Elizabeth II Bridge, and the approach on the M25, can often resemble a car park. I have had first-hand experience of such traffic mayhem, ducking on to the A13 and finding alternative routes through the Blackwell Tunnel, or else sitting it out in the queue and sweating over the ticking clock, preparing to tune in to local radio to get the team news. I have never missed a kick-off, but I did once have to hastily park the car down an alleyway and make a mad dash for the stadium, legging it over a level crossing before the barriers came down to make sure I was in my seat before 7.45pm.

■ Keeper's despair: Colchester stand-in Mike Desborough has just been beaten for the third time. Defender Paul Roberts cannot believe it while Nick Forster celebrates Gillingham's last-minute strike   Picture by WARREN PAGE

Desborough's day but misery for U's

GILLINGHAM 3 COLCHESTER 0

SCOTT BARRETT	7	MIKE DESBOROUGH	7
JOE DUNNE	7	ADAM LOCKE	7
LEE PALMER	7	PAUL ROBERTS	7
TONY BUTLER	9	MARK KINSELLA	7
RICHARD GREEN	8	TONY ENGLISH	6
RICHARD CARPENTER	7	PETER CAWLEY	6
GARY MICKLEWHITE	7	STEVE BALL	6
NICK FORSTER	8	STEVE BROWN	6
ANDY ARNOTT	6	ROY McDONOUGH	7
Sub Robert Reinelt		STEVE McGAVIN	5
30 mins)		(Sub John Richardson	
NEIL SMITH	7	46 mins)	6
NEIL SMITH	7	NICKY SMITH	8

BY CARL MARSTON

IT WAS a day to remember for Mike Desborough, and a day to forget for Colchester United.

Twenty-four year-old Desborough fulfilled the dream of a lifetime by playing 90 minutes in the Football League. Next weekend, he will be back playing for Chelmsford City reserves in the Essex and Herts Border League.

Miracle man Jimmy Saville has worked wonders in the past, promoting youngsters to celebrity status for the day. But even he would have failed to satisfy Desborough's burning desire to make a Football League appearance.

Desborough, a Telecom engineer by trade, could not be blamed for any of the

about the day he played in goal for chester for years to come, the Layer regulars will be hoping to wipe the misery from their memories quickly.

They sorely missed the influenti: Dickens in midfield, and will be that his back injury clears in t tomorrow's trip to Darlington.

Chances were few and far Steve McGavin, strangely out of recent weeks, was hauled off at and sat out a disappointing secon

Neither he nor hot-shot Ste had even the sniff of a

Flashback: Desborough's big day at Priestfield, as reported in the match report of October 1993.

Which brings me to another negative, the car parking limitations. It can be tricky to park the pool-car Porsche (okay, my own Vauxhall Meriva) within a country mile of Priestfield. It didn't help that on one occasion I forgot the name of the road where I had abandoned my vehicle, not the sort of thing you want after tracking down managers for post-match quotes, to then go on a wild car hunt in the darkness. Every street looked much the same, and the whole unfortunate episode was only resolved by a slow and painful process of elimination, going up and down street after street until the black Meriva was spotted.

Then there were two fruitless trips to Kent which I made during the 1994/95 season, following Colchester. The original Gills v U's fixture, on a Saturday afternoon, was postponed because of a waterlogged pitch (the playing surface at Priestfield has never been the best) after heavy rain. At least I managed to witness the pitch inspection, and so flesh out a story, unlike the rearranged midweek match, which was also called off for the same reason. The away coach was just drawing out of Priestfield when I arrived at the ground. That fixture was finally played in April 1995, the U's at least winning 3-1 to make up for the two aborted trips.

But one of my first visits, at the end of October 1993, stands out as clear as any, due to the one-off Football League appearance of an otherwise non-league goalkeeper. It was the stuff of comics, and while it was a day to forget for Colchester with a 3-0 defeat, it was a day to remember for Mike Desborough.

A telecoms engineer by trade, 24-year-old Desborough fulfilled the dream of a lifetime by playing 90 minutes in the Football League. He was recruited for the one game only, from Chelmsford City Reserves, which is where he returned (to the Essex & Herts Border League) after this trip to Priestfield. Both of the U's regular keepers, John Keeley and Nathan Munson, were suspended due to being sent off at Edgar Street the previous weekend, and attempts to sign an experienced stop-gap failed during the week.

Former Ipswich Town keeper Ron Fearon did agree to sign but was forced to withdraw due to a family bereavement, while McDonough's hopes of signing Mark Walton on a month's loan from Norwich City were also dashed by the U's board's reluctance to splash out on a month's wages. Even a plan to sign Chelmsford City's experienced keeper Mervyn Cawston fell through just before the deadline – Cawston was ineligible – so instead Chelmsford's young back-up Desborough was secured for the one game, even though he had missed the last couple of Clarets matches due to a trapped nerve in his shoulder. 'I'm not happy about it at all,' admitted McDonough, during his pre-match address to the press.

However, Desborough duly made his one and only league appearance and he did not freeze or have a stinker, despite the 3-0 defeat.

'The lads made me feel very welcome. I never dreamed that I would be called up. I heard the sendings-off saga on the radio but never thought anything about it until a phone call on Thursday night. I didn't know I was playing until receiving a message from my Mum at 4pm on Friday, ' enthused Desborough. His manager McDonough said, 'I thought Mickey did really well at such short notice. He had no chance with the three goals.'

Richard Green, Nick Forster and Robbie Reinelt scored for the Gills that afternoon, but this was Desborough's big day. He returned to the Essex non-league scene after his one solitary appearance in the professional game to play for Chelmsford, Braintree, Dagenham, Canvey Island, Purfleet, Burnham Ramblers and Grays.

But he could dine out on his Priestfield experience for years to come.

The ground underwent a complete facelift during the second half of the 1990s, with three of the four stands demolished, including the terracing at the Rainham End plus the old Main Stand. The fourth stand, at the old Town End with its sloping terrace (the pitch also had an appreciable slope, until it was levelled in 1955), has also been replaced by temporary seating, but with no roof, which has led to many a drenched away supporter – no wonder Priestfield does not feature highly on many visiting fans' 'most popular stadiums' lists.

It is isn't high up on mine either – but I think it tops Mike Desborough's list!

15 COUNTY GROUND (NORTHAMPTON)

Club: Northampton Town
Founded: 1897
Ground: County Ground (1897 to 1994)
First visit: 26 December 1992; Northampton 1 Colchester 0

This was a unique venue with its one open side looking out beyond the rest of the cricket field towards the cricket pavilion. Northamptonshire County Cricket Club have been based there since 1886, and still are, while the Cobblers had it as their home for 97 years, from the club's formation up until 1994. When I began visiting, which was not until the early 1990s, it had a very temporary feel to it with the former Main Stand, which had extended the length of the pitch, having been deemed unsafe and so demolished during the 1980s.

A small main stand had first been built before the First World War, flanked by terracing and superseded by a bigger new stand in 1924 which was destroyed by fire and so rebuilt in 1930. This lasted until the Bradford City fire disaster of 1985, which prompted rigid new safety regulations to be implemented throughout the land. Hence the demolition of the old structure, to be replaced by a much smaller stand, which just stood astride the halfway line. It was dubbed the 'Meccano Stand' by home fans because of all the scaffolding. It is where I occasionally sat, with notepad on lap. At one end was the Spion Kop, a small open terrace exposed to the elements, which was used by away fans, and at the other was the small but covered Hotel End, which was also a terrace. That was where most of the noise came from, the chants echoing off the low roof to create a good atmosphere.

Colchester United's last visit, in February 1994, was noted for one of the briefest of full debuts, lasting just seven minutes. It was one of the few Football League matches where I actually stood by the touchline for much of the afternoon, rather than sit in a press box, and this gave me a close-up view of U's young debutant Christian Hyslop being sent off after just seven minutes for a challenge on Efon Elad. Hyslop, 21, had only signed from Essex neighbours Southend two days before and he was thrown straight in to the team at

■ Hyslop horror: Just seven minutes into his U's debut Christian Hyslop is stunned as referee Terry Lunt brandishes the red card after a foul on Efon Elad (grounded). Even the home side felt it was a harsh verdict   Picture by WARREN PAGE

U's see red over Hyslop dismissal

CHRISTIAN Hyslop will remember his Colchester United debut for years to come. Referee Terry Lunt saw to that on Saturday.

Left-back Hyslop, the latest to make the popular move from Southend to Colchester on Thursday morning, could hardly wait to prove himself at Northampton's County Ground. But his first U's adventure lasted just seven minutes.

Nothing really happened for the first six. Hyslop did not even touch the ball, and he was destined not to during his short stay at the crease — the tumble-down arena is transformed into a cricket stage over the summer.

Cameroon under-23 international Efon Elad, the Cobblers' prize possession, sprinted down the left flank and was sent sprawling by a body-check from Hyslop.

Referee Lunt reached for his book and a card. Everyone was expecting one of the yellow variety. The crude challenge was made close to the touch-line and Elad was not through on goal.

But the colour was red and Hyslop was off. It is probably a record for a player to be given his marching orders after only seven minutes of his debut appearance. Sympathy for the 21 year-old came from all sides.

Harsh

"It was worthy of a booking, but no worse," insisted U's club captain Tony English.

"If that had been one of our players, then we would have been very disappointed with the decision," said Northampton manager John Barnwell.

And Colchester boss Roy McDonough said: "The over-reaction of the referee cost us a victory, which might prove vital come the end of the season.

"It was more than harsh. Christian was so looking forward to the game. He

BY CARL MARSTON

had just been given a nice two-year contract with us and thought that his luck had changed.

"I told him at half-time not even to think about it, and to go home if he wanted to.

"The referee told me that he didn't send him off for dangerous play or serious foul play. We will probably appeal against the decision with video evidence," added the U's boss.

The Cobblers, rooted to the basement, took the lead against the 10-strong visitors after 19 minutes.

Kevin Wilkin raced clear of a static U's back-line and coolly lobbed the advancing John Cheesewright.

"I thought that John ventured off his line too early, but he made amends with two great saves," said McDonough.

It was McDonough who netted United's equaliser in the 24th minute. The hardworking Steve Brown delivered a pinpoint cross from the by-line and McDonough headed home at the far post.

Northampton had their chances after the break but the U's defence held firm. Cheesewright tipped over shots from Elad and Mickey Bell, and the home side remain rock bottom.

However, Colchester's last trip to the County Ground — the Cobblers are moving to a new stadium next season — will be remembered for all the wrong reasons. Poor Hyslop left thinking it just ain't cricket.

Northampton 1 Colchester 1

Barry RICHARDSON	7		John CHEESEWRIGHT	8
Terry FLEMING	7		Simon BETTS	7
Ken GILLARD	6		Christian HYSLOP	4
Darren HARMON	7		Mark KINSELLA	8
Ray WARBURTON	6		Peter CAWLEY	7
Phil CHARD	7		Tim ALLPRESS	7
Kevin WILKIN	8		Tony ENGLISH	7
Efon ELAD	8		Alan DICKENS	7
Ian GILZEAN	6		Steve BROWN	8
(Sub Warren PATMORE 77 mins)			(sub Nicky SMITH 65 mins)	7
John CORNWELL	7		Roy McDONOUGH	7
Mickey BELL	7		Grant WATTS	6
			(sub Chris FRY 82 mins)	

Unused subs:	**Unused sub:**
Steve TERRY	John KEELEY (gk)
Steve SHERWOOD (gk)	

REFEREE: Terry Lunt (Ashton in Makerfield) 4
ATTENDANCE: 3,185
GOALS: Wilkin (Northampton) 19 mins, McDonough (U's) 24 mins
GOAL ATTEMPTS: Northampton 21 Colchester 10
SHOTS ON TARGET: Northampton 5 Colchester 2
SENDING-OFF: Hyslop 7 mins for foul on Elad
BOOKING: McDonough 20 mins (dissent)
CORNERS: Northampton 4 Colchester 4
OFFSIDES AGAINST: Northampton 9 Colchester 2
QUOTES: Coach Steve Foley: "The back four were top class. It's the best I've seen them play for a long time."
Roy McDonough: "We would have won the game if we had had eleven players. It just goes to show refs can cost players their livelihoods."

Flashback: Hyslop's red letter day, as reported in the author's match report from February 1994.

left-back. After a nondescript first six minutes, during which I don't think Hyslop even touched the ball, he then seemed to body check a sprinting Elad down the wing, sending the Cameroon under-23 international flying. A yellow card, surely? Referee Terry Lunt had other ideas and reached for his red.

Sympathy all round. Northampton boss John Barnwell, whose side were propping up the Football League, admitted, 'If that had been one of our players, then we would have been very disappointed with the decision.' U's boss Roy McDonough insisted, 'Christian had just been given a nice two-year contract with us and thought that his luck had changed. I told him at half-time that he could go home, if he wanted, and not to think about it.'

As it happened, even though Kevin Wilkin raced through to lob keeper Jon Cheesewright for a 19th-minute opening goal, the Cobblers were pegged back to a 1-1 draw against the ten men, McDonough equalising just five minutes later via a header from Steve Brown's cross.

After their 'coming together' at the County Ground, Hyslop went on to play just seven more games for the U's before dropping in to non-league, while Elad managed just 15 appearances in the Football League before also drifting to the semi-pro game.

So that was my last visit to the County Ground before the Cobblers moved to Sixfields later that year, leaving the cricketers to exploit the wicket – which was helpful to spinners – on their own. As I wrote at the end of my match report for Monday morning's edition, 'The match will be remembered for all the wrong reasons. Poor Christian Hyslop left thinking it just ain't cricket.'

The Cobblers, who had enjoyed one season in the top flight (1965/66), actually finished rock bottom of the Football League in their final full season at the County Ground so looked set to be relegated – but their luck was in. Kidderminster Harriers, crowned Conference champions, were denied promotion due to their Aggborough ground not meeting the new Football League fire and safety ground requirements. So rather ironically the Cobblers, still based at the County Ground (until that October) where a stray cross would sometimes fly over the nearby cricket square, and which was widely recognised as the worst ground in the Football League, enjoyed a reprieve.

16 BESCOT STADIUM

Club: Walsall
Founded: 1888 (as Walsall Town Swifts, an amalgamation of Walsall Town and Walsall Swifts)
Ground: Bescot Stadium (since 1990)
First visit: 2 January 1993; Walsall 1 Colchester 3

Handy for the M6. There can't be too many football grounds that have sprung up so close to a motorway than the Bescot Stadium, complete with its massive illuminated advertising

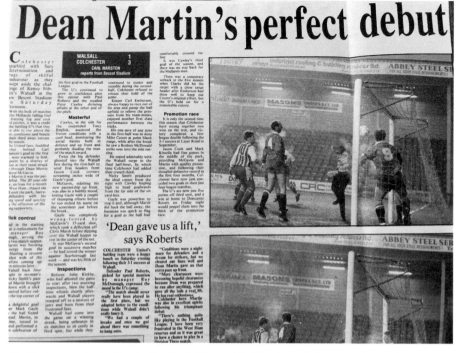

Flashback: report in the East Anglian Daily Times of the U's trip to the Bescot Stadium in January 1993.

sign, reported to be the largest of its kind to be sited next to a motorway; a fine claim to fame. The whole stadium actually looks impressive from the M6, particularly since the construction of a huge two-tiered stand at one end in 2003, which towers over the remaining three stands.

I never did get to sample the delights of Walsall's long-term home at Fellows Park, where the Saddlers were based for 94 years from 1896, just a quarter of a mile down the road. But I have often dropped off the M6 to visit the Bescot Stadium, starting from the early 1990s when both ends were standing areas. Opened in 1990 as a simple box-shaped venue, and an all-seater since 2002, the Bescot has never been the scene of much drama for me. A bogey ground, if you like, where just the odd goal has decided a match, stuck in an uninspiring location in the middle of a retail park, the stadium a blend of bright red seats, glass-fronted corporate boxes and regular supporting pillars. The press box is also tight, a small area in the main stand where you find your seat and stay there, jam-packed with other scribes. But the view is good, and the car parking is excellent.

I kicked off 1993 at the Bescot with an ice-cold visit on 2 January, again following the fortunes of Colchester United. Two memories stand out – the weather and a certain Dean Martin (the professional footballer, not the suave American actor and entertainer of the same name).

The bulk of the matches in the West Midlands that day had fallen foul to freezing fog and rock-hard pitches, but Walsall escaped the wintry grip after referee John Kirkby passed two morning pitch inspections. The U's away fans, huddled together behind their keeper Carl Emberson's goal in the first half, were at least warmed by two goals as the visitors eased to a 3-1 away win.

The aforementioned Martin marked an impressive U's debut with the opening goal on 17 minutes. Recruited on a month's loan from West Ham, front-runner Martin was a bundle of energy all afternoon, no doubt keen to impress his player-manager Roy McDonough, whom he had ironically replaced in the starting line-up. Rather predictably, McDonough was suspended. Martin's finish was stunning, bringing the ball down, from Nicky Smith's pass, before volleying into the top corner of the net past keeper Mark Gayle. To celebrate, nimble 20-year-old Martin performed a cartwheel to mark his first goal in the Football League, much to the approval of my photographic work colleague Warren Page, who captured the acrobatic image and even now proudly displays it on occasion on his Facebook page. You can't beat a happy goalscorer doing a cartwheel in front of the camera.

Steve McGavin and centre-half Peter Cawley added further goals, though neither executed or was probably capable of doing a gymnastic celebration, before ex-Wolves and Everton striker Wayne Clarke netted a late consolation for Kenny Hibbitt's Saddlers with a trademark header.

After the match, a jubilant Martin told me, 'There's nothing quite like playing in the Football League. I have been very frustrated in the West Ham reserves. I feel like my career is starting all over again.'

Well, in a way it did take off, though he never told me that he had future plans to spend most of his footballing career in Iceland! While a non-league nomad during the winter months in England, playing for the likes of Kettering, Hereford and Stevenage Borough, Martin also carved out a successful career playing club football in Iceland, eventually retiring at the age of 42 after nearly 20 years' action, and then going into coaching and management.

Perhaps that freezing afternoon at the Bescot Stadium, playing on a rock-hard pitch, had a lasting impression on Martin? The Icelandic touch.

17 SALTERGATE

Club: Chesterfield
Founded: 1866 (original club), 1919 (current incarnation)
Ground: Saltergate (1871 to 2010)
First visit: 16 January 1993; Chesterfield 4 Colchester 0

Saltergate, the home of Chesterfield in their various guises for 139 years, had the most cramped press box within which I ever had the misfortune to suffer an injury. The old

Colchester marauder Gary Bennett, who struck the bar with a first-half header, sees another goal attempt roll wide of the upright soon after the break in the 4-0 reverse at Chesterfield on Saturday afternoon. Chesterfield keeper Chris Marples, who was in excellent form, was quick to close down Bennett. The Spireites' full-back Cliff Carr is also in the picture. *Photograph by Warren Page.*

Colchester hopes are blown to oblivion

Colchester player-manager Roy McDonough refused to be despondent about Saturday's four-goal defeat at the hands of Chesterfield.

"The one disappointing aspect for me was our inability to cope with the wind at our backs in that first-half.

"We didn't exploit that advantage but, to be fair to my players, we didn't have any luck in front of goal. By contrast, the ball seemed to roll for them inside our penalty area," added the

and the reliable Paul Roberts mopping up the danger with commanding headers and timely challenges.

In fact, Emberson was not required to make a save before the interval, although Chesterfield loanee keeper Chris Marples was hardly overworked himself.

CHESTERFIELD	4
COLCHESTER UNITED	0

From CARL MARSTON at Saltergate

wrong-footed Tony Brien. He swung over the perfect

after Cliff Carr had slid ball past Emberson.

The headline in the author's match report of the U's 4-0 defeat at Saltergate in early 1993 .

wooden structure, although a delight in the antiquated Main Stand, offered only limited leg room for some of the reporters, and none at all for the others. I was usually listed among 'the others'. No football reporter should really complain about his or her lot because there are thousands of people who would willingly trade places with you (or there used to be, during the golden era of newspapers), but I did have a genuine gripe with the Saltergate press box. On one fateful afternoon, I had to watch the whole match with a twisted back. My legs could only be squeezed in sideways, so were at odds with the upper half of my body, this resulting in a back problem that was to dog me for years to come and ensure I was a regular visitor to the local chiropractors.

But enough of bad backs.

The splendid Saltergate, known early on as the (New) Recreation Ground – the name 'Saltergate' took hold during the 1920s – was never one for having lots of room. It was hemmed in by housing, only a short walk from the town centre and the Church of St Mary and All Saints, better known as the Crooked Spire due to its twisted and leaning spire. Nothing much had been done to the ground since the construction of a new brick-

and-steel Main Stand in 1936, so by the time I was a frequent visitor during the 1990s, the paint was peeling and the rust had taken hold. The other three sides were all terracing. It was a picture of decay, as if time had stood still, but it was still a fine place to watch football, if not from the rather pokey (or snug) press quarters.

While some clubs always seem to be stingy with goals, and short on entertainment, whenever I am in residence – see the preceding chapter on the Bescot Stadium – Chesterfield seemed to churn them out like they were going out of fashion. The Spireites' current ground has seen me report on a 6-0 away defeat and a thrilling 3-3 draw, while my first visit to their old Saltergate home ended in a windswept 4-0 defeat, followed a decade later by back-to-back 6-3 and 4-0 away wins, all five matches featuring Colchester United.

I have always had sympathy for goalkeepers, who have the most difficult job on the pitch after the referee, and I had a bucket-load of sympathy (not pity) for U's keeper Carl Emberson at the end of an old Third Division encounter in January 1993. A howling wind made conditions a lottery, and the Spireites made the most of it by scoring four goals in the last quarter of the game through Steve Williams (two), ex-Sunderland midfielder Paul Lemon and Dave Lancaster. A youthful Sean Dyche (21), the future successful long-term boss of Burnley, was in their line-up that day. It was a horror show for 19-year-old Emberson, who had conceded just two goals in his first five matches since his loan switch from Millwall.

U's boss McDonough was good value, as always, with his post-match summary, 'The match should never have really been played. The wind made it a farce. All you had to do was roll the ball a yard to one side and it would be blown out of play. I suppose you could say that Carl [Emberson] was to blame for three of the four goals, but I blame the elements more than Carl.'

Out of the 1990s and into the 2000s, and Saltergate suddenly became a favourite stop-off for Colchester United, none more so than on the opening day of the 2001/02 campaign. I haven't reported on that many 6-3 away wins, on my journalistic travels but an exception was on 11 August 2001, Steve Whitton's team playing what I described as 'fantasy football' to inflict an horrific debut on new Spireites keeper Nathan Abbey. Signed from Luton Town the previous week, an exposed Abbey had a shocker, although he wasn't helped by a non-existent defence as goals by Joe Dunne, Martyn Booty's own goal, Mick Stockwell, debutant Kevin Rapley and Scott McGleish (two) fired the U's to the top of the Second Division table after one round of fixtures.

It had taken the U's more than two months to rattle up six league goals the previous season, but it took them just 78 minutes at Saltergate on a day of drizzle in the Peak District. Chesterfield scored three times themselves, through Roger Willis, Luke Beckett and Steve Payne, to make it 1-1, 2-3 and 3-4. It was a job keeping up with the score, although it gave the disbelieving U's away fans a chance to try out a new chant – 'We want seven!'

'It was all guns blazing,' enthused double goalscorer McGleish. 'We've answered a few of our critics, but it's only one game.'

It was a day for the record books, the first time Colchester United had scored six goals in an away league match after previous five-goal hauls at Exeter, Southend (both 1985) and Wycombe (1993). That was to be eclipsed by a seven-goal spree at Norwich City in August 2009 – more of that later – on another opening-day feast.

Funny enough, my back didn't hurt in the snug Saltergate press box that afternoon. Too busy to feel pain? Cramped fingers, from over-writing, taking the mind off the back? Not really. I just found a corner where I could squeeze my legs into a forward position, and then stay there. The more mischievous reader might suggest that I still had more mobility than the static Spireites' defence that day. I couldn't possibly comment.

All I know is that I still kept my appointment for the chiropractors on the following Monday morning.

18 PRENTON PARK

Club: Tranmere Rovers
Founded: 1884 as Belmont FC (adopted current name in 1885)
Ground: Prenton Park (since 1912)
First visit: 23 January 1993; Tranmere 1 Ipswich 2

Tranmere Rovers, despite being in the shadow of the mighty Merseyside duo of Liverpool and Everton, basked in some of their own glory during the days when I was starting out as a rookie reporter.

This was *Roy of the Rovers* comic book material with unfashionable Rovers getting within a whisker of gatecrashing the Premier League on more than one occasion, as well as enjoying a sequence of stunning cup runs.

Football can be a very fickle business, however, and Rovers have had just as many lows as they have had highs over the last four decades. They have mixed with the best, beating the likes of Everton, West Ham and Southampton in FA Cup ties, in addition to walloping Ipswich a couple of times in the second tier during the 1990s, by 5-2 and 3-0 scorelines, both in 1996. But then I have also seen proud Rovers grapple with the unfamiliar surroundings of the non-league scene following their relegation out of the Football League in 2015, most notably a couple of visits to Braintree Town's humble home at Cressing Road. Their introduction to the National League in 2015 included an uninspiring 0-0 draw away at The Iron (I remember that well!). It took Tranmere three seasons to clamber out of the National League, very speedy when compared to the likes of Cambridge United, Lincoln City and Wrexham.

Prenton Park is a place I have always enjoyed visiting, and not everyone can say that about Birkenhead and its surroundings on the Wirral Peninsular. I always like a club with a good car park (Prenton Park has one of the best), a good fish and chip shop nearby (another box ticked), a cracking view of the pitch and beyond to the rows of houses

Flashback: The Town splash in the East Anglian Daily Times following a win at Prenton Park in January 1993.

behind the much lower Borough Bridge Stand opposite (the press box is perched high up in the main stand), and a sense of history (the ground is dripping with the memories of the glory days under manager Johnny King and his successor, John Aldridge).

Rovers have a proud FA Cup tradition, reaching the quarter-finals three times following the turn of the century in 2000, 2001 and 2004, but they found Ipswich too tough a nut to crack when I walked up to the Prenton Park press box for the first time, in January 1993 to cover a full-blooded fourth round tie.

King's Rovers finished fourth in the second tier that season and John Lyall's top-flight Town side had to really scrap to claim a 2-1 win on a sticky pitch, in windy conditions. Rovers had not lost at home in the league all season, and were a particular menace down both flanks due to the flair of Pat Nevin and John Morrissey, with Nevin giving them a 1-0 lead at half-time. A spectacular equaliser from Jason Dozzell, whose pinpoint shot flew into the top corner of the net, was followed by Bontcho Guentchev tapping home a 77th-minute winner after Chris Kiwomya's shot had rolled back off the post.

'The pitch was very heavy and was certainly the winner,' explained Rovers' long-term boss King. 'We are a team that needs a good surface.'

I have since been back to Prenton Park on many occasions, usually with Colchester United, though with a dreadful record amounting to just one solitary win in 12 visits with the U's. That success, among a mass of draws and defeats, came via the unconventional 4-3 scoreline on a Friday night on 26 September 2008, a few months after the U's had been relegated from the Championship back to League One.

It was Kit Symons's first match in charge as caretaker boss following the departure of former manager Geraint Williams at the start of the week, and it developed into a crazy night on the back of a torturous journey up the congested M6 which involved me finding another route to the north-west. I'm not saying this alternative route was slow, but I was overtaken by more than one barge inching its way along the canal running parallel to the road.

We did arrive at Prenton Park before kick-off, having finally overtaken the barges and got out of first gear, at a much-changed ground to the one that I had first frequented with Town in 1993. In fact, three of the four stands had been demolished and redeveloped at the end of the 1994/95 campaign. The Bebington Kop Stand, previously a terrace which had been closed for safety reasons in more recent times, was reincarnated as a towering single-tier all-seater, with more than 5,600 seats, and the opposite Cowshed Stand, a former terrace with a roof resembling that of a cowshed, was also replaced by an all-seater stand. The Main Stand, housing the press box, was the only original stand which was still intact, built in 1968 at a cost of £80,000 to replace an old wooden one.

The aforementioned seven-goal thriller, which at one stage had the visitors coasting with a 4-1 lead, ended with Symons being put through the mill by his new charges. Two long-range strikes by Tranmere's two full-backs, Andy Taylor and Ryan Shotton, set up a nervous finale at 4-3, and threatened to make a mockery of my already composed match report, which was fitting just perfectly in the space allowed in the following morning's newspaper. Fortunately, the U's did hold on grimly thanks to earlier goals from David Perkins, Mark Yeates (a wonderful 30-yard free kick), Clive Platt and Johnnie Jackson, to strengthen Symons's case to become the next manager. As it happened, the Welshman missed out on the job to Paul Lambert, although he did later get one chance as a full-time manager at Fulham, one of his former clubs as a player.

I'm happy to report that my journey home during the early hours was much quicker. No barge passed me, but then that was always an unlikely scenario along the M6.

19 PORTMAN ROAD

Club: Ipswich Town
Founded: 1878 (as Ipswich AFC, became Ipswich Town in 1888)
Ground: Portman Road (since 1884)
First visit: 30 January 1993; Ipswich 2 Manchester United 1

This is where I watched most of my football as a schoolboy, standing beside my dad, Eric, on a wooden crate at the front of the West Stand, from the mid-to-late 1970s and into the early 1980s. Paul Mariner, Alan Brazil, Kevin Beattie, Alan Hunter, Mick Mills, Eric

The author outside Portman Road during his time covering Town in the Roy Keane era.

Gates, Paul Cooper, Arnold Muhren, Frans Thjissen. The names roll off the tongue. One of my clearest memories was of a Tuesday night top-flight fixture on 16 February 1982 when front-runner Brazil plundered all five goals in a 5-2 win over Southampton. The Scotsman just seemed to spring the offside trap at will and convert one-on-one chances with effortless ease.

From the West Stand with my dad, I later switched to the rowdier North Stand with my school-mate Tim Horswill, before ending up in the press box high up in the West Stand. I have enjoyed that lofty vantage spot for more than 100 games, but not many surpassed my first proper matchday as the main Town scribe, a visit of Premier League leaders Manchester United on 30 January 1993. I was deputising for my boss, Tony Garnett, a culture shock from my more recent visits to the likes of Hereford, Northampton and Walsall.

It was the first time in seven years that Town had played host to Manchester United in a league match, and it was also the first time that Portman Road had boasted a sell-out crowd since it had become all-seater during the close-season. United had beaten lowly Brian Clough's Nottingham Forest in midweek, but then Town had notched a good win of their own away at Tottenham, prompting United boss Alex Ferguson to admit during his pre-match press conference, 'This is a really difficult game for us.'

And so it proved. Town ran out 2-1 winners in front of a sell-out 22,068 (the official capacity at the time was 22,600, but that has since been boosted to 30,311 following major development during the 2000s), helped by a rare blunder from Peter Schmeichel. The big Dane attempted to hoof the ball away from just outside his penalty area, only to completely miss his kick. Striker Chris Kiwomya simply sailed past the stricken figure of Schmeichel to steer the ball home, with a despairing Steve Bruce joining the ball in the back of the net. Full-back Frank Yallop crashed home a 20-yard special to double Town's lead in the 47th minute before Brian McClair gave United hope with an 85th-minute close-range effort into the roof of the net, via Eric Cantona's set-up. Town keeper Clive Baker denied Mark Hughes from point-blank range at the death to ensure there would be no sting in the tail.

The post-match press conference was heaving, a bit different to the half-dozen or so hacks who were milling around after games on my recent visits to the County Ground and Bescot Stadium. As usual, the questions were led off by my colleague Dave Allard, of the *Evening Star* newspaper, who always liked to get in with the first question, even before the manager had settled into his chair. Ferguson was gracious in defeat, though he did look a little stunned. 'I have no complaints whatsoever,' he insisted. 'I knew before the start that Ipswich are the hardest team to beat in the Premier League.' Town head coach Mick McGiven, naturally playing second fiddle to his opposite number, was next on the podium. 'This is a great result for the club,' said McGiven.

Indeed it was.

But for me, this was just a flash in the pan. I was back covering fourth-tier football the following week.

Alas, when I did finally get to report on Town full-time just over 16 years later, the club were already in the doldrums. The FA Cup triumph of 1978, when little-known Suffolk-born midfielder Roger Osborne netted the winner in a 1-0 victory over Arsenal at Wembley, and the UEFA Cup glory of 1981, when Dutch club AZ Alkmaar were defeated in the two-legged final, were just distant memories, as were a couple of second-placed finishes in the top flight to Aston Villa and Liverpool in 1980/81 and 1981/82 respectively. Town, under Bobby Robson, were one of the best teams in the land. The fans were spoilt rotten. I was in the crowd, on the terraces at the North Stand (now Sir Bobby Robson Stand) when they put six goals past keeper Gary Bailey to destroy title-chasing Manchester United 6-0 in March 1980, while to this day the Suffolk club have a proud unbeaten home record in European competition, with 31 games played, 25 wins and six draws.

Such giants of the European stage as AC Milan (European Cup, 1962/63), Real Madrid and Lazio (both in the UEFA Cup of 1973/74), Barcelona (twice, in the late 1970s), Saint Etienne (UEFA Cup of 1980/81) and Inter Milan (more recently in the UEFA Cup of 2001/02) have all lost at Portman Road, at the home of Suffolk's only professional club. But by the time I was watching from the press box, and indulging in the fortnightly diet of steak pie and chips in the spacious media lounge, Town's golden era had long since faded. Instead of Barcelona, Madrid, Milan and Manchester United leaving Portman Road with their tails between their legs, I was reporting on away wins for such footballing giants as Plymouth, Barnsley, Reading and Hull during the eras of Roy Keane and Paul Jewell.

My Portman Road days as a Town correspondent were largely spent alternating between disappointing Saturday afternoons in the press box and busy Friday mornings in the press lounge, listening to epic 45-minute recordings of Roy Keane press conferences, fuelled by filter coffee and complimentary biscuits.

Such is life. My timing was always a little bit off.

20 SINCIL BANK

Club: Lincoln City
Founded: 1884
Ground: Sincil Bank (since 1895)
First visit: 6 February 1993: Lincoln 1 Colchester 1

The Sincil Bank press box. Here lies one of the best views in the country, but you have to work for it.

You've got to be fit to frequent the press area at Sincil Bank, or at least share some of the nimble-footed qualities of a mountain goat. I always brace myself for the long climb up to the press seats from ground level at pitchside because the steps are many and steep, especially if you are also carrying a laptop in one hand and a cup of coffee in the other. I tried it once, back in the early 1990s before I knew any better, with a Cornish pasty balanced on my cup of coffee, and almost came to grief, which would have no doubt given

The expansive view from the press box at Sincil Bank. (CM)

rich entertainment to the watching home supporters seated in this portion of the ground. This is the St Andrews Stand, which is very tall and yet very short, extending either side of the halfway line for only half the length of the pitch. It replaced an old 1930s wooden stand, unluckily built in 1987 when the Imps had just dropped into the Conference. Luckily, they returned to the Football League as Conference champions the following year.

Thinking about it, while on the subject of stiff climbs up to press boxes, I reckon Sincil Bank rivals Crewe Alexandra's Gresty Road for the hardest approach to a press seat. There are other lofty viewpoints, such as at Newcastle United and Leicester City, but you can opt for the lift, rather than the stairs, at such well-equipped stadia. Taking the lift is not an option at Sincil Bank.

But the view, glancing to your right and looking northwards beyond the Stacey West Stand (the former Railway End Terrace), is one of the best of all the Football League press boxes, with the formidable Lincoln Cathedral as an impressive backdrop. That view makes all the steps worthwhile, even if your coffee is nearly always cold by the time you reach your press seat.

My first visit was a couple of years before the Co-op Community Stand, on the South Bank Street side opposite the press box, was opened in early 1995. It had been uncovered terracing since the club's move from their first home at John O'Gaunts Ground during the mid-1880s, and its transformation into the biggest stand in the stadium with 5,700 red seats was the last act in the complete overhaul of the venue. The old terrace was still in place, and about to be cordoned off, when a dubious late penalty decision denied Colchester United victory in a 1-1 draw on my first trip, in early February 1993. Referee Jim Rushton adjudged man of the match Paul Roberts to have tripped City striker Peter Costello in the box, with the ball rolling harmlessly towards touch. Graham Bressington's spot-kick was blocked by keeper Carl Emberson, but he was able to ram the rebound into the roof of the net to level West Ham loanee Dean Martin's 75th-minute opener for the U's.

'Robbo is adamant that he made no contact with the player,' blasted U's boss Roy McDonough. Seeking confirmation, I sought out centre-half Roberts before he clambered on to the team coach. 'I didn't even touch him! I'm fuming,' confirmed Robbo. All in all, that was a strong case for the defence.

As an aside, West Ham-born Roberts, like several other former U's players (Alan Dickens and Peter Cawley also spring to mind), became a London cabbie after hanging up his boots. I'd like to think that Robbo has often since regaled his passengers with tales of how he never even touched Imps striker Costello in the box at Sincil Bank in early 1993.

There was another hard luck story when I paid another visit to Sincil Bank, again with Colchester United, three and a half years later in October 1996. By then the all-seater Co-op Stand had replaced the terracing on the other side of the pitch. Again the referee took centre stage, this time Alan Butler, who dished out two red cards and five yellows, and awarded two penalties. There was also a controversial goal, an own goal plus a mass brawl featuring nearly all 22 players. The match ended 3-2 in favour of John Beck's Lincoln

Lincoln Cathedral as viewed from Sincil Bank. (CM)

City and provided enough talking points to keep everyone occupied for the rest of the weekend. Simon Betts and Karl Duguid both converted spot-kicks for the U's, though these sandwiched a questionable goal from Gareth Ainsworth, the Imps striker who in more recent times has had great success as a long-term manager at Wycombe Wanderers, guiding them into the Championship. U's keeper Carl Emberson appeared to be flattened by an on-rushing Jae Martin, allowing a 23-year-old Ainsworth to prod home the loose ball more in hope than expectation. Remarkably, the goal was allowed to stand.

Birmingham City loanee Martin netted a second equaliser for the hosts, and U's centre-half David Greene then construed to divert home a header by Dutchman Gijsbert Boss for an own goal. That completed the scoring, but not the drama. U's assistant manager Whitton saw red for over-reacting to Jon Whitney's crude tackle. Whitton aimed a kick at the City defender and was promptly given his marching orders, which sparked a mass brawl, and he was followed to the dressing rooms six minutes later by Bos, who also lost his cool and was sent off. So ten versus ten, an away defeat for Steve Wignall's Colchester, and enough copy for me to fill the sports pages for Monday morning's edition twice over.

Not every player is keen to talk to the press after being sent off, but Whitton obliged. 'I feel very sorry for the fans who travelled, and I've said sorry to the lads. In my opinion, their lad came in and tried to break my leg. I've just been out of the game for a year because of a serious injury, and I didn't want another long lay-off. I admit I then lost it. I hold up my hands and say that I deserved to be sent off,' confessed Whitton.

To end on a third and final hard luck story, even a pulsating 3-0 away win for John McGreal's Colchester United on the final day of the 2018/19 season ended in utter dejection for the Essex visitors. Lincoln City, who had spent six years in the Conference (2011–2017), had already been crowned League Two champions under manager Danny Cowley's watch. A packed Sincil Bank was rocking, a crowd of 9,832 in a party atmosphere, with the exception of the 689 Colchester fans who were nursing slender hopes of gatecrashing the play-offs. Their team had to win, which they did do in sensational style through three first-half goals by Brennan Dickenson and Sammie Szmodics (two), and other results were going their way until right at the death, when Newport County's late equaliser at Morecambe nudged them out of the top seven. A sun-kissed afternoon of terrific highs and devastating lows. Rarely have I felt so subdued after a resounding away victory!

In summary: breathtaking views of the cathedral, steep steps, dodgy decisions, controversial referees, red cards, player confessions and hopes dashed. Sincil Bank rarely disappoints.

21 GAY MEADOW

Club: Shrewsbury Town
Founded: 1886
Ground: Gay Meadow (1910 to 2007)
First visit: 20 February 1993; Shrewsbury 4 Colchester 3

Some grounds tend to blend together; the same familiar structures on the edge of a town, surrounded by car parks and retail parks, usually close to a major highway or ring road. Others are more distinct, and instantly recognisable. Gay Meadow, the former home of Shrewsbury Town, belonged to the second group, for sure.

Its proximity to the River Severn, with its unusual one-way-in, one-way-out access road, gave it a personality all of its own, aided by the closeness to the town centre and its view of Shrewsbury Abbey. There were trees, nearby parks, bridges, and the possibility of enjoying a welcome pub lunch before ambling over the river via the English Bridge to Gay Meadow. I loved it, despite the Shrews' habit of knocking Ipswich Town out of the FA Cup during the early 1980s. They did it twice, both on 30 January and both in the fourth round, in 1982 and 1984.

But I still relished every trip to this small and cramped ground, squeezed between the river and the railway, with the nosiest section of home fans spanning the length of the Riverside Terrace, and the away supporters on the terrace at Station End, which apparently at one time boasted the oldest working turnstile in the country. The press area was in the Main Stand, and on one happy occasion, on 3 January 1994 there was a bottle of whisky to share in the press box to celebrate the new year. It was also not unknown for scones to be served at half-time.

The dug-outs at Gay Meadow in 2005. U's assistant manager Geraint Williams, far left, and Shrews assistant boss Mick Wadsworth (with glasses), a former U's manager, renew old rivalries. (WP)

The Shrews first moved there in 1910, having been evicted from their previous home at the army-owned Copthorne Barracks. They were probably relieved to see the back of this old ground, not least because in the final 1909/10 campaign the roof was blown off the stand, in the process bringing down telephone wires. The first season at Gay Meadow also gave a taster of problems that lay ahead, with the adjacent River Severn bursting its banks during a fixture against Birmingham City Reserves, which caused the match to be abandoned after 70 minutes. But the club went on to flourish at their new home. On the pitch, the Shrews gained renown for their cup exploits, including reaching the League Cup semi-finals in 1961 when they beat Everton in the quarters, and also spending ten consecutive seasons in the second tier during the 1980s.

Off the pitch, the famous Riverside Terrace closest to the River Severn was built during the 1970s, and the successful decade of the 1980s saw more seating installed in the Main Stand. Although both ends were simple terraces, with the Wakeman End an uncovered terrace overlooked by the old Wakeman School behind, the whole scene was a pastoral delight, certainly one of the most picturesque and satisfying sights to be enjoyed from a press box.

Regardless of the quality of the view, though, late goals are the bane of any journalist, and that curse struck on my first visit to Gay Meadow for a crazy Third Division clash in February, 1993.

This was Colchester United's first visit since the 1978/79 campaign and it turned out to be a goal-feast with a late twist. John Bond's Shrews led 1-0 and 3-1, but were pegged back to 3-3 until deadly marksman Carl Griffiths stole the show with an 88th-minute winner for the Shropshire side, so forcing late re-writes all-round. It was his 22nd goal of the season, ending the match as he had begun it, by scoring, although his sixth-minute opener had smacked of offside. U's boss Roy McDonough rued, 'Shrewsbury's first goal was yards offside, but the linesman was well behind play.' Later that year, Griffiths was to earn himself a £500,00 move to Manchester City, having scored 31 goals in 48 appearances that previous season.

For the U's, trialist Robert Hopkins scored their first goal (it was only 1-0 at half-time), glancing home a deep cross from Dean Martin, the ball trickling over the line. Hopkins, by then aged 32, had played most of his career as a wide midfielder for Birmingham and West Brom, but had also turned out for Shrewsbury the previous season before trying his luck in Hong Kong. It was his only goal for the U's in 14 outings, before he retired from the professional game later that year.

I had no complaints with the Gay Meadow experience as a visiting member of the press, although even I would have struggled to match the glowing praise afforded to the club following the construction of a modest new stand in 1922, by the local newspaper, the *Shrewsbury Chronicle*. It read as follows, 'The club are to be congratulated on their enterprise, for the stand is a handsome structure and would do credit to almost any of the leading clubs in the country…the facilities granted to the press representatives are all that can be desired. Journalists have so often to be content with any old seat in any odd corner that the local pressmen appreciate very highly the arrangements made for their comfort.'

High praise indeed. It is always wise to keep the press happy.

22 BRUNTON PARK

Club: Carlisle United
Founded: 1904
Ground: Brunton Park (since 1909)
First visit: 20 March 1993; Carlisle 0 Colchester 2

The view from the Brunton Park press box, including the author's lunchbox and his cheap watch.

A long way away. That's what always springs to mind when I consider a trip to Brunton Park, the home of Carlisle United.

If ever there was the potential for a long, fruitless journey, then a visit to Cumbria, for most southern-based clubs, would be a strong contender.

I have had my fair share of pointless trips to the Cumbrians' abode. Ipswich Town are lumbered with a 100 per cent record in terms of failure rate with five visits and five defeats (up until 2021), and there was no longer journey for Town in the Football League than an excursion north-westwards to Carlisle, at least until the return of Barrow to the League in 2020 (the two clubs have yet to meet). It is precisely 311 miles from Portman Road to Brunton Park, and 316 miles there from Colchester Community Stadium, which equates to round trips of more than 620 miles, putting it number one in terms of distance in front of nearest contenders Plymouth Argyle and Newcastle United, although that long-standing top three was disturbed by 2019/20 National League champions Barrow at 320 miles.

Regardless, a 100 per cent failure rate for Town, at a club like Carlisle who have spent most of their years in the bottom two tiers of the Football League since their election in 1928, plus one season back in non-league circles in the Conference (2004/05), is certainly a humbling thought to occupy the weary traveller on the marathon trek back down the M6.

By contrast, I have better tales to tell of the occasional success story with Colchester United as the accompaniment, in particular a memorable last game of the 2012/13 season.

There was tension in the tiny Brunton Park press box on that late April afternoon, at least among the away press contingent, because the U's were in danger of suffering relegation back to the fourth tier. Sweaty palms, feet twitching and a tendency to hit the wrong keys on the laptop, so nothing out of the ordinary for me.

In the end, a superb 2-0 win thanks to second-half goals by ex-Watford winger Gavin Massey and centre-half Tom Eastman saw the U's stay up by one place. I described it in my Monday morning match report as a 'brave away display on a sun-drenched unforgettable afternoon. A perfect day.' And I guess it was. Joe Dunne's side did it in style, overcoming their nerves and the intense pressure that comes with playing in such a pivotal game, an all-or-nothing, do-or-die, sink-or-swim encounter. The U's would have been overhauled by fourth-from-bottom Scunthorpe if they had lost and the Iron had won. And the North Lincolnshire club did win thanks to two late goals in a 3-1 victory over Swindon. But by then Massey had headed home the rebound after Billy Clifford's short had hit the bar on 65 minutes, and Eastman had doubled the lead with a header from Drey Wright's cross just 15 minutes later.

There was no happier man in Brunton Park that day, or in fact anyone more tired, than U's chairman and owner Robbie Cowling, who had cycled to the game from Colchester's training complex at Florence Park in Tiptree. Cowling had completed the 320-mile charity cycle ride over four days as the last leg of a marathon season, which had already seen him cycle to the first away league game of the season at Preston, and also run to every home game (23 in total) from his home at Great Totham at a distance of 15 miles. Cowling had been raising money for the Teenage Cancer Trust in memory of Emily Begg, a young Colchester United supporter who sadly died of leukaemia at the age of 14 in 2006. Emily's father, Stuart Begg, also cycled with Cowling to Carlisle.

'It was a mission accomplished,' said a delighted Dunne, the boss and former Colchester full-back. 'We had a game plan which worked absolutely spot on.'

I have always liked Brunton Park, long before that 'perfect day' in 2013. It's a fine example of an old, irregular ground with four very different stands, including the distinctive triple triangular blue roof over the covered terrace at the Warwick Road End, and the Main Stand on the west side which has the small press box at the top of the middle part of the upper tier, with paddock terracing below running the length of the pitch. The central section of this Main Stand dates back to 1954, a year after a fire burnt down the original wooden grandstand due to an electrical fault. In more recent times, flooding rather than fire has been the main issue, with the Cumbrians forced to play their home games elsewhere for spells in 2005 and 2015.

The East Stand, a single-tier cantilever stand opposite the main stand, was built in 1996, three years after my first visit. It is an unusual sight because the stand extends beyond the length of the playing surface in one corner, and falls short at the opposite end, to anticipate the pitch being moved a few yards north. But the pitch has stayed where it is due to a lack of funds.

The gates at Brunton Park, home of Carlisle United. (CM)

Another unusual sight, on my first Brunton Park outing in March 1993 was the debut appearance of new keeper Fred Barber, signed on a month's loan from Peterborough United just two days previously. The extrovert Barber, as was his norm, ran on to the pitch wearing a face mask of an old man, which always guaranteed a few second looks from unsuspecting supporters. Barber went on to mark his U's debut with a clean-sheet in a 2-0 win over the Cumbrians, achieved via midfielder Jason Cook's opener and an own goal by home defender Darren Edmondson, who diverted Steve McGavin's cross past Kelham O'Hanlon. Both goals were scored inside the first 40 minutes.

Barber's goal led a charmed life at times but this didn't stop the 29-year-old former Darlington and Walsall stalwart from celebrating in style at the final whistle by donning his mask to celebrate in front of the loyal travelling fans.

'Fred [Barber] will be a real asset over the next month,' enthused U's boss McDonough. 'Now we have three talkers in the team – me, Robbo [defender Paul Roberts] and Fred.' As for Barber, he was delighted with his debut, 'I've yet to lose on my first appearance for a team that I've been on loan to. And I've been with several different clubs!'

Back at Brunton Park 20 years later, I didn't need one of Barber's face masks after surviving a nerve-wracking afternoon reporting on the U's escape from the clutches of relegation. I aged about 20 years that day, so could carry off the withered look myself. No props or masks were required.

23 SPOTLAND

Club: Rochdale AFC
Founded: 1907
Ground: Spotland (built 1920, formerly the St Clement's Playing Fields site which had hosted sport since 1878)
First visit: 27 March 1993; Rochdale 5 Colchester 2

Edgar Street maybe my favourite away ground, thanks chiefly to the title of the first away venue I visited as a Colchester United reporter, but Spotland runs it a close second. Another strange choice, perhaps, given all the other glamorous contenders, but Spotland, the home of Rochdale AFC, was where I clocked up match number 1,000 as a U's scribe, on 7 March 2015.

It is not a strict rule, but usually the 'smaller' clubs have a closer bond with their local reporters. That has certainly been my experience with Colchester, hence the welcome surprise of being presented with a signed football club shirt after the final whistle at Spotland, in front of the dugouts, by then-U's manager Tony Humes. Especially appropriate, considering that Humes was a mainstay of Ipswich Town's defence between 1985 and 1992. The watching 'crowd' was not vast. My photographic colleague Warren Page took a couple of pictures of the presentation, and a couple of other U's reporters, Jon Waldron and Glenn Speller, happened to be in the vicinity when the shirt was unveiled, although that was mainly because they wanted to grab a few quotes off the manager. The club's head of media, David Gregory, the former Ipswich Town and Colchester United midfielder, was also in attendance to oversee the 'ceremony'. But that was it. One manager, four witnesses, a signed shirt and me in my old overcoat. Short and sweet. A little subdued, perhaps, given that the U's had just lost a League One tussle 2-1 to deepen their relegation fears. But in my eyes, Spotland looked a treat that evening. And now my wife had a new shirt to iron.

Of course there are other reasons for my lukewarm love affair with Spotland, one of them being musical. The songs emanating from the stadium's speakers, in my humble opinion, have always been the best in the Football League, with tracks from Manchester bands like The Stone Roses, Inspiral Carpets, The Smiths and Oasis blaring out before kick-off. It was enough to ensure I was in my seat in the press box well before 3pm. Call it 'pure poetry', but there was always something rather apt about tapping your feet to the sound of The Smiths' 'Heaven Knows I'm Miserable Now' before reporting on another away defeat.

Glossing over the top-notch indie music, and the visiting clubs handing out signed club shirts to undeserving reporters, what else can Spotland offer? Plenty. The town might look a bit grim, especially on a cold and wet afternoon with the moors in the distance looking dark and sinister, but there's a cheerful, good old-fashioned northern chippy on the doorstep of the football ground, in among the terraced houses – the Willbutts Lane Chippy – while the away fans are housed in the adjacent single-tiered Willbutts Lane Stand. Inside the ground (the outside is a bit plain, granted), the atmosphere is usually

Carl Marston is presented with a commemorative shirt by U's boss Tony Humes, at Spotland in 2015, for reaching the landmark of reporting on 1,000 U's games. Photographer Richard Blaxall

excellent, helped by the low roofs for acoustics and the terracing for camaraderie at the Sandy Lane End. This is the only terrace area still remaining, with the other three stands having all been redeveloped during the 1990s and around the turn of the century.

The press box is in the main stand (south side), which also houses the dressing rooms and the corporate hospitality boxes. It's always an education to hear the choice words of the resident season ticket holders sitting just in front of the press desks, within touching distance. They have never been shy to voice their opinion of the match officials or the opposition, and who can blame them? Success has never come easy to the Dale, the team having spent most of their life in the fourth tier, which used to prompt some cynics to refer to the bottom division as the 'Rochdale Division'.

My favourable impression of Spotland does hide some pretty dire results in terms of away-day reporting. This benchmark was set on my very first visit, in March 1993, when Dale ran out 5-2 winners over Colchester in a fourth-tier clash, despite the U's taking the lead through Nicky Smith (who later went on to become a policeman, and captain and manage the England national police team) and being level at 2-2 at the break, thanks to a goal from teenager Paul Abrahams on his full debut. But the no-nonsense hosts powered home with goals from Alex Jones, Andy Howard, man-of-the-match Steve Whitehall, Andy Thackeray and Jon Bowden.

It was a red-letter day for U's player-manager Roy McDonough, who was sent off for the 22nd time in his career, this time for an alleged use of the elbow, although it was the linesman standing 50 yards away who spotted the incident, not referee Michael Peck.

The popular 34-year-old leader, slapped with a four-match suspension (his third ban of the season) and hampered by injuries, announced his retirement as a player the following weekend. 'It's probably just as well for all concerned at the club that I should hang up my boots. It's very difficult being a player-manager in the firing line up front,' admitted McDonough.

However, McDonough's retirement did not last long. The big man went on to make 38 league appearances the following season to finish his career on the magic 500 mark.

Twenty-two years after McDonough was presented with his 22nd red card, well on his way to 500 Football League games, I was presented with the signed shirt, on the same Spotland pitch, for 1,000 U's first-team matches (McDonough's 22nd red card occurred during game 24 of this 1,000). Some say I should have been given my own marching orders long ago.

24 PLAINMOOR

Club: Torquay United
Founded: 1899
Ground: Plainmoor (since 1910)
First visit: 6 April 1993; Torquay 2 Colchester 2

Long-distance trips like the aforementioned trek to Carlisle United often require overnight stops, or at least they did in the early days when newspaper budgets were bigger and the expenses were more generous. Torquay United, on Devon's English Riviera, was always a popular destination with lower-league hacks. The promise of some seaside entertainment, even if it was just a few beers and a plate of fish and chips, was not to be sniffed at. The bracing sea air could do wonders for the quality of the afternoon prose, as could the morning fry-up.

But I admit it was a stretch, having to celebrate New Year's Eve away from home at the start of 1996, in Torquay (or rather nearby Exeter). The ever-helpful Football League fixture 'machine' had churned up a New Year's Day fourth-tier clash between Torquay United and Colchester United, so necessitating an overnight stay at a hotel (the same one as the players). These were still the days when sports scientists and sports nutritionists were thin on the ground, especially in the nether regions of the Football League, but the U's players were as good as gold on New Year's Eve. No mingling with the other hotel guests, or strutting their stuff on the hotel dancefloor as midnight approached, even without the threat of social media sites or mobile phones with built-in cameras – the latter did not become publicly available until after the turn of the century.

No late-night partying paid off the following day when a short hop along from Exeter to Plainmoor yielded a 3-2 win, book-ended by first-minute and last-minute goals. Thankfully, I too was not suffering a hangover when the first goal flew in after just 15 seconds. The same could not be said, perhaps, of Torquay keeper Ashley Bayes, who chose

U's boss Phil Parkinson paces the touchline at Plainmoor, in 2004. His side won 3-1 that day. (WP)

not to venture off his line to gather a nondescript pass forward by willow-the-wisp winger Chris Fry. Home defender Alex Watson was also leaden-footed, allowing classy midfielder Mark Kinsella to clip the ball into an empty net. Torquay had actually kicked off, so the U's scored with only two players having touched the ball.

Eddie May's Torquay were rock-bottom of the Football League but they belied their lowly position by scoring either side of half-time to take the lead. Rodney Jack, one of a rare breed – a Saint Vincent and the Grenadines international – swept home Ian Hathaway's cross, and Aidan Newhouse, on a short-term loan from Wimbledon, poked home from Jack's header. Winger Hathaway signed for the U's just 18 months later.

The U's, though, inspired by a raw teenager in Karl Duguid, turned the tables. On as a substitute for only his second senior appearance – he went on to rattle up a remarkable 414 league games for his beloved U's and 465 in all competitions – winger Duguid equalised with a composed finish on 77 minutes. Left-back Simon Betts, an unlikely hero, squeezed home from an acute angle in the fourth and last minute of injury-time to snatch victory.

All in all, a fine start to 1996.

The U's, under manager Steve Wignall, went on to lose in the Third Division play-offs, while the Gulls, although they finished well adrift at the bottom of the table, were not relegated because Conference champions Stevenage Borough did not meet the Football League requirements with regards their ground facilities.

So the English Riviera beckoned again the following year.

And it has beckoned many times, before and after that start to 1996. The first occasion was in April 1993 when a sizzling 25-yard special from Steve Ball earned the U's a battling

Page 32   East Anglian Daily Times, Tuesday, January 2, 1996

Endsleigh League Division Three   SPORT

U's begin and end in top style

by CARL MARSTON

START well, finish well. Those were Colchester United's tactics at Torquay yesterday, and they worked a treat.

The U's promotion surge gained momentum on the English Riviera thanks to a super-brisk start and a clinical finish.

There was hardly time to blink before Mark Kinsella set the tone for a frenetic afternoon's entertainment.

The U's midfielder broke the deadlock within 15 seconds of referee Graham Barber's very first whistle.

Just a few seconds before Barber's final whistle, and 93 minutes after Kinsella's opener, up popped Simon Betts to hook home a dramatic winner from the narrowest of angles.

It was the perfect way to celebrate the New Year. In fact, 1996 could prove quite a year for Steve Wignall's side.

Unbeaten in six matches and consolidating themselves in the top five, Colchester are bang in form.

U's keeper Carl Emberson confirmed: ''I think we're good enough to stay up there, especially as the leading pack are stretching away.

''The top five at the moment are bound to be there at the end of the season,'' added Emberson, who gave

BETTS: Late winner

another confident display.

Emberson's opposite number Ashley Bayes, however, suffered a miserable afternoon, often caught in no-man's land with his defenders unable to guess his next move.

The first Bayes blip proved the most costly. Torquay kicked off and full-back Steve Winter promptly gifted possession to Chris Fry.

Fry stroked the ball forward, to no-one in particular, and Bayes should have raced off his line to clear.

But he hesitated, as did centre-half Alex Watson. While the Gulls duo dithered, the alert Kinsella stole in to clip into an unguarded net from the edge of the box.

The perfect start for Colchester, and with only two of their players touching the ball!

Bottom club Torquay, dreadfully low in confidence, could have been two-down in the 34th minute when Paul Abrahams was denied by Bayes with defenders trailing in his wake.

From one end to the other and Torquay were on level terms within a minute of that miss.

A swift break ended with Rodney Jack sweeping home Ian Hathaway's cross. Suddenly, the visitors were on the rack and they found themselves trailing when Jack headed back across goal for Aidan Newhouse to poke home.

There were still 40 minutes left on the clock when Newhouse struck. Chances continued to flow aplenty but the goals, when they did eventually come, arrived from two unusual sources.

The first was a personal triumph for raw teenager Karl Duguid, who appeared as a 60th minute substitute and added some punch to Colchester's attacks from the left flank.

Duguid, making only his second senior appearance, obliged with a 77th minute equaliser. Tony Adcock and Tony English switched play across the face of goal and Duguid calmly slotted over the advancing Bayes.

It was a finish of terrific composure from the winger

who has come up through the youth ranks at Layer Road.

The draw looked a certainty but referee Barber somehow found four minutes of injury time and, in the last of those, Betts was crowned a hero.

The U's left-back notched his third goal in six matches as Bayes was again caught napping. Betts managed to squeeze the ball home from an acute angle via the far post and Torquay were left with no time to respond.

''That was such a frenetic game,'' admitted Colchester manager Wignall within minutes of the final whistle.

''Torquay were fired up for it, as all teams at the bottom tend to be. We left it very late but I am delighted.

''We played with four up front in the second half and could have scored even more goals. Torquay may feel aggrieved, but I think we created the better chances and deserved the win,'' added the U's boss.

The year 1995 ended quietly for the U's as they prepared for this game in an Exeter hotel.

New Year's Eve may have been a sober affair, but Wignall's men were in fine spirits on the long homeward journey. Could this be the U's year?

TORQUAY UNITED	2		3	COLCHESTER UNITED	
Rodney Jack (35 mins), Aidan Newhouse (50 mins)				Mark Kinsella (15 secs), Karl Duguid (77 mins), Simon Betts (90 mins)	
			Match Rating		Match Rating
		NEW YEAR'S DAY 1996			
MANAGER: Eddie May				MANAGER: Steve Wignall	
1 Ashley Bayes			11	1 Carl Emberson	17
2 Steve Winter			15	2 Tony Dennis	15

Flashback: the author's newspaper report from the New Year's Day clash at Plainmoor, in 1996.

2-2 draw at their relegation-haunted hosts. 'I've let a few people down this season, especially manager Roy [McDonough], who has kept faith in me,' confessed Ball, who was appointed to the U's top job himself 27 years later, in the summer of 2020, after four years as an assistant to John McGreal.

Back in those days, in the early 1990s, there was an open terrace at one end – to eventually be replaced by the covered terrace of the Sparkwood Stand in 2000 – while a third of the old Plainmoor Main Stand had been destroyed by a fire in 1985. That old wooden main stand with its corrugated iron roof and yellow seats, first acquired from nearby Buckfastleigh Racecourse during the 1920s, housed the press box, which is where I spent my time opposite the long and short Popular terrace, with its rather ungainly TV gantry planted on top of the roof. Compact, basic, homely.

As I highlighted at the start of this book, in the introduction, I also spent a worrying hour or so in the Plainmoor club car park, completely stranded, after the U's team coach had left without me during George Burley's short tenure as boss in the autumn of 1994, following a thrilling 3-3 draw. Fortunately, my absence was noted before the coach had left Devon, so a quick U-turn and I was saved an uncertain, unscheduled overnight stop in Torquay.

Those were the days when a local reporter of a lower-division club could travel on the team coach and have a better-than-even chance of getting a lift home as well. Even if it meant waiting in a Torquay car park, all alone, hoping that someone would remember me. The manager, the physio, a player, anyone.

I like Plainmoor, but not enough to get stuck there for the whole weekend.

25 EWOOD PARK

Club: Blackburn Rovers
Founded: 1875
Ground: Ewood Park (built in 1882, used by Rovers since 1890)
First visit: 12 April 1993; Blackburn 2 Ipswich 1

Ewood Park was in the process of being completely revamped when I paid my first visit in April 1993, during the inaugural season of the Premier League. The Riverside Stand had been replaced in the late 1980s, and less than a year after my visit, both ends, the Blackburn End and the Darwen End, were also sporting new two-tier stands, the Darwen End construction having followed the demolition of a few terraced houses, and also Fernhurst Mill. The splendid Jack Walker Stand, the main stand, was opened later in 1994, complete with its new media and conferencing facilities. Local entrepreneur Jack Walker bankrolled the development, while Kenny Dalglish had been bringing success on the pitch as manager since 1991.

The club had certainly come a long way since its humble beginnings in 1885, and especially since its first home at the intriguingly named Oozehead Ground, which was little more than a field with a watering hole for cattle near the centre circle. Before each game, the hole had to be covered by wooden boards and laid with turf. However, success came quickly to this northern outpost, backed by the wealth of the old cotton industry,

U's keeper Aidan Davison looks stunned after his mis-kick hands Blackburn Rovers the lead in an FA Cup tie in 2005. (WP)

with many of the workers from the cotton mills becoming regulars at Ewood Park from 1890 onwards, and before that at the Leamington Road venue. One of the founder members of the Football League in 1888, Rovers had won the FA Cup five times by 1891, and had added two First Division titles and a sixth FA Cup during the first three decades of the 20th century. However, by the time of my first visit, in 1993, they had not won a major trophy for 65 years.

That first outing was a rare Monday night fixture, with relegation-troubled Ipswich Town the visitors. For me, it was part one of a two-part mini tour alongside fellow scribe Tony Garnett, my boss at the time. Part two was a slightly less glamorous visit to Scarborough's McCain Stadium just 24 hours later.

My previous appearance in the press box with Town had been a win over mighty Manchester United at the end of January, when they were flying high in fourth spot and dreaming of another year of European football. Unfortunately, that had also happened to be Town's last win of any sort, a dismal haul of four points from 12 matches seeing them flirting with relegation. And that dreadful run of results was extended by a 2-1 reverse at Ewood Park. Stuart Ripley soon had them trailing with a deadly header on six minutes, before an own goal by Phil Whelan, who deflected home Ripley's cross, doubled the lead before half-time. It was Whelan's second own goal of the campaign, following on from one against Arsenal in the FA Cup. John Lyall's Town staged a second-half comeback, helped by Simon Milton's stunning 25-yarder which beat keeper Bobby Mimms, but it was not enough to prevent a 2-1 loss.

Blackburn went on to finish fourth, just missing out on a European place, but famously went on to win the Premier League title in 1995, while Town stayed up in 16th spot, three points clear. Ripley went on to earn the first of his two England caps later that year, and qualified as a solicitor in 2010.

I was back at Ewood Park 12 years later (I have never been a regular visitor) this time for an FA Cup tie featuring Colchester United, who were going well under manager Phil Parkinson, on 29 January 2005. It was a rare footballing occasion where I was accompanied by my wife Helen and youngest step-son Harry, who were perhaps more impressed with the indoor swimming pool at our hotel in nearby Ramsbottom than the afternoon's entertainment at Ewood Park.

The U's sunk without a trace, well beaten 3-0, having never recovered from keeper Aidan Davison's air kick which saw midfielder Kevin Watson's back-pass roll into the net for an own goal. The ball did take a big bobble, but it didn't look great and the goal completely deflated the Essex side, as well as myself in the press box in the Jack Walker Stand, and also Helen and Harry in the Darwen End. Goals from Jemal Johnson (his only goal for Rovers) and ex-Liverpool and Leeds defender Dominic Matteo ensured the inevitable, namely a U's Cup exit and another Ewood Park defeat for me.

'That's the worst we have played in the three games against Premier League teams this season,' rued boss Parkinson, with reference to the previous matches against West Brom and Southampton in the Carling Cup. Parkinson added, 'I thought that our heads went down after conceding the first goal. We felt a little bit sorry for ourselves. It's just a shame that Blackburn Rovers fans have not seen Colchester at their best today.'

As for that comical opening goal, Parkinson insisted, 'I don't put any blame on Aidan [Davison] for the first goal. I blame the pitch. He didn't say a lot after the match, but he's a big enough character to move on from this disappointment.'

But Davison himself, a consummate professional for the previous 17 years, must have hoped that the ground would swallow him up after that 21st-minute howler. In fact, it was perhaps a pity that Rovers were still not playing at their first ground at Oozehead, because then he could have lifted up a few wooden planks and disappeared down the cow pit watering hole until everyone had gone home.

26 McCAIN STADIUM

Club: Scarborough FC
Founded: 1879
Ground: McCain Stadium (1898 to 2007)
First visit: 13 April 1993; Scarborough 0 Colchester 1

I endured one of my most torrid journeys as a football writer to fulfil my newspaper duties at the 'Theatre of Chips' just three days after Christmas 1993.

The snow lay thick on the ground when I left my home in Suffolk early on the morning of Tuesday, 28 December with a car-load of assorted local Colchester United media, and a boot full of radio equipment and cameras, bound for the North Yorkshire coast. Conditions deteriorated as we hit the Great North Road (or rather the A1), to such an extent that only the very bravest drivers would even venture into the outside lane.

It was a crawl. And I am not brave.

There were times when I feared we wouldn't get to Scarborough until the end of the month, let alone before 3pm. We even considered turning around at one point and so risk not attending the match, even if it managed to escape the wintry grip. Occasionally I would close my eyes and attempt a few dicey yards in the 'fast lane', so desperate were we to get to this low-key Third Division clash.

As it happened, though, the weather began to clear the further north we crawled, and we made quicker progress along the final stretch on the A64 to pull in to the McCain Stadium in good time for the kick-off. And it was all worth it. Although conditions were freezing, the pitch was just muddy (it often seemed to be muddy when the U's visited) rather than snowbound, and second-half goals from Roy McDonough and Steve McGavin wrapped up a 2-0 win.

I never actually experienced a defeat in all my six visits to the McCain Stadium – known as the Athletic Ground before McCain Foods secured the naming rights in 1988 – so in a way it was one of my favourite grounds. Sitting in the small press box at the back of the Main Stand, a proper old grandstand, and looking out over the Cow Shed opposite, with its covered terracing, and the small all-seater stands at either end (east and west), this was down-to-earth, fourth-tier football at its most pure.

My most memorable visit was in early September 1994, for Colchester United's fifth league game of the season, and their fifth under new manager George Burley. The U's had lost their first four, and scored just one goal, so my hopes were not high of success against Billy Ayre's hosts. But in the scrappiest of lower-league encounters, midfielder Tony Dennis swept home a winner with 20 minutes to go to lift the U's off the Football League basement. New manager Burley, who had begun the season playing at full-back, was happy to sit on the bench in his dual role as manager and unused substitute. Afterwards, the Scotsman told me, 'I'll just be happy to stay in the dugout and watch them do the job. It's much easier than playing.'

And that's just what he did, until leaving to become manager of Ipswich Town five months later.

It is always sad when an old ground is left to decay after a home club moves on, or in Scarborough's case is wound up due to crippling debts of £2.5m, and the McCain Stadium did suffer a humiliating fall from grace. The site was left to rot, the grass and weeds took hold – they had already started to do that while football was still being played, in one corner between stands – and the vandals made a mess of the structures. I paid a return visit a few years later while holidaying in Scarborough, and would never have recognised

The padlocked gates of the McCain Stadium, Scarborough's long abandoned home. (CM)

the place if it wasn't for the presence of the distinctive black entrance gates, emblazoned with 'Scarborough Football Club' in white letters. At least those gates have been preserved and are now on display at the new Flamingo Land Stadium, the home of Scarborough Athletic, the successor to Scarborough FC. A supermarket has been built on the site of the old ground.

I took my wife along to view what was left of the McCain Stadium, basically just those entrance gates and a few weeds, on that break. It was not Helen's holiday highlight.

27 GRESTY ROAD

Club: Crewe Alexandra
Founded: 1877
Ground: Gresty Road (since 1906)
First visit: 24 April 1993; Crewe 7 Colchester 1

If ever a stadium can be dominated and completely overwhelmed by one main stand then Gresty Road is it.

And on a personal note, if there is a stadium that can rival Gresty Road, the home of Crewe Alexandra, for providing a rude awakening on a first visit, then I don't want to know about it. My first trip to Crewe, a renowned railway town in Cheshire, ended in

The view from the lofty press box at Gresty Road. (CM)

a 7-1 defeat for Colchester United with home striker Tony Naylor banging home a club record five goals.

Gresty Road looked very different on that late April 1993 occasion. It felt small and homely, although not that comfortable for Roy McDonough's Colchester side, who saw their faint play-off hopes scattered to all four corners. The U's defence was wobbling from the first minute. It creaked, it sagged, and eventually folded as Dario Gradi's men deservedly earned the Barclay's Performance of the Week award. If there had been a corresponding Humiliation of the Week award then the U's would have been hot favourites to scoop the silverware, glassware or wooden spoon, whatever the prize.

Naylor scored 16 league goals that season, six of them against Colchester (he had also netted in a 3-2 defeat at Layer Road). He went on to enjoy seven good seasons at Port Vale, and two at Cheltenham, but his demolition of the U's was always a highlight. The pacy striker scored the first inside two minutes and added further goals on 39, 63, 77 and 86 minutes, with Dave McKearney and Phil Clarkson scoring the other two for a 4-0 half-time lead.

Crewe boss Dario Gradi joked, 'I wish he [Naylor] hadn't scored five goals. He should have scored two this afternoon and saved the others for the last few games of the season.' Originally appointed manager ten years earlier, in 1983, Gradi's reign in the Gresty Road hot seat lasted 24 years until 2007, and he had another short stint from 2009 to 2011.

For once, U's boss Roy McDonough left the post-match press briefing to his coach, Ian Phillips, who admitted, 'We had toyed with the idea of playing a sweeper, and on reflection maybe we should have done.'

I gave Naylor ten out of ten in my player ratings for Monday's newspaper, a rare accolade for an opposing player, even though I liked to think of myself as being very generous in that regard. I knew they were the best-read (or only read) item on the page. In fact, looking back through the ratings of that game, I seem to have been remarkably generous, even to some U's players. I recall Steve Ball had a good game in central midfield

The view from the lofty press box at Gresty Road looking towards the Railway End. (CM)

that fateful afternoon but to give him eight out of ten while on the wrong end of a 7-1 mauling appears rather lavish.

What I will say is that a 7-1 thrashing on a first visit makes it easier to stomach any disappointments on return journeys, and Gresty Road, with its huge Railtrack Stand opened in the summer of 1999, is like a different stadium now. About 70 per cent of the ground capacity is accommodated in this single tier cantilever stand, a sea of red seats numbering nearly 7,000 and affording an excellent view of the pitch and the adjacent railway station. The press area is at the rear of this stand, in one corner, so you can watch the trains pull in and out of the station if the football is a bit dull, while you catch your breath after tackling the long flight of stairs. Fortunately, I have had no more 7-1s to report on, so I have done my share of train spotting during some less memorable lower-division encounters.

The other stands are minute, by comparison, the away fans sitting on the opposite side in the delightfully-named Whitby Morrison Ice Cream Van Stand. This was the old Pop Side, where fans used to stand on the decaying terraces until it was demolished a couple of years after my first visit, in 1995. Above is a TV gantry, and in one of the corners is a giant clock, so there's no excuse for bad timekeeping. To the right, looking out from the press box, is the Railway End, which became all-seater in 1992, and to the left is the Gresty Road End, named after the street that also gives the ground its alternative name to Alexandra Stadium.

So it's an easily recognisable ground, but one that continued to yield very little in the way of on-the-road joy. In fact, the U's had gone 26 years without any league wins at Gresty Road, losing their last five on the bounce going into a more hopeful visit in November 2012, during the early weeks of Joe Dunne's tenure as boss. I got very excited when goals from wingers Freddie Sears and Ian Henderson put the U's 2-0 up inside half an hour, an advantage they retained going into the last 40 minutes. A first league win at Crewe since 1986, to end the drought, looked assured until Fulham loanee Lauri Dalla Valle, skipper Luke Murphy with a penalty and striker Mathias Pogba all scored past U's debut keeper John Sullivan to complete a dramatic turnaround.

I blame my own visit to the men's urinals at half-time for the capitulation on the pitch. Standing between two Crewe fans, and so privy to their conversation, I heard one say, 'I can't see us scoring three goals in the second half to win this one.' Tongue in cheek, his mate replied, 'No, I think we'll score four.' I muttered 'fat chance' under my breath. To be honest, Crewe were so bad in that first period that I couldn't see them even scoring once. At the same time, Crewe boss Steve Davis was clearly delivering an inspiring half-time speech in the home dressing room. The turnaround amazed me, and would certainly have amazed the pair of fans who flanked me in the bog. It was nearly as deflating as that dire 7-1 from 19 years earlier.

Never one to get too down in the dumps, or too bogged down by indifferent results, however awful they might be, I have always liked walking up the many steps to my press seat at the back of the Railtrack Stand, munching on a complimentary pie and looking out for the trains, while trying to forget that Tony Naylor ever existed.

Tony Naylor? Never heard of him.

28 SELHURST PARK

Club: Crystal Palace
Founded: 1905
Ground: Selhurst Park (1924)
First visit: 1 May 1993; Crystal Palace 3 Ipswich 1

The dread of relegation hung in their air when I first visited Selhurst Park on the penultimate weekend of the first Premier League season.

Visiting Ipswich Town were all but safe, regardless of the result, but Crystal Palace were desperate for the points. I remember sensing the dark fears of home fans, who were packed on to the old terraces, the dreadfully weak tea served up from a huge pot in the press lounge, the unusual sight of a Sainsbury's supermarket outside one end of the ground, and the hot, bright sunshine. It was indeed an afternoon of contrasts.

It was 1 May 1993, around the time that the ground was enjoying a much-needed facelift. The Holmesdale terrace on the south side was still standing – that was demolished a year later and replaced with a two-tier stand – but there had been work done to the Arthur Wait Stand and Whitehorse Lane. The Main Stand, where the press box was situated, with its 63 press seats, was more antiquated, having been built back in 1924. But it was bursting with character, if a little cramped, which could be said of the whole ground.

Flashback: the author's match report of Town's predictable defeat at Selhurst Park in the following Monday's newspaper, in 1993.

Passion beats pride

There was an air of predictability about this Premier League clash at a sun-drenched Selhurst Park. One team had to win; the other could afford to lose.

Steve Coppell's Crystal Palace needed the points to drag themselves clear of the relegation dogfight; Mick McGivern's Ipswich, with their Premier League status virtually secure, were playing for pride and the monetary rewards to be gained from climbing a few rungs up the ladder.

The result was never really in doubt. Palace, with pace up front and domination in midfield, were 2-0 up inside 6 minutes.

Town's band of travelling support, soaking up the sun while sweating over Palace's early forays up field, looked aghast. But gradually with some probing passes either some probing passes ere vanished.

David Gregory, who has been most of this season t reserve the reserves, registered Town's first shot on … in the 19th minute with fling volley that Nigel n was relieved to block, denly the tiring hosts match on their hands, yen Gregory's second of the afternoon flew rtyn and into the roof e's net, the carnival ere vanished.

h forced the pace in ning seven minutes t period and Jason ent Steve Palmer … to the area with a through ball. Pal- bed a cracking Martyn diverted

rs kept up the for the first ten he second half Eagles awoke slumber and

**PALACE 3
IPSWICH 1**

Carl Marston
reports from
Selhurst
Park

Town were without full-backs Eddie Youds (suspended) and Gavin Johnson (knee injury), so Mick Stockwell and Phil Whelan filled defensive roles with Steve Palmer and Gregory coming into the midfield.

A "diamond" formation was tried with Simon Milton sitting just behind the front two, but there was little shape to the visitors.

Within six minutes, Town were behind. McGoldrick swung over a corner that curled in towards Baker. Chris Coleman jumped in front of him, with Town's keeper only able to flap the ball down into the path of Eric Young, who gratefully prodded home.

A minute later, only the woodwork denied rampant Palace a second. Chris Arm-

Town stumble: Ipswich striker Chris Kiwomya tries to get the better of Crystal Palace defender Eric Young, making his 100th appearance for The Eagles, in Saturday's clash at Selhurst Park aged to redirect it over the

Tucked away in a muddle of back streets, I don't actually think I have ever approached Selhurst Park from the same direction, or via the same route. I always seem to get lost and then just stumble upon it, too proud or too foolish to resort to sat-nav.

Town stumbled to a rather inevitable 3-1 defeat at Palace on that scorching hot afternoon. Steve Coppell's hosts needed the win more than their opponents and they soon raced into a 2-0 lead. Eric Young prodded home a sixth-minute opener after keeper Clive Baker had flapped at a corner by Eddie McGoldrick while under pressure from centre-half Chris Coleman, and Chris Armstrong doubled the lead from close in. Armstrong had taken over the mantle of Palace's main goalscorer that season following the departures of Ian Wright to Arsenal in 1991 and Mark Bright to Sheffield Wednesday in September 1992.

David Gregory, who had spent most of the season skippering Town's reserves, halved the deficit by drilling past Nigel Martyn, but McGoldrick smashed home Palace's third from substitute Paul Williams's lay-off to seal the points.

Palace boss Coppell was a relieved man during the post-match press conference, 'The pressure has been on all season, so the consequences of defeat have been enormous. I'm proud to have equalled the longest spell Crystal Palace have enjoyed in the top division, but I don't want another season like this. It's certainly been the hardest of my career.'

Unfortunately for Palace and Coppell, relegation was suffered the following weekend in very cruel fashion. They ended their season with a midweek 0-0 draw at Manchester City and a 3-0 defeat at Arsenal, while rivals Oldham Athletic managed to win their last three matches – 1-0 at Aston Villa, 3-2 at home to Liverpool and 4-3 at home to Southampton on the final day. The Latics stayed up on goal difference while Palace went down despite having accumulated 49 points. That remains the highest tally for a team relegated from the Premier League. Coppell resigned shortly afterwards, so ending his nine-year stay.

I, meanwhile, left south London that evening with a touch of sunburn and milky tea still sloshing around the stomach.

It was not so sunny, although the tea was just as weak, when I surfed into Selhurst Park on the wave of Colchester United's unprecedented recent successes for a Championship fixture on 9 December 2006. Okay, so I actually arrived in a Vauxhall Meriva (not on a surfboard), once again via a mysteriously different route picking my way through south-east London, but Geraint Williams's men were surging up the second-tier table with such speed and style that it felt like we were all 'surfing'. The U's rose to the heady heights of eighth following their 3-1 win at Selhurst Park. Having survived a first-half onslaught from the Eagles, the U's scored three times in the last half-hour through skipper Karl Duguid, super-sub Richard Garcia and an injury-time penalty from Chris Iwelumo. Palace front-runner Clinton Morrison, who six years later was to end up signing for the U's on a two-year deal, had given the hosts a little hope with what proved to be only a consolation on 87 minutes. Otherwise, experienced home strikers Morrison and the ex-Town pair of Shefki Kuqi and James Scowcroft huffed and puffed to little effect. The highlight of the whole afternoon was Garcia's wonder goal, the Australian running at the home defence before crashing a 20-yarder beyond bewildered keeper Scott Flinders.

'This season just keeps getting better and better' – so began my opening paragraph in the following Monday's newspaper. The likes of West Brom, Sunderland, Norwich, Wolves, Leeds, Ipswich, Leicester and Palace were all below unfashionable Colchester in the table at the midpoint of the season. 'We were just not good enough,' rued Palace boss Peter Taylor at the end of the match, although I was more intent on infiltrating the visitors' camp. 'The players are building up some big reputations for themselves, but we are under no pressure to sell anyone,' insisted U's boss Williams.

Indeed, with just the one notable exception of Greg Halford, who left for Reading in a £2.5m deal in January 2007, the U's did not sell anyone before the end of the season. It was all change in the summer when star players like Wayne Brown, Jamie Cureton, Chris Iwelumo and Garcia all left for pastures new. Needless to say, it was no surprise that Palace doubled the weakened U's the following season, including a 2-1 reverse at Selhurst Park in March 2008.

Ground-wise, Selhurst Park itself had changed little in the intervening years since my first visit with Town, with the exception of the imposing new two-tiered Holmesdale Road Stand, with its mighty curved roof, which replaced the old bank of terracing at one end. The fans remained close to the pitch, many of the seats were still wooden, and the atmosphere could still be quite intimidating, in a 'homely' sort of way. More importantly, I still struggled to find it, and when I did, I would then have to drive a mile or so 'out of town' to find a place to park. Still, a cup of weak tea (probably one tea bag per ten cups) was always waiting for me. I might bring a flask next time.

29 FEETHAMS

Club: Darlington
Founded: 1883
Ground: Feethams (from 1883 to 2003)
First visit: 4 May 1993; Darlington 1 Colchester 0

Football at Feethams came to an end in 2003, with the ground demolished three years later, but I can still remember more about Darlington's famous first home than most modern-day, purpose-built stadia. The twin towers, the unusual walk around a cricket pitch to get to the football venue, a floodlight in the groundsman's garden, the very cheap beer on offer, and the ritual of home supporters walking from one end of the ground to the other at half-time, to stand behind the goal which their team were attacking in the second half. Feethams was full of quirks.

It was a true 'home' ground, close to the town centre and full of charm, with a main stand (East Stand) which was modernised in 1997, four years after my first visit, where

Endsleigh League Division Three

Seven-goal shambles

■ Shell-shocked: U's keeper John Keeley put up a brave perfromance

Darlington 7 Colchester 3

Darlington		Colchester	
DARREN COLLIER	6	JOHN KEELEY	7
ADAM REED	7	ADAM LOCKE	6
LAURIE PEARSON	6	PAUL ROBERTS	4
GARY HIMSWORTH	7	MARK KINSELLA	7
MARK SUNLEY	7	TONY ENGLISH	5
SEAN GREGAN	6	PETER CAWLEY	6
ANTHONY ISAACS	7	ALAN DICKENS	8
ROBBIE PAINTER	9	STEVE BALL	5
LEE ELLISON	8	(Sub. John Richardson 83)	
(Sub. Simon Shaw 89)		ROY MCDONOUGH	6
GARY CHAPMAN	8	STEVE MCGAVIN	6
PETER KIRKHAM	7	NICKY SMITH	6
(Sub. Stephen Ball 73)		UNUSED SUBS	
UNUSED SUB		Simon Betts	
Ryan Scott (gk)		David Schultz (gk)	

REFEREE: Mr Paul Harrison (Oldham) 7
GOALS: Darlington – Ellison 1, 80; Painter 20, 58;
Chapman 33, 84; Himsworth 71
Colchester – Dickens 9, McGavin 59, Kinsella 75
CORNERS: Darlington 5, Colchester 2
GOAL ATTEMPTS: Darlington 17, Colchester 12
SHOTS ON TARGET: Darlington 12, Colchester 7
BOOKINGS: Darlington – None
Colchester – Roberts (handball) 63;
McDonough (dissent) 78
ATTENDANCE: 1,299

COCO the clown should have turned up for last night's big top entertainment at Feethams. He would have left with some priceless new material for his circus act.

It was a comedy of errors from start to finish at basement dwellers Darlington and the joke was all on Colchester and their woeful defence.

The Quakers had not won in 13 league matches and scored just seven

U's defence cut to shreds at Feethams

BY CARL MARSTON

ing a one match suspension, did well to block Gary Himsworth's snap shot but striker Lee Ellison was on hand to crash home the rebound.

Despite this shock early blow, the visitors remained unrattled and dictated for 20 minutes. Steve McGavin

chester's beleaguered defence failed to deal with a Himsworth corner and Gary Chapman stabbed home inside a congested six-yard box.

That rounded off the entertainment for the first-half. The small pocket of Colchester fans consoled themselves with the belief that it couldn't get any worse — but how wrong could they be.

Darlington helped themselves to a fourth in the 58th minute. Keeley, who could not really be blamed for any of the goals, was again exposed as Painter slotted home. There was not a defender in sight.

Colchester did reply within 30 seconds when McGavin's angled shot somehow found its way through

Flashback: The headline says it all from the U's calamitous visit to Feethams in the autumn of 1993.

the few members of the press were accommodated. The River Skerne flowed just behind this stand. Opposite was the unusual and very dated West Stand with its low, curved roof making it resemble a small barn, while there was terracing at either end, the uncovered Polam Lane and the Tin Shed (Cricket Ground End). Not much changed over the years. The wooden West Stand, with its benches for seating, actually burnt down in 1960, but was quickly replaced with the same-styled structure rather than any new, modern design, apparently for insurance purposes. A roof was put on the Tin Shed at about the same time.

Entering via the turnstiles, it was necessary to walk through the twin towers (built in 1913), the proud gateway to this sporting venue, and then amble around the cricket field (Durham CCC played their first County Championship match there in 1992) to gain entry to the football ground; a happy pilgrimage. Certainly better than walking through a retail park or around a bland concourse. With the exception of a couple of early fixtures at North Lodge Park, Darlington could call Feethams their home for 120 years, from 1883 to 2003, although the venue dated back further to 1866 when Darlington Cricket Club moved there from Old Park Street, transporting much of the turf from their old ground in the process.

My first visit to Feethams ended in disappointment during the last week of the 1992/93 season. A 36th-minute goal from Sheffield United loanee John Reed, who fired past former Darlington keeper Fred Barber, an old home favourite, secured a 1-0 win for the Quakers and so ended Colchester United's play-off hopes going into the final weekend. Reed tucked home a cross by Steve Mardenborough, a much-travelled winger who ended up playing 12 games for Colchester just two years later.

But this first appearance was not half as painful as my second visit, a 7-3 drubbing on another long midweek trek up to the north-east just six months later. The headline above my story in the following day's newspaper – 'Seven-goal shambles' – hit the mark. I referred to the whole bizarre evening, wearing my U's hat, as a 'comedy of errors from start to finish', made worse by the fact that Darlington were propping up the Football League. The Quakers had not won in 13 league matches, and scored just seven goals in 1,170 minutes, before doubling their tally inside another 90 minutes on an early November evening in 1993.

Looking back, the fact that I still gave U's keeper John Keeley seven out of ten in the player ratings suggests that he had a reasonable night between the sticks, which he did. Without some of Keeley's fine saves, Colchester's club record 8-0 defeat at Leyton Orient from 1988 would have been expunged from the record books. It was a night for cool heads and calculators in the press box. The Quakers led 3-1 at half-time through goals from Lee Ellison, Robbie Painter and Gary Chapman, after ex-West Ham maestro Alan Dickens had earlier equalised with his first goal for the Essex club, a screamer from the edge of the box. Painter, Ellison and Chapman (sounding like a firm of solicitors) all scored again in the second half, as did Gary Himsworth. Steve McGavin and Mark Kinsella replied for the well-beaten and embarrassed U's, who had by then conceded 15 goals in their last three away outings, all against lowly opposition. Their defence was resembling a sieve.

What a night. I felt over-worked and under-paid.

The one salvation was a pre-match pint, purchased in the town centre for just 99p in the company of Jim French, an ardent U's supporter. To this day, whenever Jim refers to that disastrous night in Darlington, he gloats over the cheap price of his pint before he even mentions the 7-3 debacle.

I just remember it all as a crazy time. The 7-3 at Feethams happened just 17 days after a 5-0 defeat at Hereford, so at least I was getting used to all these rugby scores. I was beginning to pine for a good old 0-0.

30 RACECOURSE GROUND

Club: Wrexham
Founded: 1864 (wound up in 1884, but reformed a few months later)
Ground: Racecourse Ground (from 1864, opened 1807)
First visit: 8 May 1993; Wrexham 4 Colchester 3

Party-poopers. That was the role Colchester United wanted to play during their end-of-season clash at the Racecourse Ground in May 1993. This was my first visit, and I couldn't help but be impressed by the sheer size of the ground, especially the vast concrete terracing at the Kop (Crispin Lane End), which had been laid in 1952 to accommodate all-standing home supporters. It was a throwback to grounds of yesteryear, those spacious terraces with the colourful crowd barriers to lean on. In its heyday, that Kop could accommodate close to 9,500 fans at a push. Immense.

Reputed to be the sixth or perhaps seventh oldest association football club in the world (these lists are continually being contested and edited), Wrexham FC just screams history, although the club's foundation date has sparked some fierce debate. Recent research has revealed that Wrexham were first formed in 1864, just one year after the Football Association first convened in the Freemasons' Tavern (a well-known meeting place in the 18th and 19th centuries) on Great Queen Street in London. This was at odds with the previous assumption of 1872 as the year of Wrexham's formation, which also had pub roots with a meeting at the Turf Hotel public house on the corner of the Racecourse Ground. To complicate matters a little further, and muddy the waters, the original club disbanded in 1884, only to reform a few months later under the name Wrexham Olympic and then revert to its original name in 1888. This has led to Newton AFC (founded in 1875) claiming to be the oldest club in Wales, and not Wrexham as previously assumed. The plot thickens.

I will leave that debate here, dangling.

What is of no doubt is that the Racecourse Ground remains the world's oldest international stadium which still hosts international matches, following the first one in 1877, and although it has long since seen better days, there was a terrific atmosphere when the already-promoted

U's nearly spoil Welsh party

ESTER came within a minute of spoil-
tham's promotion party at a packed
se Ground this afternoon.
tering 25 yard drive from Mark
auled the U's back on level terms in
inute.
ve Watkin pounced with a dramatic
earn the Welsh hosts a pulsating vic-
ven goal thriller.

CARL MARSTON
reports from the
Racecourse ground

egular in the
-as given his
because Bar-
n spell from
ends this
defined with
aments.

Cawley and
moett were
rting lineup,
r Kimsella,
rip to Dar-
k to attend

iival atmo-
tacecourse
ham sup-
orate their
ion Two.
rash with
I it was
test for
vas their
son.
'rexham
Ipswich
Humes,
ng the
te pitch
el and

applaud the Wrexham
players for their promotion
feats of this season.
The home side received a
hero's welcome with a packed
crowd releasing balloons and
confetti into the air.
The Robins, needing to win
by four goals and to have
other results going their way
to clinch the title, were on the
offensive straight away and
Connolly backheaded a
corner just off target.
But there was a real hush
around the ground when Colchester threatened on the
counterattack. Smith swung
over a teasing cross and
McGavin was just inches
away from heading into an
empty net, the ball just skid-
ding off his head.
Munson had his first real
test in the 10th minute when
racing off his line to gather a
loose ball under heavy pressure from Cross.

But he was caught in no
man's land seconds later
when a low cross from Wrexham's Bennett found CON-
NOLLY in acres of space,
and all the Wrexham Number
number had to do was slot
into a gaping net from six
yards.
Only the woodwork denied
United an equaliser in the
15th minute. Kinsella timed
his pass to perfection to set
McGavin darting clear of the
Wrexham offside trap.

Cruel luck

McGavin aimed his shot
wide of the advancing Morris
but the ball cannoned off the
far post and Kinsella blasted
the rebound into the side netting.
This was cruel luck for
Colchester and McGavin in
particular. But the U's were

not disheartened and they
continued to make inroads
into the Wrexham penalty
area.
In the 18th minute,
Grainger delivered a cross
into the danger zone and
Abrahams rose high to head
narrowly over.
A minute later and keeper
Morris had to dive low to
smother a cracking shot from
Ball.
The hardworking
Abrahams outwitted his
marker and swept over a
dangerous cross that soared
over Morris' head, but there
was no Colchester teammate
on hand to get the vital
touch.
At the other end, Munson
excelled with a smart save in
the 35th minute. Bennett,
clear of the United defence,
unleashed a ferocious drive
that United's debutant
pushed away to safety.
There were a few Welsh
nerves tingling when Morris
failed to deal with a looping
cross from Smith, allowing
Ball the chance of a header
that drifted over the bar.
But the visitors fell further
behind in the 43rd minute
when the unfortunate BETTS

headed into his own net. A
corner from Cross was
flicked goalwards by Lake
and right back Betts, at full
stretch, could do nothing
more than head the ball over
his line. Half-time:

WREXHAM 2
COLCHESTER 0

Within a minute of the
restart, Roberts was in hot
water. United's player of the
season dragged down a
dangerous through ball with
his hand to prevent Watkin
from scampering clear.
The referee awarded a free
kick and summoned Roberts
over for a chat but the U's
centre half was perhaps
fortunate to escape without
even a booking.
Wrexham made all the
early running in the second
half and two corners from
Cross were dealt with by the
head of Roberts and the safe
handling of keeper Munson.
On a rare sortie upfield
Abrahams contested for a
high ball with keeper Morris
and was left sprawled on the
turf. After a minute's treatment Abrahams clambered to
his feet, although still looking
groggy.

The home supporters were
then stunned in the 54th
minute when the game's second own goal, this time
netted by HARDY, put Col-
chester right back in the contest.
Kinsella burst through
from midfield and found Ball
with a precise pass. Col-
chester's midfielder tried his
luck with a first time shot
that would have drifted wide
of the target. But his effort
bounced off left-back Hardy
and rolled over the line.
Before the game could be
restarted, following Col-
chester's strike, Abrahams
left the pitch, still looking in
a daze. He was replaced by
Hopkins.
United had temporarily
grabbed the initiative and
Grainger was able to test
Morris with two thumping
freekicks within minutes of
each other.
Morris held on to the first
thunderbolt but the second
escaped his grasp. Bennett
raced in but his effort was
blocked and the chance was
gone.
However, Wrexham were
back in command when
WATKIN pounced for their

third in the 66th minute.
Connolly's cross found Bennett in space on the edge of
the six yard box, and his
intended shot fell kindly for
Watkin to rifle into an empty
net.
Two minutes later and Colchester reduced the deficit
through BENNETT.
A superb strike from
KINSELLA sent Colchester's
away fam delirious in the
79th minute. McGavin slid
the ball across to Kinsella,
who was standing 25 yards
from goal.
Wrexham had the last
laugh when WATKIN guided
a quick reaction header past
Munson to regain the lead
and clinch a dramatic victory
in the 89th minute.

WREXHAM 4
COLCHESTER 3

WREXHAM: Morris, Jones
Hardy, Owens, Humes, Pesc
Bennett, Lake, Connolly, Wa
kin, Cross. Subsitutes: Parki

COLCHESTER: Munso
Betts, Roberts, Kinsell
Grainger, Cawley, Ball, Bent
Abrahams, McGavin, Sm
Subsitutes: Flowers and H
kins.

● Attendance: 9,705

Match report from the U's trip to the Racecourse Ground on the final day of the 1992/93 season.

Robins (they accrued a new nickname of Red Dragons at the turn of the 21st century) took on the mid-table U's to bring the curtain down on the 1992/93 season.

I was in the press box in the main Yale Stand, which was built in 1972 and backed on to the site of the former Yale College. Opposite, the old Mold Road Stand had been closed for several years, due to health and safety reasons following the Bradford City stadium fire of 1985. It was eventually demolished and replaced with a resplendent new stand, with a curved central roof, for the start of the 1999/2000 season.

Back on the final day of 1992/93, the Racecourse was a sea of red and white with more than 9,000 home fans keen to celebrate their team's promotion to the third tier, while also harbouring faint hopes of clinching the Third Division title. Brian Flynn's men needed to thump the U's by at least a four-goal margin and hope that the other automatically promoted teams, Cardiff and Barnet, slipped up. That didn't happen.

Wrexham were looking good at 2-0 up at half-time through Karl Connelly's opener and Simon Betts's headed own goal from Mike Lake's effort. But in the end, they only just squeezed home 4-3. An own goal by left-back Phil Hardy (who played more than 450 games for Wrexham, all of them under Flynn), a poacher's effort by Gary Bennett and a 25-yard thunderbolt from Mark Kinsella left it at 3-3, and the U's had the audacity to go in search of a winner until being undone by Steve Watkin's 89th-minute header past keeper Nathan Munson, who was making his Football League debut. I also remember veteran Jimmy Case, the ex-Liverpool stalwart, appearing as a second-half substitute for the triumphant hosts just a few weeks before his 39th birthday.

The Racecourse Ground was a cauldron of noise at the final whistle. The U's had come close to being party-poopers and they could slip away with their heads held high while their hosts celebrated. Alas, my head was still laid low, trying to make myself heard to the copy-takers back in Suffolk.

This trip to the Racecourse Ground, home of the 'disputed' oldest football club in Wales, brought the curtain down on my first season of covering the U's. Back in the Football League following their stint in the Conference, from 1990 to '92, player-boss McDonough was in a contented mood, despite the 4-3 defeat. 'We would have settled for finishing just four points away from the play-offs at the start of the campaign,' insisted McDonough. 'But it's been frustrating having to make do without a regular keeper all season.'

Paul Newell, Alasdair Monk, Ron Green, Carl Emberson, Fred Barber and Nathan Munson all played in goal for the U's that season. I almost considered purchasing a pair of gloves myself, just in case of an emergency. Not exactly ideal.

As for Wrexham, they went on to beat Premier League Ipswich Town 2-1 in an FA Cup tie during 1994/95, won the Football League Trophy in 2004/05, were relegated out of the Football League in 2008, won the FA Trophy in 2012/13; all these dates are set in stone. But when were they formed? 1864? 1872? 1884?

Let's just say that Wrexham FC are very, very old.

31 CRAVEN COTTAGE

Club: Fulham
Founded: 1879 (as Fulham St Andrew's Church Sunday School FC)
Ground: Craven Cottage (from 1896)
First visit: 17 August 1993; Fulham 2 Colchester 1

One of the most easily identifiable football grounds in the country, thanks to its 'Cottage' pavilion in one corner, along with the splendid red-brick facade exterior to the Stevenage Road Stand, plus its proximity to the River Thames, Craven Cottage is always a treat to visit. It has a rich history in addition to its scenic qualities, with the club having been founded in 1879 by worshippers from the local church, Fulham St Andrew's. In fact, it is the oldest London-based club to have played in the Football League, and has come a long way since those early days when Sunday School boys used to kick the ball around a field. The only surprise is that Fulham have never won a major trophy, although they did reach the FA Cup Final in 1975 when a brace from West Ham's Alan Taylor inflicted a 2-0 defeat on Alec Stock's Cottagers.

I first sat in the old Craven Cottage press box, in the upper tier of the Stevenage Road Stand and surrounded by wooden seating, for a low-key League Cup first round first leg in August 1993. It was the first of five visits I made to Craven Cottage during the 1990s, most of them ending in defeats. Actually, it was looking very promising for visiting Colchester when a Mark Kinsella volley earned them a 1-0 lead at half-time, only for a Simon Betts

Fulham's high-profile manager, Kevin Keegan, watches his side beat the U's 2-0 in 1998. (WP)

own goal and a clean header from Sean Farrell, netted within a minute of each other on the hour mark, to secure the Cottagers a 2-1 win. The proverbial game of two halves. Don Mackay's Fulham eventually won the tie 4-2 on aggregate, though it was downhill from thereon in. They lost 8-1 on aggregate in the second round to Liverpool and were relegated from the Second Division at the end of the season to drop into the bottom tier for the first time in the club's history. Mackay was also sacked before the end of the season.

However, I have clearer memories of the last of my five visits, on Boxing Day 1998, when Kevin Keegan was the Fulham manager. The day was marked by another defeat, washed down with an expensive drink and a topped by a controversial red card.

There can be no better setting for a pre-match stroll than along the River Thames and through the tree-lined avenues of nearby Bishops Park, especially around Christmas time and with Fulham enjoying such a fine season. That was the case on that particular day with Craven Cottage 120 years old and perhaps looking in need of some renovation. That was to come during the following decade. For the moment, there was still terracing at the Hammersmith End (until 2004) and the Putney End (until 2003) backing on to Bishops Park, while the Stevenage Road Stand remains the oldest surviving stand both in the Football League and in professional football.

After one of the most expensive pre-match drinks of my football reporting career, in a local wine bar somewhere off the Fulham Road – I was accompanied by long-time Colchester United reporter Bernie Webber, who never did buy a return round – it was off to Craven Cottage for some more festive cheer, although neither of us held up much hope for lowly Colchester against the league leaders.

In their first season in the third tier for 17 years, the U's were struggling in the lower reaches of the table and they were no match for Keegan's star-studded multi-millionaires, failing to even register a shot on goal during a 2-0 defeat. In fact, I could have taken over in goal from home keeper Maik Taylor and kept a clean sheet, it was that one-sided. Neil Smith headed a 26th-minute opener from Rufus Brevett's cross, and when U's keeper Carl Emberson upended German striker Dirk Lehmann, on as a substitute for Paul Peschisolido, referee Peter Walton flashed Emberson the red card and Barry Hayles, a £2m purchase from Bristol Rovers, converted the ensuing penalty. The only highlight of sorts for the U's was striker Neil Gregory pulling off a great late save to deny Lehmann – Gregory had come on as a substitute to try and snatch an equaliser, and yet had ended up in goal.

I snatched a few words from an all-smiling but sympathetic Keegan before he headed off for his car. He said, 'I can see why Colchester's manager [Steve Wignall] was annoyed. Their keeper did not deserve the red card.'

The Cottagers ended up Second Division champions with 101 points, 14 clear of second-placed Walsall. Manchester City, a distant third, won the play-offs, while Colchester finished two points clear of the drop. Keegan left Craven Cottage that summer to concentrate on the job of England manager, a position he had been given in mid-February, less than two months after the win over Colchester.

Bernie and I remained stalwarts of the Layer Road press box but we never did return to a Fulham wine bar. Our one and only other memorable pre-match drink together had taken place nearly four years earlier, but had nothing to do with Fulham. It was in a pub not far from Stonebridge Road, the home of Gravesend & Northfleet (now Ebbsfleet United). The afternoon was notable for two disasters. Firstly, I spilled a whole pint of beer, after I had unwisely balanced my glass on top of a sloping radiator; and secondly, Colchester secured a prime slot on the running order for the evening edition of TV's *Match of the Day* by crashing to a 2-0 defeat in the FA Cup at the hands of their unfancied Kent hosts, who at the time were plying their trade in the Southern League.

Losing away at the Fleet, after a spilled pint in a Northfleet boozer, felt a whole lot worse than witnessing a defeat at Kevin Keegan's Fulham, after an over-priced wine off the Fulham Road, situated some 28 miles upstream on the banks of the Thames.

32 ADAMS PARK

Club: Wycombe Wanderers
Founded: 1887
Ground: Adams Park (since 1990)
First visit: 18 September 1993; Wycombe 2 Colchester 5

The distance between the football clubs at High Wycombe and Colchester is 100 miles, so it can be somewhat perplexing to note the intense rivalry between the two factions.

David Gregory dispatches an injury-time penalty to rescue a point for the U's in a 2-2 draw at Adams Park in 1999. (WP)

It might not be a local derby, in its purist most geographical sense, but the Chairboys and the U's have harboured a grudge since their days in the Conference at the start of the 1990s. That grudge has persisted, mostly good-natured these days, but with an underlying current that has lasted since Martin O'Neill was the manager at Adams Park and Roy McDonough was the boss at Layer Road.

I visited Adams Park for the first meeting between the two clubs in the Football League in mid-September 1993. Colchester had pipped Wycombe to the Conference title in 1991/92 on goal difference, helped by securing the league double over their arch rivals including a dramatic late 2-1 win at Adams Park via a freak goal from keeper Scott Barrett, whose huge punt from inside his own penalty area took one big bounce and flew over home keeper Paul Hyde into the net.

Wycombe had followed suit the next season by emulating the non-league double heroics of the U's by winning the Conference title and the FA Trophy, hence their reunion in the fourth tier.

Adams Park is situated on the edge of an industrial estate in the Sands area of High Wycombe, on the western outskirts of the south Buckinghamshire town, which doesn't sound very appetising, but it is actually a delightful setting, surrounded on three sides by the rolling countryside of the Chiltern Hills. It is one of the few Football League clubs where you can take your stout boots, or trainers, and go for a pre-match hike or cross-country run from the car park. I have done both over the years.

As usual, it was a cracking atmosphere inside the ground for this thunderous 'derby'. O'Neill was still in charge of Wanderers – he was to be in the post for five and a half years, until the summer of 1995 and a move to Norwich – while likewise his arch rival McDonough was still at the helm for the U's. Adams Park had only been open for three years, and the bulk of a 6,000-plus crowd were anticipating a home win. Wycombe were unbeaten and had their sights set on the top three, while the U's had not yet won away from home.

But it turned into a gloriously unpredictable afternoon. There were seven goals, a dubious penalty, a dubious red card, and ultimately a 5-2 away win. Mark Kinsella, Steve McGavin, Roy McDonough, Martin Grainger (a left-footed screamer) and Steve Brown all scored for the visitors, but only after Keith Scott had given Wycombe an early lead with a controversial penalty. Referee Clive Wilkes, who was rarely out of the spotlight, had given the penalty for a foul on Scott by Paul Roberts, which led to both defender Roberts and his manager McDonough earning bookings for their protests. Wilkes sent off Wycombe skipper Jason Cousins for deliberate handball on 32 minutes, a harsh decision, and although the hosts briefly went 2-1 up through Tim Langford's shot, the floodgates then opened.

Despite the win, McDonough was scathing of referee Wilkes. 'People like him can cost players their jobs,' insisted McDonough, who as usual did not hold back with his criticism. These were still the days before political correctness took hold. Ex-Walsall and Southend hard man McDonough added, 'It could have got out of hand, but fortunately the players competed in good spirit.' However, former Nottingham Forest stalwart O'Neill had the last laugh, ultimately guiding his side to a successive promotion by winning the Third Division play-offs.

I was beginning to get used to this sort of entertainment while covering the U's during this second season. In fact, the last four games had yielded 26 goals, 13 scored and 13 conceded. No wonder my laptop was beginning to let off steam.

My second visit, nearly six years later, was just as dramatic despite a more run-of-the-mill 2-2 scoreline between two clubs who were both flirting with relegation at the wrong end of the Second Division table. The ground had been upgraded, with the former single-level Woodlands Terrace opposite the press box in the Main Stand replaced by a giant two-tier Woodlands Stand housing nearly 5,000 seats. It looked an impressive sight, built in to a forested hill. Changes had also been made at the Hillbottom Road End (East Stand), to the left of the press box, with the original terrace replaced by seats at around the same time as the Woodlands upgrade in 1996, while the opposite end was still a standing area for home fans in the Valley End.

And those supporters in the Valley End were getting particularly excited on my second stay in the Adams Park press box, on 6 March 1999, with their team desperate for points under new manager Lawrie Sanchez, who was at the start of a four-and-a-half-year reign. The Chairboys led 2-1 going into injury time through second-half goals by Andrew Baird and Keith Scott, which nullified an 18th-minute header from Jason Dozzell. There were mutterings of discontent around Adams Park when the fourth official raised a board

The view from the Chiltern Hills looking down on Adams Park. (CM)

displaying seven minutes of injury time, but the U's made little headway until the last few seconds when striker Neil Gregory was brought crashing to the ground by home keeper Martin Taylor for a penalty. Older brother David Gregory stepped up to send Taylor the wrong way with a precision penalty, his eighth successful spot-kick of the season, and so snatch a 2-2 draw. It meant that new U's boss Mick Wadsworth, recently arrived from Scarborough, had extended his unbeaten start to five matches, while leaving the Chairboys five points adrift of safety with just 13 games left.

Naturally, re-writes were required in the press box. I was sitting in the box, rather than outside in the press overspill, so space was at a premium. Tempers were frayed because of the lateness of the equaliser, and Wycombe's current plight, but I wasn't expecting one of the 'home' club's scribes to brush past me with quite such vigour and force before hammering the desk with his fist as he exited the box in frustration. The desk wobbled, my laptop wobbled, my half-re-written intro wobbled. Stoppage-time goals can indeed be a test for the supposed neutrality of the press.

But everything turned out just fine. The desk survived – though Wycombe's previous claim-to-fame as the 'furniture capital of England' would surely have assured a swift replacement – Wycombe Wanderers survived the drop under Sanchez by one point, the U's survived the drop under Wadsworth by two points, and my rewritten intro made the edition of the Saturday evening *Green 'Un* newspaper.

An old rivalry put to be bed, until the next time.

33 DEEPDALE

Club: Preston North End
Founded: 1880 (originally founded as a cricket club, in 1863)
Ground: Deepdale (hosted football since 1878)
First visit: 2 October 1993; Preston 1 Colchester 0

Deepdale is still dripping with history, despite the whole stadium having been redeveloped during the late 1990s and early 2000s. This is the home of Tom Finney and Bill Shankly, and the scene of the earliest successes in the Football League. Founder members in 1888, Preston went unbeaten when winning the inaugural championship in 1888/89 and became the first team to win the double by also winning the FA Cup, the latter trophy coming without conceding a goal, so earning the nickname of 'The Invincibles'. They retained their league championship the following season and were the runners-up for the next three years. Not a bad start to life as a football club.

It has not exactly been downhill all the way since then – the Lilywhites did win the FA Cup in 1938 by beating Huddersfield Town 1-0 – but they suffered relegation from the top flight in 1961, the year after Tom Finney, the 'Preston Plumber' and scorer of a club record 187 goals in 433 league games, retired, and have not been back since. The past lives on in the stadium. The main West Paddock stand, which was built in the early 1890s and initially included a tent in one corner of the ground for the players to change, lasted nearly a century. It was replaced by the impressive Sir Tom Finney Stand in 1995, with a distinctive statute of the great man outside. The press area was accommodated in that stand, and in my experience the press have always been well catered for, the sign of a

Karl Duguid is mobbed by his U's team-mates after scoring a late winner at Deepdale in 2000. (WP)

fine traditional club. Hot food, courteous stewards, parking next to the ground, the whole package, though I have overstayed my welcome on a few visits and so have been forced to finish my reports in the front passenger seat of the car, with the heater cranked up on a cold Lancashire evening.

My first few visits were all before the stadium was revamped, from the early 1990s, and all ended in defeats. Deepdale still had the dreaded plastic pitch on my first appearance, a 1-0 defeat for Colchester United in early October 1993. Preston had been the third club to install an artificial playing surface in 1986, around the same time as Oldham, both following on from trailblazers QPR and Luton, although it was finally ripped up after eight seasons in 1994. Not too many tears were shed.

Colchester had suffered seven successive defeats at Deepdale when the tide finally turned when I least expected it, on a March evening in 2000. It has remained one of my most memorable matches for the fact that it was so unexpected, and so dramatic. And for the matter of balance, I will follow this up with one of my most expected and undramatic of visits, with Roy Keane's Ipswich Town a decade later, one of my most forgettable matches.

Back in 2000, Steve Whitton's struggling U's caused a major upset at Deepdale, claiming a 3-2 win against a Preston side second in the Second Division. It really was a stunning result, helped by a new teenage sensation in Lomana LuaLua and a late winner from Karl Duguid. The result was all the more remarkable because after the U's had outplayed their illustrious hosts and taken a 2-0 lead through Joe Keith's header and a pearler from LuaLua, that deficit was then wiped out by a close-range brace from poacher Brett Angell, who had been unleashed as a late substitute. The U's defence simply could not handle 6ft 4in Angell's big physical presence from set pieces.

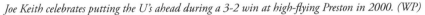

Joe Keith celebrates putting the U's ahead during a 3-2 win at high-flying Preston in 2000. (WP)

I delayed writing my introduction for the following morning's newspaper, despite the pressures of deadline, because I sensed that there would be a late winner from David Moyes's rampant Preston to complete the comeback. I was half-right. There was a late winner, on 86 minutes, but it was bagged by Colchester through Duguid's delightful volley over the head of keeper Teuvo Moilanen. The match, though, was also notable for one of the best individual goals I have ever seen, netted by the richly talented LuaLua, who turned one defender near the halfway line and beat two others before rounding Moilanen to score. The goal even drew applause from the Preston supporters. It was that good, although to be honest most of LuaLua's goals were rather special.

Preston did go up as champions that season, finishing seven points clear of the field, but that Tuesday night in March belonged to Colchester.

Ten years on, the feeling was very different after I had reported on Ipswich's subdued 1-0 defeat at Deepdale on 11 December 2010. Manager Keane cut a forlorn figure at the end of that defeat, which was his team's sixth straight league loss. Preston were rock-bottom of the Championship but still had enough to take all three points through Iain Hume's 50th-minute winner. Keane had a look of resignation about him during an unusually low-key post-match press conference, knowing that owner Marcus Evans could act at any moment to bring his 19-month reign to an end. A month later, the Irishman had indeed vacated the Portman Road hot-seat.

Deepdale, despite all its wonderful history, can be a very unforgiving place.

34 BELLE VUE

Club: Doncaster Rovers
Founded: 1879
Ground: Belle Vue (1922 to 2006)
First visit: 20 November 1993; Doncaster 2 Colchester 1

I was in the Belle Vue press box, which by then was actually just a makeshift table in the Main Stand rather than a proper press box, at least for the away reporters, on the day that Doncaster Rovers' 75-year stay in the Football League came to an end.

It was a sombre afternoon, a hotchpotch of emotions for the Doncaster faithful, encompassing sadness, anger, blame, resignation and despair. It felt like something or someone had died that afternoon, which indeed it had, to such an extent that the home fans had staged a mock funeral earlier in the day with a coffin being carried along Carr House Road. I also dimly recall a bugler playing the Last Post. It really was a sad occasion.

Bizarrely, I was primarily at Belle Vue to cover a far more cheerful subject, namely Colchester United's promotion bid. Steve Wignall's men (Wignall, by coincidence, had begun his playing career as a centre-half at Doncaster, and was to go on and manage the club briefly), nursed faint hopes of finishing in one of the three automatic promotion slots,

Mounted police keep their eye on fans during a peaceful pitch invasion at Belle Vue Ground in 1998. (WP)

so I had to wear my blinkers for much of the day, trying to shut out all that was happening around me, which included two pitch invasions. As it happened, the U's, in their bit-part role, did win the game 1-0 but had to make do with a play-off berth. Meanwhile, back in my Ipswich-based office, the printing of the Saturday evening *Green 'Un* newspaper was delayed by the two pitch invasions at Belle Vue, to ensure we included the result and that I managed to top-and-tail the 'runner' report with a quick intro and concluding paragraph.

Rovers had only mustered 20 points during an utterly miserable season, with a meagre four wins to their name, and they finished with a -83 goal difference after ex-Ipswich Town striker Neil Gregory's 56th-minute goal condemned them to a predictable final-day defeat. Gregory's goal did spark a mini pitch invasion, but the 'real one' took place just 12 minutes into the match, home fans spilling on to the pitch in their hundreds. The playing surface had been renowned for being the biggest pitch in the Football League, so there was a lot of space to fill!

There were soon more fans on the pitch than in any of the other three terraced stands, including the open terraces behind either goal, at the Town End and the Rossington End, and the long, shallow Popular Stand opposite the Main Stand. Ironically, given that just two months earlier Belle Vue had played host to the Yorkshire club's record lowest attendance for a Football League fixture – a mere 739 for the 2-0 defeat to Barnet on 3 March 1998 – a season's best 3,572 had turned up to experience the final curtain, before they plunged into non-league.

There were numerous banners and placards, most of them advertising a dislike (to put it mildly) for then-owner Ken Richardson, who the following year was to be jailed for his role in plotting to burn down the Main Stand. Both sets of players disappeared into the dressing rooms, preparing to sit it out following the invasion, and I must admit that for a while I thought there was a danger of the match being abandoned with the home fans refusing to budge, many of them sitting down resolutely near the centre circle. But the demonstration was peaceful, with Colchester fans lending vocal support to Rovers' cause from their vantage point on the Town End terracing behind their keeper Carl Emberson's goal, and eventually supporters began to drift away from the centre circle and return to the stands. Play was resumed after a delay of about 20 minutes.

The inevitable was accepted. Doncaster lost the game, facing up to a new uncertain life in the Conference as a part-time club (they returned to the Football League five years later), and once the dust had settled and I had finally finished relaying my match report back to Suffolk, I was one of the last to leave Belle Vue that night. It was eerie, a tumbledown stadium, looking tired, empty and spent. The old Main Stand, with its raised empty red seats, a row of red pillars, the paddock terracing in front, and its shoddy rear exterior, was on its last legs. There were holes in the roofs, and holes in the car park.

But at least there wasn't a hole in the newspaper where my report should have been.

'The pitch demonstrations certainly affected my players, but I understood the frustrations of the Doncaster supporters. They made their point,' explained U's boss Wignall.

I haven't experienced first-hand many of Doncaster Rovers' chapters in their long history, mostly due to having been born too late. They played at the briefly-named 'Deaf and Dumb Ground' on a field at the rear of the Yorkshire Institute for the Deaf and Dumb in the mid-1880s, before it became better known as the Intake Ground. They stayed there until the outbreak of the First World War, during which time the main stand was sold to a local butcher for firewood, hastening their move away. There then followed 84 years at Belle Vue, formerly a swampy six-acre area on Low Pasture opposite the racecourse, with all its many trials and tribulations. Among the many quirks, the club arranged the first floodlit match outside the south of England in March 1952, with a friendly against Scottish champions Hibernian, while in 1975 Chris Balderstone became the only man to play in a first-class cricket fixture and a Football League match on the same day, turning out for Doncaster Rovers in a home match against Brentford on the evening after playing for Leicestershire against Derbyshire at Chesterfield.

I never saw Balderstone play for Rovers, but I did see him bat for Leicestershire, against Essex. And 23 years on from Balderstone's busy day of cricket and football, I did at least make it to Belle Vue to hear the bugler, watch the pitch invasion and beat the revised newspaper deadline on a depressing day for a proud club. Still, Rovers did eventually bounce back, and later flourish at a new stadium, while 20 days later and the U's clinched promotion to the third tier by beating Torquay 1-0 in the play-off final at Wembley.

I like a happy ending.

SECTION TWO –
THE MID-1990s

35 GLANFORD PARK

Club: Scunthorpe United
Founded: 1899
Ground: Glanford Park (since 1988)
First visit: 22 January 1994; Scunthorpe 1 Colchester 1

There are two ways of looking at Glanford Park, the home of Scunthorpe United since 1988, and the first new ground to be built since Southend United's construction of Roots Hall 33 years earlier, in 1955. It can be seen as drab, colourless, uniform, grey, simplistic, characterless, cheap, soulless; or it can be viewed as neat, tidy, cheerful, functional, accessible, cosy, intimate. I can see both sides of the argument, and usually it just comes down to what sort of experience you have on matchday.

For instance, I visited twice during 2010 for a pair of uninspiring 1-1 draws featuring very limited Ipswich Town teams. And yet 15 years earlier, on only my second visit to Glanford Park since The Iron's move from their former Old Showground (their home from 1899 to 1988), I witnessed one of the most thrilling comebacks of my reporting career when Colchester United recovered from a 3-0 deficit inside the first quarter of the game to win 4-3.

Glanford Park, dour and uninviting when I had my Town hat on in 2010, box-like and low on thrills (the design was kept simple to keep the construction costs down to £2.5m), was anything but when the U's, with a little-known Canadian striker as a catalyst, rammed home four unanswered goals on 4 February 1995. That day, the claret-coloured seats seemed to gleam, the straight-edged stands looked architecturally beautiful, and even the breeze-blocks had an air of grandiose. Such is the power of an away win, especially one snatched from the jaws of defeat.

'The Great Escape at Glanford Park' was how the headline read above my match report. I even used the word 'miraculous' in my opening paragraph, a term I have rarely used in

Endsleigh League   SPORT

The Great Escape at Glanford Park

Super su' show by '

BY CARL MARSTON

THE great escape of the weekend, and probably the great escape of the season – that sums up Colchester United's miraculous victory at Glanford Park on Saturday.

U's manager Steve Wignall, keeping his fingers crossed for a first victory in charge, was shaking his head in disbelief after just 18 minutes as in-form Scunthorpe stormed into a three-goal lead.

An embarrassing defeat loomed large, maybe verging on the 7-3 disgrace at Darlington last season. The U's travelling support could barely watch.

Adam Locke pulled a goal back soon after Scunthorpe's third – you could have heard a pin drop inside the spanking new ground. Three minutes later and Tony English gave the U's real hope with his first league goal of the season.

Suddenly, with even not even half-an-hour played, Wignall's men had transformed a one-team procession into a competitive clash. There was light at the end of the tunnel.

Wignall blasted his players at half-time, but still Scunthorpe looked to be coasting to victory when substitute Niall Thompson and Dave Moore's side were blown away.

Hobbled

Thompson appeared in the 70th minute as a replacement for midfielder Adam Locke, who hobbled to the sidelines with a hamstring injury.

Within minutes, the lively Canadian had warmed Mark Samways' hands with a ferocious angled drive that the home keeper did well to block.

The warning bells were sounding inside Glanford Park. Thompson, making mincemeat of Scunthorpe's flat-footed back-line, then struck twice inside three minutes with first the equaliser, and then the glorious winner.

Thompson the predator pocketed his first League goal in the 82nd minute. Steve Whitton's low drive cannoned back off a post and Thompson swooped from close-in to force home the rebound.

He celebrated in real style with a mazy run that left his team-mates struggling to keep up with him. Three minutes later and he left Scunthorpe's defenders trailing in his wake.

Simon Betts delivered the perfect free kick high into the danger zone and Thompson nipped in at the far post to stab home over the prostrate Samways.

Celebration

It was a wonderful moment for the 20-year-old trialist striker, and the band of U's fans sitting behind the goal. Thompson duly started his second celebration in front of them.

This unlikeliest of wins keeps the United promotion pot simmering – it was their first victory in five games, steering them back into ninth spot, and more importantly just one point away from the play-off zone.

Saturday's performance on Humberside was like a breath of fresh air after the dismal home defeat at the hands of Wigan from the previous weekend.

Wignall was a happy man: "Scunthorpe just couldn't cope with Niall's pace in the final 20 minutes.

"He was champing at the bit to get on. He is so keen to do well, which is what I want from my players.

"Last week it was obvious that some of the players just felt their place in the side was secure. We need competition for places and Niall did himself no harm with that performance.

"At one time, it looked like we were facing an embarrassing defeat. After 20 minutes I would have

been happy to just keep the scoreline down to three or four.

"But my players showed real character and we deserved the win. We could have score five or six by the end," added the U's boss.

Scunthorpe manager Dave Moore was on a high after receiving the manager of the month award for January before the match.

He was positively animated after seeing his side steamroller into what seemed an unassailable lead.

John Eyre, on loan from Oldham Athletic, broke the deadlock as early as the fourth minute. He slid home Steve Thornber's low cross from inside the six-yard box.

Deceived

Carl Emberson was picking the ball out of the net again in the 16th minute after being deceived by Wayne Bullimore's glorious chip from 20 yards out.

Two minutes later and Eyre notched his second of the game, and his eighth in just over a month.

He combined with fellow striker Stuart Young before bursting clear to beat the advancing Emberson with a calm finish. Eighteen minutes gone and the game was effectively over – or so everyone thought.

Locke pounced onto Steve Brown's intelligent through pass to reduce the arrears with a sweet finish in the 25th minute. The U's midfielder lifted the ball over Samways from a narrow angle to score his first goal for the club.

Three minutes later and the score was 3-2. Steve Whitton headed Mark Kinsella's corner goalwards and English rammed home the rebound from eight yards out.

That completed the scoring until Thompson's late cameo role. The Scunthorpe faithful trooped out of the ground in a state of shock. – they still probably can't quite believe it.

STEVE Wignall compared Niall Liverpool super sub David Fair... match-winning performance.

"Fairclough used to come off for Liverpool, and that's what today," said a delighted Wignall.

Thompson will never forge Football League. His two late str... vital points and could have ear...

"I was so disappointed to be... last two games," explained appeared as a 70th minute sub

"I had hit the bar twice in knew I could score today. I w... I thought we were going start Scunthorpe made. But this was such an important v...

"The results had been weeks, and we had some ca into the promotion race.

"I can't remember much just came back off a post keeper, although he got a le

"For the second I punis... Betts' free kick," added 20

"When George left the going to happen. I felt a li... a contract.

"Now I want to est... England, having turned Malaysia," continued T...

Born in Birmingham to Canada when he w youngest professional League at the age of 1 name for himself in thi...

"I first met up with l Frank Yallop at th... Vancouver three years them whenever I have

Surely Thompson' will earn him a Layer

MATCH FACTS   ENDSLEIGH LEAGUE DIVISION THREE AT GLANFORD PARK

SCUNTHORPE UNITED 3
John Eyre (4 mins, 18 mins), Wayne Bullimore (16 mins)
Manager: Dave Moore

COLCHESTER UNITED 4
Adam Locke (25 mins), Tony English (28 mins), Niall Thompson (82 , 85 mi...
Manager: Steve Wignall

STATISTICS

CORNERS — 8

FREEKICKS — 14

GOAL ATTEMPTS — 15

OFFSIDE — 4

BOOKINGS — Young for foul – 44 mins

U's NEXT ACTION

PLAYER RATINGS OUT OF 10

1 MARK SAMWAYS	7
2 TONY FORD	6
3 PAUL MUDD	6
4 STEVE THORNBER	7
5 ALAN KNILL	7
6 MATT CARMICHAEL	6
7 GRAHAM ALEXANDER	8
8 WAYNE BULLIMORE	7
9 STUART YOUNG	7
10 JOHN EYRE	8
11 MAX NICHOLSON	5

SUBS
...AN THOMPSON (for Eyre, 73 mins)

MAN OF THE MATCH

NIALL THOMPSON

NIALL was only on the pitch for 20 minutes, but that's all it took for him to change a likely defeat into a superb victory.

So keen to prove himself to manager Steve Wignall, and so keen himself a contract, trialist Niall showed his goal-poaching instincts with two late strikes, both from close range.

In fact, he could have bagged a hat-trick but for a smart... keeper Mark Samways. His fresh legs ensured... Mark Samways' ...e's terrible defence.

PLAYER RATINGS OUT OF

1 CARL EMBERSON	
2 TONY ENGLISH	
3 SIMON BETTS	
4 PETER CAWLEY	
5 GUS CAESAR	
6 ADAM LOCKE	
7 CHRIS FRY	
8 TONY DENNIS	
9 STEVE WHITTON	
10 MARK KINSELLA	
11 STEVE BROWN	

SUBS
12 NIALL THOMPSON (for Locke, 70 mins)
14 PAUL STONEMAN (not used)
GK JOHN CREESEWHICH (unused keeper)

Flashback: the author's match report from the U's dramatic comeback 4-3 win at Scunthorpe.

any story relating to the U's over the last few decades. A double blast from John Eyre, on loan from Oldham, sandwiching a superb chipped goal by Wayne Bullimore, had Dave Moore's Scunthorpe flying into a 3-0 lead inside 18 minutes. I braced myself for a heavy defeat while beginning to feel sorry for Steve Wignall, who was still waiting to record his first win as U's manager.

You could have heard a pin drop inside the still-shining, seven-years-old Glanford Park when a long-haired Adam Locke pulled a goal back on 25 minutes, and suddenly there was light at the end of the tunnel after Tony English bagged his first goal of the season from Mark Kinsella's 28th-minute corner to make it 3-2. But what about this 'little-known Canadian striker'? Niall Thompson, unleashed as a substitute with 20 minutes remaining, was Wignall's last throw of the dice. Thompson immediately caused a stir with some spritely runs through the middle, and his 'catalyst' role was soon in full swing as he scored not once but twice, on 82 and 85 minutes to complete a remarkable comeback. They were Thompson's first goals in the Football League, and they were registered from point-blank range. A poacher's paradise.

'Niall was champing at the bit to get on,' confirmed Wignall. 'That's the most remarkable turnaround I have ever witnessed, either as a player or a manager.' His opposite number Moore confessed, 'I still can't believe it. In all my 19 years involvement in the game, I have never been connected with a side that has lost when leading 3-0.'

So what happened to Niall Thompson? Spearheading that 'Great Escape at Glanford Park' as a 20-year-old was probably the highlight of his club playing career, at least in England. He scored three other league goals for the U's, and later had short stints at Brentford and Wycombe, but without adding to his tally of league goals. But he did win nine caps for Canada, and continued his playing and managerial career in that country.

I have been back to Glanford Park several times but it's all been a bit tame when compared to that stunning fightback of early 1995.

The stadium holds few surprises, although I have always been grateful for its proximity to the M18. Four single-tier stands, with just one terrace at the Doncaster Road End, home to the more vociferous home supporters. The other stand behind the goal, where the away fans congregate at the Railway End, began life as a terrace before being converted to seating in 1991, while the press cram in to a small area at the rear of the main stand on the west side of the stadium. It can be like a game of sardines, with newspaper hacks and radio commentators sitting shoulder-to-shoulder along the couple of rows of seats designated for the media.

This can make it tricky to leap from your seat if inspired by a 'Niall Thompson moment' due to being wedged in, although these moments have been few and far between in more recent visits. Fifteen years after Thompson's dramatic introduction as a substitute, I did at least have the pleasure of witnessing another 'superb sub' intervention, this time with Ipswich for an otherwise drab 1-1 draw on a freezing cold Tuesday evening on 23 February 2010. It was so cold that I was actually grateful for the close proximity of fellow football scribes in the Iron's tight press quarter.

Town boss Roy Keane was getting more animated by the minute as his side struggled to break down the wall of claret and blue going into the last quarter of the game. Jon Walters had rattled the bar twice for Town during the opening 20 minutes of this scrappy Championship duel, but it was the Iron who inched ahead through defender Cliff Byrne's close-range header. David Healy, Northern Ireland's all-time record goalscorer with 39 goals, had appeared as a substitute just three minutes before Byrne's opener, and the Sunderland loanee, without a goal for more than a year, ended his lean spell with a swift equaliser from the narrowest of angles. It ended up being Healy's only goal for Town.

A moment of delight for Healy, and relief for Keane, though nothing to rival the U's 'Great Escape' of 1995. That was a once-in-a-generation experience.

36 SPRINGFIELD PARK

Club: Wigan Athletic
Founded: 1932
Ground: Springfield Park (1897 to 1999)
First visit: 5 February 1994; Wigan 0 Colchester 1

It always amazed me how a press box could be situated so as to deny journalists a clear sight of one of the two penalty areas. A serious design fault, I would suggest. Some press sections afford unobstructed views of the whole pitch, a panoramic treat from the lofty tops of main stands often looking out over terraced streets, car parks and perhaps rolling hills beyond, or even a stretch of the North Sea if you're lucky. At Springfield Park, the former home of Wigan Athletic, and the handful of clubs that existed before the Latics came into being, the press box views were restricted at best, and awful at worst.

The press were accommodated in one far corner of the main stand, and to follow the action to your right, in the nearest penalty area, you had to try and peer through a grubby side window of the stand. The window had not been cleaned for decades, or at least had not seen a sponge, cleaning pole or any cleaning solution for several seasons. That grubby sheet of Perspex was the bane of many a football writer, causing much discussion among fellow hacks who were frantically trying to work out who scored and how. Sometimes, if there was space, I would move out of the press box and down towards the bottom of the stand to get a better view of that elusive penalty area.

In short, it was easily the most restrictive view from any Football League press box that I have ever graced. Unique, certainly, but not in a good way.

I only started visiting Springfield Park during the final decade of its existence, when I appreciate that it wasn't looking at its best. Swathes of open terracing, an unusual grassy bank at one end, one old main stand (Family Stand) and rows of houses in the background. This was as far removed from the Premier League as you could possibly get. It was even possible to go for a leak in the outside urinal at one corner of the ground and still watch the action, if you were tall enough. I think it's fair to say that the place was in a state of disrepair, waiting for the inevitable.

The stadium had been hosting football since 1897, and at one time had boasted a capacity of 40,000, although across its 102-year life span it only featured 32 seasons of

Gavin Johnson, who scored a brace in Wigan's 2-0 win over the U's at Springfield Park in January 1996. (WP)

Football League action. The main stand had been burnt to the ground in 1953, with a new one built the following year, large, chunky and imposing. Opposite was the St Andrews Terrace, or Popular Side, which was very close to the pitch and had a low-covered roof, while the famous grassy bank at the Shevington End saw fans often standing here, rather than on the terracing below, until the rear section was fenced off in later years. There was a makeshift covered shed at the back, while on particularly wet days (and I believe there are many of these in Wigan) it was common for fans to lose their footing on the greasy, grassy surface, or even deliberately mud-dive down the slope.

A meat pie was often the highlight of my handful of visits to Springfield Park, although I did have a Colchester United away win to report on during a cold Saturday afternoon in early February 1994. 'Under-stated' is how I would describe the whole experience. Road signs for Wigan Athletic FC were in short supply and, with sat-nav not yet in common use and my road map woefully inadequate due to several missing pages, I stumbled on Springfield Park by accident, perhaps down First Avenue, or Second Avenue, or Third Avenue. There was hardly anyone around, even though it was only an hour to kick-off. The locals did not begin to appear until 2.30pm, and all talk on the terraces was not about the Latics, but rather about Wigan's 27-12 victory over arch-rivals Widnes in the previous night's rugby league clash, and in particular a fine debut from former All Blacks rugby union star Va'aiga Tuigamala, better known as 'Inga the Winger'.

The locals were still talking about Inga the Winger at half-time because the fourth-tier clash had offered little in the way of entertainment or talking points. And that did not change until ten minutes from the end when Kevin Langley's scuffed back-pass enabled former West Ham midfielder Alan Dickens to sneak in and round keeper Simon Farnworth to score the only goal of the game.

It was Dickens's third goal of the season, a player enjoying life in the twilight of his playing career, although this was destined to be his last goal for Colchester and his last in the Football League. 'The first half was a complete non-event, but we dominated in the second half. This win keeps our season ticking over, with the play-offs still in sight,' enthused a quietly-spoken Dickens, who had chalked up 231 games for West Ham during the 1980s, and later had a couple of seasons at Chelsea before his switch to the U's.

Dickens's professional career came to an end at the end of the season, at the age of 29, while Roy McDonough's U's side only won three of their last 16 games to finish down in 17th spot. Wigan, meanwhile, were left wallowing fourth from bottom, Kenny Swain's men only winning six games at Springfield Park all campaign. In fact, that 19th spot in the bottom tier remains Wigan's lowest league finish since their promotion to the Football League in 1978.

Peter Cawley, the U's centre-half, had a fine afternoon during that 1-0 win, ruling the airwaves at the back while also rattling the crossbar with one of his trademark thunderous free kicks. However, the big man blotted his copybook on a return visit to Springfield Park two years later, after describing the home ground as the 'Dustbin of the World' in the Essex press.

The home players got wind of Cawley's stinging criticism and pinned the headline from that newspaper on the wall of their dressing room, which proved a sufficient incentive for them to go out and soundly beat the play-off chasing U's 2-0 on an ice-cold Tuesday, 30 January 1996. The Latics were on the start of a journey which would see them grace the Premier League within the next ten years, backed by millionaire chairman Dave Whelan, and were already shedding their old-fashioned, distinctly northern, strapped-for-cash image with the likes of Spaniards Roberto Martinez and Isidro Diaz lighting up Springfield Park, although it was Suffolk-born Gavin Johnson, the former Ipswich Town left-back, who netted both goals.

The U's were well beaten that night, within the frozen confines of the 'Dustbin of the World'. As Cawley probably realised, after his controversial critique of Wigan Athletic's rather unfashionable home – sometimes, things are best left unsaid.

37 GIGG LANE

Club: Bury
Founded: 1885
Ground: Gigg Lane (from 1885)
First visit: 19 March 1994; Bury 0 Colchester 1

It always seemed quite apt that you could see the cemetery from the Gigg Lane press box, in the old wooden Main Stand, before that particular corner of Bury FC's ground was filled in down at the Cemetery End. Many was the time that I would report on a Colchester United defeat from that very press box spot with Shakers supporters in fine spirits just in front of me, celebrating their team's glittering performance to a backdrop of silent, dreary tombstones. There was a real family atmosphere about the place (the football ground, not the cemetery), with the sense that generations of the same family would watch from their favourites seats, year after year, probably after first stopping off at the adjacent BFC Social Club for a pre-match drink. And it was that community spirit which made the 2019 demise of Bury, and the closure of Gigg Lane, all the more poignant, the first club to be expelled from the Football League since Maidstone in 1992. A way of life, a Saturday afternoon family ritual, all gone.

Gigg Lane, one of the oldest football grounds in the world, had been a home to Bury since the club was formed in 1885. The land had been leased from the 15th Earl of Derby's estate before the club's first season, at the time just a field, but from which a football-specific stadium was built to accommodate a capacity of 30,000. The Lancashire club won the FA Cup twice, in 1900 and 1903, and graced the top flight for most of their early history, until losing that status for a final time in 1929. Like most grounds, the stadium was redeveloped during the 1990s, with the Cemetery End being the last to be completed in 1999.

It is situated over a mile from the centre of Bury, a former cotton mill town, close to the Manchester Road (A56) with just one access road – Gigg Lane – to the ground, so simple

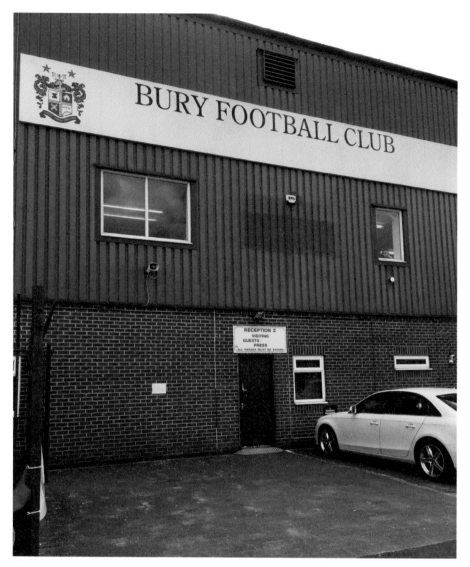

The press entrance to Gigg Lane. (CM)

that even I would struggle to get lost. A residential area, in keeping with the community spirit. I know the area quite well, often staying with my old long-distance walking friend John Davies in nearby Ramsbottom whenever I have had a Saturday afternoon date at Gigg Lane. I have also occasionally warmed up with a walk up to Peel Monument on the edge of Ramsbottom, a memorial statute to Sir Robert Peel on top of Harcles Hill, the 19th-century prime minister who oversaw the formation of the Metropolitan Police Force (Great Scotland Yard) in 1829. Nothing to do with football, but it clears the mind.

Shortly after the 1990s development of Gigg Lane, I vividly remember my first two visits of the new millennium, both with Colchester United, for very different reasons.

The view from the press box at Gigg Lane. (CM)

The first, on a Tuesday night on 12 September 2000, ended in a drab goalless draw which would usually leave me struggling to fill my allotted word count. But not that night. Rumours were rife that U's star front-runner Lomana LuaLua was about to sign for Newcastle United for a club record £2.25m, shattering the former high of £150,000 for the sale of Mark Kinsella to Charlton in 1997. Most of my match report in the following morning's newspaper was given over to this topic. In fact, my preoccupation with LuaLua, who did at least play for 70 minutes that night, meant that I didn't watch much of the game, if any (or in other words, even less than usual), but I was helped by U's chairman Peter Heard obliging with a few quotable quotes after the final whistle. With every respect to Bury, I could have been anywhere that night. The football was immaterial. And LuaLua did end up moving to Sir Bobby Robson's Newcastle later that week, so the distraction was merited.

My second Gigg Lane experience of the new century centred on another Colchester striker, although this one was at the end of his league career, not the start of it. Adrian Coote, a then-joint record £50,000 signing from Norwich City, never really lived up to expectations at Colchester. Even the one time he did hit the headlines, with a brace of goals in a 3-1 away win at Gigg Lane on 13 April 2002, he was left with mixed emotions. Most of the away fans in the Manchester Road Stand, opposite the Cemetery End, didn't know what to make of Coote's display. I was the same. Two clinical goals, but a spate of missed chances. 'I should have had a hat-trick, which is a little annoying,' confessed

Coote, who was only 23 at the time. 'That would have been the first hat-trick of my senior career. You don't get great chances like that in every game.'

Substitute Coote did score on 72 and 87 minutes, but missed an absolute sitter in between these two goals, slicing wide with just keeper Paddy Kenny to beat. Although he had won six Northern Ireland caps during his time at Norwich, Coote bagged just four goals in 35 league outings for the U's and eventually dropped into non-league.

Alas, Bury's story is much sadder, the club effectively ending up in the cemetery next door after being expelled from the Football League in August 2019.

38 FIELD MILL

Club: Mansfield Town
Founded: 1897 (as Mansfield Wesleyans)
Ground: Field Mill (hosted football since 1861, home to the Stags since 1919)
First visit: 2 April 1994; Mansfield 1 Colchester 1

Field Mill has several claims to fame. Firstly, it is the oldest ground in the Football League, having hosted football since 1861; secondly, it is the oldest ground in the world to have staged professional football; and thirdly, it is the second oldest of any football ground in the world, after Sandygate Road in Sheffield, the home of non-league Hallam FC since 1860. Moreover, the likes of Mansfield Greenhalgh, Mansfield FC and Mansfield Mechanics all played there before Mansfield Town moved in after the First World War.

I didn't know these facts during my early visits to Field Mill. I should have done, I know, but as a young reporter I was more concerned with current team news, possible team formations and whether the press would get any pre-match food rather than with club histories and away ground statistics.

However, I was aware of the origins of the name Field Mill, after the large water-powered textile mill nearby, because the mill pond and old mill manager's home are still standing on the other side of Quarry Lane, by the River Maun. I have eaten packed lunches by the mill, and visited the old mill manager's home when it used to be a public house. So I have rubbed shoulders with the Stags' distant past, which saw local textile firm Greenhalgh & Sons start by playing works' cricket games on the site in the mid-19th century when it was little more than a field with a cricket pavilion. Greenhalgh Ground became Mill Field, and was then known as Field Mill from about 1885.

My most memorable visit came 111 years later, at the end of the 1995/96 season, a few years before the stadium was modernised. The old West Stand, the main section of the ground, had been erected in the early 1960s having previously stood at Hurst Park racecourse in West Molesey, Surrey. The stand was transported up to Nottinghamshire in lorries and re-assembled, Hurst Park having hosted its final horse races in 1962. There was still terracing at both ends, a covered North Stand terrace and an open Quarry Lake End

Field Mill, pictured by the River Maun, the long-standing home of Mansfield Town. (CM)

terrace. Both ends were to become new, seated stands, four years later, decked in amber and royal blue.

There was much riding on Colchester United's trip to Field Mill, at the end of April 1996, at least for the U's, if not the Stags. Steve Wignall's visitors were in the fourth-tier play-off race going into the penultimate weekend but they really needed a win and other results to go their way to stand a fighting chance of making the top seven. It was looking like the U's would fall short, locked at 1-1 with the Stags going into injury time on a nervy afternoon.

In short, there was 'Trouble At T'Mill' for the U's. Scott Eustace had headed the hosts in front early in the second period, before Robbie Reinelt nodded home a 68th-minute equaliser. My introduction for the 'runner' report in that evening's *Green 'Un* had been penned, and was ready to be sent, when full-back Joe Dunne, not accustomed to scoring goals, popped up with a 93rd-minute winner. Dunne headed gleefully past keeper Ian Bowling from Adam Locke's cross to snatch all three points. And with the U's play-off rivals Hereford, Chester and Wigan all losing, and Barnet only drawing, it turned into the perfect afternoon.

My intro was hastily re-written, and the U's did secure seventh spot a week later by beating Doncaster 1-0 at Layer Road before losing in the play-off semi-finals to Plymouth. Mansfield ended that season in mid-table. Defender Dunne went on to rattle up 160 league appearances for Colchester, and later became the U's first-team boss for two years

There was never any excuse for not knowing how much time had elapsed, on more recent visits to Field Mill. (CM)

from 2012. Ironically, he ended up back at Field Mill to become Mansfield Town's assistant manager at the end of 2019.

Field Mill is much changed from my early visits during the 1990s. The old West Stand, from the 1960s, is now a neat two-tier stand of royal blue and amber seats completed in 2001, affording a fine view from the press box, while both ends are all-seater affairs, the Quarry Lane End predominantly amber and the North Stand (for away fans) mainly blue. Opposite, the West Stand, where the Bishop's Street Stand used to be the main structure in the ground, has been awaiting redevelopment and so is largely open with a massive electronic scoreboard and clock near one corner. There's no excuse for not knowing the score, or how many minutes are remaining.

Which brings me to a later visit, on a Friday evening on 1 November 2002, just a year after the West Stand had been opened, when time seemed to be racing. In fact, five goals were scored during a breathless first 31 minutes. My mind does play tricks, but I seem to recall reporting from a temporary press area near the touchline that evening. My recollection isn't quite so hazy when it comes to the destructive display of Stags striker Iyseden Christie, who had the game of his life by plundering four goals in a 4-2 demolition of Steve Whitton's Colchester. Mansfield were rock bottom of the Second Division, and were to eventually suffer relegation, but they easily tore the U's to sheds. Christie helped himself to a ten-minute hat-trick, between the 19th and 29th minutes, the U's responding with a Joe Keith penalty and a Kevin Rapley lob for a 3-2 scoreline with an hour still to play. It was rich entertainment, but Christie added his fourth in the second half to settle the issue before U's centre-half Alan White was sent off late on.

Not a great evening to be a Colchester supporter, or Colchester reporter, which is why whenever I think back to Field Mill, I picture Joe Dunne's dramatic winner from 1996. Selective memory – there's a lot to be said for it.

39 DEVA STADIUM

Club: Chester City
Founded: 1885 (as Chester FC)
Folded: 2010
Ground: Deva Stadium (from 1992)
First visit: 9 April 1994; Chester 2 Colchester 1

Farmyard smells and unhappy managers is how I remember my visits to Deva Stadium, the tiny box-like home of Chester City, with its capacity of under 6,000, from 1992 until the club's demise in 2010.

A small, very compact and undistinguished ground, situated among warehouses in Sealand Road Industrial Estate, just off the delightfully-named Bumper's Lane, the Deva Stadium does at least have an unusual claim to fame. Its pitch is in Wales (Flintshire),

Steve Wignall, who was the U's boss for a 3-1 defeat at the Deva Stadium in 1998. (WP)

but the main entrance plus the bulk of the club offices are in England, hence its official English address.

The border between the two home countries runs along the back of the main stand (East Stand), but what was more evident to me was the waft of cow dung or some other form of animal manure that drifted across my nostrils and swirled around the blue-and-white-decked stadium. I like such smells, having been brought up on a farm in Suffolk where pigs were kept, as well as wheat and barley grown, but I prefer the whiff to be confined to the countryside rather than in and around a football stadium.

Chester had spent two seasons in exile at the opposite end of Cheshire, ground-sharing at Macclesfield Town's Moss Rose nearly 50 miles to the east following the sale of Sealand Road, which had been their home for 84 years until 1990. The original grandiose plan for a big stadium of 15,000 to 20,000 as part of a sports complex was soon shelved, and later intentions of a 12,000 and then 10,000 venue were also scaled down. In the end, due to the pressures of time, a compact 6,000-capacity stadium was constructed in just 30 weeks at a cost of £3m, in time for the grand opening on 24 August 1992, and the first match against Stockport County in the League Cup just a day later.

It was a remarkably quick turnaround from the time that 200 or so fans watched the turf-cutting ceremony at the end of January, on a farm field. True, the stadium would never win any beauty contests, and it can be nippy at times with the open corners failing to curb the swirling winds, but 'basic' can be beautiful.

Meanwhile, the 'unhappy manager' of the opening paragraph refers to Steve Wignall, who was the Colchester United boss when he took his promotion-hunters to the Deva Stadium on 18 April 1998, the last time the Essex club visited the ground before Chester folded in 2010. The U's have yet to play Chester FC, the phoenix club that quickly arose from its ashes.

I often turn up at a ground before the away coach has pulled up, but on this occasion I was at the Deva a good hour before the frustrated U's crawled into the city for what was a very important fixture. Some players like to stay in a hotel overnight, while others prefer to travel up early on the day of the match, but on reflection it was probably the wrong decision to tackle such a journey in one day, to Chester and back. The U's did get up to Cheshire in good time to have a scheduled pre-match meal in a hotel, and they did arrive at the Deva just under an hour before kick-off, but it was not the ideal build-up to a big match, as confirmed by Chester racing into a 3-0 lead inside the first 36 minutes. The U's looked tired and travel-weary, although the players remained tight-lipped about the impact of a five-hour journey on the morning of a match, having left Layer Road at 7.45am.

Wignall was not happy, although he was diplomatic during his post-match interview, 'It is a policy of the club to travel on the day, and we had no traffic problems. I am certainly not using that as an excuse for our defeat, though some of the players might think differently.'

A freak opening goal by centre-half Spencer Whelan, whose long hopeful ball forward completely deceived Carl Emberson and ended up in an empty net, set the tone. Left-back Neil Fisher crashed home a superb 30-yarder to double Chester's lead, and Stuart Rimmer added a quickfire third. The U's did improve after the break, but the damage had already been done before Paul Abrahams fired home a consolation goal in a 3-1 defeat.

Fortunately, although the U's went on to miss out on automatic promotion by just one place and one point, they did win the play-offs to reach the third tier. Chester City, with manager Kevin Ratcliffe in his third of four full seasons at the helm, finished up in mid-table.

Having felt jaded myself in the press box after a morning slog up the M6, I did have sympathy for the U's that day. My prose suffered, as did the U's form on the pitch. And my nose suffered, due the delights of the nearby dung.

40 GRIFFIN PARK

Club: Brentford
Founded: 1889
Ground: Griffin Park (1904 to 2020)
First visit: 23 August 1994; Brentford 2 Colchester 0

Another one of my favourite football venues, I liked the way that Griffin Park almost sneaked up on you, hidden behind a maze of residential streets. The floodlights were visible from a distance, but the stadium almost played hide-and-seek behind rows of houses in this popular pocket of west London, not far from the River Thames and Kew Bridge. In fact, I have often travelled to games on the central line of the underground and walked the mile or so to the stadium from the tube, including a stroll along the Thames, usually with a bag of chips. If I arrived early enough, there was a choice of four pubs stationed in each of the four corners of the ground, a quirky feature that was unique to Football League venues. The quartet of pubs were The Griffin, The Princes Royal, The New Inn and The Brook (formerly The Royal Oak).

The Bees were at Griffin Park for 116 years, until 2020; a long and proud history that perhaps did not appear possible when, after several temporary homes, the club settled on a site that used to be the apple orchard of a local brewery. A gypsy camp even had to be removed before the stadium could be built, with the orchard being cleared by volunteers. Much work was done in the 1920s and 1930s, with a new grandstand usurping the old Cow Shed on the Braemar Road side of the ground, with terracing at both ends, at Brook Road and Ealing Road. Later, a quaint double-decker stand was erected at the Brook Road End in 1986, nicknamed the 'Wendy House' by Bees fans, with steep rows of seating on the top tier and standing below. It almost looked like it might topple over. The Ealing Road Terrace remained uncovered during my early visits, often leading to a good soaking for away fans, until a roof was added in 2007.

117

Mark Yeates is lifted aloft after scoring at Griffin Park in a 2-0 win for the U's on New Year's Eve 2005. (WP)

I used to collect my press pass from the gate outside the forecourt of the Braemer Road Stand, and walk behind the stand to the small but cosy press lounge (the Eric White Room, named after the club's former press officer and statistician). There you were always guaranteed a cup of tea and a selection of biscuits (the kind of assortment you would eat at Christmas), and could get computers connected and phones charged. The press area, in the main stand with its very low roof and several pillars, was a little cramped, but if felt homely and the atmosphere in the ground was usually electric, especially under the lights for a midweek game.

It wasn't that invigorating on my first visit, due to the fact that it was a League Cup second leg tie. Brentford had already won the first leg 2-0 at Layer Road, and they repeated the scoreline on home turf on a warm August evening in 1994 to beat Colchester 4-0 on aggregate. In fact, it was a depressing evening. The attendance was a small 2,315, and the match wasn't much of a contest after ex-West Ham midfielder George Parris drove home a spectacular shot for a 3-0 aggregate advantage, and Paul Smith poked home on the hour. For new U's boss George Burley, it was his fourth defeat from four starts (coincidentally all by 2-0 deficits), a miserable run which was to extend to six over the following week. Burley, 38, reluctantly introduced himself as a substitute after just 22 minutes after the sad sight of seeing his skipper Tony English being stretched off and then whisked away in an ambulance for an X-ray on an injured leg, although fortunately there was no break. It really was a deflating night for the Essex club.

However, I have much fonder memories of one of my many return visits, the best of them coinciding with the U's promotion campaign of 2005/06. It was the last day of

2005 and Brentford, managed by Martin Allen, were on top of League One, while the U's were making rapid progress up the table under boss Phil Parkinson. That New Year's Eve encounter was a cracker, lit up by two quality strikes from winger Mark Yeates, who was on loan from Tottenham, in a 2-0 away win. After Yeates had broken the deadlock with a slick shot beyond keeper Stuart Nelson on the half-hour, the crowd were then treated to a superb second half of end-to-end football with both two teams playing at the top of their game. Eventually, Yeates ran clear on to Chris Iwelumo's flick to beat Nelson for a second time with four minutes remaining. As a result, the U's rose to fifth in the table, and the Bees dropped to third behind Swansea and Southend.

Bees boss Allen, always good for a quote, blasted, 'Our back four displayed more formations than the Red Arrows!' Match-winner Yeates told me, 'I don't know about the top two, but we must have a good chance of making the play-offs.'

The U's did make the top two, to win promotion to the Championship, while Brentford missed out in third slot and lost in the play-offs. Yeates, who was 20 at the time, later signed permanently for the U's and has gone on to have a productive career at various different clubs. I, meanwhile, will miss my occasional trips to Griffin Park, the Thames, the chips, the pubs and the press box biscuits.

41 ST JAMES PARK (EXETER CITY)

Club: Exeter City
Founded: 1901 (as St Sidwell's United, 1904 as Exeter City)
Ground: St James Park (throughout the club's history)
First visit: 30 August 1994; Exeter 1 Colchester 0

There was nothing quite like the old-style St James Park, with its pastoral scene of yellow primroses sprouting from the grassy bank in front of the Cowshed, opposite the main stand. In more recent years, the one and only home of Exeter City has undergone a major facelift, and those primroses are now just a pleasant memory, along with the terracing behind which provided a raised view of the pitch as well as accommodating the more raucous elements of the home faithful, affectionately known as the 'Cowshed Choir'. I was enchanted by the place during my early visits, or at least the long bank of grass and flowers on the opposite side to the press box, and also the small, shallow, open terracing to the right at the St James End, which was home to the away fans. The terraces might have been crumbling but the open feel of the ground was appealing, as were its classic deep red turnstiles and matching red doors.

My first two visits were squeezed into the second half of 1994, offering the full range of footballing emotions for travelling Colchester United. There was the misery of a long away-day defeat on a Tuesday evening in late August to finish the night propping up the whole of the Football League, and then the joy of an FA Cup triumph in early December, made even sweeter by a late winner. I viewed both from the cramped quarters of the press box, situated behind a wooden partition plus a few rows of seated home fans.

St James Park, sitting next to St James Park Railway Station, with the railway line running behind the grandstand, was playing host to sporting fixtures well before Exeter City emerged as a club in 1904 as an amalgamation of Exeter United and St Sidwell's United, although in effect the former was disbanded and absorbed into St Sidwell's. It was a home to St James Institute Cricket Club from 1878 and rugby matches had been played there during the 1880s, if not before, while historically the old field had been used for the purposes of rearing livestock, fattening pigs, grazing sheep and alike.

There were primroses, but no signs of snorting pigs, when I travelled down to this corner of Devon on the team coach for that long midweek trek on 30 August 1994. Both teams were at the bottom of the league, George Burley's U's having lost all of their first five league and cup matches since the Scotsman took charge over the summer. It was one of those depressing nights when nothing went right. I did get my match report telephoned across before the 11pm newspaper deadline but the U's had lost for the sixth time on the trot, by a 1-0 scoreline after midfielder Danny Bailey had smashed home a 30-yarder to record the Grecians' first league goal of the season, after 287 barren minutes. Bailey's strike gave Terry Cooper's troops their first points of the season on what was a wet Devon evening. To make matters worse for the U's, young central defender Andy Partner exited the stadium in an ambulance with a suspected broken leg while attempting to net a late equaliser.

This meant the long trip back to Essex was delayed by a detour to the local hospital to collect the unfortunate Partner, who had suffered a cracked knee cap (although that was only diagnosed a few weeks later) which effectively ended his professional career at the age of 19. That night at Exeter was his second and last league appearance, although after more than two years of recuperation he did get back to playing a few games for the U's reserves before dropping into local non-league football.

Fortunately, my return visit in early December was far more cheerful all round. It included an overnight hotel stop, and being interviewed by BBC Essex radio gurus Jonathan Overend and Neil Kelly during the morning of the match, in Exeter city centre. We staged it as though we had just happened to bump into each other, as if by accident, along the bustling High Street, though in fact the whole cringing episode had been carefully planned, by 'consummate professionals'. It was a 'fancy-meeting-you-here' sort of interview. Inevitably, Neil or Jonny would have asked me for a score prediction. I can't remember my response, but I'm sure it was along the lines of – a fine 2-1 away win, with Colchester United skipper Tony English netting a later winner. Well, that's my story and I'm sticking to it.

In fact, English's 84th-minute winner was one of the most memorable moments of the mid-1990s for Colchester's loyal away following. English steamed in to power home an unstoppable header past teenage keeper Ross Bellotti after Steve Whitton had nodded the

A relaxed scene at St James Park, the home of Exeter City, as the author, left, and Jon Waldron, of the Colchester Gazette, catch up with former U's player Pat Baldwin. (WP).

ball into the danger zone from Adam Locke's corner. It was the culmination of a thrilling encounter between an Exeter club riddled with big debts of £1.25m and in the hands of the administrators, and a Colchester side almost unrecognisable (in terms of form if not personnel) from their earlier visit as Football League basement dwellers. Troubled Exeter were desperate for the win, to have a chance of a money-spinning third round tie to ease their financial worries – they had already sold their ground to Beazer Homes – but there was to be no fairy tale for them and they stayed in administration until the summer of 1996.

The match ebbed and flowed in true FA Cup tradition, with 38-year-old assistant manager Trevor Morgan, playing only his second game of the season due to an injury crisis, firing the Grecians into the lead midway through the first half. However, the game turned just three minutes later when keeper Andy Woodman, in a moment of madness, inexplicably smothered the ball from striker Steve Brown having strayed well outside his penalty area. Woodman was duly sent off for deliberate handball, trudging off the pitch to a chorus of boos from home supporters. Certainly, ex-Crystal Palace trainee Woodman was far from the flavour of the month in Devon, not least because he had also been sent off the previous weekend against Scarborough for violent conduct. On came 16-year-old Bellotti, who was beaten by Steve Whitton's equaliser two minutes into the second half and then by English's late headed winner.

Rookie Bellotti's two back-to-back substitute appearances were to be two of his only three outings as a professional footballer. His Football League career was effectively ended by a broken leg sustained in training. Woodman, meanwhile, had burned his bridges at St James Park after the red card against Colchester. He signed for Northampton, but ironically ended up playing for the U's at the turn of the century, under manager Whitton, with some success.

In short, these were unsettling times at St James Park. Exeter went on to finish bottom of the Football League that season but were spared relegation because Conference champions Macclesfield Town could not satisfy the Football League's ground requirements. As for the U's, they had gone from basement dwellers to FA Cup conquerors in the blink of an eye – a few months can be a long time in football.

42 ST JAMES' PARK (NEWCASTLE UNITED)

Club: Newcastle United
Founded: 1892
Ground: St James' Park (since 1892, but hosted football since 1880)
First visit: 26 November 1994; Newcastle 1 Ipswich 1

Sandwiched between my first two visits to Exeter City's St James Park, I made my first appearance in the press box at Newcastle United's St James' Park, with the distinctive apostrophe after James. The two grounds share very little in common, apart from the name. There aren't so many lifts, escalators or panes of glass inside Exeter's home stadium, and the exterior isn't as awe-inspiring, especially with regards the stunning view looking towards Newcastle's Gallowgate End and Milburn Stand (main stand).

There has been much redevelopment since I first nipped down to Newcastle's swanky footballing venue, while at university in Edinburgh in the 1980s, to coincide with visits by Ipswich Town. These days the whole stadium looks a little unbalanced, with one half rising high above the other two sides. But it has always been an impressive amphitheatre in which to watch football, especially from the lofty press box with its unobstructed views in the Milburn Stand. It is an exhilarating experience, especially when Mark Knopfler's 'Going Home' (theme of *Local Hero*) is played as the club anthem as the players emerge on to the pitch. *Local Hero* just happens to be my favourite film.

The appointment of Sir John Hall as chairman in 1992, coincidently 100 years after the club was founded as Newcastle United, led to some much-needed investment in both the team and the stadium after the ups and downs of the previous decade. Kevin Keegan, as manager, guided Newcastle back into the top flight as second-tier champions in 1992/93, just a year after they had struggled to avoid relegation into the third tier. Keegan had replaced Ossie Ardiles in February 1992 and guided the club to safety by the skin of their teeth, even though 20th spot in the second tier was the lowest finish in their history.

Keegan's exciting brand of football, with a youthful Andy Cole and the more experienced Peter Beardsley forming a prolific strike force, earned the team a new

A head for heights: Ipswich Town fans in the top tier at St James' Park, the home of Newcastle United. (WP)

nickname of 'The Entertainers', a tag that was to stick following the arrival of dazzling foreign imports David Ginola and Faustinio Asprilla a few years later, while St James' Park was undergoing big changes with the new Leazes End opened in 1993 at the north end, close to Leazes Park. Newcastle had finished third in the top flight in 1993/94, behind Manchester United and Blackburn, before my first appearance in the press box the following campaign, this time as an impoverished reporter rather than an impoverished university under-graduate.

I was on Ipswich Town duty for a Premier League clash on 26 November 1994, with relegation-haunted Town not expected to get anything out of Keegan's Toon army. Bottom of the table, Town had occasionally surprised the big guns earlier that season with home wins over Manchester United and Tottenham, but Newcastle on their home patch in front of their fanatical supporters looked an altogether bigger challenge. Yet two factors combined for John Lyall's men to snatch a 1-1 draw. Firstly, Town defended with spirit, despite rarely venturing out of their own half throughout the second period; and secondly, the likes of Cole, Ruel Fox and Robert Lee all squandered chance after chance after chance.

Eventually, King Cole did break the deadlock when finally finding a way past defenders Eddie Youds and Frank Yallop to sweep Newcastle into a 1-0 lead on 86 minutes, but Claus Thomson silenced the St James' Park faithful with a shock equaliser just seconds before the final whistle, the big Dane curling a shot beyond keeper Pavel Srnicek.

Keegan was not amused, especially when it came to mentioning Town's tactics. 'No one can enjoy watching stuff like that,' he snarled during the post-match press conference.

'Ipswich hoofed the ball anywhere and it was basically a waste of a Saturday. It was like playing a non-league club in the FA Cup.'

Sour grapes?

Keegan continued, 'I'm surprised at the way Ipswich played considering some of the respected people they have at the club. It pained me to watch it.'

Charming!

Newcastle's two dropped points ultimately cost them a European place as they finished one point and one place outside the top five. I think it's safe to say, therefore, that Keegan did not shed a tear when rock-bottom 'hoof the ball' Town were relegated at the end of the season.

43 VILLA PARK

Club: Aston Villa
Founded: 1874
Ground: Villa Park (since 1897)
First visit: 30 January 1995; Aston Villa U18 4 Colchester United U18 0

This is the exception to the norm among this list of 120-odd grounds; the only time I have frequented a press box for a youth team game rather than a first team fixture. Villa Park, the home of Aston Villa since 1897 when it was initially known as Aston Lower Grounds, has witnessed some great occasions down the years. The Birmingham-based club, founder members of the Football League in 1888, are one of only five English teams to have lifted the European Cup – doing so in 1981/82 – while Villa Park has hosted 55 FA Cup semi-finals, more than any other ground, and presided over seven top-flight title seasons. However, my visit was slightly more low-key, for an FA Youth Cup fourth round tie on a cold Monday night in late January, 1995 against a Colchester United side hoping to reach the quarter-finals of the competition for the first time.

My memories of the match are understandably sketchy, other than Villa's young guns easing to a 4-0 win. But the ground, with its outer red-brick facade, made a big impression, even though the massive stands were empty, as did the staircases and the hanging pictures of former Villa legends adorning the walls of the corridors, although all that was overshadowed somewhat by some post-match car trouble. In short, my ageing VW Golf would not start in the near-empty main car park, leaving me marooned until a midnight visit from an employee of the Automobile Association. The episode took the edge off my Villa Park experience. I eventually arrived home with the milk floats (again, a sign of the times).

Villa Park had been enjoying a new lease of life. The Witton Lane End, opposite the Trinity Road Stand which houses the press area, had been replaced with a new structure and renamed the Doug Ellis Stand at the start of 1994, while the famous Holte End,

Villa Park, the proud home of Aston Villa.

which had previously been a vast terrace banking, was transformed into two seated tiers by January 1995, predominantly blue seats in the bottom tier and claret seats in the top tier. In short, it was stunning.

The stadium certainly befits a club with such a glorious history. Villa, in fact, were the most successful club in England during the Victorian era, scooping the First Division title five times and the FA Cup three times before Queen Victoria's reign came to an end in 1901. They won the double in 1897, the year they moved to Villa Park from their old Wellington Road home, situated in Perry Barr. From the earliest days, despite players having to cope with an uneven playing surface at Wellington Road, while also changing in a nearby blacksmith's shed due to a complete lack of facilities, success soon came Villa's way. The FA Cup was won for the first time in 1887 with a 2-0 win over West Brom at the Kennington Oval in south London.

Speed on nearly a century, 95 years to be precise, and Villa were the toast of Europe when winning the European Cup in 1981/82, Peter Withe's goal securing a 1-0 victory over Bayern Munich in Rotterdam. I remember that Villa squad well, not least because they had pipped Ipswich Town to the First Division title the previous season by four points, helped by only using 14 players throughout the campaign. Those were the days of keeper Jimmy Rimmer, defenders Kenny Swain and Ken McNaught, skipper Dennis Mortimer, midfielder Gordon Cowans, winger Tony Morley and strikers Withe and Gary Shaw, to name but a select few. They won Villa's first top-flight title in 71 years.

But enough of the first team, I was at Villa Park to watch Villa's potential stars of tomorrow and hopefully a few gems in Colchester United's own youth team.

Not surprisingly, Villa's lethal finishing won the day. When they first lifted the FA Youth Cup in 1972 they had the likes of Brian Little and John Gidman in the side, while 1980's cup-winning team featured such future stars as winger Mark Walters and Noel Blake. The class of 1994/95 likewise included some big names of the future, Villa's first goal being smashed home by Lee Hendrie just before the break. That goal had actually come against the run of play with the young U's, coached by Steve Foley, peppering the target through strikers Tony Lock and Dean Francis, plus midfielder David Dowdeswell.

Villa netted three more times in the second half, staging an exhibition in the art of lethal finishing. Lee Burchwell ran on to Hendrie's through ball to double the lead, and this was followed by further goals from front runner Darren Byfield, who went on to play for the likes of Walsall, Rotherham and Gillingham, and Richard Burgess, who made just three appearances in the Football League, for Port Vale. In the U's camp was Karl Duguid, who proceeded to play 414 league games for the Essex club, plus future first-teamers Nicky Haydon, Tony Lock, Ben Lewis and Tony Cook. I reckon I went on to report on more than 400 of Duguid's 414 league games for the U's, though without ever returning to Villa Park.

Yet it was Hendrie who was the star performer in a near-empty stadium that night. The midfielder went on to have a long career with Villa, rattling up 308 senior appearances, 251 of these in the Premier League. As an aside, nearly 12 years later Hendrie provided a good story for me (and members of the national press) during a visit to Layer Road while playing for Stoke City on loan from Villa in a Championship clash on 16 December 2006. Stoke were trailing 2-0 at half-time, on their way to a 3-0 defeat, when a frustrated Hendrie let rip at rival midfielder Kem Izzet as the two left the pitch at the interval. It was a showdown of the two little guys. A petulant Hendrie bragged about his car, a Ferrari, as Izzet was to reveal during the post-match interviews in front of the dugouts.

Izzet announced, 'He [Hendrie] said, "You can come and wash my Ferrari if you like." What can you say? I certainly haven't got a Ferrari so I said, "Just give me a sponge and I'll do it!" I hope he's got a red one because if it's any other colour I won't be happy.'

Back at Villa Park, in January 1995, stuck in the car park with a broken-down pool car, I could have done with a Ferrari myself. It didn't need to be red. I wasn't choosey.

44 UNDERHILL

Club: Barnet
Founded: 1888
Ground: Underhill (1907 to 2013)
First visit: 18 February 1995; Barnet 0 Colchester 1

A mishmash of many stands, with a notorious sloping pitch, Underhill had bags of personality though perhaps with more of a non-league than a Football League feel. But

Ipswich Town boss Roy Keane seated at Underhill, casting his eye over the youth team during an FA Youth Cup clash against Arsenal. (WP)

it was the proud home of Barnet for 106 years and a friendly place to watch football despite the odd problem with crowd segregation caused by the inadequacies of the ground layout.

I was fortunate enough to attend an assortment of matches there, at the bottom of Barnet Hill in Chipping Barnet, including league fixtures, FA Cup ties, a play-off semi-final and even an FA Youth Cup tie which didn't even feature Barnet. The latter was a clash between the youth teams of Arsenal and Ipswich Town.

There were seven stands in all; the East Terrace split into three sections while the main stand, where the press area was sited, was flanked by two smaller stands. The old North Terrace backed on to Westcombe Drive, with the houses behind enjoying a fine view of the pitch, and there was a cosy clubhouse, built in 1920, in the corner at the bottom end of the stadium where home fans used to congregate. A splash of amber and black, Underhill was vibrant, if a little tatty and frayed around the edges. You felt that the Bees (nicknamed after a nearby apiary) always made the best of their humble home, despite its limitations.

My first visit featured a 1-0 win for Steve Wignall's Colchester United in February 1995. It was a special occasion for 22-year-old striker Carl Asaba, who marked his U's – and Football League – debut with the winner. Asaba had been playing in non-league for Dulwich Hamlet the previous autumn, and was loan at Colchester from Brentford, but that goal at Underhill was the start of a fine career which totalled 397 appearances for the likes of Reading, Gillingham, Sheffield United and Stoke.

Three years later my most memorable trip to Underhill actually featured a Colchester away defeat, by a 1-0 margin, although that only told half the story of an ill-tempered fourth-tier play-off semi-final first leg. I had travelled down to Hertfordshire from the Lake District earlier in the day to attend this big Sunday afternoon showdown. Defender Greg Heald scored the winner for the Bees early in the second half, although the key moment arrived with just eight minutes remaining.

Guy Branston, on loan from Leicester City, had been relishing a ding-dong battle with Barnet striker and talisman Sean Devine all afternoon. This culminated in an off-the-ball scuffle between the two, which resulted in referee Eddie Wolstenholme sending off both players for violent conduct. Although the pair received the same punishment, it had far more serious repercussions for Devine, who was automatically suspended for the second leg. Branston, by contrast, was not eligible for the second leg anyway due to his loan spell from Leicester expiring after the weekend. Naturally, conspiracy theories soon emerged, implying that this had been Branston's ploy all along to get the Bees' star man sent off. It was certainly a strange atmosphere at the final whistle at Underhill, home fans pleased that their team had won the first leg but furious that Devine had seen red.

The U's ended up winning the second leg 3-1, in Devine's absence, to go through 3-2 on aggregate and then they beat Torquay in the Wembley final to clinch promotion.

As a big footnote to this Underhill chapter, although Ipswich Town never played a competitive match there, I did go along during the 2009/10 season with my reporter's hat on, to pursue 'The Mystery of Connor Wickham'. It was a tale of would he play or wouldn't he play in an FA Youth Cup fourth round tie between Arsenal's under-18s and Town's under-18s, a case of intrigue to rival any Miss Marple tale or Hercule Poirot plot.

Seated in the press box, surrounded by flaking amber (in reality, bright orange) and black paint, I witnessed a 2-0 away win, courtesy of goals from Ronan Murray and – Connor Wickham.

I paused before mentioning Wickham, because the much-talked-about 16-year-old was not even supposed to be playing, at least not according to the team sheets circulating Underhill. There were several scouts from Premier League clubs in the stadium that night, all waiting to cast their eye over a talented striker who was already causing a stir in the professional game. Wickham had made his first-team debut at the end of the previous season as a substitute during the 3-1 home defeat to Doncaster Rovers on 11 April 2009, at the age of 16 years and 11 days. In the process, he became Ipswich's youngest-ever player, beating the previous record by 46 days, which had been held by Jason Dozzell.

Before that youth team match at Barnet, Wickham had already scored his first senior goals, netting twice in a 3-3 draw against Shrewsbury in a League Cup tie in August 2009. Later that season, he was to score four goals in the Championship. But back at Underhill,

The groundsman crosses a soggy pitch at Underhill, an FA Cup tie against the U's having been called off following a pitch inspection. (WP)

a little display of gamesmanship was on show. According to the team sheet, Wickham was not starting, and he was not even on the bench.

Perhaps those top-flight scouts had endured a wasted journey into the wilds of Hertfordshire? Yet when Town, alongside the young Gunners, walked on to the pitch before kick-off, a big lad who drew a striking resemblance to Wickham was in the long line of blue-shirted teenagers. I raised my eyebrows and grabbed for my pen to change the team sheet, while my photographic colleague Warren Page sprung into action, taking pictures of the ghost that was Connor Wickham.

After the match, Town academy boss Sammy Morgan admitted to me that a 'little gamesmanship' had taken place in leaving Wickham's name out of his original squad that morning. He gave two reasons: firstly, Wickham was carrying an injury, while secondly he also didn't want to give away his team to the intrigued Gunners.

The original team sheets that were handed out to the press, and all supporters at the turnstiles, had Caolan Lavery playing in the number nine shirt for Town, not Wickham, although it later transpired that the all-important official team sheet handed to the referee did have Wickham in accordingly.

As another footnote to this long footnote, the mere fact that the match took place at Underhill, rather than the Emirates, also had a bearing on the team sheet saga. Arsenal's request for Town's team earlier in the day may have contributed to the fact that the team sheets were probably printed at the Emirates, and then had to be transported to Barnet. Manager Morgan duly gave the Londoners his 16-man squad, with injury doubt Wickham as a glaring omission, hence all the inaccurate documents circulating in Underhill.

The plot thickened when, after Wickham had scored, the Tannoy announcer awarded the goal to Lavery. This merely added to the conspiracy theories. A script worthy of an Agatha Christie novel indeed.

45 VICTORIA GROUND (HARTLEPOOL)

Club: Hartlepool United
Founded: 1908 (as Hartlepools United Football Athletic Company)
Ground: Victoria Ground (since 1886, football club since 1908, re-named Victoria Park in 1996)
First visit: 11 March 1995; Hartlepool 3 Colchester 1

I like a press box where you can plot the slow progress of an ocean liner or container ship on the horizon as a welcome distraction from the misery unfolding on the pitch below. The press box at Hartlepool United affords such a fine view, looking out across the North Sea. Your imagination can run away with you, which is just as well because most of my appearances with Colchester United have ended in disappointing defeat.

Victoria Park was still Victoria Ground when I paid my first visit in March 1995, although the name change did happen the following year to celebrate the new look to this old venue, a home for local sport since 1886. The new Cyril Knowles Stand (East Stand) was opened in July (1995), and the new covered terracing to the Town End was also unveiled later that summer. It is now a smart, tidy, compact ground, although during the mid-1990s there were a lot of portable cabins on-site to act as temporary dressing rooms and club offices in the period between demolition and renovation. It was among these Portakabins where I conducted my first post-match interviews at the stadium.

The dug-outs at Victoria Park, with U's boss John Ward, second right, and Hartlepool manager Mick Wadsworth, a former U's boss, in the background, in 2011.

The ground is well placed, very close to the town centre with an abundance of welcoming pubs nearby, which tends to inject more passion (joy or anger, depending on the state of the game) among the home faithful. There is a paddock area of terracing in front of the west side, where the press box sits at the back of the seated tier, although most of the noise usually comes from the Town End terracing to the right, on the south side. This is the club's only home, having originally been the site of a limestone quarry owned by the North-Eastern Railway Company and later given over to allotments, before becoming the early home of West Hartlepool Rugby Club. So tradition runs deep in these parts. There's usually a tray of sandwiches at the back of the press box as well. Simple pleasures.

My first visit, for a Third Division encounter, was an eye-opener. Hartlepool United (they were known as Hartlepools United until 1968, when the 's' was dropped from the name, as was 'United' until its return nine years later) had been going through a rough patch on and off the field, but the hardy hosts dealt a blow to Colchester's play-off hopes with an impressive 3-1 win, achieved with brawn and simple endeavour.

Hartlepool chairman Harold Hornsey, new to the job, had circulated a written message to all members of the local press before the weekend game, urging hacks and commentators to abandon the current trend of referring to his club as 'minnows', 'hard up', 'cash-strapped' and 'in crisis'. His battle cry was for greater optimism. And it certainly worked, culminating in a first win in 13 attempts for the third-from-bottom Pools. Crisis, what crisis?

131

At the time, there was a massive redevelopment scheme in operation at the historic Hartlepool marina. The town was on the up and the stadium was also in the process of enjoying a facelift, with a new stand. New beginnings all round.

David McCreery's Hartlepool side went 1-0 up when U's keeper Carl Emberson dropped a clanger, or rather dropped a high ball, while under pressure from 34-year-old Keith Houchen, whom he tugged back right under the nose of referee John Kirkby. Nicky Southall dispatched the resultant penalty, and although Chris Fry equalised just four minutes later, Pools were back in front through Southall's accurate free kick before half-time. Winger Southall, who went on to have four spells at Gillingham later in his career, completed his hat-trick by burying his second penalty of the afternoon after ex-Arsenal defender Gus Caesar had upended Stephen Halliday.

'Hartlepool were giants, and we were mere boys,' rued U's boss Steve Wignall. 'We were simply overpowered.'

I enjoyed my view of the North Sea, and I appreciated the sandwiches which were curling at the edges, but in truth I wasn't sorry to leave.

Return visits, usually punctuated by away defeats or scrambled draws, sometimes included a night on the town, gliding or staggering from bar to bar in Hartlepool's vibrant town centre. BBC Essex commentator Neil Kelly, a native of Hartlepool, provided the accommodation for his fellow U's press colleagues at his old family home, where his mum would cook hearty Saturday evening suppers after we had spent the afternoon in the Victoria Park press box, and before embarking on a pub crawl to drown our sorrows.

I always found myself overdressed on these occasions, wearing a heavy raincoat to combat the north-east cold and heavy drizzle. By contrast, the locals, unfazed by the wintry conditions, sported short mini-skirts (young ladies) and sleeveless shirts (young lads). I was the perfect example of the soft southerner, an image often heightened by my inability to drink quickly on a heavy stomach after a massive dinner of two pork chops, mash and two veg cooked by Mrs Kelly. Our stay in each pub would only last 15 minutes. The bar would be full one minute, and nearly empty the next as, if by magic, groups would suddenly disappear and rock on to the next pub, usually leaving me to gulp down a half-pint, button up the coat and jog up the road to catch up with the rest. By the end of the night, my memory of the fourth tier clash at Victoria Park of a few hours before would be very hazy.

One notable exception was a visit to the north-east during Colchester United's promotion-clinching season of 2005/06, when Jamie Cureton squeezed home the only goal of the game from a near-impossible angle on the hour mark. It was the U's fifth win on the bounce as Phil Parkinson's men stepped up their successful push towards Championship football. Doubling Hartlepool that season contributed to Pools going in the other direction, suffering relegation to League Two. I remember the night well, not just for the rare away win at Victoria Park, but because it didn't end in a huge supper and a bleary-eyed pub crawl in arctic conditions. And the reason? It was a midweek fixture on a terribly damp Tuesday evening, on 6 December 2005, and by the time my reports had been filed, the pubs were shut and the A19 and A1 beckoned. For once, I had to forgo the pork chops and the copious amounts of lager. But at least I was still wearing my sensible raincoat.

46 SIXFIELDS

Club: Northampton Town
Founded: 1897
Ground: Sixfields (since 1994)
First visit: 17 April 1995; Northampton 1 Colchester 1

Built in a dip at the western edge of the town, it is possible to see most of the pitch from the top of the grassy hill in front of all the food outlets, if so inclined. Sixfields Stadium, Northampton Town's home since the autumn of 1994, is actually quite an airy place. It is not hemmed in, like so many new stadiums built in and around industrial estates, squatting instead in the valley below with the four corners of the ground open. It is a simple structure, with small stands at both ends, while the press area is in the main West Stand among a sea of maroon seats. It's not particularly appealing to the eye but it's functional, unlike the former cricket-dominated County Ground, the Cobblers' home for the previous 97 years.

There have always been close connections between Northampton and Colchester, none more so than on my debut outing in the Sixfields press box in mid-April 1995, six months after its opening. The Cobblers were managed by former U's manager Ian Atkins, while home scorer Ian Brown, in a 1-1 draw, used to play on loan for Colchester. Cobblers keeper Andy Woodman went on to play 54 league games for the U's, and home defender Scott Daniels had played for the U's during the late 1980s and the first year in the Conference.

The afternoon was lit up by player-coach Steve Whitton's pearler on 66 minutes to earn a point for the U's. Whitton started and finished the move, chesting down a cross by Chris Fry before sending an unstoppable volley screaming past Woodman and into roof of the net. It was his 12th goal of a 13-goal season, making him the U's top scorer. In fact, three of Whitton's strikes featured in my U's top ten goals of that season.

'It would be nice to just score a simple tap-in for a change,' joked ex-West Ham maestro Whitton, who was still a class act at the of 34, and a future U's manager.

Unlike Sixfields, built at a cost of £5.25m on a 65-acre site, there was rarely anything simple and functional about any of Whitton's goals.

I think it's fair to say that Northampton have led more of a yo-yo existence than most other clubs, rebounding between the bottom two divisions in recent times, although the 1960s bucked the trend with a remarkable rise and fall from bottom to top, and top to bottom, all inside the space of eight years. From the nether regions of the Football

Ian Sampson (No.4) nets an own goal as the Cobblers suffer a 3-2 defeat at the hands of the U's at Sixfields on Boxing Day 2001. (WP)

League, the Cobblers won three promotions (1960/61, 1962/63 and 1964/65) to grace the top flight for their one and only season before nosediving with successive relegations in 1965/66, 1966/67 and 1968/69 back on to the bottom rung.

Relegation fears were often swirling around Sixfields on my later visits – along with the occasional high winds, which usually helped the goals to fly in. Two trips spring to mind.

The first, on 24 April 1999, was a thunderous 3-3 draw between two clubs embroiled in a third-tier relegation battle, played in front of a 6,000-plus Sixfields crowd with a few extra looking down from the adjacent hill through an opening in the north-west corner.

There was hardly time to catch your breath. Paul Buckle lifted a ten-yard shot into the net inside three minutes to put Colchester United 1-0 up, but the Essex visitors later had to rally twice with equalisers to snatch a point. As midfielder Buckle, a former Torquay player and a future Torquay manager, revealed after the match, 'It was an exciting game to play in, but the manager [Mick Wadsworth] gave us a rollicking at half-time.' Referee Graham Frankland did not have one of his better afternoons, awarding a contentious penalty to each side and then missing a more clear-cut third when Karl Duguid was wrestled to the ground by Ian Sampson. In the end, substitute Duguid's 71st-minute header completed the scoring. Wadsworth's U's side stayed up, but Northampton, with Atkins still at the helm, were duly relegated after only drawing their last three matches. Naturally, they were back up the following season.

The second memorable trip, on Boxing Day 2001, was an afternoon for Graham Barrett, on loan from mighty Arsenal, to shine, and an afternoon for the aforementioned Sampson to curl up in a darkened room. Poor Sampson netted an own goal and made two costly errors for Dubliner Barrett to bag his brace in Colchester United's 3-2 away win.

This was an error-strewn third-tier clash, Northampton propping up the division under manager Kevan Broadhurst, although they ultimately escaped the clutches of relegation. A bubbly Barrett, who had just turned 20, did not let a shocking first-half miss prey on his mind.

'Michael Owen doesn't worry when he misses a chance, so why I should?' insisted a smiling Barrett to the small huddle of press after the match.

Never one to ignore a chance myself, I delighted in incorporating 'Michael Owen' into my match report for the following day's newspaper. Opportunities like that don't come around very often.

47 ASHTON GATE

Club: Bristol City
Founded: 1894 (as Bristol South End)
Ground: Ashton Gate (since 1904)
First visit: 22 August 1995; Bristol City 2 Colchester 1

Like many young lads of my generation, I used to collect football stickers in the late 1970s, and I always remember Bristol City players featuring heavily in these collections. The club were top-flight dwellers at this time, until suffering relegation in 1980, and many of their team were club stalwarts rather than big names. Keeper Ray Cashley, midfielder Gerry Gow and defender Geoff Merrrick spring to mind, all loyal servants. Not very glamorous, or particularly pleasing to the eye, but reliable performers, City through-and-through.

Ashton Gate has been the home of Bristol City since 1904, situated just to the south of the River Avon in the south-west of the city, though I didn't show up in the press box in the old Williams Stand (the current Lansdown Stand) until the mid-1990s, initially with Colchester and then a little later with Ipswich. The ground was in the process of being revamped, with covered terraces replaced by seating in the old Wedlock Stand (built in 1928) and also the Williams Stand (built in 1958) during the 1990s, before a major redevelopment was completed in 2016 with two completely new stands.

Pies, pasties and cups of tea were a welcome sight in the press room Portakabin behind the stand, situated conveniently or rather alarmingly close to the toilets, and many post-match press interviews used to take place near the dressing rooms, in the weights room, at the back of the Ateyo Stand at one end of the ground. An unusual set-up, but it was warm and dry. Named after club legend John Ateyo, who scored a club record 351 goals in 645 appearances, this now smallest stand in the stadium replaced an open terrace in 1994.

I have never found it the easiest stadium to reach by car, especially when grappling with the city centre traffic. A better bet has been to approach from the A4 (Portway), following

Teenager Josh Carson scores the winner for Ipswich at Ashton Gate in 2011. (WP)

the River Avon past the Clifton Suspension Bridge, or maybe come in via the undulating A369 (Rownham Hill) and parking at Bedminster Cricket Club before joining the crowds walking to the ground.

My first visit was a midweek one, when a 'Seal' proved too slippery for Colchester United in a League Cup first round second leg in August 1995. The U's had beaten their second-tier hosts 2-1 in the first leg, and were heading for a major upset when winger Michael Cheetham, of former Cambridge United fame, smashed home a glorious shot on the hour to make it 1-1 on the night and 3-2 on aggregate. David Seal had earlier broken the deadlock and it was the Australian-born striker who was to drag the tie into extra time, and ultimately a penalty shoot-out, with a late headed goal. Bristol City won the shoot-out 5-3 with Simon Betts skying his penalty over the bar for the visitors. Inevitably, it was Seal who netted the conclusive kick.

Still, the U's did themselves proud that night, chairman Gordon Parker making a point of finding me in the press box to deliver a quote that I managed to squeeze into my match report for the following morning's paper, 'The team played some of the best football I have seen from a Colchester side,' insisted Mr Parker. High praise indeed.

As for Seal, after stints with City and then Northampton he returned to the Bristol area to drop into non-league, becoming a mainstay of Mangotsfield United for several years. He achieved the feat of being the top scorer in the FA Cup in 2001/02 after netting 11 goals for Mangotsfield during their run, which ended at the fourth qualifying round stage .

Roll on 16 years from my first visit in 1995 and I was back at Ashton Gate with Ipswich to see the end of a fine week for wonderkid Josh Carson, and a blunder from ex-England keeper David James. In fact, it was arguably the best few days of Carson's career, despite the academy product still only being aged 17. Having scored a brace of goals in only his third senior appearance, a 2-1 home win over Crystal Palace the previous weekend, teenage sensation Carson smashed home his third goal in eight days to seal Town's 1-0 win at Keith Millen's Bristol City on 16 April 2011. Carson, a Northern Ireland under-21 international, deceived and embarrassed keeper James with a 30-yard shot early in the second half. It was an impressive result for Paul Jewell's Town, when considered that they had to play with ten men from the 28-minute mark due to Lee Martin's two-footed lunge at City's Kalifa Cisse.

Millen was fuming, 'I'm disappointed, frustrated and angry. We should have done much better against ten men for so long.' By contrast, Jewell was gushing in his praise of young Carson, 'Josh is not fazed by playing in the first team, I think you can see that. He already has the confidence to try things like that.'

In all, Carson only scored five league goals for Town, and seven for York City, before returning to Northern Ireland to continue his career at the still-young age of 22. But I did get to interview him, as well as Jewell, in the Ashton Gate weights room. It remains the closest I have come to lifting a dumbbell while posing a question to a professional footballer. A specialist category.

48 KIRKLEES STADIUM

Club: Huddersfield Town
Founded: 1908
Ground: Kirklees Stadium (since 1994)
First visit: 9 September 1995; Huddersfield 2 Ipswich 1

I had mixed feelings about my regular early visits to the Kirklees Stadium, known at the time as the Alfred McAlpine Stadium and now the John Smith's Stadium. Thumbs up: the place looked great, oozing character, full of curves rather than harsh edges. Thumbs down: the mobile phone connections and later the Wi-Fi were dreadful, which caused panic.

Ignoring the latter – I usually ended up sending my match report by leaving the ground and perching my laptop on the roof of my car, before returning to the stadium to chase up some interviews – Huddersfield Town's home really is impressive. No boring, straight-edged, rectangular-shaped soulless stands, the Kirklees Stadium proudly boasts semi-circular stands on each side, topped by large white steel tubing archways. The result is striking, and instantly recognisable as the Terriers' home, which it has been since the West Yorkshire club left its former Leeds Road home, across the road, in 1994. It is aesthetically one of the most pleasing grounds in the country.

Steve Palmer, 'The Professor,' who was sent off as Town suffered a 2-1 defeat at the McAlpine Stadium in 1995.

Only the two side stands were in operation when the stadium first opened in August, 1994, the main Riverside Stand and the Kilner Bank Stand, although the South Stand, built into a bank, was also being used by the time that I paid my first visit to report on Ipswich Town's 2-1 defeat on 9 September 1995. The North Stand was completed by 1998. All were decked in the blue of Huddersfield Town and the claret of fellow hosts Huddersfield Giants, the town's rugby league club.

'First early bath for the Professor' was the intriguing headline on one of my stories in Monday's newspaper, following the defeat to Brian Horton's Huddersfield in a First Division encounter. 'The Professor' was a reference to Town's centre-half, Steve Palmer, who was sent off for the first time in his career, midway through the first period. Palmer was flashed the red card by referee Eddie Wolstenholme after making shoulder-to-shoulder contact with Terriers striker Andy Booth. At the time I thought it was a harsh decision. Palmer had been a student at Cambridge University, obtaining a degree in software engineering at Christ's College, hence the nickname, but he carved out a successful career for himself as a professional footballer, going on to play 280 games for Watford and nearly 150 for QPR.

As luck, or bad luck, would have it, Palmer watched the second half from a seat near the press box, in the West Stand, so it was not difficult to grab a word with the softly-spoken defender. 'I will have to watch the incident again on video, but at the time I was disappointed that the referee had even awarded a free kick against me. But these things happen in football,' said a typically diplomatic Palmer. His manager, George Burley, commented, 'Steve is one of the game's real gentleman. It's not the decision I would have made.'

After winger Simon Collins had given Huddersfield the lead from close in, Town defender Steve Sedgley then netted a bizarre own goal just before half-time when diverting home a cross with home striker Ronnie Jepson in close attendance. Ex-Tottenham stalwart Sedgley later converted an 80th-minute penalty as a consolation, but not enough to affect the tone of my match report.

The availability, or rather unavailability, of Wi-Fi or even a decent mobile phone connection did not really apply until the following decade when laptops and internet access became more prevalent. Eleven years on from my first visit with Town, I was back at the McAlpine Stadium (on 11 February 2006) with promotion-chasing Colchester United for a high-flying League One clash which I can recall vividly, for all the wrong reasons. I knew it was going to be one of those afternoons, when photographer and travelling companion Warren Page left his prized camera in a nearby restaurant following a pre-match pizza, and had to scurry back to retrieve the expensive equipment before it ended up on the West Yorkshire black market for stolen goods. A photographer without a camera is of no use to anyone.

The afternoon did not improve. The U's, under Phil Parkinson, were just one week away from a mouth-watering FA Cup tie at José Mourinho's Chelsea, and so were perhaps a little distracted. They were also on the back of a club record run of ten straight wins which had propelled them into the top two. However, the sequence came to an abrupt end with a luckless 2-0 defeat. The U's had two goals disallowed, hit the woodwork three times, had teenage centre-half Garry Richards harshly sent off for a professional foul on home striker David Graham, and were the victim of a bizarre opening goal when Gary Taylor-Fletcher's wayward shot hit team-mate Jonathan Worthington to completely wrong-foot keeper Aidan Davison. As manager Parkinson was to later rue, 'I couldn't believe what I was seeing. It was a day when everything went wrong for us.'

As soon as the final whistle sounded it was time to grapple with the technical hitch of not being able to publish my report due to the lack of any phone connection, a dilemma that never concerned the newspaper reporters of Huddersfield Town's earliest days, of close to a century ago. In fact, when the club was founded in 1908, there were more worries about where the players were going to change than concerns over how the local press were going to dispatch their reports. An old tramcar was used as the dressing room, plus ticket office, at the Leeds Road ground, while failing that it was off elsewhere to don the kit in the pub or a tent. By comparison, the press had it easy.

Returning to the U's ill-fated visit of February, 2006, when the visitors were dogged by misfortune, my own struggle with technology could not be resolved inside the McAlpine Stadium. Instead, as soon as the players drifted off the pitch, I was out of my seat in the press box in search of a phone connection, which I finally secured on the roof of my car,

Triple helping of bad luck for Town

SEEING RED: Steve Palmer has just been dismissed by referee Eddie Wolstenholme and Ipswich Town are up against it at Huddersfield on Saturday

First early bath for the Professor

IPSWICH Town centre-half Steve Palmer, known as the Professor at Portman Road, was understandably devastated by his sending-off at Huddersfield.

The softly-spoken former Cambridge University skipper had never been shown the red card before, and few will agree that he deserved an early bath on Saturday.

In fact, referee Eddie Wolstenholme should have blown up a few seconds before when Kenny Brown chopped down Stuart Slater on the edge of Huddersfield's box. But he didn't and the rest is history.

Palmer, one of a rare breed of footballers with a degree – in science – watched the second half from the Press box in a sombre mood.

"I will have to watch the incident on video, but at the time I was disappointed that the ref— had even awarded a free kick against

just ten men, but the referee made some very strange decisions throughout the match," added Palmer.

Few were arguing with Palmer's assessment.

What they said

Town manager George Burley: "It's not the decision I would have made. Steve is one of the game's real gentlemen. I will be studying the video and might appeal against the verdict."

Assistant boss Dale Roberts: "I thought there was a foul against Stuart Slater at the other end, but the referee waved play on and within seconds Palmer was off. I don't want to say too much, but I thought it was a very questionable decision."

Huddersfield manager Brian Horton: "Who am I to comment?. I thought the penalty was harsh, let alone the sending off. Ipswich are a good scalp for us. We were

BAD luck comes in threes, so the saying goes. Ipswich won't disagree after Saturday's fruitless trip to Yorkshire.

Town arrived at Huddersfield's sparkling new McAlpine Stadium in good spirits, fresh from three straight home victories.

A win, as it happened, would have rocketed George Burley's boys to the top of the Endsleigh League Division One. But three slices of cruel luck took the wind out of their sails before half the match had been played.

First, striker Alex Mathie was stretchered off, in some pain, after just 13 minutes with a dislocated shoulder. At one fell swoop, Ipswich were stripped of their biggest asset.

Twelve minutes later and Town were struck by a second bolt of lightning. Referee Eddie Wolstenholme was well behind play as centre-half Steve Palmer raced side-by-side with Terriers striker Andy Booth.

Palmer, with a show of strength, appeared to win possession as the two made shoulder-to-shoulder contact. Booth ended up on the deck and Mr Wolstenholme, to the amazement of all

by CARL MARSTON

around him, effectively kissed Town's chances goodbye by waving the red card at Palmer.

Ten-man Town were forced to reshuffle with striker Ian Marshall dropping back to central defence alongside Steve Sedgley, and winger Stuart Slater attempting to give more support to Lee Chapman up front.

Huddersfield, feeding off Town's misfortune, didn't need a second invitation and by half-time Brian Horton's side were two-up.

Winger Simon Collins broke the deadlock in the 33rd minute from close range, and Town's dreaded third slice of bad luck came a minute before the break.

Sedgley, in attempting to divert Booth's low cross away from the onrushing Ronnie Jepson, gave his keeper Craig Forrest little chance as the ball flew in at the near post.

There was no way back for the visitors, or so everybody thought. But Huddersfield took their foot off the pedal in the second period and almost paid for it in a nail-biting finale.

Terriers keeper Steve Francis didn't have a shot to save all match, but at least

he was
Sedgley'
Subs
sparklec
naive i
died o
Scully,
ly as
stretch
were l
For
Hudd
earne
be up
side.
In
perfc
Tow
save
ing
Ye
top
the
tri
fo
P

HUDDERSFIELD		2		1

Collins (33 min), Sedgley og (44 mins)

MANAGER: Brian Horton		Match Rating	SATURDAY
1	Steve Francis	14	SEPTEMBER 9, 1995
2	Kenny Brown	14	
3	Tom Cowan	16	PLAYED AT
4	Darren Bullock	15	THE McALPINE
5	Pat Scully	14	STADIUM
6	Lee Sinnott	15	
7	Paul Dalton	16	CONDITIONS
8	Paul Reid	14	DRY AND SUNNY
9	Andrew Booth	19	
10	Ronnie Jepson	15	ATTENDANCE
11	Simon Collins	18	12,057
	Baldry (for Cowan 68 mins)		REFEREE
	Rowe (unused)		EDDIE
	Dunn (unused)		WOLSTENHOLME
			(Blackburn)

11		GOAL ATTEMPTS	
	3	CORNERS	
11		FOULS	

CARL MARSTON'S VERDICT

Alex Mathie has been the key man for Town this season. T leading scorer will be sorely missed over the next few recovers from a shoulder injury. Where the goals will con absence remains a worrying point. Nothing went right fo

Flashback: the match report in the East Anglian Daily Times following Town's defeat at Huddersfield in 1995.

200 yards from the main reception in the main car park. I was on tiptoes pressing the appropriate keys, the laptop and mobile phone threatening to slide off the roof of the Vauxhall Meriva at any second.

Ten minutes later, the deed was done. The relief was immense. The day ended with Warren still in possession of a camera, me delighted to have conquered the Terriers' terrible mobile phone service, and the Us, despite the defeat, still on course for promotion to the Championship.

Football stadiums nestling in dips or hollows, banked by tree-clad Yorkshire hills, might look scenic, but spare a thought for the poor journalist haunted by a weak phone signal.

49 NINIAN PARK

Club: Cardiff City
Founded: 1899 (as Riverside FC)
Ground: Ninian Park (1910 to 2009)
First visit: 28 October 1995; Cardiff 1 Colchester 2

Broken glass and explosives. This place had a wonderfully colourful history, with a hint of danger in the early days, though thankfully it was as safe as houses by the time that I started visiting.

They had problems with the pitch during the early years at Ninian Park, the home of Cardiff City from 1910. It had been an area of wasteland, and a former rubbish tip, before work started to level the surface and erect a small 200-seater wooden stand, and this led to several accidents. Occasionally, debris such as glass would rise to the surface, even though players were paid to arrive early for a match to clear the pitch of any objects. One of the most serious incidents took place the first time the stadium hosted an international match in 1911, with Scotsman Peter McWilliams suffering such a badly gashed knee that the injury ended his playing career. Ground improvements were slow to arrive, with the home and away teams even having to share the one solitary changing room until a second one was built in 1913.

Moving on, the old wooden stand was burnt down in 1937 as the result of thieves using explosives to try and break into the club's safe. It was rebuilt before the Second World War, with stone and brick, and new concrete terracing was added in front of the main stand in 1947. The press box had been housed there since 1960, with the vast terraces of the Popular Bank on the opposite side. It was a huge stadium, enveloping the small crowd of just over 3,000 who were in attendance for my first visit, a fourth-tier fixture against Colchester United in late October, 1995.

Despite the small crowd – the record attendance for a club match was a mighty 57,893 for the visit of Arsenal in 1953 – it still felt quite intimidating for away supporters. I managed to blend in among the local press and curbed my excitement even though Tony Adcock struck twice with bewitching chipped goals inside the first quarter of an hour. The Welsh crowd were confident, Bluebirds manager Kenny Hibbitt was buzzing, and home keeper Dave Williams was no doubt expecting a quiet afternoon, but none had banked on the intervention of a 32-year-old striker, who was feeling his age, ruining the party. Adcock's two goals were awesome. He left Williams red-faced with his first delicate chip before repeating the dose just 60 seconds later with an even better effort.

Soccer

Magician Adcock simply awesome

Cardiff City 1 Colchester United 2

by CARL MARSTON

IT WILL take a long time for the people of South Wales, and Cardiff keeper Dave Williams in particular, to forget the name of Tony Adcock.

Bluebirds manager Kenny Hibbitt, buzzing from a rare victory at Lincoln from the previous weekend, was confident of continuing the winning run in his pre-match build-up.

But he didn't bank on a 32-year-old Colchester marksman crossing the Severn Bridge and making a mockery of his prediction in devastating fashion.

Adcock was simply awesome. The U's front runner conjured up two breath-taking strikes, both of them delightful chips, in the space of a minute.

The opener, after 13 minutes, left keeper Williams red-faced as a precise chip from Mark Kinsella's excellent knock-down took a slight deflection on its way into the roof of the net.

Williams, still blushing, could hardly believe it as Adcock had the audacity to repeat the feat just 60 seconds later.

That second magical chip, if it had been delivered by a Cantona, Bergkamp or Ginola, would have been talked about for weeks to come. It was that good. Poor Williams had no chance.

There was a fear, no doubt shared by many in the Colchester camp, that the U's had rocked the boat too early. Cardiff had 76 minutes to tear into the visiting defence.

On the half-hour, the deficit was halved when Darren Adams found the back of the net with a deflected drive from 15 yards out.

But Steve Wignall's side refused to buckle under the .... despite referee Jim Rushton's unnerving habit

huffed and puffed a lot, but we lost this match in th first 15 minutes."

It was a frustrating afternoon for the Cardiff faithfu who don't shirk from throwing verbal abuse at the own heroes when the going gets tough.

But it was also rich entertainment for the neutra and in particular the loyal band of Colchester supp ers – there were enough talking points to keep every amused during the long trip home.

It was Mark Kinsella's 99th consecutive lea appearance; Steve Mardenborough's first start Colchester shirt; Robert Boyce's League debut (s 80th minute substitute); the U's second away win o season; and the 189th and 190th League goa Adcock's career.

Colchester, on the strength of just one defeat in last eight league games, are now fourth in Di Three, equal on points with second-placed Presto

That represents the best U's position since returned to the Football League in 1992.

The one worry that still hangs over Wignall is the wafer-thin nature of the squad at Layer R

First teamers Steve Whitton, Robbie Reine Ball, Adam Locke and Chris Fry were all mi Saturday. Worse still, Kinsella limped off injur

It promises to be another backs-to-the-wa mance at Fulham tomorrow. But who would b the U's in their current mood – and Adcock another flash of brilliance?

■ Torquay player-manager Don O'Riordan sacked following the 8-1 home defeat by S

Flashback: The author's match report following the U's 2-1 win at Ninian Park in 1995.

Boss Steve Wignall insisted, 'If French stars Ginola or Cantona had scored two goals like that, then everyone would have been talking about it for weeks. Tony has the ability to go cold when everyone around him is hot.'

Adcock himself, enjoying his second spell at Layer Road, declared, 'That was probably the best 60 seconds of my career when those two goals went in. Jimmy Greaves liked to pass the ball into the net; I like to chip it in.'

Adcock scored his 103rd and 104th league goals for Colchester that afternoon. He ended his career on 126 league goals for the U's and 249 career goals from just over 700 appearances all told, although his last senior goal was rather forgettable, a late consolation in a 4-1 thrashing at little-known Bedlington Terriers in the FA Cup three years after his sweet brace at Ninian Park. I was at Welfare Park to tell the tale of that sorry performance, in late 1998, which was a world away from the backs-to-the-wall display at Ninian Park where the U's held on, despite Darren Adams having halved the deficit on the half-hour for Hibbitt's Bluebirds.

Carl Emberson pulled off some miraculous saves, while the U's defence were left clinging on and walking a tightrope with all three centre-halves, Peter Cawley, Tony McCarthy and Gus Caesar, having been booked inside the first hour.

My next six trips to Cardiff, all with the U's, featured just one defeat and three more wins, plus a smash-and-grab late equaliser from full-back Joe Dunne in a 1-1 draw on a cold Tuesday night in early November 2001. That was notable because it was one of only seven league goals that defender Dunne scored during his Football League career, and because the Dubliner's lethal finish was the one and only effort on target recorded by the Us all night. 'That's the worst we've played on our travels all season,' admitted manager Steve Whitton. Daylight robbery on a cool Welsh evening.

So a lucky ground indeed, despite those early tales of jagged glass and errant explosives.

For me, Ninian Park, the home of Cardiff City for 99 years until its closure in 2009, will be best remembered for those two Adcock chips during the autumn of 1995. Collector's items, both of them. Even Cantona would have been proud.

50 MANOR GROUND

Club: Oxford United
Founded: 1893 (as Headington)
Ground: Manor Ground (1925 to 2001)
First visit: 28 November 1995; Oxford 1 Colchester 2

I will always associate the Manor Ground with the front passenger window of my car. Slightly unusual, I know, and it was no fault of hosts Oxford United or their home of 76 years, but on my second trip there I ended up driving home in the freezing cold with no passenger window. It had been smashed during a Saturday-afternoon theft of my car radio, while I was reporting on Ipswich Town's dismal 3-1 defeat inside the Manor Ground. Harsh, perhaps, but the episode has rather tainted my memories of this by-then dilapidated stadium.

Oxford's home was in a sorry state during the 1990s, full of antiquated terracing and ageing stands, surrounded by residential streets which made modernisation an impossibility. It was certainly no oil painting.

The press box was in the Beech Road Stand, the main seating area of the ground which had at least been spruced up in 1975 with the unveiling of new dressing rooms, boardroom, a players' tunnel and the aforementioned press box. Opposite was the Osler Road side, which incorporated three separate stands, and both ends had terracing. London Road housed the home fans under a large iron roof, while Cuckoo Lane End had a distinctive angled shape to it, much narrower at one end than the other, and open to the elements for the unfortunate away supporters. The pitch was also renowned for its appreciable slope towards the London Road End, which encouraged the home side to kick downhill in the second half towards their own fans.

According to the note left on my car windscreen by a friendly neighbour, my car had been broken into (down an attractive, leafy, residential street) at around 4pm, which would have been during the half-time interval of the First Division clash on 2 November 1996. George Burley's Ipswich side were already trailing 3-1 at this point. No more goals were added after the moment my car radio was whisked away by a couple of young 'entrepreneurs'. Naturally, they never were caught.

Flashback: The author's spread in the local newspaper following Town's 3-1 defeat at the Manor Ground in 1996.

It was not a great afternoon. The main opening to the ground, off London Road, was pleasant enough, in terms of a vulnerable-looking faded yellow-and-blue N-shaped entrance sign. It was an under-stated announcement to a ground that had seen better days, not helped by the presence of a petrol station next door.

On the pitch, Town defended 'like schoolboys', at least according to my match report. They were three down inside 44 minutes, the trend set early on by Tony Mowbray's own goal from Joey Beauchamp's free kick. Poor Mowbray was suffering from the flu and was substituted at half-time. Ex-Nottingham Forest striker Nigel Jemson and defensive lynchpin Matt Elliott both scored before the break, with Adam Tanner netting Town's consolation. It was a comfortable afternoon for Denis Smith's side.

Off the pitch, my colleague Dave Allard, the life and soul of many a press box, was uncharacteristically ruffled by a stubborn steward who appeared determined to make the ritual gathering of post-match quotes as difficult as possible while we all loitered beside the players' tunnel after the final whistle. It is never very easy speaking to players who have just had an ear-bashing from the manager in the dressing room after a comprehensive defeat, and a 'rules are rules' steward can make the exercise even more unpleasant.

In fact, it was not to be Dave's finest hour. True, he did resist the temptation to clout the steward, while picking up the odd quote, but worse was to follow. On returning to the car, and inspecting my smashed window, he was resigned to sitting on the back seat all the way home, shivering, teeth chattering, mumbling about how he'd like to get his hands on a certain over-officious steward. Even the many colourful fireworks displays which lined our route along the M25 and A12, just three days before Guy Fawkes Night, failed to lift Dave's spirits. It really was icy cold, exposed to the elements in the back seat of my damaged VW Polo, a very effective form of torture.

Still, under such circumstances it is usually best to turn on the car radio and listen to some tunes, to take your mind off the cold...!

By contrast, my first visit to the Manor Ground, in 1995, had been for a low-key midweek Auto Windscreens Shield southern area quarter-final against Colchester United, which attracted a small crowd of 1,943, the sort of late November fixture which only diehard fanatics and diligent members of the press bother to attend. It was notable for Colchester's 2-1 win, and full-back Simon Betts laying some ghosts to bed. Earlier in the season, Betts had missed the crunch spot kick in the penalty shoot-out which saw the U's bow out of the League Cup at Bristol City, but he made amends by beating keeper Phil Whitehead with a 68th-minute penalty. Ironically, Betts had only taken the penalty because regular taker Tony Adcock, who had been chopped down in the build-up by Stuart Massey, was receiving treatment from physio Brian Owen. Earlier, Adcock had headed the U's (Colchester) into a 26th-minute lead, with Mark Angel equalising for the U's (Oxford) via a deflected long-range shot.

Unlike my second return journey from Oxford a year later, for this one I was heartened by both an away win and four unbroken car windows. Alas, Dave Allard was not in attendance to appreciate it.

51 LONDON ROAD

Club: Peterborough United
Founded: 1934
Ground: London Road (from 1934, opened in 1913)
First visit: 9 January 1996; Peterborough 3 Colchester 2

Peterborough United's London Road has often been a scene of desolation whenever I have visited, and it was certainly not one of Roy Keane's favourite grounds.

Colchester United always seemed to lose on my early trips into north-west Cambridgeshire, the standard set by an Auto Windscreens Shield southern area quarter-final in early January 1996. Posh won 3-2 on a pudding of a pitch, with players slipping and sliding over the treacherous surface. Posh striker Gary Martindale scored a brace that night. The U's lost on my next few visits as well, before enjoying better fortune after the turn of the century, while even my days with Ipswich Town were sorry affairs. Most of the time, the press conferences were held in a deserted bar/social room, like a scene out of Peter Kay's *Phoenix Nights*. It was fairly grim, and there was no beer or buffet

Packed in at the away end, Town fans let off a flare during a 3-1 defeat at London Road in 2010. (WP)

available. It always felt like you had arrived too early for the most low-key of wedding receptions.

Ground-wise, both ends were terraced at the time of my early visits, at the London Road End and Moy's End. The Main Stand (North Stand) had been opened in 1957 with rows of wooden seating, and terracing in front, although it was overhauled with more seats added to replace the terraces during the early 1990s. The low roofs helped generate atmosphere, and an impressive new two-tiered all-seater stand was opened at the opposite side (Glebe Road) by the close of the 1995/96 season. An old-feel stadium, especially from the outside, and from the adjacent car park where only the luckiest members of the press could gain access.

The stadium itself did not start hosting Football League action until 1960, when Posh followed up five successive Midland League titles from 1955 by finally securing election at the expense of the unfortunate Gateshead, who had finished third-bottom above both Oldham Athletic and Hartlepools United. Posh had scored well over 100 goals in each of their five Midland League championships, and they proceeded to plunder a divisional record 134 goals on their way to the Fourth Division title in their first season, 1960/61, in the Football League, helped by an amazing 52 goals from centre-forward Terry Bly.

Fifty years on and Peterborough were in a rut, crying out for a striker of Bly's ilk, although that was no consolation for visiting manager Keane. In fact, one of Keane's low points – and there were many – during his 18 months as Ipswich manager was a visit to London Road for a lowly Championship battle on 16 February 2010. I was not exactly brimming with confidence when I took my seat in the cramped and rather stale quarters of the London Road press box, at the rear of Block C of the Main Stand, but even I didn't expect Town to slump to a dismal 3-1 defeat at the home of the basement dwellers.

Despite the woeful result, and woeful performance – and perhaps because of it – I have always remembered this particular encounter, maybe also because it happened to be a Tuesday evening. In fact, I have often found the misery of a midweek defeat on the road and under floodlights harder to stomach than a similar result on a run-of-the-mill Saturday afternoon. I guess the journey home, often in the dead of night, gives you too much time to stew over such a miserable experience.

I've lost count of the number of times I've written the phrase – 'a game of two halves' – but I could well have penned those familiar five words about Town's demise from early 2010. As so often happened under Keane, there were glimmers of hope for a brighter future, not least following the arrival of target man Daryl Murphy on loan from Sunderland. Murphy headed home his third goal in as many games to put Town 1-0 up at London Road, a lead they maintained until half-time.

Alas, there was always a calamity lurking around the corner, during the Keane era, and so it proved in the second half as Posh steamrollered to victory, beating keeper Arran Lee-Barrett on three occasions. Liam Dickinson, Lee Frecklington and defender Craig Morgan were all on target for the hosts, who had a new manager at the helm in Jim Gannon. He lasted for just two months, unable to stave off an inevitable relegation.

An angry Keane, who spent another 11 months in the job at Ipswich, was dismayed by his team's second-half surrender, conducting post-match interviews in an otherwise near-deserted stadium, although the lights from the press box still shone brightly. Keane fumed, 'It's criminal really when you are 1-0 up away from home and you start the second half by conceding a crazy goal after one or two minutes. I have defended the players this

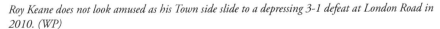

Roy Keane does not look amused as his Town side slide to a depressing 3-1 defeat at London Road in 2010. (WP)

season as they have always given their all, but we died out in the second half and I need to put my finger on why. There is no hiding place. In any walk of life you have got to show some character and we had none.'

Mercifully, it is not far from Peterborough to my home in Bury St Edmunds, so I didn't have time to dwell on Town's plight during the midnight trek along the A14. Keane only had a bit further to travel to his East Suffolk home, but I'm guessing he had more of a sleepless night. A midweek horror show at London Road can bring on nightmares.

Not all my visits to London Road, though, have ended in misery. An exception was a Good Friday afternoon on 25 March 2005 when an appropriately-named Marc Goodfellow marked his second appearance for Colchester with the opening goal in a 3-0 win. The opposition were not great. Posh were second from bottom of League One and 24 hours earlier Barry Fry, the chairman and manager, had announced his intention to stand down as boss at the end of the season. But the U's, under Phil Parkinson, were still impressive, further boosted by second-half goals from Neil Danns and Marino Keith (a penalty).

'I rarely fail to put those sort of chances away,' enthused winger Goodfellow, who was on loan from Bristol City for the month. Alas, that was to be his only goal for the U's, so I'm guessing no more of 'those sort of chances' came his way. A few weeks later and Posh were duly relegated, Fry went upstairs to become director of football and Goodfellow signed for Swansea City.

Football never stands still, though the venue for Posh's post-match interviews, with that Phoenix Club northern feel, stayed the same. I never did spot anything as much as a sandwich in that room, let alone a sausage roll. And although the catering at Kay's Bolton-based working men's club might have been just as poor, at least there was often bingo or cabaret on offer to the punters. Instead, London Road merely offered a depressed away manager to grill after a defeat.

52 HOME PARK

Club: Plymouth Argyle
Founded: 1886 (as Argyle FC)
Ground: Home Park (since 1901)
First visit: 20 January 1996; Plymouth 1 Colchester 1

The most westerly and southerly club in the English Football League, the trek down to Devon is a long and arduous one for most clubs in the country. The journey home can feel even longer after a Home Park defeat, none more so than after the anguish of a play-off semi-final loss, which is something I experienced first-hand with Colchester United at the hands of Neil Warnock's Pilgrims in 1996.

The ground has been completely reconstructed since the turn of the 21st century, but back in the 1990s most of it was given over to terracing. The original venue was destroyed

Fans stream past the turnstiles outside Home Park, the home of Plymouth Argyle. (CM)

by German bombers during the Second World War, the victim of the 'Plymouth Blitz' of 1941. A new double-decker grandstand was built in 1952, running the length of the pitch, which offered the only seating area until the end of the 1960s. The press box was sited there, at the back of the Mayflower Stand, while the first tier was for standing room. The Barn Park End remained uncovered and the Devonport End was also terracing, although the Lyndhurst Stand opposite the Mayflower Stand did become all-seater.

I was in the overspill section of the press box, perched on a wooden seat with a computer on my lap, for what was my second visit of the year, having enjoyed a debut outing in January 1996 when Colchester United centre-half David Greene celebrated his first senior goal with an 89th-minute equaliser in a 1-1 draw, turning home a cross by winger Paul Abrahams; a sweet moment. It was especially sweet for the few U's fans who had stood in the rain on the open terrace at the Barn Park End and were bracing themselves for a 300-mile return journey to Essex.

Under four months later I was back at Home Park for a thunderous Third Division Three play-off semi-final second leg. Although always impartial in the press box, I must confess to feeling utterly devastated after this match, a 3-1 defeat which saw the U's lose 3-2 on aggregate. An 85th-minute header by defender Paul Williams won the tie, meaning the U's (and me) missed out on a trip to Wembley and potential promotion. It was gut-wrenching, and collecting some post-match quotes from forlorn U's players as they boarded the team coach was a miserable task.

Mark Kinsella, whose wonder strike had won the first leg at Layer Road, had put the U's on course for success with another 25-yard beauty after 66 minutes of a helter-skelter second leg. That made the aggregate 2-2 following first-half goals from Michael Evans and Chris Leadbitter. Extra time loomed, while the U's had a decisive away goal if the aggregate scores should stay level, but all those hopes were dashed by Williams's late header. Plymouth fans invaded the pitch after the final whistle, chanting 'Wembley, Wembley'. A great night for them – their side went on to win promotion, by beating Darlington 1-0 in the final – while U's boss Steve Wignall was left to admit, 'The big game found a lot of people out. Four or five of my players did not perform.'

One incident from that night did stay with me. On 81 minutes, U's keeper Carl Emberson kicked the ball out of play to allow a Plymouth player to receive some treatment. But instead of Argyle giving possession back to the U's from the restart, they retained the ball from the throw-in. To this day, that lack of sportsmanship has rankled me.

Still, no point in bearing grudges.

I have returned to Home Park on many, many occasions since, enjoying overnight stays, drinks in vibrant pubs by the harbour, morning runs along The Hoe promenade, and walks from the city centre to Home Park for the football, yet I have never witnessed an away win, either with the U's or Town.

And not giving the ball back from that throw-in – it still bugs me.

53 BRISBANE ROAD

Club: Leyton Orient
Founded: 1881 (as Glyn Cricket Club)
Ground: Brisbane Road (since 1937)
First visit: 2 March 1996; Leyton Orient 0 Colchester 1

One of my happier hunting grounds, in terms of the ease of travel plus the number of away victories, Brisbane Road has changed much over the years (as has the club's name!). In fact, the East Stand was previously the main stand, largely built during the 1950s with the addition of a structure from the derelict Mitcham Stadium. Here was the press box and the main office buildings, until the emergence of the impressive new West Stand in 2005 which saw the main club headquarters shift across to this Oliver Road side of the ground.

The press box is now perched on the fifth floor, over-hanging the stand and guaranteeing a terrific view of the action, and the nearby plush apartments. It's a neat set-up for the press, with even a little kitchen to make your own tea or coffee, and a microwave to heat up your previous night's Indian takeaway.

But Brisbane Road was a starker place when I first visited in March, 1996. I parked a mile or so away on Green Road and then ambled along the Leyton High Road, past Leyton Cricket Ground plus an array of grocery stores and car washes, and up Osborne

Leyton Orient fans invade the pitch at Brisbane Road after 84 minutes of their home match against the U's in 2017. (CM)

Road (the stadium was originally called Osborne Road) into Brisbane Road. Colchester United won the game, a fourth-tier clash against Pat Holland's O's, courtesy of Tony Adcock's 41st-minute penalty, much to the delight of the U's travelling support on the South End terrace. That same terracing was to be ripped up later in the year, to be replaced by a short-term car park before a new seated stand was erected in 1999.

Speed on 21 years and my most memorable visit to Brisbane Road, by this time a bumper stadium with red shiny seats and black lettering, was a very sombre occasion for the hosts. It was also the only match that I have attended which was abandoned and then restarted on the same afternoon.

Hundreds of Leyton Orient supporters had been staging protests against club owner Francesco Beccheti during the pre-match build-up on the penultimate weekend of the regular season. The proud O's fans were angry at their club's relegation out of the Football League, which had been finalised the previous weekend before Colchester's visit for a League Two match on 29 April 2017. I attended one of these rallies in the adjacent Coronation Park before kick-off, a peaceful but passionate affair.

The U's were leading 3-1 after 84 minutes when a mass pitch invasion caused a stoppage in play. A single red flare was thrown into the Leyton Orient penalty area just four minutes after Macauley Bonne had tucked home the U's third goal to effectively seal victory. The flare seemed to be a premeditated signal for home supporters to start spilling on to the pitch, first a trickle and then a flood, to congregate by the centre circle. And there they remained, for more than an hour, despite repeated messages for them to return to the stands, including a plea from manager Omer Riza. They were determined to get the match abandoned, no doubt to bloody the noses of the football authorities who, they believed, had failed to intervene to stop the slow, painful demise of their club.

Eventually, when it was announced over the Tannoy that the match had been abandoned – although the term actually used was 'cancelled' – the fans began to clear the pitch and leave the stadium. I sent over my match report and ducked outside to hover by the away team coach in pursuit of players' quotes, only to then learn that the match was about to restart.

So I had to slip back in, sneaking past a couple of stewards to climb the five flights of stairs back up to watch the surreal ending to the match. The two teams had remained in the dressing room, waiting for the go-ahead from referee Carl Boyeson before playing out the final six minutes (plus two minutes of injury time) inside an empty stadium. Both sets of players just went through the motions, with Leyton Orient merely passing the ball between themselves, and the U's letting them have possession. A match that had kicked off at 3pm therefore eventually finished at 7pm.

For the record, earlier in the afternoon Reading loanee Tarique Fosu's superb header had given the U's a lead, with Sandro Semedo equalising with a long-range thunderbolt past Sam Walker before the east Londoners were condemned by late goals from strikers Chris Porter and Bonne (the latter was to end up signing for Leyton Orient later that summer, and was to prove a big hit).

Then came the pitch invasion and the temporary abandonment.

It was a sad, eerie way for Leyton Orient to bring the curtain down on their last home game as a Football League club, after a tenure of 112 years – though they did win promotion back up two years later – with no fans in the ground to witness a sham ending.

I doubt whether Brisbane Road had seen anything like it, since Leyton Orient took up residence 80 years earlier, under the name Clapton Orient, in 1937.

I guess it was, and will always be, the 'longest' match I have ever reported on, and certainly the only one where I have left the ground before the final whistle and then had to worm my way back in, unnoticed in the shadows.

54 THE HAWTHORNS

Club: West Bromwich Albion
Founded: 1878 (as West Bromwich Strollers)
Ground: The Hawthorns (since 1900)
First visit: 3 September 1996; West Brom 1 Colchester 3

West Bromwich Albion, one of 12 founder members of the Football League, have played at The Hawthorns since 1900, the first stadium to be built in the 20th century after a swift four-month construction. It was named after the old Hawthorn Estate, where hawthorn bushes had to be cleared to make way for the new stadium.

And it just so happened that I was expecting a very 'thorny' night for rank outsiders Colchester United when I paid my first visit to this famous West Midlands landmark for a League Cup second round second leg on a Tuesday evening in early September 1996. The fourth-tier U's were already trailing 3-2 from the home leg at Layer Road, so a big aggregate success appeared the likely outcome in favour of the First Division Baggies.

Not for the first time, I was proved to be way off the mark.

I had been determined to enjoy the evening at such an impressive stadium which, like so many up and down the country, had been transformed from a rather dilapidated state in the 1980s to a swanky all-seater by the mid-1990s. The terracing at both the Smethwick End and Birmingham Road End (next to the A41) had been demolished and replaced with seating, while the press box was actually in the oldest surviving stand, the West Stand, formerly known as the Halford's Lane Stand. The crowd was under 10,000 that night, with the tie seemingly already done and dusted. The locals were certainly in a relaxed frame of mind and the adjacent good old-fashioned public house, The Woodman, was doing a brisk trade (unfortunately it was demolished just seven years later, with the land incorporated into a car park).

'Amazing' is how I described Colchester's stunning performance, overturning a 3-2 deficit to win 3-1 on the night and 5-4 on aggregate, especially as the Essex visitors had played the whole of the second half without a recognised goalkeeper. Instead, assistant manager Steve Whitton, deputising for the injured Garrett Caldwell, a Canadian keeper

Jamie Guy salutes away fans after scoring in the U's 2-1 defeat at The Hawthorns in 2006. (WP)

who only played eight times in English football, abandoned his striker duties to don a pair of gloves and play in goal. Another *Roy of the Rovers* tale was about to unfold.

The U's had levelled the tie by half-time, penalty box predator Robbie Reinelt having stuck out a boot to divert Simon Betts's long-range shot past Nigel Spink. But when 37-year-old Spink's opposite number, Caldwell, pulled up sharply with a leg injury after half an hour, and then did not appear for the second half, it only seemed a matter of time before Alan Buckley's West Brom took charge.

Yet, incredibly, it was the visitors who stepped up another gear, and while makeshift keeper Whitton had very little to do, the U's scored two more goals through Reinelt and a spectacular volley from full-back Joe Dunne, who often delivered on the big occasion. Whitton was beaten by a late header from Paul Groves, but it was not enough to spare the Baggies' blushes.

To the home fans' credit, they joined in with the small U's contingent to clap and cheer the visitors off the pitch at the end. It really was a remarkable evening.

As an aside, the following season, two-goal Reinelt hit the headlines by scoring a vital equaliser for his new club Brighton in a 1-1 draw at Hereford on the final day of the season, which saved the Seagulls and condemned the Bulls to relegation from the Football League. He thus secured his place in Brighton folklore.

Many years went by before I made a second visit to The Hawthorns. Well, ten actually. This time both clubs were plying their trade at the same level, having been two divisions apart just a few months before. While Colchester had clinched automatic promotion from League One in 2006, the Baggies had suffered relegation from the Premier League, resulting in an early-season Championship duel in the West Midlands on 21 August, the first league meeting between the teams.

To be honest I, like the U's, was still getting to grips with the rarefied atmosphere of the second tier. I had taken to wearing smart ties to every away game, and made sure that I arrived early to do justice to the hot food on offer in each press lounge, while in turn the U's were finding their feet on the pitch and getting used to the bigger crowds. A gate of 17,509 witnessed a 2-1 defeat for Colchester, their fourth from four league games – though they were still being kept off the bottom by Niall Quinn's Sunderland – but a far heavier loss had looked on the cards when Bryan Robson's Baggies eased into a 2-0 half-time lead through a penalty by Nathan Ellington, a £3,000,001 purchase from Wigan (contractually, he could only leave the Latics for a fee in excess of £3m, hence the rogue pound), and a fierce strike from Ronnie Wallwork, who celebrated what was only his second West Brom goal in four years.

Yet, as a sign of things to come for the rest of a wonderful season, Geraint Williams's Essex visitors suddenly took the initiative in the second half. Wayne Brown struck the post with a header, fellow centre-half Garry Richards had a shot cleared off the line, and substitute Jamie Guy duly halved the deficit within a matter of seconds of his introduction. Youth team product Guy hooked home a powerful shot on 83 minutes to notch his first senior goal, past Swiss international keeper Pascal Zuberbuhler.

Guy, 19, therefore achieved what the might of France, Togo, South Korea and Ukraine had all failed to do during the previous summer's World Cup. Namely, score a goal against Zuberbuhler. In fact, Switzerland remain the only team in the history of the finals of the World Cup to have been knocked out of the competition without conceding a goal, having lost 3-0 on penalties to Ukraine after a 0-0 draw.

Alas, the U's could not find another route past Zuberbuhler during the closing minutes. 'Fair play to Colchester. They pushed us back in the second half,' confessed Robson. 'They gave us something to think about.'

That they did, but when I think of The Hawthorns, I prefer to dwell on the League Cup shock of 1996, not the near miss of 2006, when those two unlikely heroes, plucky striker Robbie Reinelt and emergency keeper Steve Whitton, combined to deflate the Baggies.

55 VETCH FIELD

Club: Swansea City
Founded: 1912 (as Swansea Town)
Ground: Vetch Field (1912 to 2005)
First visit: 4 October 1996; Swansea 1 Colchester 1

Occasionally, during my early days of newspaper reporting, I would do a little radio work as well, either sending the odd bulletin over to BBC Essex during the match or providing some summarising alongside the main commentator. I mention this because one of my rare sorties into the world of radio was at the Vetch Field, where the actual route to the broadcast gantry was more demanding than the radio work itself.

The gantry could only be approached via a rusty, rickety, ageing metal ladder, situated in the North Bank which just happened to house the most vociferous home supporters in the stadium. It required good balance and a degree of bravery to clamber up those metal steps, especially if you were carrying a load. It was not for the faint-hearted, and you certainly didn't want to do the journey more than once, or drop anything on to the terracing below.

I only braved this gantry once, on my first visit with Colchester United on a Friday night in October 1996. After that, I always stuck to the press box (for the print journalists) on the other side of the ground, not for the better views, but for the lack of danger.

Vetch Field, the home of Swansea City for 93 years from 1912 to 2005, was instantly recognisable. It was in a rather decrepit state when I began visiting, with the capacity drastically reduced by the demands of health and safety measures, but the place oozed personality from every corner, especially the two corners which were only a few feet away from the neighbours' back gardens. That was a feature of the Vetch Field, hemmed in by residential streets and hampered by the pitch running diagonally to those neighbouring roads, as if it had just been plonked there.

Expansion was impossible, and at the East Stand End there was the unusual sight of one floodlight jutting out over the roof at a weird angle to adhere to the objections of the local residents living in William Street, who didn't want any further intrusions. The overall impression was of a ground lop-sided, with the two gaping corners and the stands not running the length of the pitch. An uncomfortable fit in its surroundings, and with HM Prison Swansea, a Victorian building, also in the vicinity. In short, it was a million miles away from the standard, symmetrical, out-of-town stadiums of the modern era.

The golden era at the Vetch was during the late 1970s and early 1980s, when ex-Liverpool striker Josh Toshack made the move from Anfield to take over as player-boss, at the young age of 29. Three promotions in four years followed as the Swans, bolstered by several ex-Liverpool players, finished third three times in the Fourth, Third and Second Divisions to reach the top flight in 1981 for the first time in the club's history. Former Reds stars Ian Callaghan, Tommy Smith, Colin Irwin and Ray Kennedy all donned the white and black of the South Wales club during these years, as did ex-Everton centre-forward Bob Latchford and household names such as Leighton James and Robbie James.

Tipped for relegation, the Swans actually launched an unlikely title bid in 1981/82 before five defeats in the last six fixtures saw them drop to sixth. Still, fellow top-six sides Liverpool (champions), Manchester United, Arsenal and Tottenham were all beaten at the Vetch in front of frenzied crowds of 20,000-plus, with runners-up Ipswich the only rivals to enjoy success with a 2-1 win, courtesy of Eric Gates's 88th-minute goal.

My first visit to Vetch Field, though, was to be 14 years later. Having lugged the radio equipment up the aforementioned rusty steps to the exposed gantry, I watched a 1-1

The brilliant Lomana Lua Lua, deceiving home keeper Roger Freestone at Vetch Field in 2000. (WP)

draw between Jan Molby's Swans and Steve Wignall's U's on a Friday night under the lights on 4 October 1996, in front of a small crowd of just 2,531 (the record attendance at the ground was 32,796 for an FA Cup tie against Arsenal in 1968). The U's had the luxury of a second-minute opener, centre-half David Greene stabbing home a free kick by Richard Wilkins past keeper Roger Freestone, only for striker Steve Torpey to rifle home an equaliser before half-time. The Swans, relegated to the fourth tier the previous season, went on to lose 1-0 to Northampton in the play-off final.

But of greater value was a return trip to Swansea's old ground which I made in late August 2000, when Colchester were again the visitors, this time with manager Steve Whitton at the helm and ex-Chelsea boss John Hollins in charge of the Swans. Everything revolved around Lomana LuaLua, the U's African gem who scored both goals in a 2-0 win. This time, I was relieved to be watching from the sweaty press box rather than a dangerous radio gantry, though I would willingly have ignored health-and-safety protocol to climb a 100 rusty steps, if it had allowed me to witness LuaLua's ten-out-of-ten performance.

I rarely gave full marks in my post-match ratings (as I have stated many, many times) for the following day's newspaper, but LuaLua was an exception. I think I awarded him a perfect score at least twice, if not three or four times, during his brief time with the U's. He was that good.

You know you have been entertained when even some of the rival fans start applauding some of your tricks, twists and turns during the match. LuaLua, still aged just 18, commanded such respect after such a complete performance. Clearly a Premier League player in the making, LuaLua scored a goal in each half, the second a fine solo effort, as well has hitting the bar in between.

It was all too much for 50 or so Swans fans who chose to invade the pitch in menacing fashion after LuaLua had doubled the lead. Hollins had to walk over to them to restore peace. However, the vast majority of the Vetch Field crowd, which numbered more than 6,000 that hot summer's afternoon, although angered by their own team's display, were quick to applaud LuaLua. Hostile towards their own players, but appreciative of an opposing striker. It was an extraordinary afternoon.

'LuaLua is a bit special,' admitted Hollins. 'Lomana is really worth watching,' insisted U's boss Whitton.

I couldn't agree more. It was a privilege to be at the Vetch Field, with all its eccentricities, that day.

56 GOLDSTONE GROUND

Club: Brighton & Hove Albion
Founded: 1901
Ground: Goldstone Ground (1902 to 1997)
First visit: 26 December 1996; Brighton 1 Colchester 1

Steve Whitton was an assistant manager when he scored in the U's 1-1 draw at Goldstone Ground in 1996.

I only just made it to the Goldstone Ground before Brighton & Hove Albion left their home of 95 years, to initially ground-share with distant Gillingham at Priestfield, 70 miles away, following the controversial sale of their old home to help meet some of the club's debts. My one and only visit was for a Boxing Day 1996 clash in the fourth tier, with Brighton stuck on the Football League basement and facing the realistic prospect of being relegated, to coincide with their new nomadic existence. Needless to say it was not a happy time to be a Seagulls supporter.

Situated not far from the sea on the Old Shoreham Road, next to Hove Park in Hove, the Goldstone Ground was on its last legs when I visited, as if awaiting its fate of a few months down the line like a prisoner on death row.

The main section of the West Stand had been built in 1958, stretching about two thirds of the way alongside the pitch, with a family area added later. Opposite was the big bank of open, sloping terracing of the East Stand, split into different-sized sections of varying heights, and overlooked by houses and their back gardens behind. Both ends were covered. The press area was in the West Stand, pale blue and brown.

The crowd was under 5,000 for Colchester United's post-Christmas visit. At the time, the sorry Seagulls still had no guaranteed home for the following season and they also looked odds-on for the dreaded drop into the Conference, having parted company with their manager Jimmy Case, of former Liverpool fame, earlier in the month. A few days after Case's departure, the club were also hit with a two-point deduction as punishment for a pitch invasion by home fans, who were protesting against the sale of the Goldstone Ground, during a match against Lincoln at the start of October. Hence festive spirit was in short supply and the end result, a 1-1 draw, gave little cheer to either team. It really was a grim afternoon all round.

Assistant manager Steve Whitton, a future U's boss, put the visitors ahead with a 25-yard free kick which skidded past the defensive wall and in at the far post beyond keeper Nicky Rust. In truth, the U's should have gone on to record a comfortable win over what looked like a very, very ordinary Brighton side. And yet the East Sussex hosts equalised via Denny Mundee's 34th-minute penalty to secure an unlikely point. The final hour was dour, with neither side having the guile to threaten a winner. In truth, time was beginning to drag.

This happened to be the U's 13th draw from 25 games, the most in the Football League, while it left Brighton a distant seven points adrift of safety at the bottom, below Darlington and Hereford. 'I think we must be going for the world record for the number of drawn games in a season,' rued U's manager Steve Wignall.

Remarkably Brighton, who had been 13 points in arrears earlier in the campaign, recovered to cheat relegation on the final day of the season. Ex-Colchester striker Robbie Reinelt, who had ironically been a U's substitute at Brighton on Boxing Day before completing a move to the south coast in February, scored the equaliser in a 1-1 draw at Hereford, in the most crucial of all bottom-of-the-table clashes, to send the Bulls out of the Football League on goal difference. The previous weekend, a sell-out crowd of 11,341

An aerial shot of the Goldstone Ground.

had witnessed the final game at the Goldstone Ground, a 1-0 win over Doncaster which kept Brighton's survival hopes alive. Fans spilled on to the pitch after the final whistle on that damp afternoon, many of them to claim souvenirs of the famous stadium, like seats and bits of turf.

These days, the Goldstone Ground is Goldstone Retail Park.

And the next time I reported on Colchester away at Brighton was exactly a year later for another draw. But this time the venue was Priestfield, the home of Gillingham, and it was a 4-4 thriller, not a dour 1-1. It was also a shorter journey home. Time did not drag that day.

SECTION THREE –
THE LATE 1990s

57 BOOTHFERRY PARK

Club: Hull City
Founded: 1904
Ground: Boothferry Park (1946 to 2002)
First visit: 15 April 1997; Hull 1 Colchester 2

Another of the lost grounds of England, Boothferry Park was home to Hull City for 56 years, although it initially took 17 years to build from the original planning to the grand opening. Financial difficulties, and then the Second World War, delayed matters before the stadium reached the height of its powers in the 1960s with the construction of the new South Stand. Alas, by the time I made my first visits in 1997 and 1998, the rot had long since set in, with ageing stands, rusty roofs, a shrinking end (due to a supermarket) and an illuminated sign that was beginning to lose its letters.

Still, I found it to be an intimidating (in a nice way) place, a proper 'home' football stadium where home advantage counted. In short it had atmosphere, even in a semi-derelict state with only a small crowd.

The original plans were laid in 1929 but work did not begin for another three years on a site not far from the Humber Estuary. Just the pitch and some terracing had been completed when financial problems held up the project. Then came the Second World War, which left the pitch in a poor shape (tanks were even repaired on the playing surface). Finally, Hull moved into their new stadium for the start of the 1946/47 season with just one stand completed, the West Stand, which housed the changing rooms, directors' room and, most importantly of all, the press box!

It was from the West Stand that I reported on Colchester United's later visits to Boothferry Park. The simple, yellow and black box-like stand was looking very tired, with its windshields at either end (although they didn't hinder the view, unlike at Wigan

Fans on the pitch after the last-ever game at Boothferry Park.

Athletic's Springfield Park). Opposite was the East Terrace, which was covered with an intended temporary roof that ended up never being replaced. This part of the ground was popular with the locals, and was widely known as the Kempton Stand on account of the Kempton Road that ran the other side of the railway station (Boothferry Halt).

The rest of the ground was made up of the South Stand, which was the pride and joy of the club when opened in the mid-1960s to replace the former Bunker's Hill Terrace. A two-tiered structure with a cantilever roof, it had black and yellow seats in the top tier and terracing on the lower tier. Finally, the North Stand, not quite so resplendent, to say the least, especially by the time that I visited. To ease the club's debts, a supermarket was built behind that end, which resulted in the stand being demolished to leave just a small section of terracing at the front.

Boothferry Park was therefore already a scene of decay when I turned up on the coat-tails of Colchester for a Tuesday night fixture in April 1997, while the U's could have been excused for having their minds elsewhere. Steve Wignall's men were due to appear at Wembley just five days later in the final of the Auto Windscreens Shield, so a midweek trip to Humberside for a fourth-tier fixture was something they could have done without. Injuries were to be avoided, to ensure no late absentees for Wembley, while there were many other distractions, including the recording of a special CD single with Colchester-based punk band Special Duties, to mark their Wembley outing.

The players turned up at the Springvale Studios, near Ipswich, to record the anthem – 'Wembley! Wembley (Wembley Here we Come)' – and then-BBC Radio 1 DJ Steve Lamacq, a lifelong U's fan, made sure he played it regularly on his *Evening Session* programme during the week. Pop stars one week, off to Boothferry Park the next!

The U's had actually lost their first four matches on the spin since qualifying for the Wembley final, to almost kill off their promotion hopes, but they did rally with a home win over Swansea City the previous weekend, and then followed this up with a 2-1 success in front of a sparse crowd at Boothferry Park.

Mark Sale, at the time the second tallest outfield player in the Football League, below Birmingham City's Kevin Francis (6ft 7in), made the biggest impression at Hull that night. Fresh from scoring his first goal for the U's just three days earlier against Swansea, target man Sale cracked home a right-footed drive to record the winner against the Tigers in a 2-1 win after home striker Duane Darby had earlier given his side the lead before being sent off early in the second period.

'I could have scored a hat-trick, with a little more luck,' insisted 6ft 5in Sale after his Boothferry Park adventure, and in the build-up to a Sunday appearance at Wembley. 'I was just about to head home the first when Tony Adcock nipped in to beat me to the cross, and I had another disallowed before half-time.'

A £20,000 purchase from Mansfield, Sale was looking forward to the continued build-up ahead of Wembley. 'There are plans to play golf and to go clay-pigeon shooting,' said Sale. Alas, the U's lost the Auto Windscreens Shield Final to Carlisle in a penalty shoot-out after a goalless draw. They also missed out on the play-offs, by one place and one point. Hull, in decline, finished ten points clear of the drop.

Meanwhile, a sign of Hull's decline, quite literally, could be seen in the illuminated sign behind the back of the yellow main stand. In red lettering, it was supposed to spell 'BOOTHFERRY PARK' although an O had dropped off to make it 'BOTHFERRY PARK'. In later years, the only illuminated letters spelt 'FER ARK'. It 'elt time for the club to 'ove on.

58 KENILWORTH ROAD

Club: Luton Town
Founded: 1885
Ground: Kenilworth Road (from 1905)
First visit: 26 August 1997; Luton 2 Colchester 1

Kenilworth Road, the home of Luton Town since 1904, has always been instantly recognisable. It is like no other ground, with a row of executive boxes on one side of the pitch instead of terracing or a seated stand, and a very unusual approach for away supporters at the Oak Road End via a hidden narrow entrance in among a row of houses, through a back garden and then a short climb up some fire escape-like stairs to the stand above.

Situated less than a mile west of the town centre, in the Bury Park area, the ground is rather hemmed in by terraced houses and provides a big headache with parking. In

Aidan Davison, who delivered a 10-out-of-10 performance for the U's in a 1-1 draw at Luton in 2006. (WP)

the early days I used to be able to secure a priceless press parking pass for a small car park nearby, but in more recent times I have preferred to street park a mile out and trust that the car would still be there, and in the same condition, when I returned. It always was, despite my scepticism, unlike of course one of my aforementioned visits to Oxford United's Manor Ground, when parking down a leafy suburban street gave me a misguided sense of security and culminated in the loss of my car radio.

I witnessed one of the best displays of goalkeeping I have ever had the privilege of reporting on, back in Colchester United's first of two seasons in the Championship in 2006, thanks to the heroics of Aidan Davison at Kenilworth Road. By then I had already visited this corner of Bedfordshire several times, watching the action from the wooden press box in the Main Stand, the oldest stand in the ground having replaced the original one which burnt down in 1921 (that had a press loft and balcony). There is terracing below with seating in the top tier and a small structure, the David Preece Stand, bolted on in one corner as a family enclosure, which makes a total of five stands inside the stadium.

Opposite is a row of 25 executive boxes, a quirk of Kenilworth Road and a prominent feature of the stadium, with a line of terraced houses clearly visible behind. These boxes, which have a few blue seats in front of them for guests, replaced the old Bobbers Stand, so named because entrance used to cost a bob (one shilling). To the left of the press box is the Oak Road End, topped with an electronic scoreboard and usually filled with away fans, and far to the right is the Kenilworth Road End, which became all-seater just a year before my Aidan Davison tale of 2006.

The view from the press box at Kenilworth Road, looking out towards the rows of executive boxes opposite. (CM)

I have always liked the ground, especially as the press could usually grab a cup of tea from one of the comfortable suites at the back of the stand.

My first visit had been for a League Cup first round second leg on a warm late-August evening in 1997. A 1-1 draw, with Tony Thorpe scoring for the Hatters (he was to sign a short-term contract with Colchester United, in 2006) and winger Ian Hathaway equalising for the U's, was enough to see the hosts through 2-1 on aggregate. But I'd prefer to dwell on a visit of nine years later when I awarded another of my rare ten-out-of-tens, this time for away keeper Davison. It was another 1-1 draw, in mid-September 2006, but this was no typical 1-1.

It was just one of those nights when everything stuck for an inspired Davison. He caught every cross, kept hold of virtually every shot, and by the final whistle he had succeeded in completely demoralising Mike Newell's Luton, who had dominated the whole match. The 38-year-old custodian was applauded off the pitch by home fans as well as away supporters, after delivering a one-man show to keep the Hatters at bay.

Striker Sam Parkin, on loan from Ipswich Town, had headed Luton into a 31st-minute lead from future Portman Road star Carlos Edwards's cross, with Jamie Cureton equalising for the U's nine minutes later. In the second half, Hatters' Richard Langley smashed a penalty against the bar, and ex-U's loanee Rowan Vine had a goal disallowed for offside, before Davison took centre stage. 'An unforgettable night of top-quality saves' is the phrase

I used alongside Davison's perfect player rating in the following morning's newspaper. By contrast, I described his opposite number, Marlon Beresford, as 'a virtual bystander'. Davison went on to play 110 times for Colchester, before moving out to America with his family to pursue a successful career in coaching and other football-related work. But my guess is that he still remembers that night at Kenilworth Road, when he could do no wrong.

59 MILLMOOR

Club: Rotherham United
Founded: 1925 (as a merger of Rotherham County and Rotherham Town)
Ground: Millmoor (1907 to 2008)
First visit: 29 November 1997; Rotherham 3 Colchester 2

For many, Millmoor topped the list of the worst Football League grounds in the country, or at least made many top threes. Countless away supporters dismissed it as one of the worst grounds to visit in the land at around the turn of the 21st century, not helped by the rather basic amenities in the away end, the Railway End, a predominantly tin structure which could only be approached along Millmoor Lane, the narrowest of very narrow alleyways. The stand was named after the long-closed Rotherham Westgate railway station.

But for me, nothing beat Millmoor, the home of Rotherham United, for the good old-fashioned footballing experience. A less-than-perfect stadium to put it kindly, a few disjointed stands and some of the bleakest surroundings (and outside latrines) imaginable, but there was usually a cracking atmosphere and a friendly welcome to boot.

The old wooden main stand, built during the 1950s, always seemed on the verge of falling down. The seating was cramped, with virtually no leg room, and I recall the rickety old press box perched in one corner of the main stand, looking very out of place, with even a few old bus seats to sit on in the back row.

Town's Jim Magilton takes a free-kick during a visit to Rotherham's antiquated Millmoor ground. (WP)

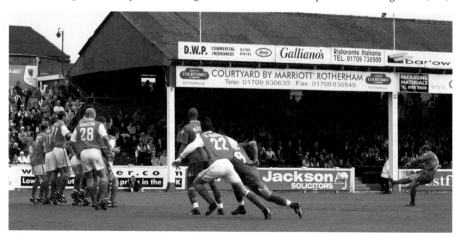

There was no room to swing a cat and I often had difficulty making out the goalscorers at the far end (a lame excuse, I know). Opposite was the Millmoor Lane End, split into three uneven sections of varying heights, with the Tivoli End, a former terrace which was transformed into a seated area during the later years in the Championship, facing the Railway End. The ground was certainly not pleasing to the eye from any vantage point, inside or outside. The main entrance was under-stated and a bit tatty, and the place was surrounded by scrapyards and long-forgotten industrial works. Parking up the car in or near one of these yards, and walking to the ground in the dark for a midweek fixture was always precarious.

My first visit was for a Saturday afternoon fourth-tier encounter in late November 1997, after the Millers had been relegated the previous season. I remember it well. It rained, and it rained, and Colchester United blew a 2-1 lead to lose 3-2, scoring a couple of fine goals and then conceding two scrappy goals.

'We threw it away,' rued U's boss Steve Wignall. 'I don't think anyone in Rotherham would kid themselves that we did not at least deserve an equaliser.' Rotherham match-winner and centre-half Alan Knill agreed, 'The luck is with us at the moment. Colchester made it very difficult for us.'

After Lee Glover, of former Nottingham Forest fame, had netted a candidate for goal of the season at Millmoor with a 20-yarder on 11 minutes, Aaron Skelton upstaged him with a glorious 25-yarder for the equaliser. Skelton's goal was actually the first in the league netted by a Colchester player at Millmoor after 677 fruitless minutes of league action, a period spanning 24 years since their first league visit.

It was almost worth the trip alone. Almost.

Mark Sale put the U's ahead with a 61st-minute header from David Gregory's cross, only for front-runner Glover, who had been purchased for a Rotherham record £150,000 from Port Vale the previous summer, to equalise from close in with a sucker punch from a free kick that was not cleared. Likewise, when the U's failed to deal with a corner, Knill, a future Rotherham manager from 2005–07, was on hand to drill home the winner. Veteran keeper Bobby Mimms, best remembered for his days at Everton, Tottenham and Blackburn, then kept the visitors at bay with some fine late stops.

All in all, then, it was not a great day in South Yorkshire.

As a footnote, Millmoor has not hosted professional football since 2008, when the owners of the stadium and the club owners failed to reach a lease agreement, leading to the Millers' temporary stay at the Don Valley Stadium in Sheffield, and eventually a new home at nearby New York Stadium. The planned new development of the main stand at Millmoor (the old one had survived, warts-and-all, since the 1950s) remained unfinished. Work was halted several times, including famously after the discovery of Japanese knotweed on site, and in recent years Millmoor has merely hosted the occasional youth football match.

Yet, for all its faults, I did like Millmoor, honest.

60 MEADOW LANE

Club: Notts County
Founded: 1862
Ground: Meadow Lane (since 1910)
First visit: 21 March 1998; Notts County 0 Colchester 0

There was one press box in particular, from the many all over the country, where I would always ensure I wore my best trousers, and sometimes even a tie.

Where was that, I hear you ask? Perhaps the posh surroundings of Old Trafford, Anfield, Stamford Bridge or the Emirates? Sensible guesses, all of them. Or maybe the Etihad, Villa Park or Craven Cottage? Again, plausible answers.

And yet the press box in question, where I used to make sure I donned at least a decent shirt (with collar) and sensible trousers, is not even currently hosting Football League action. At the time of writing, this proud club was plying its trade in the National League, the first tier of non-league.

Meadow Lane, the home of Notts County, is a place steeped in history, sited on the north bank of the River Trent just 300 yards away from Nottingham Forest's City Ground, which lies south of the river. Founded in 1862, Notts County is the oldest professional football club in the world, predating even the Football Association, that most popular of institutions.

The Magpies went on to become founder members of the Football League in 1888, finished as high as third in the top flight in 1890/91 (that remains their highest finish) and won the FA Cup in 1894 when they beat Bolton in the final. With the exception of one year, they were ever-present in the First Division from 1897 to 1920, and again spent three seasons in the top flight in the early 1980s.

Neil Warnock, the football equivalent of a magician (on occasions), guided County to successive play-off promotions in 1990 and '91 to propel the famous old club back into the top tier. Alas, they were relegated the next year, and so missed out on playing in the first Premier League season in 1992/93. That was six years before my first visit.

All well and good, but what were all the worries with my wardrobe?

Smart casual dress – that was my policy whenever I headed for Meadow Lane.

It doesn't really apply now, but back in the 1990s I recall a fellow journalist being refused entry to the press lounge because he was wearing a pair of tracksuit bottoms. Journalists occupied the same area of the stadium frequented by the club's directors, board members and VIP guests, in the resplendent Derek Pavis Stand, so that's why I suppose there was the existence of a dress code.

I passed the 'dress test' because, more by luck than judgement, I had chosen to wear a smart pair of strides that day. My fellow hack was not so fortunate, and in the end he had to borrow a pair of trousers for the duration of the match, supplied to him by the

The author's view from the press box at Notts County's Meadow Lane. (CM)

club. Now call me old-fashioned, but I have always preferred not to wear communal trousers when it comes to covering football matches. I prefer to stick with my own. And that's why I have always made sure I have respectable trousers, and even a tie, whenever I roll up at Meadow Lane. It keeps the stewards happy.

Sometimes, though, it's down to who you are. For instance, on one of my later visits, I bumped into the imposing figure of Brian Kilcline, a former Notts County centre-half renowned for his long hair and moustache. Kilcline had retired from professional football – he captained Coventry City against Tottenham in the FA Cup Final of 1987 – and was working for the media. He still had his familiar long hair and moustache, and, more to the point, he was wearing tracksuit bottoms. Yet no one bat an eyelid.

I guess it was one rule for one, and one rule for a powerfully built local football legend.

Meadow Lane was already a smart-looking all-seater stadium by the time that I started paying annual visits to the press box. It is always a pleasant place to rest your laptop, on long wide benches at the back of the Derek Pavis Stand, with power points aplenty, always a reassuring sign. Refreshments in the small press lounge were often shared by a few of the home players who were not in the matchday squad, usually because of injuries.

But before the major refurbishments, which completely transformed the ground during a frenzy of demolition and rebuilding in the summer of 1992 when the Meadow

Lane End, Spion Kop and County Road Stand were all replaced, the stadium had been in a state of neglect throughout the 1970s and 1980s.

It had not been helped by the removal of the famous old wooden stand at the Meadow Land End, which had previously been owned by Nottinghamshire County Cricket Club and had been floated across the River Trent to its new home at Meadow Lane when the Magpies changed homes in 1910. By the 1970s, this 1,400-seated stand was reputed to be the oldest stand still in active use in England. In its place sat an ugly building, acting as a social club, meaning the stadium was just three-sided with no stand behind one of the goals until the arrival of the Family Stand in 1992.

In truth, though, Meadow Lane deserves better than to just stage lower-league football. It is aesthetically pleasing, with four smart, tidy stands accommodating mostly black seats, interspersed with yellow and white lettering. The Derek Pavis Stand was the last to be revamped in 1994. Opposite is the Jimmy Sirrel Stand, which has a fabulous triangular gable on top, proudly displaying the club name and foundation date. These gables used to be common sights at old football grounds and are still on show at places like Craven Cottage and Brisbane Road. The terrace at the Spion Kop was superseded by a seated stand at the same time.

It all looked very plush when I turned up on 21 November 1998, for my second visit of the year. Actually, anywhere would have looked impressive after the previous weekend's humbling experience at Welfare Park, the home of non-league minnows Bedlington Terriers. I was up in Northumberland to report on Colchester United's humiliating 4-1 defeat in an FA Cup first round tie, and seven days later I was still feeling chastened by the whole sorry episode. The U's had secured a prime slot on *Match of the Day* that night, so the whole nation got the chance to share in the Essex club's misery. It was standing room only for most of the visiting press, and I recall BBC Essex reporters Neil Kelly and Glenn Speller standing on a small table, which was gradually sinking into the wet turf, to get a good view of the match, played on a pudding of a pitch. The magic of the cup!

It was a new low for me, and for Colchester United.

Seven days later and my hopes were not high for a U's backlash at Notts County, in the third tier. I parked up in the adjacent Cattle Market, made sure my trousers looked smart, and headed for the main entrance, bracing myself for another away-day defeat. But football is full of surprises and I had soon forgotten all about Bedlington after centre-half David Greene had netted a brace of headers inside the first quarter of the game. Midfielder David Gregory scored a third, early in the second half, and the U's ran out 3-1 winners despite a consolation from Shaun Murray.

It was a remarkable transformation. Now, whenever I think back to that dismal day at Bedlington, I also think of the following weekend's successful backlash at Meadow Lane. Chalk and cheese. Wet, scruffy jeans to well-ironed trousers.

61 DEAN COURT

Club: AFC Bournemouth
Founded: 1899 (as Boscombe St John's Institute FC)
Ground: Dean Court (from 1910)
First visit: 11 April 1998; Bournemouth 2 Colchester 0

There was an occasion when I encountered two types of bucket on a visit to Bournemouth, or to be precise the adjacent suburb of Boscombe. A pre-match stroll along the promenade overlooking the long, sandy Manor Steps beach where young children were clutching on to spades and bucket-loads of sand; and then a few hours later a few well-intentioned football fans shaking buckets full of loose change, outside Dean Court, the home of AFC Bournemouth. Two extremes. The Dorset club was in danger of going out of business during 2008, with debts of around £4m hanging over it, hence the collection buckets. I think I even hurled a few coins into one of these containers. The club survived, the buckets were shelved, and seven years later the Cherries were in the Premier League.

Despite those dark days in administration, there has always been a middle-class feel surrounding Dean Court. A summer's day here, flanked by the wide open expanses of King's Park, with its bowling green, athletics track, cricket pitch and pavilion, plus the sea less than a mile down the road, is a world away from a winter's afternoon at Luton's Kenilworth Road or Gillingham's Priestfield, choked by surrounding terraced houses with precious little space to breathe.

Dean Court was the sort of footballing destination that I usually made a point of arriving at several hours before kick-off, not to gain entry to a deserted stadium so that I could shuffle a few papers or drain the battery on my computer, but instead to go for brunch with work colleagues at the cricket pavilion, which doubled up as a cafe; or, if I was feeling more adventurous, to go for a run on the cliffs high above Boscombe beach, and all those buckets of sand.

Colchester United have had many happy days on the road at Bournemouth, including a vital 2-1 win to keep the promotion-to-the-Championship bandwagon on track in April 2006, thanks to Scott Vernon's second-half winner. That was a great day, but it's not always a bed of roses on an away day, as any football fan will testify, which is why I have chosen to recall one of the more depressing days for the U's at the Cherries.

It was during Mick Wadsworth's brief tenure as Colchester manager, which lasted a mere seven months (this included the summer break), that the U's were thrashed 4-0 at Dean Court. Wadsworth actually resigned just four days later, on 25 August 1999, after just three league games of the season, having caused controversy over the summer by releasing such club favourites as Tony Adcock, Joe Dunne, Paul Buckle and Carl Emberson, while recruiting highly paid replacements such as Jamie Moralee, Brian Launders, Sagi Burton and Steve Germain. None of the latter group made a very big impression.

Scott Vernon celebrates his crucial winning goal at Bournemouth to keep the U's promotion bid on track in 2006. (WP)

I didn't know it at the time but that 4-0 loss, during which centre-half Burton was sent off, was to be Wadsworth's last league game at the helm. I always found him a rather awkward boss to interview at the end of a match, and sometimes even an elusive one. I had chased after him out of Blackpool's Bloomfield Road on the final day of the previous season to grab a quote after another defeat, which didn't do much for my street credentials, with sweat streaming down my face and a scruffy laptop bag bouncing off my shoulder.

At least we members of the visiting press managed to corner him on the pitch at Dean Court. But just a few seconds into a radio interview, conducted by Neil Kelly, my regular travel companion on so many U's away-days, Wadsworth suddenly walked away to go and have a chat with someone else. True, that 'someone else' happened to be Lawrie McMenemy, the former successful manager of Southampton who was the Northern Ireland boss at the time, but it did rather leave us in limbo. We felt like lemons, or social outcasts left alone in the kitchen at a party.

On the pitch, earlier in the afternoon, ex-Chelsea striker Mark Stein's first-half opener was followed by Burton's red card. Danish midfielder Claus Jørgensen soon doubled the lead, and a late brace by big target man Steve Fletcher completed the rout. Fletcher went on to become Bournemouth's record appearance-maker with 726 outings, 628 of which were in the league. Wadsworth left the U's later in the week, after 209 days in charge, so at least my days of chasing after a quote were over. His successor, Steve Whitton, was much easier to pin down.

As for Dean Court, this was still two years before the big rebuild when the pitch was rotated 90 degrees from its original position and three smart new all-seater stands were opened. One end was left open for a while. In the late 1990s, though, it was still chiefly terracing at the South Stand and Brighton Beach End, while the Main Stand, opened in 1927, still had the steel frame purchased from the British Empire Exhibition at Wembley from four years earlier.

There was more than one press section in the Main Stand, with the away hacks sitting in a separate corner in the overspill, like a mini leper colony. There were usually two of us, which filled this section to capacity.

We knew our place. Under-paid, under-staffed and over-worked away-day journalists. In fact, I considered bringing a bucket to start a collection, for the unfortunate few cast out to the colony in the press overspill. A case of – if you can't beat them, then join them.

I don't think I'd have got very rich out of it.

62 BOOTHAM CRESCENT

Club: York City
Founded: 1908 (as an amateur club); 1922 (re-founded)
Ground: Bootham Crescent (1932 to 2020)
First visit: September 5, 1998: York 1 Colchester 2

One of my coldest evenings spent reporting on football was an FA Cup first round replay at Bootham Crescent in late November, 2001. Frozen toes and numb fingers. That's how I remember my second and ultimately last trip to York's home of 88 years. And naturally, because it was so cold, the tie went into extra time and then to a penalty shoot-out, just to ensure that all feeling had been lost in both sets of fingers. There was also no happy ending for visiting Colchester United because they lost a very poor quality shoot-out 3-2. Other than that, and a long 195-mile drive back home to Suffolk in the dead of night, it was a fine way to spend a Tuesday evening!

Bootham Crescent, not far from the city centre, had a tricky first few years at the start of its life as a Football League venue after the Minstermen made the move from their previous home at Fulfordgate in 1932. Fulfordgate had been in a rural eight-acre setting out to the south-east of the city, initially surrounded by hawthorn bushes, so was not easily accessible for supporters. Early on an old army hut was used for dressing rooms, and eventually there was a swell of opinion towards a ground move. York Cricket Club had vacated Bootham Crescent, which was much closer to the city centre and offered a more welcome urban setting. In fact, the stadium was encircled by terraced houses (on the east), a barracks (on the west) plus a school and almshouses to the north.

Within four months, the stadium was completely renovated to prepare for football with the erection of the Main Stand and also the Popular Stand opposite, while both ends

Steve Forbes is all smiles after scoring a late winner for the U's at Bootham Crescent in 1998. (WP)

were banked terraces which were concreted after the Second World War. Attendances were not as good as first hoped during the early seasons, while the poor state of the pitch drew criticism, especially the regular sight of pools of water on the playing surface. Gradually, though, Bootham Crescent became a good place to watch lower-league football.

The Main Stand, where the press box sat, was extended in 1955 although it still only spanned two thirds of the pitch. The corners were open at both ends, with small windshields at the rear of each end, while there was a TV gantry above the lower Popular Stand opposite. The Grosvenor Road End was an open terrace for away fans, with a gymnasium built behind it during the 1980s, and the Shipton Street End (renamed the David Longhurst Stand from 1991) was covered terracing.

The ground was, however, fraying at the edges when I first visited for a third tier fixture in early September 1998. There were a few holes in the roof of the Main Stand, and the rear of the away terracing was cordoned off due to cracks in the wall. Still, Colchester United, freshly promoted, won 2-1 thanks to a late winner from substitute Steve Forbes, who headed home Simon Betts's deep cross. Earlier, Neil Gregory's opener inside 70 seconds had been matched by York's player-coach Neil Thompson's equaliser from the penalty spot. Thompson had been an effective left-back at Ipswich during the first half of the 1990s.

There had been no further visible investment in the ground when I turned up for that bitterly cold midweek FA Cup tie in the late autumn of 2001. The toilets still looked the same

Goal! The U's score with poacher Neil Gregory in the danger zone during a 2-1 win at York in 1998. (WP)

to me, as did the press area, although a flurry of goals did temporarily warm me up towards the end of the initial 90 minutes. Chris Brass had given the Minstermen an early lead before the U's completely dominated. They didn't equalise until the 80th minute, through Scott McGleish's header, and although future Swansea and Brighton manager Graham Potter restored York's lead, Karl Duguid squeezed home another equaliser on the stroke of full-time from close-in following Colchester's 23rd corner of the night (yes, I had been counting!).

And so to the delights of extra time. Ironically, fourth-tier York did not earn their first corner of the night until the 118th minute, but they went on to triumph in the penalty shoot-out. The standard was poor, and by then I couldn't feel my feet due to the cold, with the newspaper deadline almost upon me. The first three penalties were missed. McGleish's spot-kick was saved by Alan Fettis, and Gavin Johnson blasted his over the bar, while York's Mark Maley rattled the bar with his effort.

By contrast, the next five were scored, making it 3-2 to the hosts, before Duguid, a hero with his late equaliser, turned villain when ex-Hull City stopper Fettis saved his kick. The U's were out of the FA Cup. It brought back memories of the U's losing a penalty shoot-out to Carlisle at Wembley in the Auto Windscreens Final of 1997, when the unfortunate Duguid had also missed the vital kick. Ironically, Duguid had a wonderful career with Colchester, despite those occasional spot-kick lapses and, looking back at my match report of that night in York, I did make him the man of the match.

I was destined never to return to Bootham Crescent. But the fingers and toes did eventually thaw by the time that I reached the Grantham North Services on the A1 at about 2am.

63 MADEJSKI STADIUM

Club: Reading
Founded: 1871
Ground: Madejski Stadium (since 1998)
First visit: 19 September 1998; Reading 1 Colchester 1

It looks good, and it works well. I have nothing but admiration for the Madejski Stadium, the home of Reading since 1998, especially as most of my visits have yielded points for the away team.

Easy to get to off the M4, it is an impressive oval-shaped stadium which catches the eye both from the outside and the inside. It has a futuristic look from the motorway, all modern and shiny, while inside, from every vantage point, the views across the pitch are sweeping. The acoustics are superb due to the enclosed nature (the four corners are all occupied) of the stadium, and it's also light and airy with a gap between the backs of the stands and the roofs. All four stands are a sea of blue and white seats, with good leg room, highlighted by the West Stand which is two-tiered and topped by an attractive curved roof. The press box, situated in the West Stand, features rows of double desks, and the press lounge is spacious and comfortable, usually with a good selection of pies and pasties.

No wonder I don't mind trundling down the M4 into Berkshire.

My first outing at the Madesjki Stadium was in Reading's first season at their new home, for the visit of Colchester United in September 1998. Tommy Burns's Royals were considered one of the pre-season candidates for promotion following their relegation the previous campaign, but they were held to a 1-1 draw by the newly-promoted U's. True, Steve Wignall's men did leave it very late to equalise via Karl Duguid's scrambled close-range goal on 89 minutes, but they were good value for the point. Ex-Celtic boss Burns kept his players locked in the home dressing room for an hour after the final whistle, I suspect to deliver an ear-bashing.

His opposite number Wignall declared, 'My players would love to play at a stadium like this every week.' Despite the draw, Reading still protected their unbeaten record at their super new bowl-shaped all-seater home – they went 11 games there before suffering a defeat – while the U's had understandably looked a little overawed by the plush surroundings during the first quarter of the game, which made the final result all the more satisfying.

Two years later I actually reported on a U's 1-0 win at the Madesjski Stadium thanks to a 30-yard thunderbolt from Gavin Johnson, a goal worthy of winning any game. I was beginning to really like the stadium.

A more turgid, even torturous affair, but equally memorable, was when I returned there with one of Johnson's former clubs, Ipswich Town, in early November 2009. Two managers were struggling to kick-start their clubs' seasons to such an extent that it was a real bottom-of-the-table clash in the Championship. Brendan Rodgers, the Reading boss, was left more frustrated than Town supremo Roy Keane after a predictable 1-1 draw, which says a lot when considered that the Portman Road club had gone 16 league matches with just one victory.

A fierce shot by Town striker Tamas Priskin is blocked during a 1-1 draw at fellow strugglers Reading in 2009. (WP)

That win had been notched the previous weekend, against Derby County, and Town's travelling supporters, who numbered 2,400 in the South Stand, were dreaming of back-to-back scalps when Jon Stead gave them a ninth-minute lead from skipper Ivar Ingimarsson's poor headed clearance. Reading had not actually won a home league match since January, more than nine months previously, but they salvaged a point through Simon Church's equaliser early in the second period. Church, a Welsh international, knew little about it, the ball ricocheting off him from Gylfi Sigurdsson's wayward shot.

Re-reading my match report, I think I got a little carried away that day, perhaps under the spell of the resplendent Madejski Stadium and also swayed by Keane's post-match optimism. In addition, I was probably heartened by the fact that Ipswich had clambered off the bottom rung, to be replaced by Peterborough.

I wrote, 'There is an air of optimism funnelling through the hallways of Portman Road these days. Town have begun to turn the corner.' I later added a phrase that I didn't repeat very often, 'The strike force of Jon Stead and Tamas Priskin were a genuine threat to the opposition.'

In the end, both Reading and Ipswich recovered to enjoy better second halves of the 2009/10 campaign. In Reading's case, they soared to a final position of ninth, while Town inched up to 15th. Rogers, destined for a successful career in management, had actually left the Royals that December, with his successor Brian McDermott plotting a swift climb up the table and then promotion to the Premier League as title winners in 2011/12.

But it never did get any better for Ipswich, in the long-term. Not for the first time, my words of optimism were ill-founded.

64 BOUNDARY PARK

Club: Oldham Athletic
Founded: 1895 (as Pine Villa)
Ground: Boundary Park (from 1896, revamped 1904)
First visit: 3 October 1998; Oldham 1 Colchester 0

Having previously described a night at Bootham Crescent, York, as one of my coldest experiences as a journeyman football reporter, I must admit that Oldham's Boundary Park would be another contender for a 'plunging temperature' award, although the press box in the Main Stand does offer more protection than most other areas in the ground.

It has often been referred to as Ice Station Zebra, a term coined by long-term manager Joe Royle who presided over one of the most successful periods in the club's existence, when opposing teams used to hate playing on the dreaded 'plastic pitch' at Boundary Park. The Latics, during Royle's 12-year reign from 1982–'94, lost to Nottingham Forest in the League Cup Final and to Manchester United in the semi-finals of the FA Cup in 1989/90, and won promotion to the top flight the following season. Royle went on to manage Ipswich Town for four years, from 2002.

Approaching Oldham in a westerly direction on the M62 over the Pennines, including passing the highest point of any motorway in England at the well-named Windy Hill, near Denshaw (1,221 feet), I have always felt that Boundary Park must be one of the highest and most exposed grounds of the 92 in the Football League and Premier League, at the mercy of high winds and driving rain/sleet/snow. Many is the time I have got soaked just walking from the main car park to the back of the Main (South) Stand. It is actually number two on the elevation list at 526 feet, below West Brom's The Hawthorns (551) and just ahead of Vale Park (520), the home of Port Vale, but it does give the impression of being the highest of them all.

There is nothing grand about the entrance to Boundary Park. The press entry is via a small flight of stairs, with a downstairs loo for anyone immediately 'caught short'. But the Main Stand is steeped in history, a survivor of the time when the stadium was revamped in 1904. It is a small, two-tiered structure, which used to have terracing in front – some of the old terracing can still be seen on one side of the stand – before the ground became all-seater in 1994/95. Some of the wooden seats remain, with the press box behind a Perspex front. The Chadderton Road End, affectionately known as the Chaddy End, with its low overhanging roof, tends to house the noisier members of the home support.

My first visit to Boundary Park coincided with Colchester United's first game there for 17 years, in early October 1998. I remember it well. The U's fired blanks all afternoon and duly lost 1-0 in what was their first season back in the third tier since 1981. It was a familiar tale of many of my return trips to Oldham. In fact, I only reported on two U's wins in my first 13 visits, spanning 15 years.

Geraint Williams, right, a future U's manager, shows his battling skills during a 1-0 defeat at Boundary Park in 1998. (WP)

The opening paragraph in my match report for Monday morning's newspaper was not short on irony. It read, 'Boundary Park stewards were dismantling the goalposts within five minutes of the final whistle at Oldham on Saturday. But they could have done it at half-time.'

I guess I was implying that the U's shooting was rather awry.

The lowly Latics scored the only goal of the game on 20 minutes. Substitute Adrian Littlejohn crossed for Paul Rickers to prod home from close in. There was still plenty of time for Steve Wignall's men to respond, but their shooting was so off target that home keeper Gary Kelly had precious few saves to make.

'We have to be more ruthless in front of goal,' rued U's assistant manager Steve Whitton. Midfielder Geraint Williams confirmed, 'I just thought that sooner or later we would find the back of the net.'

The U's never did, but at least they could take heart from the fact that only a little over six years earlier, there had been four divisions between the two clubs. While Oldham were relishing their membership in a select club in 1992, as one of the founder members of the new Premier League, the U's were successfully plotting a way out of non-league by lifting the Conference title. At the time, a league visit to Boundary Park was still the stuff of dreams, albeit not the most thrilling of dreams.

65 BRITANNIA STADIUM (STOKE GROUND)

Club: Stoke City
Founded: either 1863 or 1868 (as Stoke Ramblers)
Ground: Britannia Stadium (from 1997, renamed Bet356 Stadium in 2016)
First visit: 23 January 1999: Stoke City 3 Colchester United 3

On the subject of ice-cold grounds in lofty positions, Stoke City's home at the previously named Britannia Stadium (now bet365 Stadium) can be as uninviting as most, at certain times of the year. Opened in 1997, the stadium is an imposing structure from a distance, perched on top of a hill in an isolated position, well away from too many other buildings. It can be seen from several miles away on the approach roads (A50 and A500), while the views from the stadium itself are expansive looking out over the city, the Trent Valley and also the Trent and Mersey Canal.

None of the corners had been filled in during the early years, so after being caught out on my first visit in January 1999 when a cold, swirling wind had blown right through the press area at the back of the Main Stand, I have since always come prepared, wrapped up and ready to combat that cold draft.

I never did get to Stoke's former home, the nearby Victoria Ground (1878–1997), and as yet I have never reported on an away victory at the Potters' new home. Five visits have yielded a couple of hard-fought draws, and three defeats, all featuring Colchester United.

'Brave hearts' was the headline emblazoned above my match report for the first of those trips, on 23 January 1999. Colchester were managerless at the time, former boss Steve Wignall having resigned just two days earlier, so hopes were not high of any reward from the Essex club's first away clash at Stoke. Personally, I was very impressed by the stadium, a splash of red and white with four cantilever stands and a fine vantage point from the press box in the upper tier of the Main Stand. The players looked tiny, from such a lofty position, and the task ahead appeared just as daunting for the U's, with assistant boss Steve Whitton in caretaker charge, especially when trailing 3-1 towards the end of the first half. Yet the response was magnificent and the home team were booed off by their supporters at the final whistle after a surprise 3-3 draw.

'That's the most excited I've been at a football match all my life,' enthused 38-year-old Whitton. 'The adrenaline was really going today. I definitely want the job.'

Whitton did eventually get the job, but not this time around. Instead he was appointed later in the year, in August, after Mick Wadsworth's short tenure on the hot-seat.

As for the match, the U's took a shock lead when wing-back Simon Betts's ferocious half-volley soared past keeper Carl Muggleton, only for Stoke to respond with three unanswered goals. David Gregory diverted Graham Kavanagh's cross past Carl Emberson for an own goal, and this was followed by Kyle Lightbourne's accurate header from Kevin Keen's cross (Keen was another future Colchester manager, in 2015/16, though not a successful one),

Paul Abrahams competes for the ball at the Britannia Stadium, the managerless U's earning a surprise 3-3 draw in early 1999. (WP)

and another header by Larus Sigurdsson. Then came the rally, David Gregory drilling home his ninth goal of the season just before half-time before substitute Jason Dozzell levelled with ten minutes remaining via a stooping header from Joe Dunne's corner.

From where I was sitting, and shivering, at the top of the Main Stand, this felt like an away victory, not a draw. I always try and remain impartial at games, but I must admit feeling very happy for Whitton, and the way his team responded after such an unsettling week.

The U's ended up avoiding relegation by two points, while Brian Little's Stoke missed out on the play-offs by two places and seven points. Little left that summer, soon ending up at West Brom, home to the highest ground in the Football League. But to me, the Britannia Stadium felt the highest of the lot. It was certainly draughty.

66 MEMORIAL STADIUM

Club: Bristol Rovers
Founded: 1883 (as Black Arabs, named after Arabs rugby team)
Ground: Memorial Stadium (from 1996)
First visit: 30 January 1999; Bristol Rovers 1 Colchester 1

It's old, shabby, a bit smelly, a bit noisy, quirky, authentic, colourful, irregular, with a few open terraces and a few secret corners. But it's also a delight.

It always felt like I was about to watch a game of rugby (the grass was a bit too long), or even a game of cricket (the stand opposite resembles a cricket pavilion) rather than a football fixture whenever I took my seat in the press section of the ageing but wonderfully charismatic East Stand at the Memorial Stadium.

And that was hardly surprising because, for most of its life the 'Mem', as it is sometimes affectionately known by the locals, was a home to Bristol Rugby Club. When Bristol Rovers moved from their famous old Eastville Stadium in 1986, via ten years at Bath City's Twerton Park to the Memorial Stadium for the start of the 1996/97 season, they were again mere tenants. Eastville had been Rovers' home for 89 years, from 1897, until financial difficulties caught up with them.

The rugby club and football club continued to share the same home, although Rovers bought the ground in 1998. Bristol RFC, these days known as Bristol Bears, moved out in 2014 to play their home games across town in the south-west of the city, at Bristol City's Ashton Gate.

That rugby feel was certainly around at the end of the 1990s when I paid a few visits to the 'Mem'. They were all memorable affairs, with several challenges to overcome. Parking the car was often a headache with the stadium tucked away in a residential area, surrounded by houses; the small bars and toilets were a bit cramped; and the various stands, dotted around the pitch, all looked very higgledy-piggledy.

But, as I say, I rather liked it.

The East Stand, the tallest of all the various structures, has seating to the rear with the press quarter in a corner, and terracing in front and on either side. Opposite, the distinctive West Stand, with its cricket pavilion feel, has a TV gantry and scoreboard tucked beneath the roof and hospitality boxes at the top, above a few rows of seats and then an open terrace below. There is a family area near the Thatchers End terrace, while the South Stand End has a peculiar looking small, temporary stand nicknamed 'The Tent' by fans.

My first visit to the 'Mem' came in January 1999, a fortnight after my first trip to the Britannia Stadium, both with Colchester United. Steve Whitton was still at the helm in a caretaker capacity, although this was his last fixture before returning to assistant manager duties alongside new boss Mick Wadsworth, who was watching from the stands. It made for a slightly strange afternoon, in strange surroundings, not helped by the misty conditions. So after another highly satisfactory away draw, 1-1, I didn't know whether to wave my Dictaphone in the direction of caretaker Whitton or new man Wadsworth.

My second visit to the Memorial Stadium came in December 1999, by which time Whitton was the permanent manager of the U's.

Back in January, penalty-taking expert David Gregory secured a point for the U's as late as the 87th minute. Ex-Ipswich man Gregory won the penalty, a soft one for a foul by defender Andy Thomson, and then converted it past keeper Lee Jones for his tenth goal of the season. At the time, Gregory's haul represented more than a third of the U's league goals total of 29, not bad for a player who had spent half of the season in central defence.

Neil Gregory dives forward to head goalwards at Bristol Rovers in 1999. The U's drew 1-1. (WP)

It was certainly a good result against a Rovers side who boasted one of the best strike forces in the third tier, in the shape of Jason Roberts and Jamie Cureton. Ian Holloway was the player-manager at the time. Roberts had broken the deadlock with his 14th goal of the campaign, having been set up by Cureton's header. Roberts, who had celebrated his 21st birthday just five days earlier, went on to command big-money moves to West Brom (£2m), Wigan (£1.4m) and Blackburn (£3m) during a fine career. Cureton, meanwhile, ended up helping Colchester win promotion to the Championship seven years later, and then claimed the Golden Boot for his 23 goals in the second tier in 2006/07.

After the clash at the Memorial Stadium, new U's boss Wadsworth began with a conventional quote, 'I didn't think the penalty was controversial.' But he then veered into the weird and wonderful, informing me, 'If I take my players up to 25,000 feet and then give them parachutes to jump out of the plane, then that might be a problem, but they shouldn't be nervous about playing football.'

That quote caught me on the hop. Wadsworth was to do that fairly often over the next few months.

67 MOSS ROSE

Club: Macclesfield Town
Founded: 1874, dissolved 2020
Ground: Moss Rose (since 1891)
First visit: 13 March 1999; Macclesfield 2 Colchester 0

When Colchester United clinched promotion to the third tier via the play-offs in the early summer of 1998, one of my first thoughts was that I would get a rare and, as it turned out, only chance to visit Maine Road, due to Manchester City's relegation from the second tier at the same time. Alas, this never materialised, because when the new fixture list was published and the date of 31 October was revealed as the U's away-day at Manchester

Flashback: the author's match report in the East Anglian Daily Times following the U's 2-0 defeat at Moss Rose in 1999.

City, it soon became apparent that I had double-booked. I was due to spend much of late October and early November on a trekking holiday in the Himalayas. More fool me.

But to soften the blow I did get a chance to visit Macclesfield Town's Moss Rose for the first time that season, sited 20 miles south of Maine Road. The Silkmen had just completed back-to-back promotions out of the Conference and the Third Division, and I had missed the U's away game in Cheshire the previous season due to Ipswich Town reporting duties, a deeply depressing 2-0 home defeat to Stockport County on a Tuesday night at the same time as the U's were drawing 0-0 at Moss Rose.

Okay, so it didn't really 'soften the blow'. The U's once in a lifetime trip to Maine Road, five years before City moved to the Etihad, was played in front of a crowd of 24,820 and, by all accounts the unfashionable visitors did themselves proud in a narrow 2-1 defeat. The later trip to Moss Rose, in March 1999, was a poor substitute. A crowd of 2,796 witnessed Mick Wadsworth's under-performing Colchester slip to a 2-0 defeat at the hands of a club who were destined to finish bottom and suffer relegation.

Even so, Moss Rose did make a favourable impression on me.

A modest, unassuming stadium, squeezed between side streets a mile south of the town centre, Macclesfield's home was quaint and old-fashioned, and in fact one of the oldest Football League grounds in the country. I say 'was' because the club was unfortunately wound up in the late summer of 2020 due to debts of £500,000. In the same week as

Mick Wadsworth, who was the manager when the U's suffered a 2-0 defeat at Moss Rose in 1999.

the Silkmen's liquidation, Welsh wizard Gareth Bale completed a loan move from Real Madrid to Tottenham with Bale having reportedly been on a weekly wage of more than £500,000 at the Bernabeu Stadium. The contrast in stories could not have been more acute. The former barely got more than a mention outside of Cheshire, while the latter dominated the back pages of all the nationals and filled the airwaves of all the major broadcasters for several days.

But this is a chapter about Moss Rose, not Gareth Bale. There was a small grandstand, plenty of terracing and, best of all, the hills of the Peak District were so close that they were almost on top of you. That view towards the southern end of the Pennines was a welcome sight, but was of scant consolation to away supporters getting soaked to the skin on the open terracing of the Silkmen End, if it happened to be raining on that particular afternoon. And it does rain rather a lot in these parts (though the sun shone brightly on my visit).

Creature comforts were in short supply at Moss Rose, which used to be the fifth highest of the 92 Football League/Premier League grounds, at 513 feet, until the club's relegation and subsequent liquidation. There was no press room to lounge in before kick-off, at least during the late 1990s, but the Main Stand on the east side of the ground was a classic design, with a small staircase leading up to a raised seating area, with terracing in front and open terracing to either side. It looked old and well lived in, but was in fact only opened in 1968. Furthermore, it was not particularly big, stretching only about a third of the length of the pitch, from a central position on halfway.

While on the subject of the pitch, the playing surface was awful for the U's visit in March 1999. A mixture of mud and sand, Moss Rose left the U's in a quagmire as Macclesfield, rock bottom of the division, won 2-0 through second-half goals by Richard Landon and Alan Bailey. Landon's opener was controversial because his header hit the inside of the far post with Carl Emberson catching the rebound, only for the assistant referee to rule that the ball had already crossed the goal line.

Wadsworth was philosophical, 'The linesman gave the goal so it was a goal. There's no point in bleating about it.' Emberson was not so convinced. 'I don't think it was a goal,' insisted the 25-year-old custodian, who was to total 231 games for the U's during the 1990s.

Ironically, I did get to report on a player on Manchester City's books scoring a goal at home to Colchester, during that 1998/99 season, despite my failure to make Maine Road. And that's because substitute Bailey, on loan from City, doubled the Silkmen's lead by lobbing Emberson in injury time.

Even so, I must confess that Moss Rose is/was no substitute for Maine Road.

68 TURF MOOR

Club: Burnley
Founded: 1882
Ground: Turf Moor (since 1883)
First visit: 5 April 1999; Burnley 3 Colchester 1

A blend of old and new, and a ground of two halves, Turf Moor is a place of contrasts. There's the scenic approach through the brooding Pennines, which gives way to the austerity of the

Kevin Watson is given a lift by Chris Iwelumo after scoring the opener in the U's 2-1 win at Turf Moor in 2006. (WP)

back-to-back terraced streets which surround the football stadium. This is an old-fashioned, typically northern experience, hardly surprising when considered that Burnley, with its proud industrial heritage as a major cotton mill town, were one of the six dominant Lancashire clubs who comprised half of the dozen founding members of the Football League in 1888.

One half of the ground is modern, with a couple of impressive two-tiered stands opened three years before my first visit in 1996, at the Bee Hole End and on the north side. Both used to be terracing, with the latter replacing the famous Longside Terrace. The press box is at the rear of the upper tier of this stand, now called the James Hargreaves Stand, and affords a great view of the pitch, and the rows of terrace houses and rolling hills and moors beyond. The other two smaller one-tier stands, at the Cricket Road End and the Bob Lord Stand, both had wooden seats. Unusually, the dressing rooms are still located behind one end, the Cricket Road End, and this is where I hovered to forage for some post-match quotes after my first visit with Colchester United in April 1999, which prompted then-Burnley manager Stan Ternent to emerge from the home changing room with a towel wrapped around his waist and suggest, in no uncertain terms, that I make myself scarce. His Clarets side had just eased to a 3-1 win over the U's, so goodness knows what he would have said to me if his team had lost. Needless to say, I made myself 'scarce'.

I've been to Turf Moor many times, with both Colchester and Ipswich, and witnessed a few away wins. One of the highlights was on 9 September 2006, when Colchester escaped with an unlikely 2-1 victory, much to the absolute disgust of Burnley manager Steve Cotterill. It was the U's first away win in the Championship, sealed by goals inside the first hour from midfielder Kevin Watson and striker Chris Iwelumo (a penalty).

Cotterill was livid during the post-match press conference. In fact, I had never seen a manager whinge and moan as much – and I have seen many!

He insisted that his team were 'better by miles' and that the result was an 'absolute travesty'. Best of all, he delivered a terrific quote on sombreros, a collector's item. 'I'm sure that Colchester players will be riding out of town with sombreros on tonight!' seethed Cotteril, suggesting his team had been victims of a smash-and-grab robbery. Actually, although his Burnley side did dominate that afternoon, U's keeper Aidan Davison played a blinder and the hosts did not actually score until Andy Gray's scuffed shot rolled in with three minutes remaining.

Four years later I had the good fortune to report on an Ipswich Town victory, under Paul Jewell, a 2-1 win achieved thanks to goals from 30-year-old warhorse David Norris and raw teenager Connor Wickham.

Midfielder Norris broke the deadlock with his tenth goal of the season, a close-range finish from Jimmy Bullard's corner, with Wickham, just two days after his 18th birthday, doubling the lead via a 24th-minute header that bounced off the ground to loop over keeper Lee Grant. It was young Wickham's 19th successive start, and his seventh goal during that period, repaying the faith that Jewell had shown in him. Jewell's predecessor, Roy Keane, had always been reluctant to start with his young starlet.

'Connor [Wickham] is a young kid. An awful lot is spoken about him and he deals with it very well. He's going to be a top player,' said Jewell during a more conventional press conference than either my 'Ternent towel tunnel' experience of 12 years earlier, or the 'Cotterill sombreros outburst' of five years ago.

I remember thinking that if the wily Norris, out of contract that summer, could be persuaded to sign a new deal, and young striker Wickham could resist any tempting offers from Premier League clubs, then the future looked rosy at Portman Road.

Perhaps a return to the top flight would be on the horizon?

Of course, once again, I was to be proved wrong. It was to be Burnley, not Town, who ended up in the Premier League, having first won promotion there in 2009 and then going up again in 2014 and 2016, when they managed to establish themselves in the top flight. By contrast, Town were heading in the other direction.

69 THE NEW DEN

Club: Millwall
Founded: 1885 (as Millwall Rovers)
Ground: The New Den (since 1993, now The Den)
First visit: 14 April 1999; Millwall 2 Colchester 0

The Den (1910 to 1993) might have been replaced by The Den (from 1993), but there is a world of difference between these two most recent homes of Millwall, despite sharing

The eye-catching view from the press box at The New Den, looking out towards Canary Wharf. (CM)

the same name. Dark, dank and foreboding, the old Den was the least welcoming of all Football League grounds. It's successor, called the New Den in its early years, is very, very different. Four smart two-tier stands of the same height, fantastic views from all sides, open corners which give the stadium air and light. The atmosphere is still intimidating, but a trip to Millwall, in South Bermondsey, south-east London, is no longer a sinister experience.

However, the New Den did provide a 'sinister' backdrop to a 6-1 mauling handed out by the Lions to timid Colchester United on one of my first visits on Boxing Day 2000. Millwall were going great guns at the top of the Second Division and they provided little in the way of Christmas charity towards the struggling U's.

Red-hot striker Neil Harris, a future Millwall manager who used to ply his trade in non-league just down the road from Colchester at Maldon Town (these days known as Maldon & Tiptree), helped himself to a hat-trick to walk off with a late Christmas present, the match ball. Remarkably, Harris also had a big hand in setting up the other three goals. My guess was that Colchester probably wished that they had paid more attention to the teenage striker playing just a few miles away during the mid-1990s, especially as Harris went on to become Millwall's all-time record goalscorer with 138 goals in all competitions.

Back on Boxing Day 2000, Millwall players actually scored all seven goals because the U's only contribution was an 87th-minute own goal by Robbie Ryan, the only goal without any Harris involvement. Paul Moody scored a brace and Paul Ifill added the late fifth for Mark McGhee's Millwall before 23-year-old Harris completed his hat-trick with a last-minute penalty. Not surprisingly, the Londoners went on to be crowned champions that season. It was also the first time that they had hit six goals in a league match since their switch to the New Den seven years before, in 1993.

Despite the result, the away performance and the painful task of interviewing a subdued manager, Steve Whitton, after the match, it was a pleasure to be at the New Den that afternoon. In fact, it is always a joy, especially when you can take your mind off the football unfolding on the pitch below you, from the spacious press box at the top of the West Stand (Barry Kitchener Stand), by looking out for the trains that regularly trundle past on the Thameslink Trunk Route railway line behind the back of the East Stand (Dockers Stand) and glide past the corner flags opposite. Beyond that there is a terrific view of Canary Wharf, which looks at its best when lit up during a midweek winter's evening. You are also guaranteed a good pre-match meal in the press lounge, which always lifts the spirits after the trek through east London and over Tower Bridge, or under the Rotherhithe Tunnel.

True, the surrounding area, just like at the old Den down Cold Blow Lane, looks a bit desolate and forlorn, resembling the backdrop of a typical 1970s London-based TV detective series, but the destination at the bottom of Zampa Road is far, far different. A jewel, if you like.

Paul Jewell might not have agreed with this, after his first match in charge of Ipswich Town ended in a 2-1 defeat at the New Den on 15 January 2011. 'A big dose of reality' was the headline above my match report in Monday morning's newspaper, after Tamas Priskin's 26th-minute opener had been wiped out by goals from Danny Schofield and man of the match Steve Morison to leave Town just three points above the Championship relegation zone.

Still, I enjoyed the train-spotting.

70 BLOOMFIELD ROAD

Club: Blackpool
Founded: 1887
Ground: Bloomfield Road (1899, permanent home since 1901)
First visit: 8 May 1999; Blackpool 2 Colchester 1

It has has not always been serene beside the seaside on my frequent visits to Bloomfield Road, the permanent home of Blackpool since 1901. The ground is almost unrecognisable from the 1990s, when parts of stands were occasionally closed and the whole place looked rundown, almost forgotten and abandoned, with the pitch often closer resembling a beach than a sports surface. The exterior was shabby, plastered with colourful posters advertising

The vantage point from the press box at Bloomfield Road, during the warm-up. (CM)

amusement arcades (like 'Funland'), theatres (including the Grand Theatre) and circuses (e.g. Tower Circus), and surrounded by corrugated iron, a mixture of browns, blues, oranges and whites. The whole sad scene was further complemented by an overgrown grass bank leading up to the backs of open terraces.

To put it bluntly, the place was ramshackle, past its sell-by date.

However, three new modern stands have since been built, of similar styles and height, and now the bowl-shaped stadium, with some of the corners also filled in, is all orange and gleaming, a proud product of the 21st century.

I have had various vantage points because the press area has moved around over the years. It is currently in the East Stand, the only side of the ground not to have been completely renovated. Erected as a temporary stand in 2010, it has often been a lonely place for the press. In fact, for three seasons the stand was vacant apart from the press, who gained access down a narrow alleyway called Back Henry Street (it is actually the back of Henry Street). There were Portakabins dotted around, with plenty of pillars to obscure the view as well, although the welcome has always been a warm one for visiting members of the press.

I have certainly never grumbled. My journalistic predecessors back in 1906 had it far tougher. Apparently, they were pleading with the club to build a press box of any sort, because they had to report on games while standing on the touchline during those early days. Hard times.

Many of my trips to Bloomfield Road, which have often begun with a stroll along the promenade, a detour along Central Pier, a mug of tea at a slightly seedy cafe, and then takeaway fish and chips, have had an edge to them.

One of the edgiest was a visit with Roy Keane's Ipswich Town on 2 January 2010.

Blackpool boss Ian Holloway, never one to mince his words, was even more straight-talking than usual in his post-match interview following a 2-1 home defeat in the FA Cup. The Seasiders were famed for their FA Cup win of 1953 in the 'Matthews Final' (a Stanley Matthews-inspired 4-3 victory over Bolton), and 57 years later Holloway was positively seething beside the seaside after Town had knocked his charges out of this same competition.

And perhaps he had good reason to use some colourful language after watching two of his players shown red cards by referee Eddie Ilderton. Ironically, Holloway too was to be sent off by Ilderton, following the home manager's over-the-top reaction to the red card flashed at the second of these players, Rob Edwards. Substitute Edwards joined fellow defender Ian Evatt in the changing room for an early bath, the duo having been dismissed on 55 and 76 minutes respectively.

From the press box (then in the West Stand), I had a good view of Holloway's antics as he left the dugout. I remember him hurling his coat, hat and gloves to the ground, before making his way up to the top rows of the main stand. He may have regretted that – not necessarily his loss of temper – but the fact that it was a very, very cold afternoon. I had arrived in Blackpool several hours before kick-of in order to have the obligatory stroll along the seafront, and I could confirm that the Irish Sea was looking in a particularly menacing mood.

The spitting cauldron of angry waves perhaps foreshadowed Holloway's rant of later in the day. Actually, I was on the side of the referee on this occasion. Both Evatt and Edwards deserved to be sent off, having committed professional fouls on Jack Colback and Jon Walters, who were homing in on goal.

Earlier, Colback, formerly of Sunderland and later to be at Newcastle, had broken the deadlock inside three minutes, after which Holloway's early frustrations were not helped by Charlie Adam's 24th-minute penalty rattling a post and staying out. Blackpool did equalise through veteran striker Brett Ormerod, early in the second half, but then came the two red cards (three if you count Holloway's) and a 76th-minute winner from young Owen Garvan, who guided a free kick beyond the defensive wall and low into the corner of the net.

Needless to say that Town boss Keane, another manager not afraid to speak his mind, was disappointed that his team had not killed off the nine men during the later stages. I recall substitute Connor Wickham missing two great chances. A passage, however stormy, was nevertheless negotiated by Town through to the fourth round of the FA Cup, although my quest to get a few words with Holloway after the match was less successful.

Holloway was nowhere to be seen for an hour after the final whistle, prompting this final paragraph to my match report for Monday's newspaper, 'Perhaps Holloway had stormed off for a toe-curling dip in the Irish Sea to cool down?'

I know, such a 'toe-curling' way to end a match report.

My first visit to Bloomfield Road, with Colchester United in 1999, was just before both the West Stand and the Spion Kop were demolished and rebuilt. It was a melancholic place, a sad relic of a more glorious past, which could refer to the town as well as the football club. But the stadium had been revamped by the time that I enjoyed a memorable return with the U's on 8 October 2005, early on in the club's successful promotion season in the third tier.

'The Halford Show' screamed the headline above the following Monday's newspaper report, and the 2-1 scoreline. Right-winger Greg Halford's first-half lob had Phil Parkinson's men in charge, but then home striker Tommy Wright scuffed home a 92nd-minute equaliser for Colin Hendry's men. I quickly changed the headline on my blow-by-blow account to 'Daylight robbery by the seaside', only to hit the delete button again just 60 seconds later when the beanpole figure of Halford arrowed a winning goal into the far corner of the net. It was a sensational finish to an afternoon that rivalled any amusement arcade or circus for sheer entertainment.

Blackpool felt like Las Vegas that afternoon.

SECTION FOUR –
FIRST HALF OF THE 2000s

71 ELLAND ROAD

Club: Leeds United
Founded: 1919 (following the demise of Leeds City FC)
Ground: Elland Road (since 1897)
First visit: 20 January 2000; Leeds U18 0 Colchester U18 0

Home advantage has always been a big feature of Elland Road, the famous stomping ground of Leeds United. You could almost sense the hostility seeping through the walls of the press lounge. The home crowds are passionate, loyal, and unforgiving, making sure that the visitors never feel comfortable in the midst of a cauldron of noise.

I have visited Elland Road on many occasions, and in the early days it was never one of my favourite grounds. The press used to be packed in to a rather cramped press lounge, almost in the attic, with the stewards professional but never smiling. It was the same for everyone; players, fans, the press. This was Leeds United, where visitors were respected but never particularly liked.

Of course that's all probably changed now – I haven't been to this corner of West Yorkshire for a few years, but I used to be a regular.

Certainly, my first experience of Elland Road probably dampened my spirits for future visits. This was due to the weather, not any antics on the pitch, in the stands or in the resplendent press box. Basically, all I got to report on from that first visit was a pitch inspection, and a failed inspection at that!

As a young and aspiring journalist at the time I was looking forward to writing a match report of the big game, a rare chance for me to cover Ipswich Town during the 1990s. But heavy rain dashed those hopes. All I mustered was a few words from the referee, which I composed in the back of the car on the way back down the motorway. The situation was rescued somewhat by an impromptu stop off on the way back with colleagues Dave Allard

Ipswich Town fans show their appreciation after their side's 2-1 win at Elland Road in 2000. (WP)

and Tony Garnett to see former Ipswich Town boss John Duncan's Chesterfield team in action at their old Saltergate ground. I can't remember much about that game, or even who were the opposition. It was probably entertaining, maybe route one football, but it wasn't Leeds v Ipswich in the Premier League!

My first Elland Road trip to report on a match rather than a failed pitch inspection, was actually an FA Youth Cup fixture on Thursday, 20 January 2000. Colchester United produced the performance of their lives that night to hold a fancied Leeds team to a 0-0 draw in the fourth round. Leeds had won the competition twice in the previous six years and were expected to stroll home, but they were lucky to force a replay with home keeper Chad Harpur saving a penalty from Sean Hillier.

'It's been a proud night for Colchester United. The boys were not overawed by the occasion,' declared director of youth football Micky Cook, the U's all-time record appearance maker with 614 league games between 1969 and 1984. The team was not full of future stars, although keeper Andy Walker, defender Jack Wignall, midfielders Marc Canham and Sam Okafor, and striker KK Opara did go on to make a few first-team appearances for the U's. Only Frenchman Thomas Pinault, though, became a first-team regular.

The replay at Layer Road a week later also ended goalless, with Leeds scraping through 4-2 on penalties.

Later that year, I was back at Elland Road, this time for first-team action in the Premier League to witness Ipswich Town's fine 2-1 victory on 16 September 2000. It was a great day all round. Not only did I finally get to file a first-team match report from Elland Road, but the home fans ended up turning against their own team, such was the lacklustre performance of the hosts.

Elland Road looked a picture, filled to the brim with blue seats, and a few yellow and white ones for good measure. The press box was in the John Charles Stand, the oldest stand in the ground, having been built in 1957 at a cost of £180,0000 to replace the previous structure which had been completely gutted in a fire the previous year when the club offices, dressing rooms, club kit, club records, directors' rooms and even the press box were all destroyed. Opposite, the Lowfields terracing gave way to the massive new East Stand in 1992/93, boasting at the time what was the biggest cantilever stand in the world. It dwarfs the other stands. At either end is the Don Revie Stand (the old Spion Kop), where the last remaining terraces had been replaced in 1994/95, and the Norman Hunter Stand, constructed in 1974 to replace the famous old 'Scratching Shed', which had been a popular sight with its wooden barrel-shaped roof since the 1920s.

A fast forward return to September 2000, and we arrive at what was a great day for Jermaine Wright, as well as Ipswich. Wright capped his then-best display in a Town shirt with the winning goal, exchanging a one-two with striker Marcus Stewart before stroking the ball past Nigel Martyn on 47 minutes. It was the midfielder's second goal for Town since his switch from Crewe for £500,000 during the summer of 1999, shortly after the departure of Kieron Dyer to Newcastle United. Earlier, Lee Bowyer's fourth-minute opener for Leeds had been matched by James Scowcroft's 12th-minute equaliser.

Being quick on my own feet in those days, I managed to catch up with a delighted Wright after the match, outside the stadium. He told me, 'We knew we could win at half-time. Leeds fans turned against their team as the match went on, and that worked for us.' Ironically, Wright opted to join Leeds from Ipswich four years later.

So perhaps Elland Road is not such a bad place after all.

As a footnote, a few years later I began reporting on Jermaine's son, Drey Wright, during his early days as a winger at Colchester United, with Jermaine often watching from the stands. Alas, leaping from one generation to the next always makes me feel that bit older, not wiser.

72 COUNTY GROUND (SWINDON TOWN)

Club: Swindon Town
Founded: 1879
Ground: County Ground (since 1896)
First visit: 12 August 2000; Swindon 0 Colchester 0

Neil 'Razor' Ruddock, who was struggling to put his shorts on around a bulging waist just a month earlier, cut Colchester United down to size on one of my first of many visits to Swindon Town's County Ground, on the first day of September 2001. The 33-year-old veteran defender caused a stir that afternoon during a 1-0 home win. More on that soon.

It is usually plain sailing to get to the outskirts of Swindon, but the main obstacle lies just before you arrive at the County Ground in the shape of the Magic Roundabout. This bewildering spider of roads comprises five mini-roundabouts, arranged in a circle

Flashback: the author's match report from the U's 1-0 defeat at the County Ground in 2001.

around a sixth. It can be a complicated business navigating your way around but the good news is that Swindon Town's long-term home is adjacent, in between County Road and Shrivenham Road, with the town centre also only a short stroll away.

The stadium is actually visible from afar due to its tall floodlights and the open spaces all around. In fact, there's a cricket ground behind the back of the main Arkell's Stand, on the northern side of the stadium, the home of Swindon Cricket Club; always a welcome

A clean-up operation on a wet and windy night before the U's 0-0 draw at Swindon Town in 2014. (WP)

sight. This too is known as the County Ground and was actually used for football during the early days, from 1893 to 1896, before the football venue was constructed. This all began with Swindon-based Arkell's Brewery (established in 1843) donating £300 towards the building of a stand. A new all-seater Arkell's Stand was built in 1971 behind the original one, and it is there that the press box is situated.

I had the good fortune, or ill fortune, to report on 'Razor' Ruddock's debut appearance for Swindon in the early weeks of the 2001/02 campaign, in the third tier. Best known for his days as a tough-tackling, take-no-prisoners central defender at Southampton, Tottenham, Liverpool and West Ham, new Robins player-coach Ruddock had made a brief outing for the reserves in midweek. He was far from fully match fit, but at least he was able to keep his shorts up (it was reported at the time that he had problems finding a pair to fit), and there was an air of predictability about him going on to score the winner, the only goal of the game against Steve Whitton's Colchester, who had begun the day sitting proudly on top of the Second Division after four fixtures.

In the blistering, red-hot Wiltshire sunshine, Ruddock won the day with a thunderous 53rd-minute free kick which flew through the defensive wall and into the far corner of the net. So a day that had begun with the U's hoping to expose Ruddock's lack of pace at the back ended with the cheeky Londoner delivering a faultless display in defence and then thumping home the winner. This was, though, to be the highlight of Ruddock's otherwise unhappy stay at Swindon, which culminated in him taking the club to an employment tribunal in December of the following year, where he received money for lost wages but also agreed to have his contract terminated. He had not played for a few months due to a knee injury.

But Ruddock, and his boss Roy Evans, the former Liverpool manager, were all smiles after that free kick. I interviewed U's centre-half Alan White after the match. 'As a Liverpool fan, I often used to watch Neil Ruddock. He's very vocal, always talking on the pitch,' explained ex-Luton defender White. U's boss Whitton was not so charitable. 'It was a disgraceful decision to award the free kick in the first place,' blasted Whitton, with reference to a harsh handball.

The two clubs have been in the same divisions for most of the last two decades, so I have had my fair share of return trips to the Magic Roundabout and the press box in Arkell's Stand. One of these, 11 years later, was a match that I never thought would even kick off. I took shelter in the tiny press lounge with a few fellow hacks under the main stand, listening to the wind howling and the rain driving across the stadium. There were a couple of late pitch inspections and I fully expected the game to be called off, which would have been a blow because it was a Friday night and it had been a difficult journey. A long way to travel just for a complimentary pie and a lukewarm cup of coffee. But the pitch was deemed playable, fans' safety was not seen to be compromised, and the U's weathered another storm to draw 0-0 despite playing 20 minutes with ten men after winger Sanchez Watt's red card.

That same year, 2014, 'Razor' Ruddock appeared in an episode of the Channel 5 TV programme, *Can't Pay? We'll Take It Away!* during which High Court enforcement agents sought to collect an alleged unpaid bill to a dog kennel off the former footballing star.

A far cry from firing home a free kick at the County Ground!

73 LOFTUS ROAD

Club: Queens Park Rangers
Founded: 1882 (as Christchurch Rangers); 1886 (as QPR, following the merger of Christchurch Rangers and St Judes Institute)
Ground: Loftus Road (1904, first used by QPR in 1917)
First visit: 6 September 2000: QPR 1 Colchester 4

Compact, fully enclosed and atmospheric. Loftus Road, a home to football since 1904, and home to Queens Park Rangers since 1917 (except for two short stints at White City Stadium), is a little gem, an intimate stadium dripping with personality and character in West London.

You may guess from this intro that I am a fan of Loftus Road, a lukewarm love affair that had its roots embedded on my first visit, thanks to the magic of Lomana LuaLua as much as the majesty of the stadium, squeezed in among residential streets. I watched from

Town fans fill one end of a packed Loftus Road. (WP)

the press box in the South Africa Road Stand as LuaLua, who I have already mentioned in glowing terms in previous chapters, almost single-handedly tore QPR to shreds during a League Cup first round second leg, held in front of a stunned but ultimately appreciative Loftus Road crowd on a Wednesday, 6 September 2000.

I have touched on the rarity of my full marks for player ratings elsewhere in this book, but Lua's Lua's perfect ten was one of the most straightforward I have given. The 19-year-old Democratic Republic of Congo (formerly Zaire) whizz-kid dazzled with a sensational hat-trick in Colchester United's 4-1 away victory on the night, which secured a 4-2 aggregate success after a 1-0 defeat in the home leg. First Division hosts QPR were left bemused by the tricks of LuaLua, who increased his price tag with this individual showcase of his talents. In fact, he even set up the U's other goal as well, for team-mate Steve McGavin. Another 19-year-old striker with different attributes, Peter Crouch, was a QPR substitute that night.

LuaLua's second goal was the pick of his slick hat-trick. He controlled Karl Duguid's powerfully hit low cross and cut inside three defenders, shaping to shoot twice before finally putting QPR out of their misery with a sweet drive into the far corner of the net past keeper Lee Harper, who was rooted to the spot. It was like watching a mischievous cat toying with a group of mice. The Londoners were being played off the park, and although ex-Ipswich Town attacker Chris Kiwomya levelled the aggregate score at 2-2 with a header on the stroke of half-time, LuaLua did not let up in the second half, setting up McGavin for the third and then racing on to Tim Breacker's poor back-pass to round Harper for a late fourth.

The Loftus Road home faithful gave the Essex visitors a standing ovation at the final whistle, with a special round of applause reserved for LuaLua, who ended up signing for Premier League giants Newcastle United for £2.25m just a week later. LuaLua had also been attracting the attention of Tottenham and West Ham, a fairytale story for the Kinshasa-born front-runner who moved to London at the age of eight, but didn't start playing football until much later. He was spotted by Colchester's assistant director of youth football, Geoff Harrop, while playing for Leyton College against Colchester Sixth Form College two years earlier, in 1998. It was a good spot!

That LuaLua-inspired first visit has meant I've always been a fan of Loftus Road, a ground which was originally built in 1904 and had amateur club Shepherd's Bush FC as its first hosts. QPR led a nomadic existence during their early years, with up to about 20 different venues used, including such diverse homes as London Scottish Ground, Wormwood Scrubs, Kilburn Cricket Ground and the Royal Agricultural Society Showgrounds. When they settled on Loftus Road from 1917, there was just an open field and a pavilion, but developments soon started with the club dismantling a stand from their previous ground, Park Royal, and re-erecting it at their new home to establish the first Ellerslie Road Stand. This provided the only shelter (a roof) until the late 1960s.

These days, the ground is all-seater and has a claustrophobic feel, with all four stands meeting at each corner to ensure there are no gaps. The current Ellerslie Road Stand dates from 1972, when it replaced the original tin-roofed grandstand from Park Royal, while the bigger South Africa Road Stand was constructed in 1968 to replace terracing. The Loft (Loftus Road End) and School End behind each goal, like the other two stands, are close to the pitch so the atmosphere can be quite intimidating.

I have usually travelled via the underground, getting off at White City on the Central Line and joining the hoards walking up South Africa Road. My first port of call, the press lounge, was long and narrow, which made for an intimate press conference, especially if Roy Keane happened to be the away team's manager. Fortunately, my midweek visit with Ipswich Town on 9 February 2010 ended in a Town 2-1 away win when first-half goals

Lomana Lua Lua, who scored a sensational hat-trick at QPR in 2000.

from David Norris and Sunderland loanee Daryl Murphy proved decisive against Ray Harford's QPR. Keane was in a good mood that night.

Loftus Road had never looked better, except when playing host to that dazzling LuaLua one-man show of September 2000.

74 JJB STADIUM

Club: Wigan Athletic
Founded: 1932
Ground: Wigan Athletic Stadium (known as the JJB Stadium, 1999–2009; now the DW Stadium)
First visit: 9 September 2000; Wigan 3 Colchester 1

After 67 years at a slowly decaying Springfield Park, Wigan Athletic moved to a spanking new stadium to the north of the Robin Park retail complex, about a mile and a half from the town centre, to team up with the Wigan Warriors rugby league club from the summer of 1999. It was a move that kick-started a golden era for the Greater Manchester club, culminating in promotion to the Premier League just six years later. It was an altogether very different experience to that offered by Springfield Park, a very different world. In fact, it felt like you were visiting a very different club, which, with owner Dave Whelan's financial backing, it was.

Originally named the JJB Stadium, it's a good-looking structure of four very similar single-tier stands, with the corners left open. It looks more impressive from the outside due to the very distinctive supporting steel frameworks which are visible from above the roofs along the two sides of the stadium. Inside it's a little blander, but it is efficient and airy. Perhaps lacking the dubious charm attached to Springfield Park, but with far better views of the pitch. There are no grubby, impenetrable windshields to peer through, trying to fathom out what the hell is going on inside one of the goalmouths. Instead, the view from the press area in the main West Stand, now known as the Springfield Stand, is glorious, with a separate media room close to the reception for the post-match interviews. All mod cons.

Although the Latics were destined for success, they were still in the doldrums when I paid my second visit to the JJB Stadium (renamed the DW Stadium in 2009) for a third-tier clash against Steve Whitton's Colchester United in November 2001. Paul Jewell had only been in charge since the summer, and the pressure was growing on the successful ex-Bradford City boss after a slow start. That pressure had intensified by the time that the U's had celebrated a 3-2 win courtesy of veteran Mick Stockwell's first-half brace and Ross Johnson's late winner.

Operating as a makeshift striker, the versatile Stockwell, who played most of his 700-plus senior appearances in midfield or at full-back, struck twice on 13 and 18 minutes, the first a spectacular volley on the turn over keeper Derek Stillie. This was one of the 36-year-old's best individual displays in a Colchester shirt during his three years and 131 league appearances at the Essex club after 18 years and 610 senior outings at Ipswich

Mick Stockwell volleys the U's into an early lead during a 3-2 win at Wigan Athletic in 2001. (WP)

Town. Back came Wigan, though, Norwich City loanee Matt Jackson and striker Andy Liddell both scoring early in the second half to make it 2-2. It was against the run of play when defender Ross Johnson, formerly of Brighton, smashed home the winner with a 25-yard shot which took a wicked deflection off defender Arjan De Zeeuw. It was 25-year-old Johnson's first goal for the U's, and in fact his only one. He had dropped into non-league by the following season.

The win ended a miserable run of seven straight away defeats for Whitton's Colchester, while it was already Wigan's fifth home defeat of the campaign. In the end, the U's finished a comfortable 15th in the Second Division table, with Wigan under-achieving in tenth spot. However, under Jewell, the Latics went on to clinch promotion as Second Division champions the following season, and then reached the Premier League by finishing second to Sunderland in the Championship in 2005.

Within six years of its grand opening, the JJB Stadium, with its mass of red (Wigan Warriors) and blue (Wigan Athletic) seats, was therefore hosting top-flight football. Grotty Springfield Park seemed a million miles away.

75 BRAMALL LANE

Club: Sheffield United
Founded: 1889 (as on offshoot of Sheffield United Cricket Club)
Ground: Bramall Lane (opened 1855)
First visit: 19 September 2000; Sheffield United 3 Colchester 0

There has always been an edge to my visits to Bramall Lane, which I assure you is not a poor attempt at a pun for a home club which began life with the nickname of The Cutlers

Joy and pain as Sheffield United poach a last-gasp equaliser during a 3-3 thriller against Town in 2009. (WP)

for the first 23 years (1989 to 1912) of their existence, before assuming the nickname of The Blades for the last 100-plus years. Rather, it refers to the often-electric atmosphere, the highly-charged fans and the heavy weight of history surrounding the place.

Sheffield United's home crowds are always passionate, and the matches are usually full-blooded affairs. No quarter is given and the Blades faithful demand high standards, to be expected for a club with such a glorious past, which includes winning the Football League in 1898 and lifting the FA Cup on four occasions by the end of the first quarter of the 20th century. That edge also takes on a personal note for me because, perched in the press box at the back of the old South Stand, I always found it nigh-on impossible to discern the identity of most of the home players, with the numbers on the backs of their shirts melting into the red and white stripes. It can be a hard life, being an away hack, or at least a guessing game at times. The partially-obscured squad numbers gave an unwanted edge to my visits.

From that old press box, approached via a short flight of stairs from the press lounge – a plate of pie, peas and gravy in this attic-like room was also a welcome sight after a long drive into South Yorkshire – I have witnessed several Ipswich Town and Colchester United sides over-powered by the opposition, none more so than on my debut appearance in September 2000 when Steve Whitton's U's were brushed aside 3-0.

But there have been better away days at this most famous of venues, which began staging football from 1862. Bramall Lane's attraction in the even earlier days, when it hosted cricket matches, was its location away from the smoke and grime of the city's industrial area, but these days it remains conveniently sited just a 15-minute walk from the city centre and the railway station. Approaching the stadium, from the city centre in the north or from the neighbouring cobbled streets, where I used to leave my car before the onset of 'residents only' parking, it always felt like I was about to attend a big event, hence that edge. This has been the home of football for countless generations and yet, very occasionally, I have reported on some fine away results, leading to the ever-so predictable 'Blunting the Blades' headline in the following days sports pages.

Here are two extremes; one of elation, the other of devastation, both common emotions at Bramall Lane.

The elation came via Colchester United's FA Cup third round victory at Bramall Lane on 7 January 2006. The U's, the underdogs, surprised Premier League hopefuls Sheffield United with a 2-1 win despite trailing to Steve Kabba's fifth-minute opener. Midfielder Neil Danns equalised just after the half-hour mark and substitute Gareth Williams headed home the winner with 18 minutes left, nodding home Mark Yeates's cross from a short corner to celebrate his first goal in almost a year.

This was no smash-and-grab win, the U's dominating for the majority of the afternoon, as Blades boss Neil Warnock admitted after the game. 'Colchester players were stronger than ours. We only had a couple of big lads, while they seem to breed them big down in Colchester!' conceded Warnock, who employed some kidology during the build-up to the cup tie by claiming that third-tier Colchester would be 'the favourites' when everyone read his team sheet. As it happened, Warnock left it very late to select his team and even then only made a few changes to his normal starting line-up. U's boss Phil Parkinson was on the offensive during his post-match interview, which made for some good copy. 'I look

Town manager Roy Keane in the Bramall Lane dug-out during his side's 3-3 draw in 2009. (WP)

in some of the national newspapers and it's almost as if Colchester United don't exist,' thundered Parkinson. 'We've just beaten a top-two side in the Championship, so I hope we finally get some credit and some recognition.'

In the end, both teams clinched promotion that season, the Blades into the Premier League and the U's into the Championship.

And so to the devastation which, not for the first time, was the over-riding emotion after Ipswich Town's 3-3 draw at Bramall Lane on Tuesday, 29 September 2009. 'Sheffield steal' was the headline on the back page of the following day's newspaper, after Roy Keane's Town slumped to the bottom of the Championship table by dint of shipping two late goals.

Town had not won any of their first nine league games of the campaign, but they looked to have the three points in the bag when moving into a 3-1 lead going into the last dozen minutes. A crowd of 28,000-plus had largely been quietened by goals from Jon Walters, Grant Leadbitter and Gareth McAuley, after Darius Henderson had given Sheffield an early lead due to keeper Richard Wright's missed punch. Henderson pulled a goal back on 78 minutes, but Town were within touching distance of a first league win when disaster struck in stoppage time. Wright failed to gather a corner kick and the loose ball was bundled over the line at the far post by defender Chris Morgan.

As I said before, there was an edge to this duel, a real Championship thriller, but it was also a heartbreak ending for Keane and his men. Plymouth's win at Peterborough on the same night saw Town drop to the basement.

'It should have been three points,' rued a weary Keane during the post-match interviews, late that night. 'We again came so close, but not close enough. We should have seen the game through.'

Harsh, gut-wrenching, cruel. This just wasn't cricket. Ironic really, at a ground that used to have one side open, until as late as 1975, to accommodate a cricket outfield and a distant cricket pavilion.

76 GOODISON PARK

Club: Everton
Founded: 1878 (as St Domingo FC, for members of the St Domingo Methodist New Connexion Chapel)
Ground: Goodison Park (from 1892)
First visit: 30 September 2000; Everton 0 Ipswich 3

I knew it was going to be an interesting day when, on parking the car down a side street, a couple of local teenagers appeared from nowhere and offered to 'look after' the vehicle for us while we were away. The 'us' referred to myself and the driver, Tony Garnett, the then-Ipswich Town correspondent and sports editor for the *East Anglian Daily Times*. I was the

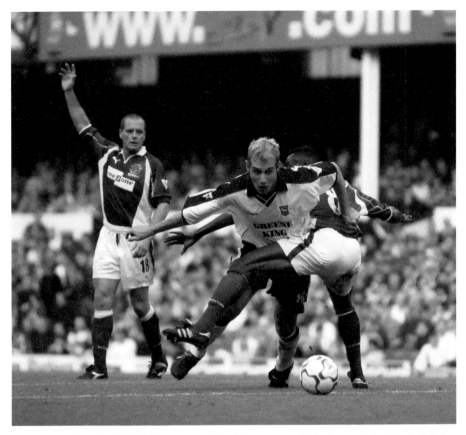

James Scowcroft in the thick of the action, with Paul Gascoigne in the background, during Town's 3-0 win at Everton in 2000. (WP)

passenger, the quotes man (to extract post-match quotes from managers and players), and most importantly the tea boy. Our destination was Goodison Park, the proud and long-standing home of Everton, for a Premier League clash between the Toffees (nickname originating from one of two, or both, toffee shops in Everton village, Ye Anciente Everton Toffee House and Old Mother Nobletts Toffee Shop) and Ipswich on 30 September 2000.

Our first task on arriving on Merseyside was to answer 'yes please' to the kind offer of 'looking after' our car.

Mr Garnett gave one of the lads a note (probably a fiver, maybe a tenner), safe in the knowledge that the car would be safe for the duration of the afternoon. If we had not coughed up, well, let's just say I may have feared for the health of one of Mr Garnett's wing mirrors.

Where to start, with regards Goodison Park?

The stadium looks huge from the outside, its lofty stands dwarfing the narrow residential streets surrounding it, with Stanley Park beyond separating Everton's home from Liverpool's abode at Anfield. Even from its earliest years, Goodison Park, affectionately known as 'The Grand Old Lady', had been turning heads. The first purpose-built football stadium in England, there was a frenzy of work before the grand opening in 1892 with the field levelled, a drainage system installed and three stands erected, the other end featuring a big bank of cinder. There was also an athletics track, until that was removed in 1909. Squeezed between tiny streets and alleyways, housing was even built into the structure at the Park End Stand (south side). The club owned these houses and used to rent some of them out to players, although by the 1990s most of them had been demolished.

Even now, Goodison Park is a grand theatre from which to watch football, a very intimidating blue-and-white-seated arena due to the proximity of the stands to the pitch. Which brings me back to my first visit, and a particular need to possess a head for heights.

The inkling that I had about this promising to be an 'interesting day' proved spot on. I remember it as if it was yesterday, my first experience of the Goodison Park press box, perched high up in the main Goodison Road Stand, a double-decker stand with two tiers on the lower deck. Opposite was the Bullens Road Stand, with the single-tier cantilever Park End Stand to the right and the noisier section of the Gwladys Street Stand to the left. I had never come across such a steep drop from the main stand to the pitch. If I had suffered from vertigo then I doubt whether I would have made it through the afternoon. The lot of a quotes-man-cum-tea-boy is not always plain sailing.

On the pitch, newly promoted Ipswich were sublime, lethal, all-conquering, despite the big presence of Paul Gascoigne in Everton's midfield. Marcus Stewart, a proven goalscorer in the Football League with Bristol Rovers and Huddersfield, showed that he could adapt to life in the Premier League by scoring a second-half brace to add to John McGreal's 19th-minute headed opener from Jim Magilton's free kick.

And after the match, I had an absolute field day with quotes. Some days, no one wants to talk you; other days, they – manager, coaches and players alike – are queuing up to speak into your Dictaphone, or to test your ropey shorthand.

On that glorious afternoon I spoke to Town boss George Burley, Everton manager Walter Smith, Town's double goalscorer Stewart, and Town's midfield maestro Magilton, who had man-marked 32-year-old Gazza out of the game.

Front-runner Stewart, recruited from Huddersfield for £2.5m in February, explained, 'I'm enjoying the Premier League after playing in the lower divisions for all my career up to now. The manager has had faith in me.' That manager, Burley, said, 'We are coming to grounds with no fear factor. I keep reading that we are two to one on to be relegated, but the Premier League has more open games and that suits us.' His opposite number Smith, a former and also future Rangers manager, was more critical of his own team than complimentary of Town. He insisted, 'If we had lost because we had been outplayed, then I would hold my hands up. But that was not the case today.'

Magilton was buzzing. 'The plan was to keep Gazza [Gascoigne] quiet. We don't usually man-mark, but we were aware of his strengths and tried to stop him.'

Marcus Stewart spins away after scoring Town's second goal in a 3-0 win at Goodison Park. (WP)

But pride of place went to Merseyside-born 28-year-old McGreal, scorer of Town's opener. It was an extra special day for him. McGreal managed to upset most of his mates who were watching in the stands by scoring against their favourite team. The ex-Tranmere Rovers centre-half was, and remains, a lifelong Liverpool fan, so to head home what was only the second goal of his career against the deadly enemy was extremely satisfying.

McGreal told me after the game, 'It was a special goal, and a special feeling. I've been a Liverpool supporter all my life, although most of my mates are Everton fans. They were all watching today, so I suppose they will be a bit subdued now. I'm staying up here for the weekend, so I'm not sure what sort of reception I will get. Hopefully, they will forgive me.' Sixteen years later, I started interviewing McGreal two or three times a week, every week, when he took over as manager of Colchester United. He still is a Liverpool supporter.

Back on 30 September 2000, a perfect day was capped by Mr Garnett and I returning to the car, later that evening, to find it was still in one piece. A fiver well spent, Mr Garnett!

And for the record, Town went on to finish fifth in the table that season, with Everton down in 16th.

77 VALE PARK

Club: Port Vale
Founded: 1876 or 1879 (open to interpretation), re-established in 1907
Ground: Vale Park (since 1950)
First visit: 14 October 2000; Port Vale 3 Colchester 1

Snow storms, muffins in the press box, corner cafes, red cards, regular away-day misery. These are my clearest memories of Vale Park, the home of Port Vale since 1950, situated off Hamil Road (opposite one of the club's former grounds, Burslem Park) in the town of Burslem, within the city of Stoke-on-Trent in the Potteries area of Staffordshire.

Port Vale score their third goal during a 3-1 win over the U's at Vale Park in 2000. (WP)

I mention the location specifically, because Port Vale is one of very few Football League clubs not to be named after a town, city or geographical location. In fact, it can be argued they are the only club, Arsenal having been named after the Royal Arsenal at Woolwich, but the whole subject is a grey area with several clubs no longer attached to their original towns or districts. A stranger to these shores might assume that 'Port Vale' is situated somewhere on the coast, surrounded by shipyards or close to a harbour, when in fact it is bang in the middle of the country, the name perhaps referring to the valley of ports on the Trent and Mersey Canal. Another theory, one of many, is that the name stemmed from the venue of the inaugural club meeting at 'Port Vale House' in the suburbs of Stoke-on-Trent, in 1876. It's safe to say that the precise origins of the name remain shrouded in mystery.

When in the early planning stages, Vale Park was intended as being the 'Wembley of the North', an 80,000-capacity stadium, but it didn't quite work out like that, perhaps just as well for a lower-league club. Instead, a 40,000-capacity home was built, including only 360 seats, with just two stands erected. There were banks of terracing at both ends of the ground, at the Hamil End and Bycars End. Furthermore, the pitch was problematic and vulnerable to both heavy rain (poor drainage) and freezing temperatures. The latter was not helped by the clay under the grass, as the site was a former clay pit, and also the exposed and lofty nature of the stadium. In fact, at 520 feet above sea level, it is the third highest English Football League stadium, behind (or rather below) West Brom and Oldham.

The pitch and the stands have improved much since then. The pitch is actually one of the widest in the Football League, conducive to expansive football, while the ground is still rather old-looking, despite a few upgrades and a new Lorne Street Stand, which was opened while still unfinished in 1999. The glass-fronted reception area is smart and shiny, but the most curious section of the stadium is a two-tiered wedge of blue and yellow seats in one corner, between the Railway Stand and Bycars End, which still has the old roof taken from the Valiants' previous home at the Old Recreation Ground in Hanley.

Colchester United usually shipped goals, whenever I rolled up at the main Port Vale car park behind the main Lorne Street Stand on my early visits. Back-to-back 3-1 away defeats were followed two years later by a 4-3 reverse, but one of the most incident-packed encounters was ironically a 0-0 draw on a cold but dry Tuesday evening on 8 March 2005. Two struggling teams, in the bottom half of the League One table and with one eye on the relegation scrap below them, this was not a match for the faint-hearted. No goals, little goalmouth action and a mere point apiece, and yet referee Paul Robinson ensured there would be talking points galore after flashing three red cards and awarding more than 40 free kicks during a bad-tempered clash. Some nights, an intrepid reporter does not need goals to fill column inches. This was one such night.

Liam Chilvers, Colchester's central defender, was the first to ensure an early bath after being sent off for two bookable offences in first-half stoppage time. In fact, Mr Robinson went card crazy before the break with four quickfire bookings, including a red for Chilvers after a foul on striker Billy Paynter near the touchline. The ex-Arsenal youth-teamer was hard done by. But if U's boss Phil Parkinson was seething at half-time, it was Vale manager Martin Foyle who was grinding his teeth during the second half. Stalwart midfielder Micky Cummins and substitute Levi Reid were shown red cards to leave it nine versus ten on the pitch and, considering all the interruptions with the countless free kicks, it was no wonder that neither team looked like scoring.

Cue for some juicy quotes.

Parkinson blasted, 'I don't believe what I have seen tonight. I've never seen anything like it in all my days as a player or manager. None of the red cards were deserved.'

Vale supremo Foyle also pulled no punches. 'I've never seen a worse referee in all my life.'

There was almost smoke coming out of my Dictaphone.

Needless-to-say, my report in the following morning's newspaper, despite the tight night-time deadline, was quotes-driven.

Despite the unsatisfactory match – fortunately both teams did avoid relegation that season – Vale Park did provide a welcome if slightly unusual experience for the visiting press. The media room doubled up as a games room for the Valiants' youth-teamers or fringe first-teamers, so you could sip a cuppa while watching a game of pool between two budding 16-year-olds, or two crocked but seasoned pros. Outside, the press box was situated low down in the unfinished but modern-looking Lorne Street Stadium, just above pitch level and towards one goal. Often, cakes would be passed around at half-time, always a highlight, especially if time had been pressing before kick-off, so preventing a quick visit to a nearby greasy spoon cafe (a favourite of my travelling photographer, Warren Page).

One other midweek night stands out for me – I guess Vale Park always served up its clearest memories after a Tuesday night in the Potteries.

There were two goals but no red cards in this one, a 2-0 home win for Port Vale on 11 February 2014 when home skipper Doug Loft, a future injury-plagued Colchester player, bagged both goals. But it was the weather rather than the League One action that stood out for me. It snowed heavily that night, although the U's were just relieved that the match actually went ahead, having not played at all for the previous 24 days due to four successive postponements. I remember returning to my car, which was smothered in snow, just after 11pm, wondering whether I would ever get out of Burslem. Fortunately, the engine spluttered into life, at the third attempt, and the wipers cleared the snow from the windscreen. It was a long journey home.

78 HUISH PARK

Club: Yeovil Town
Founded: 1895 (as Yeovil Casuals)
Ground: Huish Park (since 1990)
First visit: 18 November 2000; Yeovil 5 Colchester 1

Few grounds have featured such a personal high, and such a personal low, as Yeovil Town's Huish Park, down in Somerset. It has only been Yeovil's home since 1990, replacing the former Huish Athletic Ground famed for its considerable slope, which saw a differentiation of eight feet from one side to the other. The new venue, sited at an old army camp in the Houndstone area of Yeovil and named after the old ground, has always had strong links with Colchester United due to the fact that the U's were the visitors for the first competitive match at Huish Park, a 2-0 home win for the Glovers in an opening-day Conference clash on 18 August 1990.

My first visit was disastrous in terms of the result. Still a non-league club at the time, Yeovil thrashed third-tier Colchester 5-1 in the FA Cup first round on 18 November 2000, all six goals arriving in the second half. It came 42 years after the U's had claimed a 7-1 win at Yeovil's old Huish Athletic Ground in an FA Cup tie of 1958 (I wasn't around for that earlier clash). It's perhaps surprising, then, that my chosen featured game for this chapter should be a 0-0 draw from six years later, in 2006. It just happened to be the most glorious stalemate I have ever sat through, the most highly-rated of 0-0s, easily my favourite goalless draw of all-time. But first more on that cup woe from 2000.

It was 0-0 after 50 minutes at Huish Park, the one setback for the U's being left wing-back Gavin Johnson ending up in hospital with an ankle injury. But calamity then struck for Steve Whitton's U's. Not once, not twice, but five times! Centre forward Warren Patmore (two), front-runner Barrington Belgrave, centre-half Terry Skiverton and midfielder Paul Way (a penalty) all struck to give Yeovil, who were four points clear at the top of the Conference with two games in hand, a handsome victory. Skiverton and Way

Pat Baldwin celebrates in front of the away fans at Huish Park after the U's clinch promotion in 2006.
(WP)

went on to be Yeovil managers in later years, while the club missed out on promotion to the Football League that season, finishing runners-up to Rushden & Diamonds.

Karl Duguid, who nodded home a consolation for the U's, branded his team's display as 'disgraceful'. Manager Whitton was just as damning, 'We totally lacked effort, passion and desire in the second half. We should all be embarrassed by this performance.'

And Johnson, on emerging from hospital that evening, was shocked to discover the result. 'I couldn't find out how we got on until someone gave the kit man, who was with me in hospital, a message. I couldn't believe it. We were holding our own in the first half and it was 0-0 when I left!' said a bemused Johnson.

Fast forward six years and we come to one of the best days in Colchester United's history, again at Huish Park, where those FA Cup demons were put to rest.

Phil Parkinson's U's needed just one point from their final-day trip to Yeovil to wrap up automatic promotion to the Championship for the first time in the club's history. It was an afternoon for biting fingernails, covering your eyes, and keeping your fingers and toes crossed. The away end terracing was jam-packed with U's supporters, most of them decked in the traditional blue and white, and others sporting the yellow shirts of the team's away strip. It felt like a cup final, at least for the U's. Yeovil had guaranteed their League One survival the previous weekend by winning at Huddersfield, so they were in a relaxed frame of mind.

As for the match, it wasn't pretty. In fact, it was a stinker, but that didn't bother any U's supporter. At times the tension was almost unbearable, and I had difficulty concentrating on what I was typing on my laptop, while never taking my eyes off the action.

The most prized of all 0-0 draws as the U's pick up the point needed at Huish Park to win promotion. (WP)

U's keeper Dean Gerken, in the side because first choice Aidan Davison had been laid low with food poisoning, diverted an early shot by Yeovil's leading scorer Phil Jevons on to the bar. That combination of a fantastic save, with a slice of luck for good measure, was to set the tone for the rest of the afternoon.

Looking back at my match report, I wrote, 'The second half was certainly one of the longest halves of football I have ever endured.' And it was, that's for sure. I recall one great chance that the Glovers had to spoil the party, when David Poole scampered through on goal with 20 minutes remaining. But Gerken raced off his line and did just enough to distract Poole, who dragged his shot wide of target. When referee Andre Marriner blew his final whistle, all the Colchester players ran over to their jubilant travelling fans, and the celebrations began in earnest. And as soon as I had pinged over my match report, I too was on the pitch. It's not every year that you get to report on a promotion party.

I think I interviewed just about every U's player that afternoon, plus the manager, assistant manager, chairman, physio, and kit man. Only the coach driver might have been spared my questions.

Ground-wise, I have always found Huish Park to be a very friendly, welcoming venue, surrounded by trees and open spaces, and sporting a small press room under the Main Stand which often used to have a tray of sandwiches for hungry hacks, in addition to a row of power points for hungry laptops. But to reach the actual press box, which is situated on the other (east) side of the stadium, requires walking around the perimeter of the pitch and along the front of the open terracing at the away supporters' end. This is not easily done while scalding your hand with a cup of hot tea.

The press box is suspended beneath the cantilever roof of the single-tier stand, surrounded by home fans. The one exception for me was that glorious end-of-season goalless draw in 2006, when I was in an emergency press overspill area further along the back of the stand, in among the crowd. But I couldn't care where I was that day, to be honest.

Huish Park looked a picture, from all angles. The U's had just reached the Championship!

79 FRATTON PARK

Club: Portsmouth
Founded: 1898
Ground: Fratton Park (from 1898)
First visit: 21 August 2001; Portsmouth 1 Colchester 2

Fratton Park is iconic, unique, a proper football stadium. It has been the home of Portsmouth FC since the Hampshire club was born towards the end of the 19th century and has remained a good old-fashioned, charming, charismatic venue for football, with some wonderful old stands, a splendid mock-Tudor pavilion as an entrance and four mighty floodlights.

Above all, there's nearly always a cracking atmosphere there. The home fans are very vocal, almost snarling at the opposition, and for many decades (from the 1930s through to the 1990s) there were very few changes to the stadium. The Fratton End, previously a home terrace, was fitted with 4,500 plastic blue seats in 1997, while at the opposite end of the pitch, the Milton End was finally equipped with a roof to offer shelter to the long-suffering away supporters. That stand is reached via turnstiles down an alleyway named Specks Lane. But otherwise, Pompey's home is of a bygone age.

I have been a fairly regular visitor to the Fratton Park press box over the years, enjoying the big-match atmosphere from the back of the upper tier of the South Stand, which is the oldest stand in the ground, built in 1925. The cramped press area is behind the directors' box, while TV cameras are perched on the roof. On the subject of the South Stand roof, the one on the original stand (called the Grand Stand) was blown off in strong winds in 1901. The replacement roof only lasted 15 years before it too was blown off, causing considerable damage to nearby properties. Fortunately, I have never been at Fratton Park when it has been blowing a gale.

My last visit with Ipswich Town was in the autumn of 2010 for a goalless draw, quite a triumphant result when compared to a lot of what happened under manager Roy Keane's rather dubious stewardship. But my first trip to the south coast – Fratton Park is actually on Portsea Island, which makes up most of Portsmouth, rather than the Great Britain mainland – was far more memorable, featuring a big cup upset and also an early glimpse of a beanpole striker by the name of Peter Crouch, who was all arms and legs.

The occasion was a League Cup second round tie, Pompey entertaining Colchester United on a warm August night in 2001. The afternoon had begun in failure for me, and for BBC Essex commentator Neil Kelly, as we suffered defeat on a seaside pitch-and-putt course to golfing guru Warren Page (my trusty travelling companion and esteemed photographer), but the evening ended in glory with the U's upsetting the odds to register a 2-1 win.

A gutsy display from the third-tier U's on a balmy evening saw two of the smallest players on the pitch, Mick Stockwell and Kem Izzet, net second-half goals, sandwiching an equaliser from Crouch, the tallest player on view. Crouch hit the target with one of his trademark headers, from Courtney Pitt's cross, but only after Stockwell had headed the visitors in front on 52 minutes. And Izzet regained the U's lead with nine minutes remaining, right in front of the huddle of away fans in the Milton End, by rounding 42-year-old keeper David Beasant, the ex-Wimbledon stalwart, and sweeping into an unguarded net.

I must confess that I didn't foresee the impact that Crouch would have during his career. He was still very young at the time, just 20. Although he had been recruited from QPR for a cool £1.5m that summer, and had scored against the U's that night, I didn't dream that the 6ft 7in target man would go on to have such a fine career. I thought he would probably drop down the divisions after a couple of seasons rather than to end up blazing a trail for the likes of Aston Villa, Liverpool, Tottenham, Stoke City and England.

Portsmouth keeper Dave Beasant forces Mick Stockwell to shoot wide, although the U's won this League Cup tie 2-1, in 2001. (WP)

I guess it just shows what a hopeless judge I am!

Nine years later and I was back at Fratton Park with Ipswich who, under Keane, were remarkably riding high in the top three going into this Championship clash on 11 September 2010.

I remember the afternoon well. I munched through two pies in the press lounge before kick-off, so felt slightly bloated, before having the privilege of sitting in the press box next to Ray Crawford, the former Ipswich legend who began his career at his hometown club Portsmouth before going on to score goals galore in Town's successive Second Division and First Division title campaigns of 1960/61 and 1961/62. He was summarising for local radio, still looking fit at the age of 74. In all, Crawford rattled up 259 senior goals for Ipswich, ending his professional career at Colchester, for whom he scored twice in the U's famous 3-2 win over mighty Leeds United in the FA Cup in 1971.

On the Fratton Park pitch, Town were good value for their point in a goalless draw. Gareth McAuley played a blinder in central defence, the Northern Ireland international getting my vote for man of the match. Pompey, despite their lowly position – they had taken just one point from their previous four games – played with the pride and passion that I have come to expect from all Portsmouth sides. They remained at the foot of the Championship table after Town's visit with Leicester City just above them on goal difference.

Town nearly won it. David Norris rattled the woodwork in the second half, while defender Darren O'Dea missed a sitter from close in. But Town fans left Pompey feeling it was a good point, further cheered by the return of young prodigy Connor Wickham after a two-month injury lay-off. Wickham's cameo as a substitute was the highlight, which said all you really needed to know about the game.

Despite rubbing shoulders with such distinctive characters as Peter Crouch, Dave Beasant, Ray Crawford, Roy Keane and Connor Wickham, my main memory of Fratton Park is a structure, not a footballer. That mock-Tudor pavilion, with its black and white timber facade in the south-west corner of the ground, bearing a close resemblance to the 'Cottage' pavilion at Fulham's Craven Cottage, always captures the imagination. Its tall clock tower and spectator gallery have long gone, removed while the South Stand was being built in 1925, but at least the exterior of the original pavilion lives on as the distinctive mock-Tudor entrance to Fratton Park in Frogmore Road.

Even better, the press lounge, with those tempting meat pies, is close by.

80 WITHDEAN STADIUM

Club: Brighton & Hove Albion
Founded: 1901
Ground: Withdean Stadium (1999–2011, built in 1930)
First visit: 27 October 2001; Brighton 1 Colchester 0

U's striker Scott McGleish tries his luck with a flying header during a 1-0 defeat at the Withdean Stadium in 2001. (WP)

I only visited two 'new' grounds (personal first visits, not new stadia) during 2001, but they couldn't have been more different. The aforementioned iconic Fratton Park, steeped in footballing history spanning more than a century, and the Withdean Stadium, an athletics venue which just temporarily staged Brighton & Hove Albion home matches for 12 years, from 1999 to 2011. The contrast was acute.

As a club runner, and big fan of athletics, I did relish these trips to the Withdean, an athletics stadium situated two miles north of Brighton's city centre. It was the home track of Steve Ovett, the Brighton-born middle-distance runner who struck gold over 800 metres at the Moscow Olympics of 1980, and had a career-long rivalry with Seb Coe during a golden era of Great Britain middle-distance running. The improvised press room, on my first visit to the Withdean on 27 October 2001, was actually the clubhouse of hosts Brighton & Hove Athletics Club, with photos and running books dotted about the place. I was in my element.

As an improvised football stadium, though, the venue had its shortcomings. The eight-lane running track separated the pitch from the six stands, five of which were temporary, the only exception being on the north side where a little press area was equipped with a long, narrow table. Grin and bear it was the order of the day as fans squeezed past in front and from behind. Once in your seat, there was no budging. The whole scene was surreal, with a hammer net in one corner, seated stands kept up with scaffolding on three sides of the ground, and a surrounding area of leafy avenues, substantial houses and the tree-filled slopes of Withdean Woods.

Most supporters would arrive by bus, using the travel vouchers included in the price of the match ticket. This was my mode of transport first time around, though on later visits I would park the car outside the one-mile parking restrictions and walk to the ground. Like Fratton Park, it was a unique experience.

Brighton had ended up at the Withdean following the sale of their long-term Goldstone Ground for commercial development in 1997, and then a couple of years as tenants at Gillingham's Priestfield Stadium in the distant Medway area of Kent. Despite the woefully inadequate facilities, though, the Seagulls made the best of a bad job. A large, green-seated temporary stand was erected down the whole length of the south side, and later three stands (two large and one small) were put up on the east end, with away fans filling the west stand. None of these five stands had roofs, while the players and officials changed in portable cabins. It was all a bit of a maze but a crowd of more than 8,000 could be accommodated, at a push, and everyone seemed to adapt. It was sometimes dubbed 'The Theatre of Trees' and, as if to reinforce the surreality of the place, the park used to be the site of the short-lived Brighton Zoo until the 1950s, boasting such attractions as Russian bears, lion cubs, monkeys and parakeets.

But in the early 2000s, it was League One footballers rather than exotic birds or animals on display at the Withdean.

I did witness a couple of Colchester United 2-1 away wins during my handful of visits, but early on the U's tended to be out of luck and beaten by the odd goal, as was the case on my debut appearance at the Withdean on a sun-kissed Saturday afternoon in East Sussex on 27 October 2001.

You know when you have been unlucky when the opposing keeper wins the man of the match award and the opposing manager showers you with compliments. Steve Whitton's Colchester suffered a 1-0 defeat at the hands of second-placed Brighton, thwarted by the acrobatics of Seagulls keeper Michel Kuipers. The U's launched wave after wave of attacks against hosts who were on the crest of a wave after promotion as fourth-tier champions the previous season. They were also virtually impregnable at the Withdean, having gone 24 matches without a home league defeat stretching back to January 2000. Dutchman Kuipers, as the last line of defence, celebrated his 50th game for the club with a hard-earned clean sheet, while at the other end the highly rated Bobby Zamora scored the only goal of the game, stealing a march on defender Ross Johnson to prod home Paul Watson's quickly-taken free kick.

Brighton boss Peter Taylor, who earlier in the month had still been gracing the Premier League as Leicester City manager, confessed, 'We got away with it! There were times when we just could not get the ball. You have to give Colchester a lot of credit for that.' U's boss Whitton naturally agreed, 'We should have easily scored four or five goals. We were the better team.'

In the final analysis, Brighton ended up as Second Division champions by six points, losing just one of their 23 home matches, while the U's comfortably avoided relegation by 13 points.

The Withdean hosted its last Football League match on 30 April 2011, against Huddersfield Town. No one was that sorry to see the Seagulls fly off to their spanking new stadium, in nearby Falmer, not least the local residents. But although it was only ever a temporary measure, with a few flimsy stands and numerous portable cabins and huts, the Withdean was not all that bad.

Tellingly, when *The Observer* launched a mini survey to compile an unscientific top-ten list of the worst Football League grounds in the country back in 2004, the Withdean Stadium did not even make the top three. Priestfield, Kenilworth Road and Millmoor pushed Brighton's athletics-based temporary home, with its running track and long jump sandpit, into fourth spot.

Happily, unlike local hero Steve Ovett, it didn't make the podium.

81 REEBOK STADIUM

Club: Bolton Wanderers
Founded: 1874 (as Christ Church FC)
Ground: Reebok Stadium (1997, renamed Macron Stadium 2014–18, University of Bolton Stadium from 2018)
First visit: 6 April 2002; Bolton 4 Ipswich 1

When a player of Matt Holland's class and repute describes a match as 'the most embarrassing defeat of my career', you know it's been a bad day at the office. Midfield maestro Holland, who at the time was Ipswich Town's long-serving club captain and the first name on the team sheet every week (he was ever-present for several seasons), was referring to one miserable afternoon at Bolton Wanderers' then-named Reebok Stadium, on 6 April 2002, and more specifically a calamitous 4-1 defeat.

Personally, I have had far 'more embarrassing' days as a football journalist. There was the occasion when I got locked in at Chesterfield's old Saltergate stadium, having spent too long writing my match report, and another when I was refused a press entry to Doncaster Rovers' former home at Belle Vue, for a grim fourth-tier match. I had to make several telephone calls to establish my identity and eventually gain admittance, leaving me to conclude that it would have been easier to blag my way in to the FA Cup Final at Wembley. And there was another occasion when I forgot where I had parked the car, while attending a match at Gillingham's Priestfield Stadium.

But for Holland, who only missed one league game (because of international duty) in six full seasons with Town between 1997 and 2003, and chalked up 49 caps for Republic of Ireland, his own particular 'embarrassing' day was at Bolton Wanderers, just five days

Dejection for Town as they concede yet another goal during their damaging 4-1 defeat at Bolton Wanderers in 2002. (WP)

before his 28th birthday. George Burley's Town had really needed to win the match to have a fighting chance of avoiding relegation out of the Premier League but they ended up capitulating in dismal fashion, hammered 4-1, a result which helped to guarantee Bolton's own top-flight status.

I must say that, despite the stunning exterior of Bolton's current home, which they moved to in 1997 after a 102-year stay at Burnden Park, I have always regarded the Reebok Stadium (later Macron Stadium, now University of Bolton Stadium) as one of my 'least favourite' grounds. Much of that has to do with the depressing visit in the spring of 2002 when Town were utterly outplayed by Sam Allardyce's Bolton. I hated the whole experience, from high up in the press box on the West Stand looking down on Town's dire performance, and I didn't exactly relish the prospect of chasing up a post-match interview with one of the players.

Fortunately, a forlorn Holland, ever the gentleman, obliged, and he did not hold back. 'I think I can honestly say that this was the most embarrassing defeat of my career,' confirmed Holland. 'It was perhaps not the worst performance, but the most embarrassing. It's not as if we were playing Manchester United! It was a must-win game for us, and we weren't good enough. You can say that Bolton had four shots and scored four goals, but the table does not lie.'

Fredi Bobic had scored after only two minutes to put Town on the back foot, and by the 40-minute mark they might as well have been back on the away team coach. They trailed 4-0, German striker Bobic completing a hat-trick and classy French attacker Youri Djorkaeff scoring the other. Jamie Clapham netted a very late consolation.

The Reebok press box was a lonely place that evening for us travelling hacks. It's never easy having to write a gloomy post-match piece after a heavy defeat, especially one that had effectively consigned a club to relegation. True, Town were still only two points adrift of fourth-from-bottom Blackburn, but they had played two more games and, more to the point, three of their last four matches were against Arsenal, Liverpool and Manchester United.

The Football League beckoned.

It was another ten years before Town would be back at the Reebok Stadium, which I could describe as a 'saving grace'. But that would be far too harsh on a stadium that is still one of the most attractive sights in the English footballing world, with its eye-catching, bowl-shaped design, topped by spectacular tubular steel supports with diamond-shaped floodlights at each sweeping bend of the curve. Gleaming white, it still has that futuristic look as you approach from the M61, especially if you are travelling at night. Inspired by Huddersfield Town's Kirklees Stadium, opened just three years earlier in 1994, the resemblance is striking.

Sited at a retail park in Horwich, several miles outside Bolton town centre, it can be a long wait trying to get out of the car park at the end of the game. But by the time I had written Town's Premier League epitaph, that car park was virtually empty.

82 BLUNDELL PARK

Club: Grimsby Town
Founded: 1878 (as Grimsby Pelham)
Ground: Blundell Park (since 1899)
First visit: 8 October 2002; Grimsby 3 Ipswich 0

Blundell Park, the Cleethorpes-based home of Grimsby Town, is not always the most appealing of places to visit on a cold evening in October, and there was certainly a chill wind blowing through the press box on my first visit, on 8 October 2002.

In general, I have quite enjoyed the odd trip up to north-east Lincolnshire to report on football at this much-maligned ground, despite Blundell Park having regularly been included in lists of 'worst grounds in the Football League' by away supporters and neutrals alike.

I've always been enchanted by its unusual setting, adjacent to the Humber Estuary, tucked away among rows of terraced houses and with a railway line squeezed between the back of the stadium (just off Harrington Street) and the River Humber. I usually arrive early, mainly because street parking is the only option, and walk over a bridge spanning the railway line to have a stroll along the promenade beside Cleethorpes Beach, looking out over the estuary towards Spurn Point on the north bank, in the East Riding of Yorkshire, and the North Sea beyond.

Town boss George Burley looks on glumly as his side slump to a 3-0 defeat at Grimsby in 2002. Three days later and Burley exited Portman Road. (WP)

Perhaps I'm seeking literary inspiration for the afternoon or evening ahead? Or maybe I'm just blowing away the cobwebs after a frustrating drive through rural Lincolnshire, stuck behind tractors with their heavily laden trailers on the A17? Either way, if you can avoid the copious amounts of dog excrement that often plague this part of Cleethorpes, then a pre-match walk along the Humber Estuary can do wonders for the spirit. Alternatively, there's always the option of fish and chips. In fact, if you are going to eat a portion of cod and chips, or haddock and chips, before any game anywhere in the country, then it might as well be in close proximity to Blundell Park. Grimsby used to boast the largest and busiest fishing port in the world, back in the middle of the 20th century, and it still serves the best fish supper in the land.

Estuary strolls and fish suppers aside, there was nothing that could inspire George Burley's Ipswich Town on my first visit to Blundell Park. Already struggling at the wrong end of the First Division table, following relegation the previous season, and with the club destined to enter administration just five months hence, the 'straw that broke the camel's back' was a miserable 3-0 defeat at a desperately poor Grimsby on a bleak October evening.

Town's travelling press, me included, had an inkling that the end was nigh for manager Burley. Two down inside 20 minutes through an early opener by Steve Kabba and a penalty by Alan Pouton, woeful Ipswich never recovered and Crystal Palace loanee Kabba added his second and the Mariners' third on the hour.

Fortunately for me, sitting in the back row of the cramped press box in the Main Stand, with its low, over-hanging roof, I had a dreadful view of the debacle unfolding before me on the pitch. I had to crouch down to see across to the far touchline, below the roof line. Burley tried to put on a brave face during the post-match press interviews but it was to prove his last game in charge. He was sacked just three days later with Town down in 19th spot.

A defeat at Blundell Park is not the way that any manager would like to sign off, though a manager's exit is rarely a happy occasion. Eight years before, it had been Burley's own choice to leave Colchester United on Christmas Eve 1994 to become the new boss at neighbours Ipswich. It proved the right decision (though it created work for me, on Christmas Day!), the Scotsman eventually propelling Town into the Premier League and into the UEFA Cup. Just 18 months before the ill-fated trip to Blundell Park, Town had finished fifth in the top flight, and as little as ten months previously they had been playing at the San Siro against Inter Milan in the third round of the UEFA Cup.

Following the announcement of Burley's departure, Town chairman David Sheepshanks declared, 'He [Burley] is a man of honour and integrity and his many skills will no doubt lead to further opportunities and successes in his managerial career.' That proved correct, with Burley going on to manage the likes of Derby County, Hearts, Southampton and the Scotland national team.

Grimsby finished the 2002/03 season rock-bottom of the old First Division, with just nine wins all term, but Town picked up to finish just one place outside the play-offs under new boss Joe Royle.

That first visit to Blundell Park set the bar very low for me in terms of expectations, and since then my return trips have been more pleasant, although I have yet to report on an away league victory. Town have not been back since Burley's demise but I have accompanied Colchester United a few times, with just the odd point scrambled, here and there. I had better luck with Braintree Town in a National League play-off semi-final first leg in 2016. The Iron won 1-0, but lost the second leg 2-0 at Cressing Road with Grimsby going on to regain their Football League status with a 3-1 win over Forest Green Rovers in the play-off final.

The ground has not changed much. A small central section of the Main Stand remains from the original structure, built on the north side in 1901, and it is often claimed that this is one of the oldest surviving stands in the country. There are lots of red supporting pillars to impede the views, together with the low roof. Behind the stand is a separate press lounge, where a cold buffet is usually available, very welcome, especially if the wind is blowing off the estuary. Opposite is the bigger (in terms of height) former Barrett's Stand, which is very narrow but has two tiers, including a big upper tier, although the stand only runs three quarters of the length of the pitch straddling the halfway line. Two of its sponsored names, Findus and Young's, reflect the town's fishing heritage.

And it seems apt to end this Blundell Park chapter on the subject of fish. French midfielder Thomas Pinault, on leaving the Mariners after just one season, 2004/05, couldn't resist giving his view of the town of Grimsby. He said, 'Grimsby was a really bad place to live. The town was really old and there wasn't much to do there. It was full of fishermen and it smelled of fish all the time.'

I mention this because the previous season I had paid my second visit to Blundell Park, to report on Colchester United's 2-0 defeat on 18 October 2003, and it just so happened that Pinault played the full 90 minutes in the U's midfield that day. Clearly, the experience wasn't fishy enough to deter him from signing for the Mighty Mariners the following summer.

83 ANFIELD

Club: Liverpool
Founded: 1892
Ground: Anfield (built 1884, Liverpool moved in, in 1892)
First visit: 4 December 2002; Liverpool 1 Ipswich 1 (Liverpool won 5-4 on penalties)

A remote guest house, a late night and a penalty shoot-out featured on my first visit to the press box at Anfield, the home of Liverpool, in early December 2002.

My first visit to Anfield was actually back in the late 1970s, when I was in my early teens. Friends of the family on Merseyside had secured tickets to a reserves fixture, which was more glamorous than it possibly sounded. We had passes to the VIP lounge, where

On the touchline at Anfield in 2002, with Liverpool assistant manager Phil Thompson, left, alongside Town boss Joe Royle. (WP)

we could inspect the impressive trophy cabinet, and I also bumped into England and Liverpool centre-half Phil Thompson, who was then in his prime. Or did he bump into me? Thompson was the club captain from 1978 to 1981, succeeding Emlyn Hughes and preceding Graeme Souness. Certainly, the bump meant more to me than it did to him.

Anfield captured my imagination that day, as an easily-impressed teenager, even though the stadium was virtually empty for the second-string fixture. The place was very modest compared to the present-day Anfield, with the exception of the world-famous Kop, a mighty terrace first built in 1906 and extended in 1928 with the addition of a roof and boasting 100 steps. This immense structure loomed over Walton Beck Road, which ran behind that end. Even the famous 15-foot high cast iron Shankly Gates, with the 'You'll Never Walk Alone' sign inscribed on top of them, had yet to be erected. The great man (Shankly was Liverpool manager for 15 years) died in 1981 and the gates were opened the following summer.

Greater changes kicked in during the 1990s. I was in the away end, the Anfield Road Stand, for Town's thunderous FA Cup fifth round replay in 1993 which saw Steve McManaman net an extra-time winner for Liverpool in a 3-2 victory. The Kemlyn Road Stand, opposite the Main Stand, had been rebuilt the previous year, while the Kop became a one-tier all-seater a year later, in 1994. The intimate feel of the ground has always remained, though, with the stands very close to the pitch and the stadium completely enclosed with the corners filled in, helping to create a deafening wall of sound.

There was a time when rarely a year went by without Ipswich paying a visit to Anfield. The two clubs rubbed shoulders in the top flight for most of the 1960s, 1970s and the first half of the 1980s, right up until the 1985/86 season when Liverpool were crowned First Division champions and Town were relegated into the second flight, along with Birmingham and West Brom.

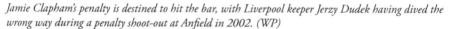

Jamie Clapham's penalty is destined to hit the bar, with Liverpool keeper Jerzy Dudek having dived the wrong way during a penalty shoot-out at Anfield in 2002. (WP)

Town's trips to Anfield have been few and far between since then, with just eight visits over more than three decades, three of them in cup competitions. At the start of the 2019/20 season the two clubs started further apart than ever before. Buoyant Liverpool, fresh from being crowned Champions League winners, went on to lift the Premier League title, while Town endured life two divisions below the Reds, in the third tier, for the first time in 62 seasons.

Back in December 2002 I was on post-match quotes duty again, with *EADT* sports editor Tony Garnett composing the main match report for a League Cup fourth round replay. Given that it was a midweek game, we had decided to book in to a guest house, which I seemed to recall was situated in the middle of nowhere. I think it may have been close to the infamous Saddleworth Moor (an hour's drive away), but I could be mistaken.

True to form, as with all long-distance away cup replays, at least the ones you hoped and prayed would finish after 90 minutes with a positive result, this one went into extra time. That's not to say it wasn't exciting. There were thrills and spills, all great value under the Anfield lights, and the upshot was a 1-1 draw and a penalty shoot-out.

Back in the second tier after relegation the previous season, Town were in dreamland when German defender Markus Babbel passed the ball straight to midfielder Tommy Miller, who duly tucked home past keeper Jerzy Dudek on 14 minutes for 1-0 to Town. Alas, Senegalese front-runner El Hadj Diouf saved Liverpool's blushes by equalising in the second half, and then scored the vital penalty in a 5-4 shoot-out success after Jamie Clapham had missed for Town, his spot-kick crashing off the bar.

By the time that Mr Garnett had penned his match report, and I had scrambled together some quotes from the respective managers, Town boss Joe Royle and Liverpool's relieved Gerard Houllier, it was past 11pm when we finally left Anfield.

'Ipswich made life very difficult for us,' admitted Houllier, who had opted to select error-prone Dudek in goal that night, despite the Polish keeper having blundered twice against Manchester United in the previous match just three days earlier, dropping the ball at the feet of Diego Forlan for the opener in a 2-1 Anfield defeat. 'If you fall off your bike, it's best to get back on as soon as possible. It's a therapy,' insisted Houllier to the hoards of press.

Dudek's presence in goal was the main story for the national hacks that night, but for Mr Garnett and myself, we needed to 'get on our bike' (or rather into the company car) after overcoming the pressures of beating newspaper deadlines to find our accommodation, somewhere on the moors. There were many questions that needed answering.

Would Mr Garnett find our guest house without the aid of a sat-nav in the dead of the night? Would the proprietor still be awake? Would the front door be locked, chained and bolted? More to the point, would there be a bar?

It was a worrying journey.

Fortunately, the answer to all of these questions, except the one about the front door, was 'yes'! We did get in and, despite the bitter taste of a Town defeat (although it was a 'glorious' defeat), we did enjoy a beer.

A few months later, Liverpool lifted the League Cup at Cardiff's Millennium Stadium, Dudek exorcising his demons with some brilliant saves in a 2-0 win over Manchester United. Town, by contrast, were by then stuck in administration, counting the cost of the previous year's relegation.

Town, and indeed myself, have yet to return to Anfield.

84 EDGELEY PARK

Club: Stockport County
Founded: 1883 (as Heaton Norris Rovers)
Ground: Edgeley Park (since 1902, built in 1901)
First visit: 1 February 2003; Stockport 1 Colchester 1

I have always relished a visit to Edgeley Park, which usually starts with a walk around nearby Sykes Reservoir (popular with fishermen) and Alexandra Park, before indulging in a steak pie in the old Main Stand, which was rebuilt in 1936 after a huge fire gutted the former structure the year before, destroying all the club records in the process. The stark exterior of the bulky stand, with its blue-and-white-painted lower half featuring a row of small windows and a red-brick top half, is strangely welcoming. The overall impression is that of an outdated but traditional, community-based stadium. Unfortunately, being located only ten miles from both Manchester United and Manchester City, the club's fanbase has remained limited.

The 1990s were the dream decade for hosts Stockport County, so I was a latecomer when visiting for the first time on the first day of February 2003. It was a year after the club had celebrated 100 years at Edgeley Park, which had originally been built in 1901 as the home of Stockport's rugby league club. The football club moved in the following year, and the rugby league club went bust in 1905.

The Hatters, named after the town's former hat-making industry, enjoyed five seasons in the second tier during the 1990s. I was working in the Portman Road press box on the night of 4 November 1997 when Stockport established a 'new low' for many Ipswich Town fans by recording a 2-0 away win thanks to a couple of late goals from Brett Angell, who was shaped out of the mould of the good old-fashioned centre-forward. A 6ft 4in menace in the air, though never very mobile on the ground, Angell bullied Town's defence with two close-range goals. It was unthinkable. A cloud of depression hung over Portman Road that night, although Stockport were in the middle of a stunning season. They went on to finish eighth that term, the highest position in their history – 28th in the football pyramid – just two places outside the play-offs.

Fast forward to 2003 and I was at Edgeley Park for a third-tier clash on an ice-cold afternoon, although the early-morning snow had cleared. Stockport's best days were behind them – they were to be relegated out of the Football League in 2011, alongside

Edgeley Park, the home of Stockport County.

Lincoln City, after a continuous stay of 106 years – while Colchester United were going in the opposite direction, slowly. The ground was dominated by the impressive two-tiered Cheadle End, a sea of blue seats with the letters SCFC emblazoned on a few white seats. The Railway End opposite was open to the elements, seats having replaced concrete terracing in 2001 (before that, old wooden railway sleepers had acted as the terrace steps). The press box was at the rear of the old Main Stand, which itself was only 75 yards long and so left gaps at both ends.

It felt as though the club's best days were indeed behind them, and for me I have yet to report on a home win in five visits to Edgeley Park, so equating to an unusually fine 'away' record. Perhaps the most likely prospect of a Colchester defeat was on my first visit, because the U's were managerless at the time. Steve Whitton had grudgingly left Layer Road by mutual consent during the week after three and a half years at the helm, leaving his assistant Geraint Williams in caretaker charge.

The U's were in the bottom four, but Stockport, with ex-Sheffield Wednesday favourite Carlton Palmer on the hot-seat, were only a couple of points better off, having been relegated from the First Division as basement dwellers the previous year.

In the end, home striker Luke Beckett was to take centre stage during a 1-1 draw which saw Joe Keith rescue a point for the Essex visitors with an 88th-minute equaliser. Outgoing U's boss Whitton had tried to sign Beckett the previous season, so it was ironic that he should stab home a 36th-minute opener in front of a nervy Edgeley Park faithful. It was his 24th goal of the season. And yet Beckett, who went on to play for Sheffield United and Huddersfield, then proceeded to squander chance after chance to kill off Colchester, so enabling Keith to bundle home a late equaliser.

After the match, Stockport boss Palmer revealed, 'Luke has been magnificent for us this season, and he's in tears in the dressing room because he could have scored five today.'

By contrast, U's caretaker Williams was a happy man, 'It meant a lot to me, to get this draw. I didn't really feel any pressure. I've been in football all my life and I know that one day you'll get the sack. I hope I get an interview for the job.'

Ex-Ipswich midfielder Williams didn't land the job this time around. It went to Phil Parkinson instead, with Williams staying on as assistant. But the Welshman's patience was rewarded with the manager's job in 2006, by which time the U's had reached the Championship. As for County, they were beaten by the visiting U's at Edgeley Park in the two following seasons, and were eventually relegated to League Two in 2005, the National League in 2011, and National League North in 2013.

Needless to say, I haven't had the chance to walk around Sykes Reservoir for a few years now, or munch on an Edgeley Park meat pie. More's the pity.

But I haven't given up hope of a return.

85 WHADDON ROAD

Club: Cheltenham Town
Founded: 1887
Ground: Whaddon Road (since 1932, built in 1927)
First visit: 22 February 2003; Cheltenham 1 Colchester 1

The view from the Whaddon Road press box, just over a mile to the north-east of Cheltenham town centre, is one of the best in the Football League. From the small press box, tucked away at the back of one corner of the Main Stand and accessible via a small flight of steps, you can see the Cotswold Hills on the horizon with the tops of trees poking above the small all-seater Wymans Road Stand opposite, and also the Prestbury Road End terrace and Whaddon Road Stand at either end. That view takes in Cleeve Hill, which overlooks the town and is the highest point in Gloucestershire, at 1,083 feet (330 metres).

The ground, home to Cheltenham Town since 1932, is small but compact, smart but unobtrusive, low-rise but close to the pitch, a blend of three new stands and an older Main Stand, a mixture of seating and terracing. It has a non-league feel, not surprising given that the capacity is only 7,000 and that the Robins have indeed spent most of their life outside the Football League.

Cheltenham is a popular place for a weekend break, a spa town famous for its Regency architecture, quaint cafes and restaurants, neat gardens and Grade I-listed buildings. I have indulged in a short stay with my wife on one of the few occasions that Colchester United have visited. She said 'yes' to a weekend in Cheltenham, and yet 'no' to Oldham, Accrington and Middlesbrough. Strange that.

Whaddon Road, not one of those Grade I-listed buildings, had to wait patiently for league football, 67 years in total until Steve Cotterill masterminded the club's promotion from the Conference in 1998/99. That was the same Steve Cotterill who, as Burnley boss

Gareth Williams celebrates with his caretaker manager Geraint Williams after netting an equaliser at Whaddon Road in 2003. (WP)

seven years later in 2006, accused Colchester of riding out of town wearing sombreros after stealing a 2-1 victory at Turf Moor. Cotterill left Whaddon Road for Stoke City after guiding the Robins into the third tier for the first time in their history via the play-offs in 2002.

This was when Colchester made their first return to Whaddon Road, since the two clubs were together for one season in the Conference, 1990/91. The Cotswolds club were relegated at the end of that campaign, and they suffered the same fate at Second Division level in 2002/03, despite remaining unbeaten in three clashes with the U's. Two 1-1 league draws sandwiched a 4-1 win in the Football League Trophy.

Like at Stockport three weeks before, 41-year-old Geraint Williams was in caretaker charge of the U's for their visit to Whaddon Road, and his namesake Gareth Williams was to give him a timely boost by netting the equaliser in a 1-1 draw, albeit against hosts who were propping up the table. It was Gareth's first goal for the club since his loan switch from Crystal Palace, rifling home from just inside the box after Julian Alsop's close-range headed goal inside two minutes. The U's players had shown their support for caretaker boss Geraint, who was to be interviewed for the full-time post the following day, by running over to celebrate Gareth's goal by the dugout.

As a footnote, Geraint was back in his former role of assistant manager following Phil Parkinson's unveiling as the new boss just three days later. Flame-haired striker Gareth, meanwhile, went on to score a hat-trick in Parkinson's first match in charge the following weekend, a 4-1 win over Port Vale, but that was probably a career highlight for the 20-year-old. He did sign a permanent deal from Palace in the summer but within two years he had dropped into non-league, primarily with Bromley.

The view from the main stand at Whaddon Road looking towards the Cotswold Hills. (CM)

My return trips to Whaddon Road have all been relaxed affairs. Football tends to take a back seat in these parts, behind horse racing, jazz, literature and even croquet (Cheltenham has the largest and oldest croquet club in Great Britain, and is the HQ of the national croquet association). Football reporters rarely flock to Cheltenham so it's a pleasant way to spend a Saturday afternoon, even though the press box can feel a little stuffy. The Main Stand, built in 1963, is a favourite of mine, straddling the halfway line with narrow terraces in front, in the Tunnel and Paddock enclosures, and open corners at either end.

And then there's always the mighty bulk of Cleeve Hill, the highest stretch of the Cotswolds, to marvel at if the football is not up to scratch. I've walked the Cotswold Way as a youngster, and run the Cheltenham parkrun (at nearby Pittville Park) in more recent times, but I have yet to wield a croquet mallet in malice, or empty my bank account on Gold Cup day at Cheltenham Festival.

Maybe one day.

86 HILLSBOROUGH

Club: Sheffield Wednesday
Founded: 1867 (as The Wednesday)
Ground: Hillsborough (since 1899)
First visit: 15 March 2003; Sheffield Wednesday 0 Ipswich 1

Every football reporter has a few 'lucky' grounds, and for me Hillsborough, the home of Sheffield Wednesday since 1899, is one of them. I love the stadium, which just sneaks into the top dozen biggest football stadiums in England, for its sheer beauty as well as its sheer size, hovering close to the banks of the River Don, a good three miles from the Sheffield city centre. It's a cracking venue to watch football, and furthermore, Hillsborough has treated me to some wonderful away successes over the years, both for Ipswich Town and Colchester United.

My first visit coincided with a Town 1-0 win in March 2003, and I returned with the Suffolk club seven years later for another 1-0 success. Even more remarkable, three of my first four trips with unfashionable Colchester United ended in victory against distinguished hosts who have lifted four top-tier titles and three FA Cups during their illustrious history. So, all in all, Hillsborough has been a home from home for me, gazing down from the press box in the main South Stand, the oldest stand in the ground dating to 1915, a complete contrast to my miserable record just four miles south at Bramall Lane, which ironically used to be the home of The Wednesday.

It is certainly worth tracing the club's early history.

One of the oldest football clubs in the world, The Wednesday were founded in 1867 and were founder members of the Football Alliance in 1889, an alternative to the

Craig Fagan opens the scoring for the U's during their 3-0 win at Hillsborough on the opening day of the 2004/05 campaign. (WP)

Football League, which was founded the previous year. The Wednesday were the inaugural champions, in the same division as clubs like Grimsby Town, Stoke, Lincoln City and Nottingham Forest, although the Football Alliance only lasted three years. The Wednesday duly joined the Football League in 1892 and changed their name to Sheffield Wednesday in 1929, by which time they had already been based at Hillsborough for 30 years.

They had been tenants at the aforementioned Bramall Lane during much of the 1880s but moved to Olive Grove in 1887 after turning professional. When another new home was required, due to the expansion of railway lines around Olive Grove, a new site was earmarked at the village of Owlerton, which although now a north-west suburb of the city of Sheffield, was at the time several miles outside the Sheffield city boundaries.

The ten-acre site was part of the Hillsborough House estate, and was effectively a meadow full of dandelions, so much work was needed to level the ground and erect a couple of stands. One of them was transported from their old Olive Grove ground, the 2,000-seated stand being rebuilt, brick by brick. This was a forerunner to the current South Stand, which houses the press box and is the largest stand in the stadium. The other stand had 3,000 seats and was swiftly built in time for the start of the first season.

The ground has undergone several facelifts over the decades, but its distinct character has remained, squeezed between the River Don (south and west), terraced houses (to the north) and the busy dual carriageway of the A61 Peninstone Road (to the east), bound for the city centre. The main entrance is close to the river, which is now spanned by a bridge connecting the football club to Parkside Road, while the massive Spion Kop, which at one time could claim to to have the largest bank of covered end terrace in the country, finally got that roof in 1986 and became all-seater by 1993. Opposite the South Stand lies the equally impressive North Stand, which was only the second stand in the country to have a cantilever roof, built in 1961. The first was at Scunthorpe United's Old Showground. The Leppings Lane End, the scene of the terrible Hillsborough disaster of 1989, when 96 Liverpool fans lost their lives as a result of crushing on a packed terrace at an FA Cup semi-final against Nottingham Forest, is a two-tier structure built in the early 1960s. It became all-seater by 1992.

My first visit, on 15 March 2003, produced an away win which, admittedly, was not all that surprising, although it did delight the long-suffering Ipswich supporters in the Leppings Lane End. I described Sheffield Wednesday as 'fallen giants' on the back page of the following Monday morning's newspaper, an apt description for a club rock bottom of the First Division with just six wins from 37 matches. Skipper Matt Holland led by example, heading home a 17th-minute 1-0 winner for Joe Royle's Ipswich, leaving his team just one place outside the play-offs although still a distant five points from that all-important top six.

'If we keep winning matches, then the others will come back to us,' insisted Holland. 'Sheffield Wednesday are fighting for their lives, so we knew at some point they would come at us. They put us under a little pressure.'

Town ended up missing out on the play-offs by just one place, while the Owls, with Chris Turner in charge, improved a little but were still relegated to the third tier, along with Grimsby and Brighton.

The following year, I twice re-visited Hillsborough with Colchester United, and amazingly on both counts Phil Parkinson's side recorded wins. Ex-West Ham trainee Joe Keith was the hero of a 1-0 victory on 24 April 2004, chipping a 20-yarder into the roof of the net early in the second half to sink Wednesday, who had been gracing the Premier League just four years earlier. Left-sided specialist Keith enthused, 'Of all the places to score, this was the best. Scoring here will be a treasured memory.' His manager Parkinson agreed, 'I never got to play here myself, so I'm a bit jealous of my players!'

Just over three months later, on the opening day of the following 2004/05 season, the U's kicked off with another eye-catching win at Hillsborough, this time a 3-0 success via three goals inside the last five minutes. A crowd of more than 24,000 were silenced by goals from Craig Fagan, Sam Stockley with a 25-yard bullet, and another Joe Keith special, this time a curling free kick. 'Silenced' was not entirely accurate. While some home fans stood up and left the ground after full-back Stockley's 88th-minute second, a few others began a chorus of 'sack the board', a chant you don't hear very often on the first day of a new season.

'No doubt the U's would love to play at Hillsborough every weekend' – that was the main thread of my match report in Monday's newspaper.

And to cement my 'lucky' ground tag, I was back at Hillsborough in February 2010 to report on one of Town's best goals scored under manager Roy Keane, a sweet long-range rocket from Carlos Edwards in a hardy-fought, scrappy 1-0 away win. The unpredictable Keane, always one to catch journalists, fans and even the opposition off guard with some surprise team selections, rung the changes and a previously out-of-sorts Edwards, back in the side, cracked home a 20-yarder on 15 minutes to celebrate his first goal in nearly three years.

Ex-Hull and Bradford City striker Dean Windass, in his role as a football pundit on Sky TV, apparently dismissed this Championship relegation scrap as being the 'worst match' he had ever seen.

A bit harsh, I thought. I had seen a lot worse.

87 NENE PARK

Club: Rushden & Diamonds
Founded: 1992 (dissolved in 2011)
Ground: Nene Park (built in 1969, revamped from 1992)
First visit: 22 November 2003; Rushden & Diamonds 4 Colchester 0

Chalk and cheese. From a first Hillsborough visit to a first Nene Park visit just eight months later; the once mighty Sheffield Wednesday, dripping in rich history stretching back to the 1860s, to the little-known Rushden & Diamonds, with a history dating back just 11 years;

Manager Brian Talbot, the ex-Ipswich Town midfielder, watches his Rushden & Diamonds side thump the U's 4-0 at Nene Park in 2003. (WP)

from a giant stadium with four towering stands accustomed to holding crowds of 30,000-plus, to a miniature home of four small stands incapable of even housing 6,500 spectators. Different worlds, Football League extremes. And yet, while the giants (the Owls) were on the slide, the minnows (the Diamonds), at least for a while, were on the rise.

Those extremes existed on a personal level as well. Basking in regular away-day glory at Hillsborough, my one experience of a Football League fixture at Nene Park ended in crushing failure.

This was the pinnacle of Rushden & Diamonds' success. Formed in 1992 as a merger between Irthlingborough Diamonds and Rushden Town, the Northamptonshire-based club made rapid progress up the non-league pyramid, winning three promotions inside four years to leap from the Southern League Midland Division (Step 4) to the Conference (Step 1). Bankrolled by local businessman Max Griggs, the owner of footwear company Dr Marten's, the Diamonds' forward momentum continued with promotion to the Second Division as Third Division champions in 2003, which led to my first short trip along the A14 to Nene Park in the late autumn, on the coat-tails of high-flying Colchester United.

Nene Park might have been small but it was very smart, close to the busy A6 and on the banks of the River Nene. Crowds averaged a little over 300 during the Diamonds' debut season of 1992/93, when they were plying their trade in the Southern League, but by the height of their powers, in their only campaign at third tier level – 2003/04 – that season average reached an all-time high of 4,457.

The old ground, opened in 1969 when home to Irthlingborough Diamonds, was completely overhauled at a cost of £30m when the new club was formed. The old South Stand, together with the old dressing rooms and clubhouse was demolished to make way for a new 1,000-seater stand, with a new pitch laid, new floodlights installed and the Diamond Centre built, all duly opened by the Prince of Wales in 1995.

I sat in the press box, which itself had shifted during the 1990s boom to a more easterly point in the North Stand to make way for some new corporate boxes, fully expecting a Colchester win. The U's had won their last six matches to sit in the Second Division play-off zone, while Brian Talbot's Rushden had lost their last three, and also exited two cup competitions.

Instead, though, the visitors were dealt a blow by striker Craig Fagan's red card for violent conduct just before the half-hour mark, and shipped goals at regular intervals to be thrashed 4-0. The U's were completely outplayed, and were indebted to keeper Simon Brown for maintaining an air of respectability to the scoreline. The Diamonds' first three goals, scored by 6ft 3in Jamaican striker Onandi Lowe, a real handful all afternoon, plus ex-Celtic defender Stuart Gray and club stalwart Andy Burgess, were all netted from inside the six-yard box. Defender Marcus Bignot volleyed home a late fourth.

'Everything that could go wrong, did go wrong,' rued manager Phil Parkinson. 'I had already spoken to Craig [Fagan] about discipline this season.' Rushden boss Talbot, the former Ipswich and Arsenal midfielder who was in his sixth year at the helm at Nene Park, enthused, 'We have done a professional job on Colchester.'

Yet Talbot, who became the first player to win the FA Cup with two different clubs in successive years, with Ipswich in 1978 and Arsenal in 1979, was also mindful of his club's uncertain future, with long-term backer Briggs having recently announced his intention to sell the club and its Nene Park site. Talbot said, 'For the moment, our main aim is to survive as a club, and we want to survive as a Second Division club.'

Unfortunately, Talbot's hopes were to be dashed. He himself left in March 2004 as a bleak set of results over the winter period saw the Diamonds eventually suffer relegation. Seven years later, back in non-league, the club was dissolved.

Nene Park had a stay of execution. Kettering Town played there for 18 months, though by then it looked a sorry state with some parts of the ground shut down. I visited with Braintree Town for a midweek Conference clash in October 2011, and couldn't even buy a beer or a cup of tea due to the closure of the refreshment stalls.

Nene Park's glory days were gone, and the stadium was finally demolished in 2017.

88 CROWN GROUND

Club: Accrington Stanley
Founded: 1968
Ground: Crown Ground (since 1968)
First visit: 3 January 2004; Accrington 0 Colchester 0

There are few more exposed terraces in the Football League than the Coppice End at the Crown Ground, the home of Accrington Stanley since the club was reformed in 1968. Up to 1,800 away supporters can be accommodated on this uncovered terrace, with fields and hills stretching into the distance. A great view, at the western edge of the Pennines, but if its mid-winter and freezing cold, or perhaps raining cats and dogs, then it can be a real test for any travelling fan.

The Crown Ground (516 feet) is the fourth highest Football League ground in the country, behind The Hawthorns, Boundary Park, and Vale Park, and it does feel like it among the surrounding hills. Opposite the press box, the very name of the old Whinney Hill terrace seemed to encapsulate the mood of the stadium. Known as 'The Cowshed', it ran along the length of the pitch on the lower slopes of the Winney Hill, a massive waste and recycling landfill site. There was a small three-row terrace, with some seating behind, although the roof only extended for two thirds of the stand, leaving the corners open. Although since replaced by a plush new stand, the tidy-looking Eric Whalley Stand, the old structure was still in place on my first visit, as was the uncovered Clayton End which, like the Coppice End, featured open terracing. The Clayton End was eventually topped with a roof in 2007/08 and seats added.

That familiar non-league feel, so common among the older, smaller grounds in the Football League, was not only all-pervading on my first visit, it was also very true.

The open Coppice End, accommodating 100 or so U's fans at the Crown Ground, with photographer Warren Page taking a picture in the foreground. (CM)

Accrington Stanley were still a non-league club when I ventured up to this corner of Lancashire in the early days of 2004, a northern outpost trying to scramble out of the Conference and gain the Football League status which had been enjoyed by the original Accrington Stanley from 1921 to 1962, before that club had eventually folded four seasons later.

Encircled by many 'bigger' clubs, likes Blackburn Rovers (eight miles to the west), Burnley (nine miles to the east), Preston (15 miles to the west), Rochdale (15 miles to the south) and the two big clubs in Manchester, it's no wonder that Stanley have always struggled to attract more than a very modest fanbase, but the Crown Ground can still create a lively atmosphere, as was the case when Colchester United visited for a hiding-to-nothing FA Cup tie at the start of 2004. There was no press lounge – there still isn't one, I believe – and the narrow press area is very cramped, or cosy, depending on your point of view, but that adds to the Accrington experience.

Like many others of my generation, I had grown up watching the TV adverts for milk from the late 1980s and early 1990s, where a couple of young Liverpool supporters discussed the merits of drinking milk. The suggestion was that if you didn't drink your milk, then you would end up playing football for Accrington Stanley. Not a bad side-effect, you would imagine, but when one of the lads says to the other – 'Who are Accrington Stanley?' – the other one replies in a thick Scouse accent and with a measure of disdain – 'Exactly!'

The advert, though clearly mocking Stanley's low status, didn't seem to do the club any harm. Instead, it boosted its profile. And under long-standing manager John Coleman, who had been appointed in 1999, Stanley were on a roll. They were to secure promotion to the Football League two years after my first visit, but they were already heading in that direction when Phil Parkinson's Colchester United entered the humble surrounds of the Crown Ground. It was a long, cold, murky afternoon, and it felt like the match went on for hours and hours, with the third-tier U's holding on grimly for a 0-0 draw and the consolation of a replay back in Essex.

This was a proper FA Cup tie. Part-time Accrington (they turned professional later that year) were great, urged on by a crowd of more than 4,000. All the ingredients were there for another U's cup flop, following the embarrassing exits at the hands of Gravesend & Northfleet and Bedlington Terriers over the previous ten years, with a bumpy pitch complementing the freezing conditions. Stanley had already disposed of Football League sides Huddersfield Town and Bournemouth in the previous two rounds, and they were thirsting for blood. The Crown Ground was awash with colour (mostly red, with balloons galore) and literally vibrating to the noise of drums, anticipating another cup upset.

It was an enthralling afternoon. There was no way you could tell that the two teams were two divisions apart, as so often happens in an FA Cup leveller. Both sides struck the woodwork, the U's twice and Stanley once, but visiting keeper Simon Brown was the busier of the two custodians. Appropriately, the mist began to descend, sweeping

The U's take on hosts Accrington Stanley, with the visiting fans in the open Coppice End, and the moors beyond. (CM)

in from the West Pennine Moors as the second half dragged on, and on. It certainly felt never-ending if you were connected with Colchester United, especially when Brown produced a wonder save in injury time to prevent former Burnley midfielder (and future Ipswich manager) Paul Cook's header from creeping into the net. If I had not been wedged between my seat and the press table, then I would have been on the edge of my seat. It was suspense all the way as the clock ticked towards 5pm and the temperatures plummeted.

'I'm bitterly disappointed not to have won the match,' declared Stanley manager Coleman. 'I've been a goalscorer all my life, and I'd like to think that I would have scored a goal today.' Meanwhile, U's boss Parkinson was a relieved man when addressing the press. 'Nothing that happened out there this afternoon surprised me. We knew that if we approached this match like we were playing a non-league team, then we would get beaten,' admitted Parkinson.

For the record, the replay back at Layer Road ten days later was even more dramatic, beginning with a 15-minute delay before kick-off due to crowd congestion. Stanley felt aggrieved to lose a bad-tempered game 2-1, with Joe Keith scoring a brace. They had Stephen Halford sent off in the 86th minute but the ten men halved the deficit through Paul Mullin late on and very nearly forced extra time. Tempers had flared in the narrow players' tunnel at half-time, which saw Stanley boss Coleman banished to the main stand for the second half after an apparent altercation with one of the stewards. 'I found it all quite amazing. I'd never known anything like it,' insisted Coleman.

The Crown Ground had enjoyed a facelift by the time that I returned for my first Football League visits in 2017, with a few extra bright-red seats on show, though the Coppice End was as delightfully open and exposed as always. Colchester were soundly beaten twice, in February and August of that year, and again lost in 2018.

Coleman, who had been back in the hot-seat since 2014, was all smiles on all occasions. Clearly, that former cup clash was all forgotten. 'Exactly!'

89 ST MARY'S STADIUM

Club: Southampton
Founded: 1885 (as St Mary's Young Men's Association)
Ground: St Mary's Stadium (since 2001)
First visit: 27 October 2004; Southampton 3 Colchester 2

A young rookie striker by the name of Dexter Blackstock put a spanner in the works during my first visit to Southampton's impressive new St Mary's Stadium, in late October 2004. Up until 18-year-old Blackstock's appearance, as a half-time substitute, everything about my trip to the Hampshire coast for a League Cup tie with Colchester United had gone swimmingly well.

St Mary's had only been open for three years, since the Saints' move from their long-term home at The Dell, situated less than a mile and a half away, and it looked fantastic from the outside as the U's travelling press corps approached down the Belvidere Road after parking the car down near the docks, albeit in some foul weather. It was a very, very wet evening, and windy as well.

Greg Halford scores for the U's at St Mary's Stadium during an exciting 3-2 cup defeat in 2004.

True, the surrounding area is not the most picturesque, full of industrial premises and various depots along the west bank of the River Itchen. But the 32,000-plus all-seater stadium, built for £32m, looks one of the best in the country, a full bowl-shaped modern structure with a striking white roof and plenty of space around each of the four stands, which are all of the same height and a similar style. It's in the heart of the city, on the site of a disused gas works, appropriately just 700 or so yards away from St Mary's Church, from where the football club originated back in 1885.

Inside, St Mary's is gleaming, a theatre of red and a few white seats. Completely enclosed, with the corners filled in, the atmosphere is excellent even though the stands are some way back from the pitch, which is surrounded by a cinder perimeter track. The press box is well-placed in the main Itchen Stand, named after the nearby river, as is the media suite for post-match interviews. It's a great place to work, and for 45 minutes of my first visit, third-tier Colchester United were on course to topple their Premier League hosts,

Not only was this the U's first visit to St Mary's, it was also the first meeting of the two clubs for 21 years. In fact, the duo had moved in different circles since their time together in the old Third Division in the 1950s, with the exception of a few cup clashes, so midfielder Neil Danns's seventh-minute opener did cause a stir among the Saints faithful, especially as the U's had beaten top-flight West Brom in the previous round.

Enter Blackstock, unleashed from the bench by head coach Steve Wigley for the start of the second half, perhaps in response to the boos ringing around St Mary's at half-time. Within the space of just nine minutes Blackstock had scored twice from point-blank range to put the Saints 2-1 up, and although Greg Halford equalised by sweeping home from Craig Fagan's lay-off, Blackstock completed his hat-trick with a header from Mikael Nilsson's free kick on 80 minutes to seal the Saints' passage into the fourth round of the League Cup.

It was a thrilling cup tie, played on a sodden surface due to all the heavy rain before kick-off, and for Blackstock it was a big statement of intent. These were his first senior goals in what was only his third appearance, although he never really went on to establish himself at Southampton, instead going on to enjoy productive long stays at QPR and Nottingham Forest.

'I really believe that we should have beaten Southampton tonight,' insisted U's boss Phil Parkinson. 'We took a Premier League team to the wire.' First goalscorer Danns, on loan from Blackburn, agreed, 'We absolutely hammered Southampton and yet we ended up losing.'

The Saints ended up finishing rock bottom of the Premier League that season, hence my next visit to St Mary's three years later was for a Championship showdown on a Friday night in March 2007. This ended up being a glorious night for the U's, but a nightmarish evening for one of their former managers, George Burley, who was in the St Mary's hot-seat. The Essex side won 2-1 courtesy of an early brace of goals from hot shot Jamie Cureton, under the glare of the Sky TV cameras.

True, the U's were indebted to some fine saves by keeper Dean Gerken that night – it was a much milder and drier evening than the League Cup clash of three years ago – but that simply made the win, and a league double over the Saints, all the sweeter for Geraint Williams's side and their away fans who loved every minute of it from their lofty position in the Northam Stand. In the build-up to the match, Cureton had revealed to me that he had set a new target of 20 goals for the season, which neatly filled a page in the paper. In fact, the ex-Norwich striker ended up exceeding that target by winning the Championship Golden Boot with 23 goals. Burley did go on to guide the Saints to the play-offs that season but they lost out to another of his former clubs, Derby County, in the semi-finals.

I didn't have quite such a fun time on a later return visit to the south coast with Roy Keane's Ipswich Town for an FA Cup fourth round tie on 23 January 2010.

The Saints, FA Cup winners in 1976 under Lawrie McMenemy, built up a two-goal lead against the 1978 FA Cup winners thanks to a sensational 25-yard strike from Wayne Thomas, and a second-half goal from substitute Michail Antonio, on loan from Reading and soon-to-be a loanee at Colchester. At least Town's travelling supporters, who numbered 3,300 that mild January afternoon, were treated to a barnstorming finish from their side. Pablo Couñago halved the deficit in the last minute of normal time and nearly equalised in injury time, but Alan Pardew's League One hosts held on for a 2-1 win.

As an aside, 38-year-old Keane disclosed in the pre-match build-up that he had no recollection of Ipswich Town's FA Cup success of 1978. 'I was six or seven when Ipswich won the FA Cup, so I don't remember it, but I keep being reminded of 1978 now I'm here!' said a smiling Keane.

I guess that meant Southampton's 1976 triumph also passed him by.

90 VALLEY PARADE

Club: Bradford City
Founded: 1903
Ground: Valley Parade (since 1903, built in 1886)
First visit: 6 November 2004; Bradford 2 Colchester 2

It pays to be physically fit when visiting Valley Parade, the home of Bradford City since the club was founded in 1903 after the Manningham rugby league club switched codes to association football. The stadium was hacked out of a steep hillside in the mid-1880s, which means some steep walking and climbing of steps, especially for away fans in the Bradford Road End, the oldest part of the ground. I guess the clue is in the title – Valley Parade.

My first visit, in early November 2004, was also Colchester United's first visit for 23 years, and so the U's first appearance at Valley Parade since the terrible stadium fire of 1985 which gutted the main stand and killed 56 fans, with a further 265 injured.

Daniel Pappoe is sent off on his U's debut, but cheekily gives a thumbs up to irate Bradford City manager Phil Parkinson at Valley Parade in 2013. (WP)

These days, the stadium boasts two massive stands, and so is a little top-heavy, with one (west) side and one (north) end towering over the more modest east side and older south end. In a way, the stadium reflects the highs and lows of the club, from the dizzy heights of winning the FA Cup in 1911 and securing promotion to the Premier League in 1999, to scraping the barrel with two spells of going into administration and a series of relegations (2001, 2004 and 2007) taking them down to the fourth tier.

If you can handle the hilly approach then Valley Parade is a rewarding destination, a colourful mix of amber and claret, the unusual club colours of the Bantams which might well have inspired Scottish club Motherwell to later assume that same colour scheme in 1913, just two years after Bradford's FA Cup victory over Newcastle United. Interestingly, club scarves have sold extremely well in recent years, helped by author J.K. Rowling and in particular the house colours of Gryffindor at Harry Potter's Hogwarts School. Described as red and gold, they bear a close resemblance to the claret and amber of Bradford City.

The press box is in the huge Main Stand, which gained a second tier in 2001 and is attached to the equally impressive two-tier Kop by a connecting section in the north-west corner. The view is awesome, almost overshadowing the much smaller single-tier of the Midland Road Stand opposite, plus the ageing Bradford Road End, a curious box-like double-decker structure with the top tier slightly overhanging the lower tier.

In five visits, I have yet to report on an away defeat, with a run of four draws. Home favourite Dean Windass and Colchester United's Gavin Johnson traded a brace of goals each in a 2-2 draw on 6 November 2004, but I have clearer memories of another 2-2 draw from nine years later, on 14 September 2013, when Joe Dunne was in his first full season at the U's helm, and former Colchester manager Phil Parkinson was the Bantams' boss.

'What a fantastic game,' comprised my whole opening paragraph for the following Monday's newspaper, which was a short-and-sweet way of describing a League One cracker. Four goals, a Bradford hit-man, a U's debutant goalscorer, and a U's debutant red card.

The 'Bradford hit-man' was Nahki Wells, who plundered a brace to boost his tally to eight goals in the first seven matches of the season; the U's debutant scorer was teenage winger Jeffrey Monkana, who kick-started his loan spell from Preston with a first-half equaliser; and the U's debutant red card was dished out to another loanee, Chelsea's Daniel Pappoe, who was introduced as an 86th-minute substitute and sent off just six minutes later for a rash injury-time challenge on former Colchester winger Mark Yeates.

Talking points galore.

An angry Parkinson, who had clinched promotion to the third tier for Bradford via the play-offs the previous summer, seven years after he had guided Colchester to automatic promotion, blasted, 'Out of nowhere this lad [Pappoe] launched himself. At the time, the way Yeatesy's leg looked from where we were, it looked like he had broken it. It was needless because it had been a great game.'

From the other camp, goalscorer Monkana announced in brief sentences, 'Colchester fans can expect a lot more from me. This is nothing. There's a lot more to come. Hopefully this is the first goal of many.'

So, what did happen, over the next few weeks and months?

Club-wise, the U's officially staved off relegation that season by thrashing already-promoted Brentford 4-1 in their last home match, while Bradford finished in 11th spot at their new level.

Player-wise, Bermudan international Wells went on to score 14 goals in 19 league matches that season before signing for Huddersfield in January for an undisclosed club record fee; the super-confident Monkana didn't score in any of his next eight matches for the U's before returning to Preston and then having an unsuccessful spell at Brighton; and centre-half Pappoe, after his disastrous debut, made just one more appearance for the U's, ironically again as an 86th-minute substitute (against Walsall) before moving on to another loan spell, at Kingstonian, and a career in non-league.

Contrasting fortunes.

And no, I haven't purchased a Bradford City scarf on any of my visits. For the record, I prefer the blue and bronze of Ravenclaw to the red and gold (claret and amber) of Gryffindor.

SECTION FIVE – SECOND HALF OF THE 2000s

91 KC STADIUM (HULL CITY STADIUM)

Club: Hull City
Founded: 1904
Ground: KC Stadium (since 2002, re-named KCOM Stadium in 2016)
First visit: 8 January 2005; Hull 0 Colchester 2

Hull City's home since 2002 is unusual in that it attracts very few critics. In fact, it is very hard to find any criticism or any negative vibes, however slight, surrounding the KC Stadium, renamed and rebranded as the KCOM Stadium in 2016. Nearly every visitor loves it, or at least is impressed by the stadium structure and the parkland setting. Despite its hidden charms, the same could not be said of tumbledown Boothferry Park, the Tigers' previous home for 56 years.

I know the city of Kingston upon Hull reasonably well. My oldest step-son, Jack, went to Hull University for three years, and on my various visits I went to a few sweaty gigs at The Welly, a music venue on Beverley Road, sampled the delights of a few cafes in The Avenues district, had a few drinks down by the marina, and occasionally took part in the Hull parkrun in East Park on a Saturday morning.

But five years before the Hull parkrun was conceived, I paid my first visit to the KC Stadium, in January 2005, to report on Colchester United's eye-catching 2-0 win in an FA Cup third round tie. What was just as eye-catching was the stadium itself, completed just over two years before, in December 2002, at a cost of £44m. It was money well spent, the fruits of a public and private collaboration, with Hull City Council as the owners. Instead of being stuck in an isolated spot on the edge of town near a busy motorway, perhaps with a retail park close by, or alternatively tucked away down an industrial estate surrounded by warehouses and depots, the KC Stadium was built in the parkland setting of West Park and so is flanked by trees, with plenty of paths and footbridges leading to the venue.

Craig Fagan scores during the U's 2-0 win at Hull City in early 2005. (WP)

The bowl-shaped structure is dominated by the West Stand, which has a second tier and so is far bigger than the other three single tier stands. The single tier of seats extend all the way around the ground, a colourful scene of blacks, whites and ambers. Hull City's club colours are black and amber stripes, while Hull FC rugby league club, who also play their home games here, are black and white hoops. The view of the pitch is fantastic, from any seat in the ground, which includes the press box in the slightly curved West Stand, which is topped by an attractive roof that curves upwards.

It's no surprise that the stadium has won awards for its design, though I must confess that on my first visit I felt that bits of the roof were going to fall off in the high winds as I made my way around the outside, searching for the press entrance. In fact, a small section outside the stadium was cordoned off, just in case of any flying debris.

On the pitch, away-day specialists Colchester United completely outplayed the Tigers, progressing into the fourth round of the FA Cup through two goals in two minutes before the half-hour from the strike partnership of Gareth Williams and Craig Fagan. Peter Taylor's side were humiliated, despite being top of League One at the start of the week.

'Colchester beat us in every department,' confessed Taylor. 'We didn't deserve anything today.' U's boss Phil Parkinson, who was to become the Hull manager 18 months later, could not hide his glee, 'That's close to the best display since I've been at the club.'

U's goalscorer Fagan signed for Hull the following month for an undisclosed six-figure fee believed to be about £125,000, and Taylor's men went on to clinch automatic promotion to the Championship that season.

Hull City manager Peter Taylor looks dejected as his side suffer a 2-0 defeat at the hands of the U's in 2005. (WP)

In fact, the KC Stadium proved an ideal backdrop for some unprecedented success at the club. Successive promotions in their first two full seasons at the new venue sparked an upsurge which culminated in a third promotion to the Premier League in 2008.

A first trip with Ipswich Town on 20 November 2010 was a much bleaker affair, both in terms of the result – a 1-0 defeat courtesy of Robert Koren's late 25-yard bullet which was deflected past keeper Brian Murphy – and also the weather, which featured driving rain and darkened skies all afternoon. It was a cold, dismal day, which rather summed up the mood of Town manager Roy Keane and his players following a third Championship defeat on the bounce. But I was used to that, and there was much worse to come in future weeks.

Dismal indeed, but I refuse to criticise the KC Stadium. It is beyond reproach.

92 NATIONAL HOCKEY STADIUM

Club: MK Dons
Founded: 2004 (changing their name from Wimbledon FC)
Ground: National Hockey Stadium (1995 to 2007, football use 2003–2007, demolished 2010)
First visit: 15 January 2005; MK Dons 2 Colchester 0

Aidan Davison is sent off during the U's 1-1 draw at the National Hockey Stadium in late 2005. (WP)

As a football reporter you can go years and years, or even decades, when work never takes you to a particular stadium. It can be 20-plus seasons before, all of a sudden, an obscure cup draw allows you to make that long-awaited trip to a far-off place. But that was not the case for me with regards the National Hockey Stadium, situated beside the central railway station in Milton Keynes. In fact, the opposite applied – I couldn't seem able to avoid it, even if I tried.

The stadium only hosted football for four seasons, and only three of these when the home club was known as Milton Keynes Dons, following a first (and last in the club's history) campaign as Wimbledon FC. And yet in the space of 19 months I visited four times, on each occasion with Colchester United to face MK Dons in two league contests, a Football League Trophy encounter and a League Cup clash. MK Dons moved to their new Stadium MK venue in the summer of 2007, and their old home was left unused and eventually demolished to make way for Network Rail's new headquarters three years later. But by then I felt I knew the National Hockey Stadium rather well.

As a sports stadium originally built with a synthetic surface to host England Hockey, for national and international matches, it is not surprising that the place never felt like football was at its core, especially as the home club, Wimbledon, had experienced a controversial 45-mile move north-westwards from south London to Buckinghamshire, and to a new town established as late as 1967. A grass pitch was laid and the club was rebranded as MK Dons in the summer of 2004.

The green-and-white-seated South Stand, which housed the press box and all the main facilities, was fit for any Football League stadium, that's for sure. It looked appealing from the outside, a pale-brick facade with three towers and a slightly raised slanting top which left a big gap between the stand and the roof. On the opposite side of the pitch squatted an unusual-looking North Stand structure which, when viewed from the side, was a chunky triangular shape with some quite steep rows of seats, topped with a few flag poles. The stand only extended for a third of the pitch straddling the halfway line. Meanwhile, the open West Stand was a temporary structure, with plenty of scaffolding and a row of trees to the rear, while the Cowshed at the other end was covered and had far more character, behind which there was a small herd of concrete cows 'grazing'.

It was an uneasy first visit for me, in mid-January 2005. Photographs of Wimbledon's glory days hung on the walls inside the South Stand, which didn't feel quite right, while on the pitch Colchester United were brushed aside by a lowly MK Dons who had begun the day third from bottom of League One. Early goals from midfielder Ben Harding and striker Wade Small, inside the first 20 minutes, accounted for a comfortable 2-0 home win, aided by some dreadful defending. Harding's goal was particularly bizarre, with U's full-back Sam Stockley taking too long to clear the ball, allowing it to bounce and then jumping too early to head tamely at the feet of Harding to score.

While Danny Wilson's Dons remained in trouble at the wrong end of the League One table, and were to only avoid relegation by the skin of their teeth on goal difference on the final day, U's skipper Wayne Brown confessed that he too feared a relegation scrap. 'Make no mistake about it, we are in a relegation battle,' warned centre-half Brown after the defeat at the National Hockey Stadium. 'The manager and the players know that. We have to hold our hands up when we are not good enough.'

The U's did stay up quite comfortably, in 15th spot, and were back at the National Hockey Stadium, as was I, for two happier visits the following season. A gutsy 1-1 away league draw in August was achieved despite keeper Aidan Davison being sent off for violent conduct after clashing off the ball with home striker Izale McLeod, with the U's 1-0 down on 69 minutes. Left-back Liam Chilvers netted an equaliser ten minutes later, heading home after Greg Halford had flicked on Neil Danns's corner. Then five days before Christmas, second-half goals by Karl Duguid and Danns overturned a 1-0 deficit in a Football League Trophy southern area quarter-final for a 2-1 victory. It was the U's tenth win in their last 11 games.

Gradually, and despite still opposing Wimbledon's controversial switch to Milton Keynes in 2003, I had grown to like the National Hockey Stadium. Guess I am fickle.

93 LIBERTY STADIUM

Club: Swansea City
Founded: 1912 (as Swansea Town)
Ground: Liberty Stadium (since 2005)
First visit: 10 December 2005; Swansea 1 Colchester 1

Although the new Liberty Stadium is located only two miles north of Swansea City's former home at the Vetch Field, there is a world of difference between the two venues. The Vetch was a mixed bag of distinct stands and terraces, seedy and run-down, and wedged between terraced streets, while its successor is bowl-shaped and uniform with four similar shiny stands and a landscaped surrounding area of trees and shrubs. There is room to breathe, away from the city centre and within easy access of the M4.

After 93 years at the Vetch Field, the Swans, plus rugby union club Ospreys, moved to their new ground in the summer of 2005 on the site of Morfa Stadium, an athletics venue which had been built in 1980 on the banks of the River Tawe. A new Morfa Retail Park on the other (east) bank of the river helped to fund the sports stadium. Although modest in size, with a current capacity of just over 21,000, it is gleaming white and pleasing to the eye. That was never the really the case with the Vetch.

Having said that, success has been in short supply on the pitch during my handful of visits. The stadium was less than five months old when I made my first appearance in the comfortable press box in the West Stand, in December 2005, and that remains my highlight in terms of a result, a plucky 1-1 draw for promotion-chasing Colchester United against the then-leaders of League One. On a sensational run of eight straight victories, Phil Parkinson's men saw that sequence ended by Andy Robinson's spectacular equaliser for the Swans, from a free kick, after Chris Iwelumo had netted early on with a right-footed shot past keeper Willy Gueret. Neil Danns had an 85th-minute penalty saved by

Neil Danns has this penalty saved by keeper Willy Gueret during the U's 1-1 draw at the Liberty Stadium in late 2005. (WP)

Town midfielder Grant Leadbitter, right, goes toe to toe with Swansea's Ashley Williams during a 4-1 away loss in 2011. (WP)

Frenchman Gueret, otherwise the winning run would have been extended. 'We can hold our heads up high,' announced Parkinson. 'We need a stadium like this one, to attract bigger crowds.'

The U's did move into their new Community Stadium two and a half years later, but Parkinson himself had left the club at the end of the 2005/06 season with promotion secured, heading for what was an unsuccessful stint at Hull City.

Back at the Liberty Stadium, I have been on the wrong end (in the press box at least) of some heavy defeats since then, including two trouncings in early 2011. The U's suffered a 4-0 reverse in an FA Cup tie in January, after which I returned to the South Wales coast in mid-April to endure a 4-1 loss on the road with struggling Ipswich Town. Indeed, I must be glutton for punishment when it comes to visiting the Liberty.

I think its fair to say that the Easter break in 2011 was not a happy one for Town boss Paul Jewell. Just four days after his side had been humiliated by East Anglian rivals Norwich City in a 5-1 defeat at Portman Road on a Thursday evening, Town crashed to another big loss at Swansea on Easter Monday, undone by a brace from Chelsea loanee Fabio Borini which sandwiched a long-range strike by Luke Moore and a second-half penalty from leading scorer Scott Sinclair. Town's only reply came via a 20th-minute goal from Colin Healy, the former and future Cork City midfielder, the one ray of sunshine for Jewell's sorry bunch. The Swans ended up clinching promotion to the Premier League via the play-offs that season.

It was a hopelessly one-sided encounter on the west bank of the River Tawe, and to be honest I couldn't wait to begin the return half of the 550-mile round trip back to Suffolk.

It was a wake-up call for Jewell, who said, 'I'm just grateful that we have enough points [59 from 44 games] not to have to worry about the last couple of games, because if we hadn't, it would have been a sticky situation. The players have said themselves that they are not good enough to get us into the top six, and that's where we want to be next year.'

For the record, Town finished 13th at the end of the season, and 15th in 2011/12. It seemed that Jewell's current crop, and the new players to come in, were indeed not good enough.

Still, the Swans promotion meant that the Liberty Stadium became the first ground in Wales to host Premier League football.

It is also one of the smallest to have hosted Premier League action, but by no means THE smallest – Bournemouth's Dean Court, Oldham's Boundary Park, Swindon's County Ground, QPR's Loftus Road, Blackpool's Bloomfield Road and Derby's Baseball Ground, to name but a few, are all higher up the list.

94 STAMFORD BRIDGE

Club: Chelsea
Founded: 1905
Ground: Stamford Bridge (since 1905, built in 1877)
First visit: 19 February 2006; Chelsea 3 Colchester 1

It's impossible not to feel a buzz of expectation every time you enter Chelsea's famous old ground, the club's only home, from the main entrance off the Fulham Road. I have been lucky enough to have sunk into my blue plastic seat in the cramped Stamford Bridge press box, with legs pinned against a shelf of plugs, and little TV screens flashing either side of the desk, on a couple of noteworthy occasions. The vantage point is very low, just 20 yards from the dugouts and so extremely close to the pitch. As a journalist you therefore always feel in the thick of the action, almost ready to win a header or tackle a winger, immersed in the whole atmosphere of the occasion. In that respect it's a different perspective to the more usual lofty press boxes in the Premier League which offer a bird's eye view from about two miles up in the very highest stand.

My two visits have been for FA Cup ties. Both ended in defeats, but were very different defeats. Minnows Colchester United had the audacity to go 1-0 up against Jose Mourinho's Premier League champions Chelsea in a fifth round tie in 2006 before losing heroically

Managers Phil Parkinson and Jose Mourinho look on intently, flanked by U's Greg Halford and Chelsea's Didier Drogba, during an FA Cup tie in 2006. (WP)

3-1, while at the other end of the scale managerless Ipswich Town were blitzed 7-0 in an embarrassingly one-sided third round tie in 2011. There was nothing heroic about that drubbing.

Back in 2006, Phil Parkinson's Colchester side were on a roll and destined to win promotion to the Championship, so the FA Cup was a welcome sideshow. Chelsea away was a dream tie, the west Londoners having won the Premier League the previous season. They were on course for back-to-back top-tier titles, to become only the fifth club in England to achieve such a feat, so they were the best team in the land by some distance. The U's, although on an upward curve themselves, were still a couple of years away from moving to a new ground, and several years further away from getting their own training facilities at the purpose-built Florence Park in Tiptree. Instead, they were training at the Colchester Garrison, having to keep to a rigid time schedule, or at the University of Essex on the edge of town. The latter was where all the pre-match interviews took place in the week leading up to the big cup tie, both tucked away in a small sports pavilion and at the mercy of the elements on windswept sports pitches.

I had tried to do my homework, mixing with all the hacks from the national newspapers who had converged on the University of Essex from the city of London. U's boss Parkinson was in top form, and the players lapped up all the attention.

As regards my homework, while the U's transfer activity of the previous summer had been restricted to the acquisition of striker Chris Iwelumo on a free transfer and winger Mark Yeates on loan from Tottenham, I found that Chelsea had spent a cool £53m on three players alone – Shaun Wright-Phillips, Michael Essien and Asier del Horno.

Also, I calculated that Colchester's annual budget of £750,000 was the equivalent of roughly two months' wages for Mourinho. And while Chelsea's playing staff was valued at £200m, the U's, apart from the £15,000 paid to Blackburn for midfielder Neil Danns, cost nothing at all in transfer fees.

And so on, and so on.

Stamford Bridge was a mouthwatering experience for U's players and supporters alike, the first time the Essex club had played against Chelsea. It would have been easy to be overawed by the magnitude of such a grand occasion, performing in front of a crowd of more than 41,000, especially when their own Layer Road ground could only squeeze in just over 6,000 supporters. Yet there was no sign of nerves. It was a day to treasure and, incredibly, there was a spell when it seemed as though Colchester could indeed topple Mourinho's men.

Stamford Bridge itself, which is actually located in the London Borough of Hammersmith and Fulham rather than neighbouring Chelsea, is rather hidden behind tall buildings, flats and a couple of hotels. But it's still a vast, oval-shaped theatre, mostly rebuilt during the second half of the 1990s when the north, south and west sides were all converted into all-seater stands and moved closer to the pitch. The old main stand, the East Stand, had been replaced by a towering three-tier structure in 1973, and the whole stadium is enclosed. Blue is the colour, and football is the name.

The locals expect – and have been used to – unrivalled success on the pitch since Russian billionaire Roman Abramovich started bankrolling the club, which is why there were murmurings of discontent at half-time with the U's holding their illustrious hosts at 1-1.

The visitors went ahead in the 28th minute when Portuguese centre-half Ricardo Carvalho could only divert a cross by Richard Garcia past keeper Carlo Cudicini for an own goal. As I wrote in my match report for the following day's paper, 'For a split-second the yellow-and-blue-decked U's fans, who were stationed at the other end of the pitch, struggled to take in the enormity of the situation. Delirium then ensued.'

It was a deserved lead as well, Yeates having rattled a post with a shot just six minutes earlier. Alas, the U's could not hold on for half-time, Paulo Ferreira equalising from close range via Damien Duff's corner. But at least they had worried Mourinho enough for the Portuguese boss to introduce England midfielders Joe Cole and Frank Lampard as substitutes at the start of the second half, with striker Hernan Crespo, a £16.8m buy from Inter Milan, also being introduced just after the hour. That proved too much for the U's, Cole scoring twice on 79 and 91 minutes to clinch the tie.

I actually composed my post-match stories outside the stadium, in a quaint little Brazilian cafe, because my wife Helen and youngest step-son Harry had been at the game, in the away end, and were in need of a meal. I listened back to the musings of Mourinho on my Dictaphone while they munched on black beans and rice, a fair trade-off.

Mourinho admitted that Colchester had 'played better' than his team in the first half. He declared, 'If you give players from a lower division so much time and space, then they

The scene on the touchline during Town's 7-0 thrashing at Chelsea, with Town caretaker boss Ian McParland, left, and Chelsea manager Carlo Ancelotti, right. The author can be seen in the press box in the background. (WP)

begin to look like you. Colchester finished the game with their players exhausted, but they gave us a proper game. They brought a lot of fans with them [6,000], and they believed it was possible to win. I don't know Phil Parkinson, but I believe he is a good manager.'

Parkinson himself said, 'We ruffled a few of Chelsea's feathers in the first half. They certainly knew that they were in a game.'

All in all, an unforgettable Sunday afternoon, and my return to Stamford Bridge with Ipswich Town on 9 January 2011 has also stuck in my memory, though for very different reasons.

It was always anticipated that managerless Town would exit the FA Cup at the hands of Carlo Ancelotti's star-studded Chelsea, and it was feared that with ex-Notts County manager Ian 'Charlie' McParland on the hot-seat, due to Roy Keane's departure on Friday, there was a good chance the Championship strugglers would be roasted on this particular Sunday lunchtime. Keane had been axed with Town in the bottom six, and caretaker boss McParland had already stated that he only planned to hang around for one game.

That one game just happened to be a trip to Chelsea! Alas, McParland's record as Town boss read as follows: P1 W0 D0 L1 F0 A7. To be accurate, though, McParland was still in the dugout for Town's next match (newly appointed manager Paul Jewell was watching from the stands) just three days later, which yielded an equally striking result, a 1-0 home win over Arsenal in the first leg of a Carling Cup semi-final. So in a way, 'Charlie' did put the record straight.

Returning to the Stamford Bridge debacle, this was Town's heaviest FA Cup defeat, a horrible surrender in a horribly one-sided third round encounter. It was actually goalless for the first 31 minutes, until three quickfire goals before half-time from Salomon Kalou, Daniel Sturridge and a Carlos Edwards own goal paved the way for an avalanche of second-half goals.

And as I wrote at the time, 'The final score could have been even worse.'

I gave the Brazilian cafe a miss that evening.

95 ST ANDREW'S

Club: Birmingham City
Founded: 1875 (as Small Heath Alliance)
Ground: St Andrew's (since 1906)
First visit: 5 August 2006; Birmingham 2 Colchester 1

I will always associate St Andrew's, the home of Birmingham City since 1906, as the venue for Colchester United first match as a second tier club, a Championship fixture on the opening day of the 2006/07 season. I even wore a tie for the occasion, the same tie that I wore for my wedding just two months previously. Which was the bigger day? Difficult to say, though I have since gone on to attend 200-plus Championship fixtures, and yet to date have not had a second wedding, so I guess I have to concede that the wedding edged it.

The result was an unsurprising away defeat – the U's lost their first four matches at this new higher level – but St Andrew's successfully whetted the appetite for what was to come for the rest of the season, playing against 'bigger' clubs in front of bigger crowds at bigger stadiums. I soon acclimatised myself to the bigger press boxes, with their greater number of power points and the occasional rows of mini TV screens showing the game live, plus the more spacious press lounges with their more extensive pre-match menus (not just a plate of stale sandwiches, a stewed tea or a stale biscuit). Yes, I soon became a little spoilt, I am ashamed to say. I actually adapted remarkably well to my more salubrious

U's away fans at St Andrew's watch their former player Neil Danns take a corner during the Essex club's first-ever Championship fixture. (WP)

Richard Garcia firing home the U's first-ever goal in the Championship, at St Andrew's in 2006. (WP)

surroundings, while the U's also soon found their feet in this higher tier, going on to finish in tenth spot, and 30th in the Football League pyramid, their highest league standing.

St Andrew's looked a picture on a warm and muggy Saturday afternoon, the shirt-sleeved U's fans in good voice at the Railway End as they embraced their new life as supporters of a Championship club. It was the start of a dream journey for them.

The 8,000 all-seater Railway End was one of three stands to be completely rebuilt during the 1990s. The Tilton Road End and the Kop, both former sprawling terraces, were replaced by continuous seating which stretched around the corner to surround half the pitch, which just left the Main Stand untouched. And that has remained the case.

The press box is in the Main Stand, with the dugouts in front, a two-tiered structure opened in the early 1950s after the previous one was accidentally burnt down during the Second World War. The stadium had been closed to football and was operating as a temporary fire station when a fireman mistook a bucket of petrol for a bucket of water, leading to the stand being destroyed by fire. The club records also went up in smoke. Although it is the oldest, smallest and lowest of the four stands, it at least leads the way in the character stakes, with its antiquated roof.

St Andrew's itself is built on a hill, in the Bordesley Green area of the city on the site of a former brickworks. So that means an uphill walk to the stadium, although there was a spring in the step of every Colchester supporter that day. Their team, with Geraint Williams in charge for the first time, lost 2-1 but made their intentions loud and clear – they were not going to be the whipping boys of the Championship.

Birmingham, with Steve Bruce at the helm, had been installed as one of the promotion favourites after a very busy summer, having been relegated from the Premier League the previous season. Bruce had been free to spend some serious cash, thanks to the sale of Emile Heskey to Wigan and Jermaine Pennant to Liverpool for a combined £13m, and they duly took the lead through striker DJ Campbell's precise header from debutant Bruno N'Gotty's cross on the half-hour mark. One down at half-time, the U's deservedly levelled on 51 minutes when Australian attacker Richard Garcia blasted home the club's first goal in the Championship, right in front of the noses of the U's supporters.

And it began to look very promising for the visitors after City substitute Cameron Jerome, a £3m recruit from Cardiff earlier in the summer, was sent off for raising an arm to Karl Duguid in the 70th minute. However, their hopes of gaining a first point in the second tier were dashed by Danish teenager Nicklas Bendtner, who had only arrived at St Andrew's two days earlier on loan from Arsenal. Rookie Bendtner's first shot was blocked by defender Wayne Brown, but he buried the rebound with precision.

'You could say it's a little bit cruel. We got caught by a sucker punch on the break, so it's a hard lesson for us. But we have proved that we can compete against one of the promotion favourites, and on their home ground,' declared U's boss Williams, with a touch of pride.

Birmingham boss Bruce admitted, 'Colchester played well. They were itching to play at this level, and they had a point to prove. This was a wake-up call for us.'

U's fans, though, did not need a wake-up call. They were in dreamland, and they stayed in that trance for what was to be a remarkable campaign.

96 WALKERS STADIUM (LEICESTER CITY STADIUM)

Club: Leicester City
Founded: 1884 (as Leicester Fosse)
Ground: Walkers Stadium (since 2002, renamed King Power Stadium in 2011)
First visit: 23 September 2006; Leicester 0 Colchester 0

Leicester City's new stadium, built just a stone's throw from their old Filbert Street home and about a 30-minute walk from the city centre, shares something in common with Colchester United's later new ground – they both welcomed Spanish club Athletic Bilbao as their first visitors, on the fourth day of August, perhaps the most obscure of all trivia facts.

The Foxes marked their short-distance move with a friendly against Athletic Bilbao on 4 August 2002, a 1-1 draw, while exactly six years later the U's also entertained the Basque club for their first game at their new Community Stadium, a 2-1 defeat.

The two clubs met on an equal footing for the first time, and in fact for their first competitive fixture, in the Championship on 23 September 2006. It was also my first visit to the then-named Walkers Stadium, a plush bowl-shaped venue of four stands,

Greg Halford goes close with this free-kick during the U's 0-0 draw at Leicester City in 2006. (WP)

all of the same ilk and with the corners enclosed. A sea of blue seats, with some white-seated lettering, and a strip of transparent Perspex across the front of a couple of the roofs to let in more light, this is a tidy-looking venue with a bold glass frontage. In fact, there is nothing bland about Leicester's current abode.

The acoustics are good, so the atmosphere is usually superb, though I confess that on my first visit the half-time cream cakes made more of a lasting impression on me than the actual match, a goalless draw. So good were the cakes in the press lounge that I was still in the lift returning to the press box when the second half started. That said as much about the high quality of the half-time refreshments as it did the low quality of the first-half action.

Although I have yet to report on an away success at the stadium, situated close to the River Saar on Filbert Way, just a few yards south of the old ground – some fans choose to refer to their new home as Filbert Way, rather than by the sponsor's name, which I think I would be tempted to do as well – I have witnessed some marginally better encounters than that original 0-0 stalemate. However, the emphasis is on 'marginally'.

I returned to the Walkers Stadium with the U's the following season, but only after Geraint Williams's men had been officially relegated during the course of the week, without even kicking a ball. Lowly Barnsley's 3-0 win at Watford on the Tuesday night had ensured the U's relegation from the Championship before their weekend trip to Leicester for a 1-1 draw. That game summed up the U's whole season, so near and

David Norris celebrates as Town equalise during a 1-1 draw at the Walkers Stadium in 2010. (WP)

yet so far, with Kevin Lisbie's 17th goal of the season putting them ahead only for substitute Iain Hume to poach an 89th-minute equaliser in a 1-1 draw on 12 April 2008. That point was enough to nudge the Foxes out of the relegation zone, on goal difference, although Ian Holloway's side ended up being relegated on the final day.

Instead, another 1-1 draw, this time featuring Roy Keane's Ipswich Town, gets the nod for my feature game in January 2010, due more to the weather than the football. We had snow showers for this Sunday clash, though I'm glad I forsook the warmth of the press lounge early to take my seat in the ice-cold press box because Town scored after just 20 seconds, which didn't happen very often during Keane's era. Strictly speaking, it wasn't an Ipswich player who scored, although David Norris did try and claim what would have been his first goal of the season. Instead, it went down as a Ryan McGivern own goal, the ball coming off the Leicester defender from Jack Colback's cross. Oh well, they all count.

The Foxes, with Nigel Pearson in charge, equalised through centre-forward Steve Howard, who charged down Damien Delaney's attempted clearance to slot home in the 38th minute. Having struggled against relegation all season, Town were at least starting to show more battling qualities, and this draw extended their run to just one defeat in 14 to create a four-point buffer between themselves and the bottom three. Any success, however minor, was worth celebrating during those lean months.

Overall, I think it's fair to say that I have yet to enjoy a fine away-day experience at 'Filbert Way,' with the exception of those fantastic cream doughnuts.

97 MOLINEUX

Club: Wolverhampton Wanderers
Founded: 1877 (as St Luke's FC)
Ground: Molineux (since 1889)
First visit: 14 October 2006; Wolves 1 Colchester 0

Molineux has a character of its own, situated just a short walk from the city centre, surrounded on matchday by a sprawl of burger vans and food stalls, and inside filled with bright orange seats (bring your sunglasses) within four distinctive stands, two of them curved. This is not out of the mould of the modern, uniform, perfect bowl-shaped structure. Molineux is unique. Alas, it is also a place where I have never reported on anything other than an away defeat, as an 'away' reporter. Wolves on home soil are a tough nut to crack.

The West Midlands club, and its famous home, can boast a long and rich history. Founder members of the Football League in 1888, Wolves were formed on a bedrock of religion and cricket, like so many other Football League clubs emerging from the late 19th century. St Luke's FC adopted the name of Wolverhampton Wanderers in 1879, two years after the club's formation, and trophies soon followed.

Wolves lifted the FA Cup for the first time in 1893, beating Everton 1-0 in the final, and during the 1950s they vied with Manchester United for the title of best club in the land. Under manager Stan Collis, they won the top-tier title three times during this period.

Likewise Molineux, the home of Wolves since 1889, has often been a trailblazer, whether it be in the form of giant terraces, floodlight installation or the emergence of European football. Nestling in a hollow, to the north-west of the city centre and reached via underpasses beyond the ring road, Molineux used to be the site of a pleasure park within the gardens of Molineux House, which was built by local merchant Benjamin Molineux during the 18th century, hence the name of the football stadium. Where the ground is now situated used to be an area of trees with a bandstand and an ornamental lake, in an era before burger vans and pizza stalls.

Wolves were one of the first British clubs to install floodlights, in 1953, which in turn helped to boost the new concept of European football, so paving the way for Wanderers to become the first English club to compete in the European Cup in 1956, just a year after the competition was introduced. And in terms of terracing, the old South Bank terrace used to boast one of the largest Kop end open terraces in the country, perhaps second only to the Holte End at near neighbours Aston Villa.

Of course these days Molineux is all-seater, benefiting from a major redevelopment overseen by owner and lifelong fan Jack Hayward in the early 1990s. When I first visited with Colchester United, in the autumn of 2006, this was the Essex club's first appearance for 18 years at the new-look Molineux. The ground looked a picture with its slightly

Wolves keeper Matt Murray spills this cross under pressure from Chris Iwelumo during the U's 1-0 defeat at Molineux. (WP)

unusual convex curved stands along both sides of the pitch, which left those sitting near the halfway line marginally further away from the action. Not always a bad thing when your team are having an off-day.

Geraint Williams was beginning to find his feet as U's boss, as were his team in the Championship, while Wolves were under the stewardship of a future Ipswich Town manager, Mick McCarthy. I must say that, watching from the press box in the Billy Wright Stand, I thought the U's were hard done by following a 1-0 defeat.

Wolves' leading scorer, Jay Bothroyd, netted the only goal of the game early in the second half. The much-improved U's pushed for an equaliser and the home fans were left sitting on the edge of their bright orange (or rich gold) seats for the remainder of the second half, to such an extent that referee Scott Mathieson's final whistle was greeted by sighs of relief rather than shouts of joy.

'There will be teams who come to us and don't create as many chances as Colchester United did today,' admitted McCarthy. 'They gave us a few problems. We scored at the right time because had it gone on for a bit longer, then it could have been difficult.'

Welshman Williams, who had scooped the Manager of the Month award for September, was guiding his team up the Championship table. Indeed, they were already above local rivals Ipswich, Southend and Norwich after 11 games, so Williams was not too disheartened by the 1-0 defeat. He explained, 'The game could have gone either way again. No team has had an easy afternoon against us so far, and I think Wolves can vouch for that.'

I was back at Molineux the following season but it was a similar story with Colchester again losing 1-0 in a midweek clash on 28 November 2007. By this time Bothroyd was down the pecking order of Wolves strikers, and instead it was Stephen Elliott who was the match-winner with a close-range header on 31 minutes. Yet the U's came within a whisker of an injury-time equaliser as Kem Izzet struck a post with virtually the last kick of the game, after being teed up by Teddy Sheringham's downward header.

Molineux might be an orange oasis, but the U's have always left feeling blue – if I get another chance, I might use that phrase in a match report one day. It might catch on.

98 RICOH ARENA

Club: Coventry City
Founded: 1883 (as Singers FC)
Ground: Ricoh Arena (2005–13, 2014–19)
First visit: 23 October 2006; Coventry 2 Colchester 1

It is virtually impossible to get lost, once installed in a football stadium, or so I thought. Embarrassingly, I proved this wrong on my first visit to Ricoh Arena, the on-and-off home of Coventry City since 2005, when I managed to hopelessly lose my bearings between the media lounge and the press box. I know, pathetic!

I arrived in good time for Colchester United's Championship clash at the Ricoh on a Monday night on 23 October 2006, leaving the car in Car Park C on the other side of the Coventry-to-Nuneaton A444 dual carriageway and crossing via a footbridge to the purpose-built stadium. The early evening continued to go well. Press passes were secured in the spacious foyer, which resembled more of an airport lounge or shopping precinct than a football club reception, and platefuls of pie and chips were consumed in the basement press lounge while firing up the laptops and digesting the official team sheets. I sat myself in one of the press booths under a sign on the wall which declared, 'The Ricoh welcomes the world press' – a tongue-in-cheek picture opportunity which my photographer colleague Warren Page could not resist, with me as the solitary hack in shot.

Thirty minutes before kick-off, myself and fellow away journalist Jon Waldron, of the *Colchester Daily Gazette*, decided to brave the cold of the press box, a simple affair we assumed, being only a short one-minute walk up the stairs and across the foyer.

However, a bemused (or mischievous) steward, who was probably on his first day in the job, directed us up an escalator and on to a higher floor, well away from the pitch area. Perhaps he thought we were late for a business function? I sensed all was not well but, having never been to the Ricoh Arena before, I just thought the press box must be high up in the gallery. We got lost, hopelessly lost. Panic set in as we paced the corridors. There were hotel rooms, an exhibition hall, and apparently a casino in the basement, but

Jamie Guy celebrates his goal at the Ricoh Arena during the U's 2-1 defeat in 2006. (WP)

where was the bloody press box, or the football pitch for that matter? In short, it was not my finest hour, and apparently Jon still has nightmares about it.

By the time that we had returned to ground level, and eventually found the press box – which was signposted and easily accessible, naturally – the teams were already on the pitch. A lesson learned. Always make sure you know where the press box is, or take a steward's directions with a pinch of salt, or just don't let the home journalists out of your sight.

That first trip coincided with a 2-1 defeat, a late goal from former youth-team striker Jamie Guy proving insufficient to save Colchester in front of the glare of the Sky TV cameras. Goals from striker Stern John and club stalwart midfielder Michael Doyle put the Sky Blues in charge, before 80th-minute substitute Guy halved the deficit within five minutes of his arrival. The 19-year-old exchanged a one-two with Jamie Cureton and slammed an angled drive past former Ipswich keeper Andy Marshall. It was only Barking-born Guy's second senior goal, following his first at West Brom during the third weekend of the season, and he was to only score once more for the U's before eventually dropping into non-league just over three years later. He has since played for about 20 different non-league clubs.

My first impression of the Ricoh Arena was that it had potential, but was really a bit soulless. The bowl-shaped, sky blue-seated stadium was three quarters empty and failed to inspire. The press box, low down in the main West Stand, the only one of the four stands to be two-tiered with an upper tier of corporate hospitality boxes plus a total of 50 hotel rooms boasting views of the pitch – personally, I prefer sea-view hotel rooms – is a fine place to work, with the widest tables I have ever encountered in all my Football League press box travels. I imagine it would be easy to take a school exam on such a huge

Ricoh Arena, the on-and-off home of Coventry City. (WP)

desk, and surround yourself with an array of lucky mascot toys, pencil cases, calculators, erasers, water bottles, vases of flowers and bars of chocolate. I felt spoilt, after all my past experiences in cramped lower division press boxes, where the desk would be too narrow to accommodate a laptop and where your legs would be stuck in the same position for 90 minutes, plus injury time, knees wedged behind the seat in front.

So a perfect place to work, if you can avoid getting lost en route, but not the best venue to watch football. No wonder it often ranks highly on fans' lists of worst football stadiums among the 92 Premier League and Football League grounds, whenever it is a member of this exclusive club, which is not very often. Coventry have ground-shared at Northampton's Sixfields and most recently Birmingham City's St Andrew's due to disputes with the stadium owners, leaving the venue to host more rugby union matches (Wasps have been based there since 2014) than football fixtures these days.

A few seasons later, when the Sky Blues were still in residence at the Ricoh, I visited with Ipswich for another Championship encounter.

The end was nigh for manager Roy Keane when Town arrived for what was a New Year's Day clash at the start of 2011. I remember that day well, and was already preparing the 'Keane as Town boss' epitaph, to be used not 'if' but 'when' the Irishman parted company with the Portman Road club.

I always wanted Keane to succeed on the Town hot-seat, not least because, as I have touched on earlier, his press conferences were always terrific value for us hacks, both pre-match and post-match. His quotes were priceless and every journalist hung on his every word. Sure, it was a circus, and sure, the football under Keane was pretty terrible, but it was still a sad day when he finally exited Portman Road. He eventually packed his bags just six days after that visit to the Ricoh, on Thursday, 6 January.

So what of that game, a 1-1 draw, on the first day of 2011?

In essence, it summed up the whole 20 months under Keane, which had almost entirely been spent grappling against the perils of relegation at the bottom end of the Championship. The writing was on the wall, although I hadn't bargained on a draw. Ironically, given that Town's previous 16 games in league and cup had yielded ten defeats and six wins, this 1-1 draw was a long time in coming, but in truth it felt like another defeat.

Coventry, in the top ten of the Championship, were attracting crowds of around 15,000 to the Ricoh, but most of a gate of 14,412 were fearing the worst when Town deservedly took the lead towards the end of the first half. It was recent signing Rory Fallon's first goal for the club, the Plymouth loanee ramming home the rebound after keeper Keiren Westwood had beaten away Jack Colback's stinging shot.

Football is often about fine margins, and if they had managed to hold on for a 1-0 win at the Ricoh, Keane's men would have been up to 16th, five points off the top six. Maybe there would have been life in the Irishman yet? However, Aidy Boothroyd's familiar style of route one football saw the Sky Blues level within three minutes of the restart via Freddy Eastwood's equaliser.

And even though the hosts were reduced to ten men following Marlon King's reckless challenge on defender Darren O'Dea on the hour mark, toothless Town could not take advantage. Some days an away draw can feel like a moral victory. Not that afternoon. The writing was on the wall.

As Keane said in one of his last press conferences as Ipswich manager, 'If it works out, people pat you on the back. But if it doesn't work out, people think you are a clown and that you don't know a thing about football.'

Keane had already held discussions with owner Marcus Evans, about possible transfers during the January window. The outcome was not encouraging. He had clearly lost the backing of his chairman, just as I had lost my way from the media lounge to the press box five years earlier.

99 CARROW ROAD

Club: Norwich City
Founded: 1902
Ground: Carrow Road (since 1935)
First visit: 31 October 2006; Norwich 1 Colchester 1

The home of Norwich City since 1935, Carrow Road was the setting for my favourite away-day press box experience. A stunning 7-1 win for Colchester United, on the opening day of the 2009/10 campaign, against a Norwich side who had just been relegated from

U's players celebrate yet another goal during their sensational 7-1 win at Norwich City on the opening day of the 2009/10 campaign.

the Championship and were, ironically, destined to win immediate promotion back to the second tier. It was the most remarkable of afternoons, verging on fantasy football, underdogs Colchester sprinting into a four-goal lead inside the first quarter of the game and maintaining their ascendancy in front of a stunned crowd of more than 25,000. I had to pinch myself to make sure I wasn't just dreaming.

There was no suggestion of what was to unfold during the build-up to this east region derby (Norwich is just 60 miles up the road from Colchester, in a northerly direction). I had visited Carrow Road many times as a youngster, and a few times as a reporter, but I had never experienced anything like what accrued that August afternoon in 2009, any time, anywhere.

The ground is impressive, the original having been built in just 82 days due to the pressure of getting it ready for a new season (1935/36). The Canaries' former home, at The Nest on Rosary Road, had been deemed unsuitable for hosting big crowds by the Football Association, not surprising when considered that a few years before, in 1926, one corner of the pitch had subsided by about 30 feet due to the collapse of an old chalk workings, a predictable consequence of the pitch having been levelled over a disused chalk pit.

A new site was found, half a mile away, owned by mustard manufacturers J & J Coleman, and Carrow Road was hastily constructed with one main grandstand and three sides of opening terracing. It was proudly billed as the biggest construction job completed in the city of Norwich since the building of Norwich Castle.

The stadium has stood the test of time, encircled in a loop on three sides by Carrow Road itself – the name of the street harks back to Carrow Abbey, perched on the river bank – and on the other side by Geoffrey Watling Way and the nearby River Wensum. It is a fine place to watch football, the two-tiered River End having been built in 1979, and the City Stand being opened six years later to replace an earlier structure which had been fire-damaged, apparently by an electric fire having been left switched on overnight. The press box is sited in this City Stand, the smallest of the four stands, and features some rotating seats which can cause unsuspecting journalists to lose their balance even when seated. There is an art to settling into your seat without causing a fuss at Carrow Road.

The ground is completed by the impressive South Stand opposite, a splendid 8,000 all-seater which is the newest of the four stands, built in 2004 with a Perspex roof and TV gantry, and the Barclay Stand at the other end. Three of the corners are filled in to give an intimate feel, and everywhere you look is decked in bright yellow and dark green. The stadium has seen some great times – the Canaries finished third behind champions Manchester United in the inaugural year of the Premier League, in 1992/93, and the club has hosted some big European nights – but it witnessed a new low when I joined the throngs for the opening day of the 2009/10 season, down in the third tier.

All talk, in the press lounge at the rear of the City Stand was of Norwich securing a winning start to Bryan Gunn's first full season as manager. Gunn had been the goalkeeper when Mike Walker's Norwich had become the first British side to beat Bayern Munich on their home patch in a UEFA Cup tie at the Olympic Stadium in 1993/94. Gunn was a hero that night, making a string of fine saves, but he must have wished the ground would swallow him up after the debacle at the hands of Colchester.

The U's, with Paul Lambert at the helm, had been busy in the transfer market during the summer, but nothing to suggest that a club record 7-1 away-day thumping was on

Two angry Norwich City fans run towards the dug-outs, with U's boss Paul Lambert trying to intercept them, during the home side's humiliating 7-1 defeat.

the cards. Everything was calm and peaceful for the first ten minutes, until all hell broke loose as the goals flew past bewildered home keeper Michael Theoklitos at breakneck speed. Goals from Kevin Lisbie (11), Clive Platt (13 and 19) and David Fox (23), the latter a sweet free kick, put the U's 4-0 up. Lisbie added a fifth before half-time, and second-half goals by midfielder David Perkins, a left-footed dipping volley, and substitute Scott Vernon completed the rout, easily Norwich's heaviest home defeat in their 107-year history. The whole experience was surreal.

And for me, the memory that lingers most from the whole day was the sight of two irate Norwich supporters running on to the pitch after the fourth goal went in and tearing up their season tickets in front of the dugout, throwing the bits of paper in the direction of Gunn and his coaching staff. A mini pitch invasion after just 23 minutes of a new season? That must have been a first.

'Sweet dreams are made of this' was my banner headline in Monday morning's newspaper, supported by a sub-heading – 'Carnage at Carrow Road will live long in the memory' – with a stream of gushing text below. I'll pluck just one paragraph from my match report, to provide some flavour:

'Where to start? How can you possibly do justice, in a few paragraphs, to such an amazing 90 minutes of football? It was as if half a season was condensed into one dramatic afternoon. Colchester were simply invincible; Norwich were simply awful.'

The press lounge after the match was full of journalists trying to get their heads around what they had just seen, while also considering what questions to ask of Canaries boss Gunn. Many were ringing up their respective sports desks to request bigger word counts so they could do the game justice in their reports.

A shell-shocked Gunn referred to the action of the two angry home fans, 'As a player, I've had lots of abuse, including coins thrown at me. I understand that can happen, but it's disappointing at the frustration they have shown.' U's boss Lambert, trying to keep a lid on his team's achievement, while attempting to hide a satisfying smile, mused, 'It's what happens at the end of the season that counts.'

Now here's where the real irony sets in. By the end of the season, Lambert was celebrating promotion and the League One title, but as Norwich manager, not the U's boss. Lambert controversially quit the U's to replace the axed Gunn a mere ten days after the 7-1 demolition at Carrow Road with the Essex club on top of the table. The Scotsman went on to secure back-to-back promotions at the Norfolk club, to reach the Premier League. The U's, who had been on the cusp of something exciting under Lambert, finished a distant eight points adrift of the play-offs and have continued to dwell in the lower two divisions ever since.

The aftermath might not make pleasant reading for Colchester fans, but even now I still find myself marvelling at what happened on that warm summer's afternoon at Carrow Road. Delight, disbelief, shock, anger, joy, humiliation, a heady mixture of emotions.

And that was only day one of the season.

100 STADIUM OF LIGHT

Club: Sunderland
Founded: 1879 (as Sunderland and District Teachers)
Ground: Stadium of Light (since 1997)
First visit: 18 November 2006; Sunderland 3 Colchester 1

As stated before, there weren't many bright moments for me, or any Town fan for that matter, while on the Ipswich Town trail during Roy Keane's era. Ironically, though, I did report on a Keane success on my first visit to the Stadium of Light, a vast ground sitting proudly on the north bank of the River Wear. It had nothing to do with Ipswich – his move down to Suffolk was still two years in the future – but rather was connected with host club Sunderland, who claimed a 3-1 home win over Colchester United in mid-November 2006.

Keane was the man charged with the job of regaining Sunderland's Premier League status following relegation the previous season. With Mick McCarthy at the helm for the first two thirds of that campaign, the Black Cats had finished rock bottom with just three league wins and 15 points gathered, setting a new record Premier League low which was surpassed by Derby County's 11 points in 2007/08. Keane arrived in late August, taking over from Niall Quinn, who remained as club chairman, and duly achieved the main aim of promotion by winning 27 of the remaining 42 matches to be crowned champions.

Sunderland had actually lost their first four league games of the season under acting boss Quinn, and had also exited the League Cup at the hands of fourth-tier Bury, but by the time that Geraint Williams's newly promoted Colchester United arrived at the Stadium of Light for the first meeting between the two clubs, the Wearsiders were beginning to slowly climb the table.

In truth, it felt like a big cup tie if you happened to be in the Colchester camp, which was true of just about every fixture in that first season in the Championship. Mighty Sunderland, six times top-flight winners, albeit the last time in 1936, could boast one of the biggest stadiums in the country and were the wealthiest club in the second tier, by far. They had a big-name manager in ex-Manchester United midfielder Keane, determined to succeed at his first crack at management, while crowds at the Stadium of the Light often topped 30,000 and three times surpassed 40,000 during the course of the campaign.

It is impossible not to be impressed by the Stadium of Light, which is visible from afar on the approach from the A19. An enclosed rectangular-shaped bowl, with an imposing white roof, it dominates the skyline and yet is only a short walk from the city centre. The U's travelling away press, which as usual could be fitted snugly within the confines of one car, usually my own vehicle, arrived ridiculously early. We were all middle-aged men, and yet all (sadly) excited about the prospect of working in Sunderland's press box, surrounded on all sides by thousands of shiny red seats (the old ones had been bleached pink by the

U's defender Wayne Brown heads just wide during a 3-1 defeat at Sunderland's Stadium of Light in 2006. (WP)

sun) in four huge stands, two of them three-tiered structures, and then attending Keane's post-match press conference. We were in the West Stand, the main stand, which afforded a cracking view of the pitch and the city beyond.

Game-wise, it all went as feared for the first 75 minutes. Sunderland, who began the day four points behind the U's, cantered into a 2-0 lead through a brace from livewire Stephen Elliott, but there was to be a sting in the tail. Chris Iwelumo, on as a 71st-minute substitute for full league debutant Jamie Guy (normally an impact substitute), netted from close range just seven minutes later and suddenly the Black Cats were on the ropes. Greg Halford, who was blossoming into a wonderful footballer, teased the home defence with some surging runs down the right flank, and both Jamie Cureton and Kem Izzet were guilty of missing sitters to equalise before David Connolly calmed the home nerves with an injury-time third to seal a 3-1 win.

'To say it was tough would be an understatement,' confessed Keane, who looked a relieved man in the press conference. 'We knew that Colchester would give it a go and come at us. When they scored, the natural instinct was for us to sit back.'

His opposite number Williams remarked, 'The scoreline looks bad, but we were worth a point.'

The result aside, it was still an unforgettable day for the U's, a rare opportunity to play at what at the time was the largest stadium to be built since the Second World War. Still, football is all about results, so it was satisfying to report on the U's out-gunning Keane's Sunderland 3-1 back at Layer Road during the third last weekend of the season, in late April 2007.

Tiny Layer Road was bathed in sunshine that day and at virtual capacity with a crowd of 6,042, all of whom of course could have sat together in just one stand at the Stadium of Light! Two different worlds colliding. Late goals from Richard Garcia and Jamie Cureton (a penalty) knocked Sunderland off the top of the table that afternoon, after veteran striker Dwight Yorke had netted an equaliser for the Wearsiders to cancel out Wayne Brown's header. The north-east club had arrived at humble Layer Road on an unbeaten run stretching to 17 matches, with 14 wins, and Keane had scooped back-to-back Manager of the Month awards.

But that afternoon, the Stadium of the Light must have felt a million miles away, for Keane and the red-and-white decked Sunderland travelling fans. To be precise, the distance is 283 miles.

101 PRIDE PARK STADIUM

Club: Derby County
Founded: 1884
Ground: Pride Park Stadium (since 1997)
First visit: 2 March 2007; Derby 5 Colchester 1

I didn't know it at the time, because I had yet to visit the Riverside Stadium, but Derby County's Pride Park Stadium bears a strong resemblance to Middlesbrough's new abode. There are obvious differences, including the colour scheme, the main facade and the unusual stack of corporate boxes filling one corner (north-west) of Derby's ground, but the basic structure and general character are the same. The two grounds, built two years apart, are 132 miles apart. Distant cousins, in industrial areas just outside their respective city centres, sitting proudly between a river and railway tracks, both with dominant main West Stands inside enclosed stadiums. Both a credit to their clubs.

I have noted a trend in past chapters, where grounds that I have visited with both Colchester United and Ipswich Town have often featured U's success stories and Town failures, but Pride Park bucks that trend. My first visit, with the U's in early March 2007, nearly ten years after the stadium was first opened, ended in a 5-1 thrashing of the visitors. That remains the Essex club's one and only experience of Pride Park, and 30 years since their only other away game at Derby, at the old Baseball Ground. By contrast, I have returned twice with Ipswich, both ending in away victories. So results have been very black and white, with no grey areas (draws), matching Derby's club colours, or at least those since the 1890s – the original club colours were actually amber, chocolate brown and blue.

Win or lose, Pride Park has always been a very welcoming ground. It was constructed in under a year, built on an area of wasteland between the River Derwent and the railway lines, with the A6 road close by and the city centre just a mile away in a north-westerly direction. The stadium itself looks good from the outside, with its sloping roof and bold

Connor Wickham slots home Town's third during a 3-1 win at Pride Park in 2010. (WP)

front entrance, especially before night games when it's glowing silver and black. The press box is in the main West Stand, which has a second tier and so is bigger than the other three stands, hence that sloping roof.

Everything felt rather daunting on my first visit, not helped by the fact that it was a Friday night fixture under the lights with the Sky TV cameras present, and with Derby intent on returning to the top of the Championship table. Even though this was the U's 36th game of a wonderful first season in the second tier, which had seen them already

Derby County are awarded a penalty for this foul by John White during the U's 5-1 defeat at Pride Park in 2007. (WP)

accumulate 52 points and so be closer to the play-offs than the relegation zone, I think the enormity of the occasion got to them. The stadium was buzzing, the press box was packed and I even had trouble digesting my pre-match meal in the press lounge. I suspected a home victory and, alas, Colchester were brushed aside in emphatic fashion, hammered 5-1 and so conceding more than three goals for the first time during an otherwise heroic season. It was certainly not a happy return to Derby for U's boss Geraint Williams, who had rattled up more than 300 senior appearances as a midfielder for the Rams during the mid-1980s and early 1990s.

Billy Davies's Derby were rampant. The match was effectively over by half-time with goals from David Jones, Arturo Lupoli and man of the match Giles Barnes putting the Rams three up. Midfielder Johnnie Jackson did pull a goal back early in the second half, but Steve Howard tucked home a penalty and U's left-back Chris Barker netted an own goal to complete the drubbing. Oh, and it also poured with rain all night!

U's defender Wayne Brown ensured that I had copy galore for a follow-up story in Monday's newspaper. Brown confessed, 'This was a great opportunity to show what we could do, playing in front of a big crowd, live on Sky. But we ended up showing nothing. There was no heart.'

Derby dropped out of the top two during the run-in, but were still promoted to the Premier League via the play-offs.

Two return trips with Ipswich Town, in 2010 and 2011, proved more fruitful. The stadium looked just as handsome, especially with the addition of a new bronze statue of the former successful management team of Brian Clough and Peter Taylor outside the main entrance. The statue was officially unveiled three weeks after my first visit with Town, honouring the duo who had masterminded Derby's first of two top division titles, in 1972.

Town, under Roy Keane, triumphed 3-1 at Pride Park in a feisty Easter Monday fixture on 5 April 2010 against a Derby side managed by Brian Clough's son, Nigel. Centre-half Gareth McAuley scored early from a corner, and substitute Carlos Edwards tapped home a late second. A deflected header from Rob Hulse gave the Rams some hope, but 17-year-old Connor Wickham ran through to slot home Town's third in injury time. Wickham had only just put pen to paper on his first professional contract, so it was the perfect way to celebrate.

Ten months later, and with ex-Derby manager Paul Jewell recently installed as Town's new boss, I witnessed another away victory at Pride Park, this time veteran Jimmy Bullard hogging the headlines with a goalscoring debut in a 2-1 victory on Tuesday, 1 February 2011. Full of energy, the charismatic Bullard crashed home a 28th-minute equaliser with a little help from home keeper Stephen Bywater, who could only fumble the midfielder's 25-yarder into his own net. David Norris drilled home the winner in the 68th minute, via a one-two with Tamas Priskin.

Pride Park looked a picture under the lights that night, capturing the glint in Bullard's eyes. Not that he ever stopped smiling, ever.

102 NEW MEADOW

Club: Shrewsbury Town
Founded: 1886
Ground: New Meadow (since 2007)
First visit: 14 August 2007; Shrewsbury 1 Colchester 0

I still pine for Gay Meadow, just as I sometimes hanker for Layer Road. Two old grounds, neither perfect but both with bags of personality, superseded by functional yet depressingly bland out-of-town structures.

I had the good fortune to report on Shrewsbury's Town first competitive match at the New Meadow, just as I also sat in the press box for Colchester United's first competitive game at their new home just one year later. I mention this, because the Shrews' New Meadow and the U's Community Stadium share so many similarities. On a good day, they are neat and tidy, safe and sound, blessed with fine views from every seat in the stadium, and can both really rock when filled to the rafters. But on a bad day, they can be cold and forlorn, lost in desolate surroundings and often two thirds empty, banished to the outskirts of town.

The Shrews' move from Gay Meadow, their delightful old home on the banks of the River Severn near the centre of town, took place in the summer of 2007. The first match was a friendly between Shrewsbury Town and an All Stars XI on 14 July, but a month later the real business began with Colchester United's visit for a League Cup first round tie on a Tuesday evening. I remember the press room in the main East Stand was not ready to

U's boss Joe Dunne is interviewed by the media after his side had lost a 2-0 lead in a 2-2 draw at New Meadow in 2012. (WP)

Karl Duguid (No. 7) cannot stop Asa Hall from scoring with a header during the U's 2-2 draw at Shrewsbury in 2012. (WP)

welcome a flood of guests, instead acting more as a temporary store room, but everywhere else looked spick and span. Four separate stands with blue seats and amber lettering, topped by four white roofs, and the corners open to the elements. A car park in front of the main stand, a railway line to the rear of the opposite West Stand, and the A5 road close at hand. It's a bit too far to walk from the town centre, amounting a two-mile slog, and in essence you could be in any out-of-town location anywhere in the country.

Certainly, it was not the dream first fixture that the Shropshire side would have wanted, but the U's were a Championship club at the time, two divisions above the Shrews, and the hosts did win the game 1-0 on a warm late summer's evening. The crowd was just 3,069 to mark the occasion, so the brand-new stadium was less than a third full, although four days later the first league match, against Bradford City on the traditional Saturday afternoon, did attract a gate of 6,413.

The League Cup tie did drag, if I'm being honest. It was 0-0 after normal time, before a dour encounter was settled by defender Darren Kempson's headed goal from a long throw in the 106th minute. That at least paved the way for an exciting finale. Centre-half Kempson, whose goal had been his first and as it turned out his last for the Shrews, turned villain when tripping Kem Izzet in the box for a U's penalty on 115 minutes, only for ex-Tottenham midfielder Johnnie Jackson's spot-kick to be saved by keeper Ryan Esson. U's manager Geraint Williams admitted, 'I think if we were still out on the pitch now, then we'd still struggle to score a goal.'

Returning from Shropshire to Suffolk, in the dead of night after an away cup defeat, is never much fun.

But I was back at New Meadow for an incident-packed League One encounter in late October 2012. This time the stadium was just over half-full, and most of the crowd left with smiling faces after some late drama saw Graham Turner's Shrews recover from a losing position to score two late goals and snatch a 2-2 draw.

Joe Dunne's Colchester were crestfallen at the final whistle having shipped two soft goals, both of them headers by substitute Asa Hall, and both from corners. Two points tossed away, much to the disgust of Dunne, who had been appointed the new U's boss just a month previously. Looking on from the press box, I felt that the U's were a little over-confident that day, having won their previous three games. The talented Craig Eastmond drilled home a third-minute opener via the inside of the far post, and his fellow Arsenal loanee Sanchez Watt doubled the lead with a sensational goal thanks to a lightning-quick run and sublime finish. But the killer blows never arrived, Hall struck twice, and the U's were left hanging on grimly for a point at the end.

Watt admitted, 'We are so used to winning that this has hurt us bad. It feels like a loss.' Neither Watt nor fellow Arsenal trainee Eastmond quite fulfilled their early promise, spending most of their careers in non-league.

Yet it was rich entertainment on that October afternoon in Shropshire, despite requiring a flurry of hasty re-writes in the press box, for me included. New Meadow was alive and well. It almost felt like the good old days back at Gay Meadow. Almost.

I can't help feeling that watching a match at an out-of-town away ground, while never even visiting or setting eyes on the town itself, is a touch depressing.

103 THE VALLEY

Club: Charlton Athletic
Founded: 1905
Ground: The Valley (1919–23, 1924–85, since 1992)
First visit: 1 January 2008; Charlton 1 Colchester 2

My beloved Uncle Len, a Londoner, used to support Charlton Athletic harking back to the glory days of the 1930s and 1940s. He still followed them in later years at a distance, from his home in Bexleyheath, Kent, so I have always taken a keen interest in the goings-on at The Valley. It was ironic, then, that my first Charlton home game as a reporter should be while they were paying rent as tenants at West Ham's Upton Park during the 1991/92 season. For the record, they lost 2-1 to John Beck's visiting Cambridge United in a third-tier clash on 23 November 1991 when Alan Curbishley and Steve Gritt were the joint managers.

Charlton thankfully returned to The Valley in 1992, after seven years of ground-sharing with Crystal Palace and later the Hammers. They had left because of safety concerns following the Bradford City stadium fire disaster of 1985. The huge East Stand terrace had been closed, and the club did not have the funds to renovate the ground having gone into administration the previous year after many seasons of virtually no investment.

Kevin Lisbie steps up to convert a penalty for the U's during a 2-1 win against his old club Charlton on New Year's Day, 2008. (WP)

It was a sad state of affairs, and consequently there was an air of triumph when the club returned to its rightful home, to a stadium which used to be the one of the largest in the country, capable of accommodating crowds in excess of 70,000 in its heyday. Under Jimmy Seed, the most successful manager in the club's history, they had finished runners-up to Manchester City in the top flight in 1937 and reached back-to-back FA Cup Finals in 1946 and 1947, winning the latter by beating Burnley 1-0. The Addicks, south London slang for the Haddocks (their nickname originates from a local fishmonger's practise of giving the team portions of haddock and chips) were one of the best-supported clubs in the land, boasting an impressive record attendance of 75,031 for an FA Cup fifth round tie against Aston Villa in 1938.

But fans from the first eight decades of the last century would not recognise The Valley as it looks now. In Uncle Len's day, the ground comprised a covered main stand surrounded by vast open concrete terraces, including that massive East Terrace which was widely acknowledged to be the biggest of its kind in England by the end of the 1930s. The whole place had become derelict during the club's temporary spell on the road at Selhurst Park and Upton Park, but thousands of volunteers cleared the site and three of the four stands were completely rebuilt following the club's return before Christmas, 1992. It still retains a good deal of character, not least in the Jimmy Seed Stand which dates back from the 1980s and houses the away fans, whose view of the action is often impeded by the one and only supporting pillar in the stadium, centrally located behind the goal.

I finally found my way up to the press box in The Valley for the first time on New Year's Day 2008 for a Championship fixture against lowly Colchester United. It was to be my one of only two 'new' grounds of that year, the other being the U's own new Community Stadium, and it was a special occasion, not least because the Essex visitors recorded a rare away victory.

Situated just south of the River Thames, near the Thames Barrier, the stadium is actually not very easy to spot. As the name suggests, it is tucked away in a valley. The original site was a disused chalk and sand quarry, known as The Swamps, with volunteers helping to level the pitch and build up earthen banks from the excavated material ready for the opening in 1919. The stadium's invisibility is also aided by the absence of any floodlight pylons jutting upwards. Instead, there are rows of lamps along the roofs of the east and west stands, while houses, shops and flats conceal the stadium quite effectively. I rather stumbled across it by accident having left the car down a side street and crossed the railway line.

Inside the ground, which is awash with red seats, the press box is one of the longest I have come across, stretching the length of the West Stand, the main stand, and accommodating more than 100 seats and individual desks. The views are excellent, looking right towards the away fans in the smaller South Stand, which is overlooked by a big block of flats from where the action can be watched for free from the balconies. To the left is the Covered End, where the most vocal of the home fans sit, while across the pitch is the lower single tier East Stand. The corners are filled in on both sides of the Covered End, and in the north-west corner can be found a plush media suite, which is where members of the press summon up the energy and enthusiasm for the short walk and long climb up to the press box.

The U's stumbled into 2008 rock-bottom of the Championship, but Geraint Williams's men lifted themselves off the bottom rung via a brace from ex-Charlton striker Kevin Lisbie in a shock 2-1 win in front of a 20,000-plus crowd. It was a grand way to celebrate the club's first visit to The Valley in 28 years. Lisbie turned the screw on his old team-mates by converting a 15th-minute penalty and then doubling the U's lead with a sublime overhead kick just before the half-hour. The Addicks did pull a goal back in first-half injury time, substitute Luke Varney netting from close in, but the visitors held on quite comfortably with many home fans booing off their team at the final whistle.

'Kevin Lisbie was on fire,' enthused U's boss Williams. 'He wishes that he could play against Charlton every week, and today proves that he should be able to do this against any opposition, anywhere. However, one swallow does not make a summer. We need more wins.'

I grabbed a word with Lisbie as he was leaving the stadium, among a swarm of autograph-hunters. It is a journalist's prerogative to pinch a few quotes, from anywhere at any time, especially when it involves the match-winner. Patience is often the name of the game and you can't just sit around in the media suite waiting for potential back-page quotes to fall on your lap. 'We proved that we are a good Championship side. We can handle it,' insisted Lisbie, who had made 176 senior appearances for the Addicks, most of them in the Premier League, before his switch to Colchester the previous summer.

Alas, whether they could 'handle it' or not, the U's did not record enough wins to stay up during the first half of 2008. They ended up bottom of the table, mustering just seven wins all season and scraping just two more victories after the New Year's Day success at The Valley, from the remaining 20 games. Lisbie led the way with 17 goals, an impressive tally in a struggling team, before switching to Ipswich Town in the summer of that year. Alan Pardew's Charlton ended up in mid-table, six points off the play-offs.

The Valley did not disappoint. I loved it, and I'm sure Uncle Len would have loved it as well.

104 COLCHESTER COMMUNITY STADIUM

Club: Colchester United
Founded: 1937
Ground: Colchester Community Stadium (since 2008)
First visit: 4 August 2008; Colchester 1 Athletic Bilbao 2

Sometimes football is all about timing, and Colchester United's move from Layer Road to their new Community Stadium in the summer of 2008 was a little awry. To be brutally honest, it came a year too late. Frayed-at-the-seams Layer Road – okay, worn-to-shreds Layer Road – was always a big home advantage for the U's, a humble abode that the big guns rarely fancied from the moment that they set eyes on the place. Two seasons in the Championship, the last two years at Layer Road, had been a graveyard for big names and dented the pride of many who graced the tiny away dressing room, including Sunderland, Derby, Ipswich, Norwich, Leeds, Wolves and so on.

Crowd limits of around 6,000, with severe restrictions on the number of away fans, meant serious financial constraints, to say nothing of the inability to cater for corporate groups or even cook hot meals on site, so a move to a new ground was long overdue. But when it did finally arrive, after some 30-odd years in the making – various alternative sites had been identified and explored from the mid-1970s onwards, well before my arrival at the newspaper – the U's had passed their peak. Relegation just three months earlier had brought an end to the most exciting period in the U's history, meaning that instead of the promise of a jam-packed Community Stadium (boasting an official capacity of 10,105) most weeks, and entertaining second-tier clubs with their large away support, the ground has usually been only half-full, at best, with just the odd exception.

I missed Layer Road, and I still do, but the Community Stadium was the way forward with its big corporate opportunities, executive boxes, conference suites, north-of-town location and sizeable car park. Without the £14m move to a new ground, on the site of

George Moncur wheels away to celebrate his key goal in the U's 1-0 home win over Preston on the final day of the 2014/15 season.

Cuckoo Farm and owned and largely funded by Colchester Borough Council, plus the building of an impressive training facility a little further along the A12 at Florence Park in Tiptree, it is doubtful whether the U's would have survived as a Football League club.

The stadium is neat and orderly, functional rather than clinical, although the atmosphere in a two thirds empty stadium on a bleak winter's afternoon can be rather lacking, just as when the wind swirls through the open corners separating the four one-tier stands, it can feel very, very cold! Furthermore, when the wind and the rain combine, the press box situated at the front of the main West Stand, next to the players' tunnel and to the left of the dugouts, is not the best place to be, trust me. I have had laptops die a death after a good soaking, and written notes washed away. In fact, for one match against Tranmere in February 2013, the press were evacuated to an empty executive box in a rear corner of the stand to watch the action for fear of drowning in the exposed-to-the-elements working area. Rovers won 5-1 that day.

I know the Community Stadium very well, having reported on hundreds of games over the last decade and a bit, but the great moments, and great games, have not been too plentiful. The days of the club punching well above their weight, against illustrious opponents in a rarefied atmosphere, are in the past, while many of the old faces and local characters from the Layer Road days disappeared with the move.

However, a few fixtures do stand out, none more so than the end-of-season thriller against Preston North End on 3 May 2015, which saw the U's fend off relegation on an afternoon of high drama. The U's began the day a point and two places adrift of safety, requiring a victory over promotion-chasing Preston and for lowly rivals Notts County and Crawley Town to both fail to win.

It was not looking good going into the final quarter of the game. Preston, targeting automatic promotion, were holding the U's to 0-0 with home striker Chris Porter having rattled the bar with a 57th-minute penalty, while Notts County and Crawley were both 1-0 up against Gillingham and Coventry respectively. But, in the glint of an eye, all that changed. George Moncur, the former West Ham midfielder, swept home from Porter's pass to send the U's home fans into raptures, and elsewhere County and Crawley kissed goodbye to their slender leads with both of them ending up defeated and so relegated into the fourth tier. It was a remarkable turnaround, and one that prompted tearful scenes at the final whistle.

U's boss Tony Humes enthused, 'The players withstood a barrage and withstood a battle.' Match-winner Moncur, a man with strong Christian beliefs, announced, 'There's no better feeling in the world than this one today.' And Porter admitted, 'For me it was a massive relief, having missed the penalty. I think we deserved it.'

My opening paragraph in the following day's newspaper simply read, 'The U's are staying up!'

Short and sweet.

As a postscript, while the media facilities are far superior to those on offer at Layer Road – although it was drier and warmer under cover in the old dingy press box – the actual

U's fans spill onto the pitch at the Community Stadium to celebrate their side's victory over Tottenham in the League Cup in September 2019, winning a penalty shoot-out after a 0-0 draw. (CM)

press lounge has led a nomadic life at the Community Stadium. It was located downstairs in the early days, near the manager's office, then went upstairs, then back downstairs again in a room close to where the away team coach pulls up outside the stadium, and then back on to the first floor to be sited in a suite behind a row of executive boxes.

Although shunted around a little, I can always sniff out the press tea and coffee, which comprised the limited menu of the Colchester United press refreshments (orange squash was an alternative), albeit for one glorious day when trays of pies, chips and peas suddenly appeared. Had the hard-working hacks finally been recognised by the catering corps for their behind-the-scenes contributions, in print and on the airwaves? Was this a culinary turning point in the life of a Colchester United reporter?

Alas, no. A TV celebrity duo by the names of Chris and Kem, *Love Island* mega-stars from the 2017 TV series (although I didn't know this at the time; I didn't recognise them from Adam and Eve) were at the Community Stadium, which coincided with a home match against Swindon Town in November, 2018, filming footage for their Challenge TV Series. This involved Chris Hughes and Kem Cetinay taking part in a penalty shoot-out during the half-time interval, and also apparently required the TV crew to be supplied with hot meals to keep them going.

I didn't linger in the press box to watch their efforts at the interval. Instead, while hearing a few jeers from the U's faithful in the background – I don't think everyone appreciated the presence of Chris and Kem as the half-time entertainment – I slipped out to scrounge a leftover portion of pie and chips from the press lounge.

Just as with matchday quotes, I can happily live off scraps.

105 STADIUM MK

Club: Milton Keynes Dons
Founded: 2004
Ground: Stadium MK (from 2007)
First visit: 12 January 2009; MK Dons 1 Colchester 1

The smart-looking, bowl-shaped Stadium MK is a terrific venue to watch football, and a great place to work, although I do have one gripe. Too many goals going in the wrong end!

What is it about Colchester United facing MK Dons during the month of November? I recall a 5-1 home drubbing at the hands of the Dons on 19 November 2011, and then an awful 5-1 reverse at Stadium MK just 370 days later, both painful experiences. But both were to be upstaged by another November nightmare, two years later, a humiliating 6-0 defeat on 30 November 2014.

I still shudder to think about it. With the exception of a smooth journey across country on the A421, and an excellent pre-match balti pie in the spacious press lounge, it was an away day from hell.

Will Packwood during his nightmarish U's debut at Stadium MK in 2014. (WP)

It was MK Dons' biggest victory in their short history (having been known as such since 2004), featuring a hat-trick from Benik Afobe and a class performance from Dele Alli, and the U's heaviest defeat for 21 years, since a 7-1 roasting at Crewe in 1993. It also

285

The view from the press box at a sparsely populated Stadium MK before the visiting U's take on the Dons. (CM)

featured the worst of all debuts, from American defender Will Packwood, and left the U's facing up to a season-long struggle to avoid relegation. This was achieved, as the previous chapter on the Community Stadium revealed, by the skin of their teeth with a late 1-0 home win over Preston.

The ground is affectionately known by some locals as the 'Moo Camp', a nod towards Barcelona's famous Nou Camp and more specifically a reference to the town's iconic sculpture of concrete cows. Just like at their former National Hockey Stadium home, one of the stands is nicknamed 'The Cowshed', where most of the more vocal home fans sit in the South Stand.

Outside, the stadium's frontage is gleaming black and silver with reflective panelling and mosaic tiling, surrounded by vast car parks with a hotel, indoor arena, cinema and a selection of restaurants all nearby. Hotel guests and football fans mingling, the 'Moo Camp' offers a very modern experience, right down to the wonderfully comfortable padded seats and generous leg room found throughout the bowl. In fact, many visiting fans make a point of commenting on the padded quality of the seats, on various football ground-related websites, after many unhappy years of squatting on unforgiving wooden or plastic alternatives. Sometimes the simple pleasures in life make all the difference.

So say what you like about MK Dons, whether it be the original club's controversial move from Wimbledon, in south London, or the uninspiring out-of-town location in the

Denbigh district of Bletchley, but you cannot knock the seats, or the views from them. The 'Moo Camp' is among the best in the land on both counts. And rest assured, you won't be getting piles after sitting through 90 minutes at an MK Dons home fixture.

Stadium MK always looks an imposing structure, even when most of the seats are empty. A crowd of under 8,000 witnessed the U's dire afternoon in November 2014, and most of them loved every minute of it, with the exception of a few hundred visiting fans in the North Stand and a posse of away reporters in the press box high up in the West Stand. In fact, the Dons could have scored far more than their six goals, having also struck the woodwork and been denied by some smart saves from U's keeper Sam Walker. I totalled up 27 goal attempts, the goal avalanche started by teenage midfielder Dele Alli, an England under-21 international at the time, breaking the deadlock with a 25-yarder. A £5m move to Tottenham was just around the corner for Alli, a home favourite who was born and raised in Milton Keynes and progressed through the youth system from the age of 11.

Arsenal loanee Afobe, destined for future big-money moves to the likes of Wolves (twice), Bournemouth and Stoke, tucked away two goals before half-time, and he had completed his hat-trick before the hour. A penalty by Ben Reeves and a late rocket from defender Lee Hodson rounded off one of the most one-sided third-tier contests I have ever seen.

And what about the aforementioned Will Packwood? Signed on loan from Birmingham City, where he had successfully graduated from the youth team to chalk up 20-odd first-team outings, the Massachusetts-born centre-half endured a torrid afternoon in an inexperienced U's defence that also included rookie full-backs in Cole Kpekawa and Elliot Hewitt, the latter on loan from Ipswich.

Packwood was given the task of trying to keep the talented Afobe quiet, and I think it's fair to say that the 21-year-old failed in that mission, although he didn't get much help from his team-mates. His afternoon was eventually cut short by the double whammy of a red card and an injury, and a triple one if you also include giving away a penalty, all happening on 67 minutes. The luckless Packwood brought down powerhouse Afobe for a clear-cut spot-kick, injuring his groin in the process. He was promptly sent off by referee Scott Mathieson, leaving the U's debutant to hobble off the pitch, and Reeves to slot home the Dons' fifth goal from the ensuing penalty.

I felt very sorry for Packwood that day. His progress at Birmingham had been hindered by a badly broken leg the previous year, and a loan spell at Cheltenham, after his brief loan stay at Colchester – that dire debut at MK Dons was to be his only U's appearance – was also cut short by a pulled hamstring. No wonder he returned to America later that summer, after his Birmingham contract was not renewed.

Looking back, Packwood's ill-fated Colchester debut was probably the saddest I have witnessed from a press box. I have seen many Colchester players sent off on their debuts over the years, several of them only lasting a few minutes, such as Southampton loanee left-back Stephen Hunt (sent off within 59 seconds of coming on as a substitute at

Chesterfield in 2004) and young Chelsea loanee Daniel Pappoe (sent off against Bradford in stoppage time, after just four minutes as a substitute, in 2013), but Packwood's debut packed an extra punch with the added injury and the penalty conceded.

Ever since, I have approached an away game at Milton Keynes with extreme caution, fearing the worst. And with a calculator to keep track of the goal count.

But at least I know that I won't get piles.

106 KEEPMOAT STADIUM

Club: Doncaster Rovers
Founded: 1879
Ground: Keepmoat Stadium (built 2006, opened 2007)
First visit: 19 September 2009; Doncaster 3 Ipswich 3

The Keepmoat Stadium, the home of Doncaster Rovers since the beginning of 2007, hosted the briefest post-match press conference I have ever attended in 30-plus years as a sports hack. It lasted precisely one minute and comprised precisely one question, with no answers. The fixture in question was a Championship duel between Rovers and visiting Ipswich Town, which the latter won by an emphatic 6-0 scoreline thanks primarily to a hat-trick by young striker Connor Wickham; the date was Tuesday, 15 February 2011; and the home manager, Sean O'Driscoll, was the central figure in the enactment of the shortest of all post-match press interviews.

It was a night to forget for dreadful Doncaster but a memorable one for Town boss Paul Jewell, and Wickham in particular. The only downside was that Wickham's three-goal cameo would raise a few more eyebrows among the bigger clubs and perhaps hasten his departure from Portman Road. Indeed, the teenager, who was still only 17 at the time of his hat-trick at the Keepmoat, did end up leaving in the summer, signing a four-year deal with Premier League club Sunderland for a fee of £8m.

I remember it was a filthy night in South Yorkshire, with persistent rain from the moment that we pulled up at the Keepmoat, a neat-and-tidy bowl-shaped stadium with four modest stands of the same height, adjacent to a smaller stadium which boasted a six-lane athletics track. In fact, we got soaked on walking the short distance from the spacious car park to the club entrance, behind the West Stand, drying off in the press lounge before kick-off.

It is unusual to get a view of the pitch from any press lounge, but the Keepmoat Stadium is an exception. It is perfectly possible to watch the whole match in comfort without actually taking your seat in the press box, very tempting on a wet and cold evening. The whole pitch is visible through massive windows and there's a good supply of tea, coffee and pies. However, we all did brave the elements to sample the atmosphere and get up close to the action among a sea of red seats. And we didn't regret it, gorging on a goal feast before reconvening for the bizarrely short post-match gathering back in the press lounge.

Inside the comfortable press lounge, overlooking the pitch at the Keepmoat Stadium. (CM)

Town were 3-0 up at half-time, helped by an opening own goal from centre-half Sam Hird, the ball looping off his head from Grant Leadbitter's long-range shot and dropping under the bar and into the net. Colin Healy doubled the lead with a well-worked team goal, and Wickham bagged his first of the night just before the interval, slamming home the rebound after keeper Gary Woods had spilled a rasping shot from Healy. Rovers were on the ropes and they were eventually knocked out by Wickham's second and Town's fourth on the hour. Centre-half Gareth McAuley headed home the fifth from Jimmy Bullard's free kick, and Wickham completed his hat-trick from the penalty spot on 90 minutes.

Wickham walked off with the match ball, while I hastily sent over my match report and scurried off to the press lounge in search of quotes to beat the tight 11pm deadline. As you would expect, after a resounding away victory, Town boss Jewell was out quickly to address the huddle of reporters. And as you would expect, most of our questions concerned Wickham.

'Connor is 17 and there's a lot of people talking about him. He's got huge potential, everyone knows that. Life's good for him at the moment, and if he had my good looks then he would have everything!' joked Jewell.

Connor Wickham celebrates one of his hat-trick of goals during Town's 6-0 win at Doncaster in 2011.

But what about Rovers boss O'Driscoll? He was not so quick out of the dressing room to meet the press, and he was not in the mood for jokes, understandably. But I didn't dream that he would be so 'short' with the journos.

He addressed the gathering by warning us that he would walk out as soon as someone asked him a 'stupid question'. One of the reporters, not me I hasten to add, kicked off proceedings by asking O'Driscoll how disappointed he was. That was all it needed for him to turn on his heels and storm out of the press lounge.

Luckily, I didn't have the equivalent of a book to write on O'Driscoll's post-game analysis for the back page of the following day's paper. Just space for one paragraph at the end of the copy. Fitted like a glove.

107 CARDIFF CITY STADIUM

Club: Cardiff City
Founded: 1899 (as Riverside AFC)
Ground: Cardiff City Stadium (since 2009)
First visit: 29 November 2009; Cardiff 1 Ipswich 2

It was at the Cardiff City Stadium, home of the Bluebirds since 2009, where Jimmy Bullard bagged a brace, prompting Ipswich Town manager Paul Jewell to compare me (nothing to do with footballing prowess) to the all-smiling veteran midfielder just two days later, at a Portman Road press conference. These are not the sort of incidents that you tend to forget.

I have had the pleasure of several visits to the imposing Cardiff City Stadium, built just a quarter of a mile away from the club's former ground at Ninian Park on the site of the old Cardiff Athletics Stadium in the Leckwith area of the city. I reported on Town's 2-1 win during City's first season at their new home, on a Sunday afternoon in late November 2009, when late goals from Jon Walters and substitute Jon Stead clinched all three points for Roy Keane's men. And I've also had the distinction of sitting in the press box in the Grandstand, one of three stands to share the name from their old Ninian Park counterparts (along with Canton End and Grange End), for a Friday evening FA Cup tie against Colchester United which featured the smallest attendance for a competitive game at the stadium. A mere 4,194 saw Cardiff's comfortable 3-1 win on 2 January 2015. However, Bullard's brace of early March 2011 demands the closest scrutiny, if only for the subsequent hair-raising comparison.

Jimmy Bullard celebrates his second goal during Town's 2-0 win at the Cardiff City Stadium in 2011. (WP)

Before I recount the awkward moment of Jewell's surprise Bullard/Marston jibe, or compliment, depending on your point of view, I need to back-track a couple of days to Town's comfortable 2-0 win at the Cardiff City Stadium. It was a Sky TV tea-time feast and, true to form when the TV cameras are around, Bullard rose to the occasion by scoring twice, on 67 and 86 minutes, to keep Cardiff stuck in third spot in the Championship, one point behind deadly rivals Swansea.

Hull City loanee Bullard had netted on his Town debut at Derby County in a 2-1 win a month earlier, when Stephen Bywater was in goal. And it was Bywater, by now on loan from the Rams to Cardiff, who was again beaten by Bullard to upset the form book. An away victory had seemed very unlikely at half-time with Cardiff in the ascendancy. Town keeper Martin Fulop, the man of the match, kept the scores level with a string of fine saves, and the big Hungarian also made several good blocks late in the game, but by this time Town were 2-0 up. Bullard broke the deadlock with a 25-yarder and doubled the lead from even further out with a free kick which deflected off the defensive wall and wrong-footed Bywater.

Fast forward two days and we come to the Portman Road press conference, looking back on the success at Cardiff.

I never usually switched off during an Ipswich Town press gathering, despite having the safety net of the Dictaphone switched on, but I must confess that I was feeling a little bit sleepy as Jewell replied to the usual flood of questions regarding injuries, away wins, extinguishing relegation fears, hopes of a top-ten finish and so on. Then, all of a sudden, the names 'Marston' and 'Bullard' were uttered in the same sentence by Town's forthright manager.

It was enough to give me a right start.

'He reminds me of another Jimmy Bullard, him there, Carl,' declared Jewell to the listening press corps. 'He's got that same type of hairstyle. He stands out in a crowd, and his [Bullard's] price stands out more than anything,' added Jewell.

Now I am not used to being compared to a former Premier League footballer, especially one who had commanded a fee in excess of £5m following his switch from Fulham to Hull at the start of 2009, and was also reported to have weekly wages from his parent club – the Tigers – of a cool £45,000. It did not sit easy with me.

And I doubt whether Bullard would have been very chuffed with being compared to a local scribe with dubious hair, especially one with two left feet, as opposed to two good feet!

I had been minding my own business, hoping to get a story about the possibility of Town signing man-of-the-moment Bullard on a permanent contract, with Jewell waxing lyrical about the midfielder's attributes, but I hadn't bargained on this. A reference to my 1970s hairstyle.

Fortunately, I don't think Bullard ever got wind of the comparison.

Meanwhile, my last trip to Cardiff City Stadium was for that record low attendance, a paltry crowd watching what proved to be awful game, a woefully one-sided FA Cup third round tie. I have never found City's new home to be even half as intimidating as their old Ninian Park, even though it is completely enclosed with the corners filled in, but it didn't

Jimmy Bullard prepares to celebrate his second goal during Town's 2-0 win at the Cardiff City Stadium in 2011. (WP)

need to be very partisan that night in early 2015. Colchester never did themselves justice in a 3-1 defeat, played in front of nearly 30,000 empty blue seats – the stadium capacity had just been increased to 33,280 by the expansion of the Ninian Stand, with its vast overhanging roof.

The game was televised live on BBC Two Wales, hence the Friday evening kick-off, and after Cole Kpekawa had netted a first-half own goal, further goals from Kadeem Harris and Kenwyne Jones eased Cardiff to victory despite a late consolation from Freddie Sears. Still, the press food was excellent.

The last word, though, should go to Bullard. Four years after his brace at Cardiff, and the subsequent press conference, I happened to be at Fetcham Grove in Surrey reporting on a non-league contest between hosts Leatherhead and visiting Leiston in October 2016. Bullard had just taken over as the boss of Isthmian League side Leatherhead and he oversaw a fine comeback from the Tanners, who trailed 3-1 going into injury time before scoring twice at the death for a 3-3 draw.

Bullard looked his usual dapper self that night. I, however, still resembled a throwback to the 1970s. Even Paul Jewell would have struggled to see the likeness.

SECTION SIX –
THE THIRD DECADE AND A BIT

108 RIVERSIDE STADIUM

Club: Middlesbrough
Founded: 1876
Ground: Riverside Stadium (from 1995)
First visit: 7 August 2010; Middlesbrough 1 Ipswich 3

My first visit to the Riverside Stadium, visible for miles around from the splendour of its River Tees setting, coincided with the opening day of a new season, which is always a time of renewed hope and usually a misguided belief that this could be the season when success comes to your club. More often than not the first day ends in huge disappointment, a summer of expectation ruined by an opening-day defeat and the knowledge that it could be a long nine months ahead.

The 2010/11 season at Ipswich Town was indeed destined to be a long, slow uphill struggle, although Town's first-day clash at Middlesbrough suggested otherwise. A heart-warming 3-1 away win, thanks to three second-half goals, prompted the headline 'Town flow at Riverside' in the following Monday morning's newspaper. It was too good to be true, Town third in the Championship table (okay, after just one game) and manager Roy Keane already smiling.

It was a surprise result, that's for certain, and I don't think many Town fans (from the official number of 740) who made the trip up to the north-east on that wet August afternoon were expecting anything other than a defeat. The previous season it had taken Keane's men nearly three months to record a league victory, while hosts Middlesbrough had been billed as one of the early favourites for promotion by all the major bookmakers, with manager Gordon Strachan having splashed out more than £6m in transfers during the year and securing seven new players over the summer.

Despite the heavy showers on Teesside, the Riverside Stadium still looked very enticing as we approached from the A66. Built in only 32 weeks and opened for the start of the 1995/96 campaign, the stadium is striking from the outside, an imposing bowl-shaped

Town's Tamas Priskin scores with a diving header at the Riverside Stadium on the opening day of the 2009/10 season.

structure that often (if you are lucky) has the unusual sight of a huge ship docked behind it as a backdrop, with the distinctive Grade II-listed Tees Transporter Bridge in the more distant background. Sure, the surrounding Middlehaven area, to the east of the city centre, resembled a desolate wasteland, a sprawl of empty yards and derelict industrial buildings, but the stadium shone like a beacon from this otherwise apocalyptic scene (the area has since enjoyed a period of regeneration).

What catches the eye are the red entrance gates to the stadium, emblazoned with 'MIDDLESBROUGH AFC' in white lettering, which were salvaged from Ayresome Park, the club's former home for 92 years. The gates were erected in 2005. Inside these famous wrought iron grill gates is the decorative modern entrance to the stadium, which is where I headed as a member of the travelling Town written press corps, a select group which fitted into one car, with the promise of a hot meal served in the cosy press lounge in the West Stand. The stadium itself can generate a good atmosphere with the noise drifting across the River Tees, which flows just behind the North Stand, otherwise known as the New Holgate End as a reminder of the famous Holgate End at Ayresome Park.

On the pitch, Boro nursed a 1-0 lead at half-time via Scott McDonald's close-range header on 22 minutes. No surprise there, but the scoreline was a little harsh on the visitors, one felt, and Keane's men duly made their own dominance felt in the second period with three unanswered goals by Tommy Smith, Tamas Priskin and Jon Stead.

This was no smash-and-grab opening-day away win. True, New Zealander Smith's opener, the centre-half's first professional goal, was a shade lucky as his shot took a wicked deflection off defender Matthew Bates, but otherwise there was nothing fortuitous about this victory. It was an especially important day for Priskin, who had mustered just one goal in 17 league outings for Town since a £1.7m move from Watford the previous summer. The Hungarian's header from Carlos Edwards's cross put the visitors ahead, before a transfer-listed Stead volleyed home the third.

So far, so good. My matchday report culminated in the short paragraph, 'All the pre-season scepticism has vanished already.'

Unfortunately, I was a little premature. Just four days later, Keane announced a big fall-out with his skipper Jon Walters, who had requested a transfer after the win at Middlesbrough. Stripped of the captaincy and dropped from the first-team squad, Walters didn't play for Town again, instead moving to Premier League Stoke City, where he flourished. 'He has gone about things the wrong way,' insisted a brooding Keane during the midweek press conference, with reference to Walters's wish to cut his ties with Town. It was the latest example of an alleged fall-out featuring Keane, who had reportedly had a dressing room bust-up with striker Pablo Couñago the previous week, leaving the Spaniard to train with the under-18s and eventually move out on loan to Crystal Palace.

Town stayed in the promotion race for several weeks but then began to slide down the table, with Keane becoming even more and more the centre of attention, while also cutting more and more of an isolated figure. As he would regularly remind us, the press, on a weekly basis, he was never one to court public relations. 'I didn't come here with my own PR people, and I don't have pals in the media. I don't have people working for me, putting out positive messages all the time,' announced Keane.

By then, the opening-day joy at the Riverside Stadium was just a distant memory.

Keane was gone by the following January, though he did last longer than Strachan, who had vacated the Boro hot-seat by October. Managers sink or swim at the mercy of the tides, none more so than beside the Tees.

109 EMIRATES STADIUM

Club: Arsenal
Founded: 1886 (as Dial Square, in Woolwich)
Ground: Emirates Stadium (since 2006)
First visit: 25 January 2011; Arsenal 3 Ipswich 0

Wow! In my humble opinion, and in my line of work, there is no better club football stadium in England than the Emirates, the home of Arsenal since 2006, at least in terms of comfort and indeed sheer luxury.

The ground is known by many names: 'Ashburton Grove' before the sponsorship deal with Emirates kicked in; 'The Arsenal Stadium' in the eyes of UEFA for European competition; the 'Arsenal Terminal' because of its close association with Emirates Airlines,

Cesc Fabregas tucks home Arsenal's third against Ipswich in a 3-0 win in a League Cup semi-final tie at the Emirates. (WP)

who now have the rights to the stadium name until 2028; and 'The Library', a hangover from the Highbury days and a nod towards the silent corporate and business clients who make up a large proportion of the home crowd, housed in the middle two tiers of the impressive quartet of four-tiered stands.

The stadium looks dramatic from the outside, especially from passing trains on the adjacent East Coast Line. It is an amazing structure of glass and steel, which gleams in the sunlight and glows under the floodlights, a massive bowl-shaped amphitheatre topped by a dish-like white oval roof which dips inwards slightly. The place screams 'Arsenal', the exterior walls proudly surrounded by eight huge murals which give the effect of warmly embracing the whole stadium with 32 legends of Arsenal's history emblazoned on them, standing arm in arm in a huddle, interspersed with images of the club badge.

Predictably, the Emirates attracts views that are polar opposites, from those who condemn the whole corporate package to those who just love the majestic beauty of this 60,000-plus all-seater footballing temple. Personally, I have never had a better away-day press experience. From the wonderfully red-and-white-decked interior, with the exquisite vantage point looking either end towards the evocatively named North Bank and Clock End (two ghosts of Highbury), to the three-course pre-match meal (choice of chicken, salmon, or a vegetarian option on my first visit) served in the bustling media suite, below ground level, with the half-time cones filled with fish and chips, the Emirates is top-notch, world-class.

And yet I would not like to work here every other weekend, because I'd put on about four stone in weight every season, and also probably end up a spoilt brat. I do prefer the more down-to-earth, shabby, less formal vibe that characterises my more mundane visits

Ipswich Town fans enjoy their big night out at the Emirates for a League Cup semi-final second-leg tie in 2011.

to Layer Road, the Abbey Stadium, Moss Rose and alike, but the Emirates is fantastic, the best-looking of all footballing venues. Padded seats inside, wide concourses to walk around on the outside. Space to breathe, despite the stadium having been constructed within a tight 17-acre triangular, constrained by railway lines to the east and west, and Queensland Road to the south.

In summary, the Emirates is living life in the fast lane, without having forgotten its past. The atmosphere might be hushed at times, with often more noise coming from the kitchens underground than from the seats encircling a perfect pitch, but it's still footballing heaven.

And Ipswich Town must have felt like they were going to heaven and back (or at least to Wembley) after successfully protecting a 1-0 lead from the first leg of their League Cup semi-final against the Gunners for the first hour of a highly-charged second leg at the Emirates on Tuesday, January 2011. Hungarian striker Tamas Priskin, much maligned, had steered home the only goal of the game at Portman Road 13 days earlier. But I must confess that I didn't give the visitors much chance of holding on to that slender advantage as I made my way to the Emirates for the first time via the Piccadilly Line, disembarking at the Arsenal station and walking the short distance along Gillespie Road and Drayton Park, and then over the Ken Friar Bridge to be drawn to the warm glow of red and white in the London night.

Roy Keane had been axed as Town boss just five days before the first leg, with Paul Jewell officially taking over the day after Town's 1-0 win. Cesc Fabregas had stoked the fire by likening Town's first-leg tactics to those of the rugby field rather than the football pitch, in particular accusing the Suffolk side of punting the ball upfield at every opportunity.

'I don't know if it's a long ball or if it's a rugby kick, but it worked for them. Ipswich played well, but Arsenal played the football,' insisted midfielder and skipper Fabregas, who also criticised the state of the Portman Road pitch. In all truth, it sounded like sour grapes from the Spaniard.

Fabregas was no doubt also a frustrated man on home turf as plucky Town held Arsene Wenger's Gunners to 0-0 until after the hour, in front of a near-capacity crowd of 59,387. Town fans delighted in renditions of '1-0 to the rugby team', making the most of it before the inevitable happened. A trip to Wembley was looming large, but Town were near the bottom of the Championship for a reason – they were not a great team – and they finally succumbed after 151 minutes of shutting out the Gunners over the two legs, Nicklas Bendtner curling home a delightful right-footed shot following 19-year-old Jack Wilshere's slick pass. Three minutes later Arsenal were 2-0 up on the night, and 2-1 ahead on aggregate, keeper Marton Fulop unable to intercept Andry Arshavin's corner with centre-half Laurent Koscielny nodding home. Suddenly the mood within the Emirates had completely changed, from one of increasing anxiety to one of unbridled joy.

Yet Town were still in the tie until Fabregas broke through on to Arshavin's pass to slot home the third on 77 minutes. Their resistance was finally broken, though the 9,000 away fans certainly appreciated their side's efforts.

And so to the eagerly-awaited press conference, staged in the media centre within a 150-seater theatre, the tiered black seats looking down on the platform below. I felt like any minute a university professor would walk in and deliver a lecture on Tolstoy, or Einstein. Instead, we were treated to Arsène Wenger, whose arrival was typically cool and calm, as was his response to a barrage of questions. 'For us it is the perfect night,' said Wenger. 'Our season depends on our performances, our results and our consistency. We needed to be patient, calm and mature, and you have to credit Ipswich as they defended with great spirit.'

Next entered Jewell, though by then many of the national hacks had left the theatre to type up their Wenger quotes before the dreaded deadlines. I stayed put.

'We knew Arsenal would have all the ball and we would soak it up and make it difficult, but we have held them and also had that bit of luck. For an hour we looked all right, however the manner of the goals were disappointing. We always knew we were going to be under the cosh here, but you have got to give the players credit because they were not disgraced over two games,' enthused Jewell.

Then it was time to beat my own deadline, eat a tub of vanilla ice cream saved from my many earlier visits to the buffet, and then return to the joys of the underground. For the record, Arsenal lost 2-1 to Birmingham City in the League Cup Final on their first visit to Wembley since 1998, while my belt felt a little tighter around my midriff for a couple of days after my Emirates adventure.

110 B2NET STADIUM (CHESTERFIELD FC STADIUM)

Club: Chesterfield

Founded: 1919 (several earlier incarnations, including 1867 and 1884)

Ground: b2net Stadium (built 2010, renamed Proact Stadium in 2012, Tecnique Stadium in 2020)

First visit: 1 October 2011; Chesterfield 0 Colchester 1

Goal feasts and gentle curves, two reasons why I like Chesterfield's post-Saltergate home.

Whenever I attend a match at the Spireites' new ground, whether it be called the b2net Stadium, the Proact Stadium or by any other future sponsored name, it always feels like I am either at Colchester United's Community Stadium or Shrewsbury Town's New Meadow. All of them are out of the same mould; four single-tier stands with predominantly blue seats and a capacity of around 10,000, sited out of town and opened within a few years of each other.

Chesterfield's new home, though, has the edge in my eyes, helped by the aesthetically pleasing shape of the roofs along each flank, on the east and west sides, with their gentle curves topped by white steelwork. It feels a little more homely and compact than the U's or Shrews' abodes, and it has the added bonus of being sited on a busy street (Sheffield Road) with a good choice of eateries. The stadium also tends to guarantee goals whenever I am stationed in the press box, not necessarily a good thing, but it keeps me busy.

The U's scramble a late equaliser in a 3-3 draw at Chesterfield in 2015, the ball flying in off defender Charlie Raglan (No. 16) for an own goal. (WP)

A night to forget for keeper Chris Lewington, who shipped six goals on his U's league debut at Chesterfield in April 2015. (WP)

Two quickfire visits in 2015, in April and September, both featured six goals, with Chesterfield netting nine of the 12 and Colchester the other three. Both matches were crazy affairs.

I will gloss over the first, a 6-0 thrashing on a Tuesday evening in mid-April. The relegation-threatened U's were 3-0 down insides 17 minutes through an opener by ex-Ipswich midfielder Gary Roberts and a brace by Sam Clucas, and Tony Humes's men shipped three more goals in the second period to leave them second-from-bottom of League One with just four fixtures remaining. It was a torrid U's league debut for Chris Lewington, who was given a long-awaited chance in goal due to Sam Walker's knee injury. Walker had been ever-present throughout the league campaign, and the former Chelsea trainee chose a good game to sit out. Lewington, signed from Dagenham & Redbridge the previous summer, had a nervous first touch when scuffing an attempted clearing kick, and was then exposed by a crumbling defence for the rest of the night. Enough said.

Remarkably the U's managed to avoid relegation, and they were back at the Proact Stadium as it had been re-named in 2012, for another League One clash five months later. This time the six goals were spread evenly on a mad afternoon. The U's completely dominated, playing against a Chesterfield side reduced to ten men after just 15 minutes, registering 29 goal attempts and enjoying two-thirds of the possession. Yet it needed an injury-time own goal to rescue even a point for the Essex visitors in the hot Derbyshire sunshine.

I described the match, in my opening paragraph of Monday's newspaper, as 'one of the craziest Colchester United games I have ever witnessed, a ten out of ten for entertainment, but a three out of ten for defending'. Spireites right-back Drew Talbot was sent off for a professional foul on U's debutant Marvin Sordell on quarter of an hour, after which the U's rained in shots from all angles, only to be let down by some woeful finishing. Instead, Chesterfield built up a 3-1 lead with goals by Dan Jones, Lee Novak and Sam Morsy, with a lone reply from Gavin Massey, going into the final 15 minutes. Substitute George Moncur reduced the deficit but it was not until the 92nd minute that an equaliser was found, Moncur's shot cannoning back off the bar and defender Charlie Raglan diverting Callum Harriott's cross into his own net for the most unfortunate of own goals.

'Sometimes you can't just believe what you are seeing,' admitted a bewildered Tony Humes. I had to agree with him.

111 AMEX STADIUM (FALMER STADIUM)

Club: Brighton & Hove Albion
Founded: 1901
Ground: AMEX Stadium (full name American Express Community Stadium, since 2011)
First visit: 25 February 2012; Brighton 3 Ipswich 0

The fourth entry from Brighton & Hove Albion, following my previous visits to the long-term Goldstone Ground, Gillingham's Priestfield and the athletics-orientated Withdean

Stadium, the Falmer Stadium (its unsponsored name) has been well worth the wait, despite all the deviations. A deservedly proud home for the previously unsettled Seagulls, in one of the most beautiful parts of the country.

I walked the South Downs Way as a student, a 100-mile National Trail extending from Eastbourne, on the East Sussex coast, through to Winchester in Hampshire. I didn't imagine that a 30,000-plus all-seater football stadium would end up appearing within a few miles of the rolling hills of the Downs, but that's what happened with the construction of the AMEX Stadium (an abbreviation for American Express Community Stadium) over three years between 2008 and its opening of 2011.

The South Downs Way route, which crosses the busy A27 near Lewes, is just a few miles away, and the stadium enjoys an isolated, tranquil setting, squatting low down in the landscape – 138,000 cubic metres of chalk were excavated in its construction – with the rolling hills as a backdrop. It is three miles away from the hustle and bustle of Brighton seafront, with the University of Sussex campus as its main companion on the other side of the A27 Brighton bypass. Falmer itself is no more than a small village, best known for its large pond and parish church before the arrival of the football stadium, so its perhaps no surprise that there were problems with planning permission and legal challenges before the green light was given for the ambitious project to proceed.

Results-wise, the AMEX has not been kind to me on my couple of visits. I have sat in the press box reporting on Ipswich Town, during Paul Jewell's regime, and Colchester United, under John McGreal, and both ended the same way – heavy defeats and no goals. A 3-0 reverse for Town came in the Championship on 25 February 2012, followed by a 4-0 EFL Cup exit for the U's in August 2016.

The impressive AMEX Stadium, the home of Brighton & Hove Albion.

On both occasions, the venue rather than the match was the highlight. It's captivating. The graceful white curves of the stadium, with its attractive tubular steelwork on top of a transparent roof, gives it an elegant, dignified look, which sits well with the surrounding slopes of the chalk Downs. Inside, the two stands alongside the pitch are striking, with their top tiers following the contours of the semi-circular pattern of the roof above. Both ends have smaller, single-tier stands, with their roofs slanting downwards from the bigger West Stand, which gives the place a slightly unbalanced look. But the acoustics are good in such an enclosed environment, and it is on the other end of the scale to the Withdean Stadium with its motley collection of temporary stands and support scaffolding.

Although a second-tier clash, if felt like I was entering a Premier League ground when arriving with Ipswich in early 2012. The stadium was still in the process of being finished, with the East Stand opposite waiting to welcome a second tier, but the main West Stand was stunning with a few images of white seagulls breaking up the decks of blue seats. The media suite screamed Premier League, as did the hot food, and the open press box is in a prime position, centrally low-down above the players' tunnel and the two dugouts.

Alas, Town failed to inspire in late February 2012, during Brighton's first season at their dazzling new home. A first-half opener from energetic striker Craig Mackail-Smith and a second-half brace by the talented Ashley Barnes, the first of these aided by a dreadful clearance from keeper Arran Lee-Barrett, halted a run of four straight wins which had seen them shake off the threat of relegation. Town were no match for the crisp passing and fluent attacks of Gus Poyet's men, who had been promoted as League One champions the previous season.

The East Sussex club were clearly on an upward trend after years in the doldrums. The opposite could be said of Town.

As I wrote in my concluding paragraph, for Monday's *Ipswich Star* newspaper, 'Nice ground, good weather, big crowd, good game. Shame about the result.'

A return visit for a lower-key EFL Cup first round tie in early August 2016, was more memorable for a few hours spent on the pebble beach near Brighton Pier than the action on the Falmer Stadium pitch. I travelled down to the south coast with my wife and youngest step-son Harry in tow earlier in the day, to amble around the warren of narrow, twisting alleyways that make up The Lanes, before heading down to the beach with an early tea of takeaway fish and chips. The distance to the football ground is only about three miles but it took nearly as long to get from the centre of Brighton to the AMEX for the early evening kick-off than it did to get from Suffolk to Sussex earlier in the day. Two hours in rush-hour traffic jams and in the end we only just made the kick-off. A brisk walk/jog from the car park and I just had time to scoop up a team sheet from the media suite before heading straight to the press box, while Helen and Harry joined 250-plus U's fans in a crowd of under 7,000.

The League Two U's held their own for more than an hour, within the resplendent if four fifths empty AMEX, before three goals in a ten-minute spell by Sam Baldock, Jamie

Murphy and Elvis Manu killed off the tie. Murphy added a late fourth in a 4-0 win, while I made Kazenga LuaLua, the younger brother of former Colchester star Lomana LuaLua, as my man of the match. The young trickster set up the first two goals, but in truth I would have made him MOM for just simply being the younger brother of one of my all-time favourite footballers!

The fish and chips sat heavy in the stomach that night, and the sunburn on the arms and neck soon began to throb, a punishment for those few hours on the beach, but my admiration for the AMEX and the surrounding South Downs remained undiminished.

112 BROADHALL WAY

Club: Stevenage
Founded: 1976 (as Stevenage Borough)
Ground: Broadhall Way (built 1961, used by current club since 1980)
First visit: 20 March 2012; Stevenage 0 Colchester 0

Funfairs and Duracell bunnies.

There's rarely been a dull moment whenever I have veered off the A1 at junction seven to report on a match at Stevenage's Broadhall Way, located within a stone's throw of a busy roundabout but with an inviting expanse of woodland and parkland just beyond.

The funfair entertainment, across the A602 road from the football ground, often reduces the car parking options in the Fairlands Valley Park, especially if the circus is in town. That can present a challenge to sneak the pool car into the car park even a couple of hours before kick-off, but I have usually managed to squeeze in among the adjacent trucks, caravans and funfair attractions. Feeling smug about this small achievement, which then ensures only a short walk across the busy dual carriage or via the underpass to the home of Stevenage FC, I have usually swung open the car door and planted both feet straight into a deep puddle. In the sphere of lower-division football reporting, success is usually swiftly followed by a reality check.

As for the battery-fuelled 'Duracell bunnies', well that was a phrase coined by then-Colchester United manager Joe Dunne after the U's first of several triumphs at Broadhall Way, this particular one occurring on my second visit, on 2 March 2013.

One of the smallest grounds to grace the Football League, I have always been fond of Broadhall Way, which has been named the Lamex Stadium for sponsorship reasons in recent years. Away fans, although not bowled over by the overall experience, do tend to refer to the Hertfordshire venue as 'neat', 'tidy', 'modern' and 'compact'. It is all of these things, but with a little bit of extra character thrown in for good measure. The non-league roots are clear for all to see, especially from the outside, but the four separate stands are small and cosy, and the press box in the main West Stand is more than adequate. Furthermore, there's a charming little triangular clock tower jutting out

The view from the press box at Stevenage's Broadhall Way, with the author's lap-top in the foreground. (CM)

from the top of the roof in the East Terrace opposite, to add a touch of personality. I am easily pleased.

By the time of my early visits, the South Stand had already been converted into a single-tiered all-seater to house the away fans, although the North Terrace still amounted to just seven steps of terraces (that has since been superseded by a new covered all-seated stand, opened at the end of 2019). The ground is very intimate, given its small size, with hosts Boro so used to playing the role of underdogs since their promotion to the Football League in 2010. In fact, their size had counted against them four years previously when lifting the Conference title in 1995/96, only to be denied promotion because of their poor facilities and specifically their failure to meet the required ground capacity of at least 6,000, with at least 1,000 seats.

The 'Duracell bunnies' quote came after Colchester's hopes of avoiding relegation from League One were boosted by a second-half brace from burly striker Jabo Ibehre in a 2-0 win in early March 2013. Ibehre headed home Chelsea loanee Billy Clifford's 61st-minute free kick and then steered home winger Gavin Massey's low cross, both goals netted in front of the South Stand housing the jubilant U's away fans.

'We had a meeting during the week about playing high-energy football. We just feel that we have to be like Duracell bunnies. We have to run and run and run, as well as pressing and harrying,' insisted manager Dunne. That high-octane approach ended up paying dividends for the U's because they duly escaped the clutches of relegation on the final day of the season, thanks to a 2-0 win at Carlisle.

Double goalscorer Ibehre, who used to ply his trade at Leyton Orient and MK Dons, was full of beans after his Stevenage success. He told me, 'We don't do draws, as everyone knows, so you would say we need five more wins to get safe.'

As it happened, Dunne's men only won three of their remaining ten matches, but managed to draw four others, so avoiding the drop by three points. Ibehre, therefore, was a little off the mark with his assessment, although I would never have disagreed with the big man, especially as he ended the season as the club's top scorer with eight goals.

Future visits to Broadhall Way have often been just as fruitful, both in terms of parking the car and witnessing away-day wins, such as a helter-skelter 4-2 victory on New Year's Day 2017, when John McGreal's side lost a two-goal lead before late goals from substitutes Chris Porter and Tarique Fosu, on loan from Reading, sealed victory in a breathless finale.

Despite all these happy days, I haven't yet been in the Big Top, braved a rollercoaster ride or purchased some candy floss from the adjacent funfair. And just to confirm, I have never left Stevenage with my face painted, or with a prize from the Hook-a-Duck stall in my car boot.

Maybe next time.

113 BROADFIELD STADIUM

Club: Crawley Town
Founded: 1896 (as Crawley FC)
Ground: Broadfield Stadium (since 1997)
First visit: 1 January 2013; Crawley 3 Colchester 0

'Just Like Heaven', a song from the extensive repertoire of alternative rock band The Cure, who happen to be one of my favourite bands and who also happen to hail from Crawley (the band's founder members were school-mates in the town), is as good a place as any to start with regards Crawley Town. I mention this with a heavy dose of irony because the Red Devils' Broadfield Stadium has been anything but 'just like heaven' over the years, at least for me and for Colchester United.

You could be excused for getting Stevenage and Crawley mixed up. Broadfield Stadium is not unlike Broadhall Way in more than just name. Both are small, compact venues, mostly decked in red and white with restricted capacities of between 6,000 and 8,000; both are sited about a mile from their respective town centres and respective railway stations, nestling close to wooded areas; both clubs represent 'New Towns' spawned from the New Towns Act of 1946; both have only won promotion to the Football League in recent years, Stevenage in 2010 and Crawley in 2011; and curiously both grounds squat next to big roundabouts.

The view from the press box at Crawley Town's Broadfield Stadium. (CM)

For me, Stevenage is an hour's drive across country and usually ends in an away win, whereas Crawley involves crossing the Thames and grappling with the M25 and M23, and usually culminates in an away defeat. The trend was set by a New Year's Day tanking for Colchester at the start of 2013, a 3-0 loss representing a seventh defeat on the trot for Joe Dunne's men, a miserable run that was to be extended to nine defeats on the spin over nearly a ten-week period.

In fact, I only reported on one away win in my first seven outings to Broadfield Stadium, situated just seven miles south of Gatwick Airport, the one bright spark arriving on Boxing Day 2017.

The Red Devils had only moved to the purpose-built ground a decade earlier after 48 years at their rather shabby but homely Town Mead ground, two miles across town. Four years later the West Sussex club were promoted to the Football League as Conference champions under manager Steve Evans, who also laid the foundations for an immediate promotion to League One before his departure for Rotherham. Around the same time, in April 2012, the ground was upgraded with the rapid construction of a new rather makeshift 2,000 all-seater East Stand, complete with a few supporting pillars to impede views, which upped the capacity to 5,500 (it is now just over 6,000), with new floodlights and turnstiles also installed.

But the West Stand opposite is the main feature of the whole ground, running two thirds of the way along the pitch. The small two-rowed press box is at the rear of this modest-sized structure, to the right of the dugouts closest to the South Stand. Once wedged into the press box, it is difficult to get out, unless you happen to be planted at one end. It is a case of tucking in the legs, breathing in, and making sure you don't spill your tea over your neighbour's laptop.

Actually, although the press area is very snug, it is a fine place to work, boosted by the presence of a tiny press room at the top of the flight of stairs behind the press box. Trays of sandwiches, a big teapot and a friendly welcome are always assured. The view from the box is also unobstructed, the whole stand being raised a few feet above pitch level, which requires fans to scale a few steps to reach their bright red seats. And on top of the stand are three rather unusual mini floodlights, perched on slender red pylons.

My one away-day success, on Boxing Day 2017, put home-grown Sammie Szmodics firmly in the spotlight. The talented 22-year-old bagged the second goal in Colchester's 2-0 victory, a result which propelled John McGreal's side up to fifth in the League Two table. It also increased the transfer speculation surrounding Szmodics, who had been at the Essex club since the age of seven and worked his way up through the youth ranks to become hot property in the lower divisions.

Conditions were awful in West Sussex for this post-Christmas fare. Broadfield Stadium was rainswept but the U's had fun in the rain against Harry Kewell's hosts. Frenchman Mikael Mandron scored after just four minutes, capitalising on hesitancy by left-back Cedric Evina to slam the ball into the net from ten yards out, and Szmodics doubled the

The exterior of Crawley Town's Broadfield Stadium. (CM)

lead by running on to Brandon Comley's through ball and lifting his shot over advancing Turkish keeper Yusuf Mersin.

'It's going to take a big bid for Sammie to go,' insisted boss McGreal, after the dust (or rather wet turf) had settled at Crawley's neat home. 'He is one of our own, we are playing him regularly and he is enjoying his football. It would have to be a huge offer to come in.'

During the subsequent January transfer window there was speculation that Premier League club Bournemouth had tabled a £1m bid for Szmodics, but he ended up staying with the U's for another 18 months until his final contract wound down, enabling him to move to Bristol City for an undisclosed compensation fee following previous interest from both Hull and Leeds. So ended 16 years with the U's.

U's fans were sad to see Szmodics, 'one of our own', leave the club. Yet there were no tears. As Robert Smith, lead singer of The Cure, reminds us in one of the Crawley band's more famous singles and albums, 'Boys Don't Cry'.

114 VICTORIA ROAD

Club: Dagenham & Redbridge
Founded: 1992 (merger between Redbridge Forest and Dagenham)
Ground: Victoria Road (built 1917)
First visit: 3 September 2013; Dagenham & Redbridge 4 Colchester 1

Whenever I think of Victoria Road, I rather oddly dwell on the name of Magnus Okuonghae, the subject of the most queries I have ever received from fellow journalists and radio commentators concerning the precise pronunciation of a player's name. I mention this because Okuonghae, the most likeable of centre-halves, used to be a mainstay of Dagenham & Redbridge's defence before completing a successful move to Colchester United. Fittingly, he was to be the centre of attention when I paid my first visit to the Victoria Road press box, for a Football League Trophy duel, then known as the Johnstone's Paint Trophy, in the late summer of 2013. But more of that later.

Under-stated and well hidden, Victoria Road has been a no-nonsense home to non-league football and occasionally the lower echelons of the Football League ever since two clubs, Dagenham FC and Redbridge Forest FC, merged to become one bigger, stronger entity in 1992. That was the same year Colchester regained their Football League status after two years in the Conference wilderness. So a good year.

I have arrived via car, and parked in one of the side streets, and also via the underground, because the Dagenham East Station on the District Line is only 400 metres from the ground. Either way, it's all very laidback, as reflected by the short walk up the quiet Victoria Road, just off the A112 Rainham Road. There is nothing pretentious about the ground, or the area; a motley collection of stands and terraces with walkways in front and old-fashioned turnstile blocks outside. A very tiny car park, small club offices and some

Colchester United right-back Brian Wilson is brought crashing to the ground by this challenge by Afolabi Obafemi at Victoria Road in 2013. (WP)

eccentricities are thrown in for good measure. For instance, the players emerge from a tunnel at one corner of the ground, not via the main stand, and Victoria Road remains the most unlikely place where I have been treated to a complimentary cream cake at half-time.

Actually, the place has hosted football in this corner of east London since 1917, starting off with works team football, although during these early years it was just a playing field rather than a recognised stadium. Sterling Athletic, representing Sterling Telegraph & Electrical Company, who had a factory next door, were the first to play there, before Briggs Sports (representing Briggs Motor Bodies) also staged home games on the site. The pitch finally became fully enclosed in 1955, when Dagenham FC left the Dagenham Arena to take up residence at Victoria Road, after which a wooden stand was erected and new toilets and turnstiles were installed.

The biggest transformation, however, was prompted by the emergence of Dagenham & Redbridge as a new club in 1992. A new main stand was up and running by 2001, replacing the old wooden stand, equipped with 800 seats and a press area, while eight years later the tallest stand in the venue was opened at the Pondfield Road End with

'DAGGERS' emblazoned in white lettering on otherwise banks of red seats. Elsewhere, the stadium has clung on to its non-league feel with the small open terrace at the Bury Road End, to the right of the main stand and topped by a fairly basic electric scoreboard, and the low-roofed north stand with its mixture of seats and terraces.

The current capacity is small, just over 6,000, although the ground did accommodate 7,200 fans for an FA Cup tie between Dagenham and Reading in 1967. However, the biggest home attendance for Dagenham & Redbridge was in the same competition against Ipswich Town in January 2002. I remember that day well, because George Burley's Town were trailing 1-0 early on, perhaps ruing the fact that the match had passed an earlier pitch inspection after the covers had been removed.

American-born Junior McDougald gave an early lead to the Daggers, who were plying their trade in the Conference and went on to finish as runners-up behind champions Boston United that season. Town were a Premier League outfit and the away contingent in a crowd of 5,949 were gearing themselves up for the horror of an FA Cup shock until a brace from Argentine attacker Sixto Peralta, one from future Town manager Jim Magilton and a fourth from goal poacher Marcus Stewart settled the tie.

Alas for Town, they were drawn at home to Manchester City in round four. City were destined to win the First Division (now Championship) title that season, and they brushed aside their opponents 4-1. Burley's boys, who had an evergreen Finidi George patrolling the right flank for much of the campaign – no one quite knew the exact age of the veteran Nigerian international, who was widely regarded as a £3.1m flop – were relegated at the end of that season.

In my experience, although my stays in the Daggers' press box have been few and far between, the team taking the lead is usually the team that ends up being beaten.

That was also the case when I visited with Colchester for a Football League Trophy fixture on a warm Tuesday evening on 3 September 2013. The U's were 1-0 up at half-time only to end up being hammered 4-1.

Which brings me to the aforementioned Magnus Okuonghae, playing for the U's against his old club. The big man with the bold name endured the ignominy of being sent off that evening, much to the delight of the locals. It was looking good when new club skipper Brian Wilson crashed home a 38th-minute free kick to put the U's 1-0 up at half-time, at which point I was surprised by the offer of a cream cake, but the evening went downhill from there on in.

In fact, the second period was nothing short of calamitous. Ex-U's winger Medy Elito equalised for the Daggers, before Okuonghae was dismissed for two bookable offences, the second yellow earned for chopping down winger Zavon Hines. Ten-man U's then leaked three more goals to defender Brian Saah, skipper Abu Ogogo and substitute Louis Dennis.

Manager Joe Dunne, who always wore his heart on his sleeve, confessed, 'It's a bad night for the club. We were ragged in the second half. We were there to be put to the sword, and we were. It could so easily have been five or six.'

The scene at Victoria Road before Ipswich Town's FA Cup tie in 2002, with the covers being removed. (WP)

Whether a Dagger or a sword, it hurt all the same. Okuonghae had been Dagenham's player of the season four years earlier, in 2008/09, before his switch to Colchester. The Lagos-born defender went on to play 215 first-team games for the U's, over six years, and enjoyed a spell as club captain.

But I think it's fair to say that his evening's return to Victoria Road was a low point. I don't think he even got a cream cake.

115 NEW YORK STADIUM

Club: Rotherham United
Founded: 1925 (merger of Rotherham County and Rotherham Town)
Ground: New York Stadium (since 2012)
First visit: 2 November 2013; Rotherham 2 Colchester 2

Last-gasp equalisers. They can be so joyful, and yet at the same time so exasperating, especially for those toiling away in the press box. Any reporter wanting an easy life hates late, injury-time, last-kick-of-the-game goals, especially if they completely alter the whole complexion of the afternoon and potentially alter the whole tone of a match report. Although remaining neutral and non-partisan at all times (and so politically correct), a local or regional scribe secretly hopes for a victory or positive result from the team they happen to watch week in, week out, up and down the country. They hope for goals to be flying into the opposing net. That is until the last few minutes, when stories have been

Elliot Lee pops up with a last-gasp headed equaliser for the U's at the New York Stadium in 2013. (WP)

written, headlines have been finalised, introductions have been composed. Then, and only then, are goals unwelcome.

Which brings me to New York Stadium, the smart, all red-and-white home of Rotherham United since 2012, following on from 101 years at Millmoor and an intervening four years at the temporary base of the Don Valley Stadium in neighbourly Sheffield.

Built beside the River Don, not far from the old Millmoor ground to the west of the town centre, the Millers' new stadium is very impressive from the outside, and also the inside. It was constructed on the site of the former Guest and Chrimes foundry and brass works, which had a long and distinguished history in the town for more than 150 years from the 1840s until its closure in 1999, so it is close to the hearts of many local residents. This area of the town is historically known as New York, hence the name of the stadium, while the old foundry also had strong links with New York City in America, for whom it made fire hydrants.

The resplendent football stadium, built at a cost of nearly £20m, is a worthy successor on this site. I visited during the Millers' second season at their new home, in early November 2013, once again following the fortunes of Colchester United. I didn't hold up much hope of a positive result for the visitors so I even went for a pre-match run along the River Don and adjacent canal (I occasionally pack my trainers and running kit for such a window of opportunity) before entering the stadium via the striking West Stand, expecting that jog to be the highlight of the afternoon. At the time, the press lounge was next to the players' dressing rooms, which meant a heady mix of dance/jungle/hip-hop/rap/grime – I am no expert in musical genres – penetrating the walls and infiltrating the minds of the seated

Outside the New York Stadium.

members of the press, most of whom were calmly sipping cups of tea and discussing the possibility of Rotherham securing back-to-back promotions.

Larger-than-life manager Steve Evans had guided the Millers to second spot in League Two the previous season, and they were to eventually celebrate another promotion via the play-offs in 2012/13, but not before kissing goodbye to two points in a smash-and-grab 2-2 draw at the hands of the U's. Despite a seventh-minute opener from ex-Brentford midfielder Marcus Bean, who directed a diving header from Everton loanee Luke Garbutt's cross into the net via the inside of a post, the Millers were soon in charge and following the script. Goal poacher Matt Tubbs, on loan from Bournemouth, chalked up his first goal for the South Yorkshire club to equalise just two minutes later, and Kieran Agard bundled the Millers ahead from close in.

Sitting in the back of the press box, in the West Stand – the largest stand in this fully enclosed stadium, looking out towards two rather futuristic floodlights hovering over both ends of the roof of the East Stand opposite – I braced myself for a heavy defeat. Rotherham looked far too powerful, and should have been well out of sight instead of nursing a slender 2-1 lead going into injury time. They had battered Colchester.

Then, with my story top-and-tailed and ready to be published online, up popped diminutive striker Elliot Lee, in the fifth minute of stoppage time, with the most unlikely of equalisers. Some head tennis followed Garbutt's delivery from a corner, before West

Ham loanee Lee sneaked an instinctive header over keeper Adam Collin, the ball clipping the underside of the bar and dropping over the line before a desperate Collin could attempt to clear. Lee could hardly contain himself. It was the 18-year-old's first senior goal and he celebrated in front of the U's fans by taking off his shirt, which ensured a booking to go with his last-ditch equaliser. Of course he didn't care about the yellow card, and was also no doubt oblivious to the number of hasty re-writes that he had prompted in the press box. It was time for me to make use of the delete button and begin a rapid revision.

'It felt like I had scored the winner,' enthused a breathless Lee, after I had belatedly posted my revamped report and headed for some post-match reaction down by the empty dugouts. 'Moments like this, you have got to cherish, and I know that we celebrated like we had won,' added Lee, the son of former England midfielder Rob Lee.

Predictably, Millers boss Steve Evans was seething, 'I'm as down as I've ever been. We've absolutely battered Colchester from start to finish!'

An emotionally draining afternoon for all concerned on the banks of the River Don, and a memorable first visit for me. A day of contrasts. A peaceful jog along the canal, followed by the thumping music from the dressing rooms; the delight of a late equaliser, tempered by the thought of a quick re-write; a buzzing Elliot Lee, at the start of his footballing career, and an angry Steve Evans, midway through his managerial career.

Who needs New York City, with its Yankee Stadium, Madison Square Garden and Citi Field, when you can spend the afternoon in New York Stadium, the home of the proud Millers? And don't leave early. There might be a sting in the tail, and a dreaded re-write.

116 HIGHBURY STADIUM

Club: Fleetwood Town
Founded: 1908 (current incarnation, 1997)
Ground: Highbury Stadium (since 1939)
First visit: 25 April 2015; Fleetwood 2 Colchester 3

Fleetwood, on the Fylde peninsular, has always been better known as a centre for deep-sea fishing and fish processing rather than as a hotbed for football. But that is all changing.

There aren't many football clubs in the land, if any, that have enjoyed such a meteoric rise as Fleetwood Town, especially as the latest incarnation of the club was only born in 1997. Off the pitch, the ground has been completely redeveloped; on the pitch, the Cod Army soared from the ninth tier to the third in just a 17-year period, a phenomenal effort for a club with such shallow roots and such a small fanbase. That amazing run of success included a crazy period of six promotions in just ten seasons, between 2004 and 2014.

Stuck out on the Lancashire coast, just eight miles up the road from the bigger and more established Blackpool, Fleetwood re-emerged as a then ninth-tier club in Division Two of the North West Counties League in 1997. The fishing industry might already

Chris Porter converts a penalty at Highbury Stadium to keep alive the U's hopes of avoiding relegation in 2015. (WP)

have declined, especially during the 1960s and the 1970s, hastened by the damaging 'Cod Wars' with Iceland over fishing rights in the North Atlantic which brought the town and the port to its knees, but the Cod Army has done the place proud at a new-look Highbury Stadium.

Fish processing is still a big industry in the town, and the docks and the waterfront have enjoyed facelifts, but the biggest success story has been down in the south-west corner of Memorial Park, where Fleetwood ply their trade in front of modest crowds of around 3,000.

My first visit for a Football League match was in late April 2015, by which time the club had already propelled themselves into League One by dint of clinching promotion via the play-offs and a Wembley victory over Burton Albion the previous year. But I had actually graced the Highbury Stadium press box previously, earlier on in the Cod Army's rise, when a young-ish striker by the name of Jamie Vardy was banging in the goals. Vardy did not disappoint on my first appearance, while reporting on the fortunes of unfashionable Braintree Town in the National League, then known as the Blue Square Premier.

Fleetwood had been languishing in the ninth tier, in the North West Counties Division One, just seven years before I braved a midweek round trip of 560 miles. There was a buzz about the place, and Highbury Stadium had already benefited from a big renovation period. Everywhere was red and gleaming, with new stands on all four sides. Players, fans, officials, directors, stewards, all were smiling. It's remarkable what success can do to a club.

One player in particular ran rings around Braintree that night. The distinctive figure of Vardy, a striker with a big attitude and a shiny crop of dyed hair, capped a dynamic display by bagging the second goal in a comfortable 3-1 home win on 24 January 2012, just one of 31 league goals he netted that term. Vardy had celebrated his 25th birthday just a fortnight earlier. Four months later, his career really took off with a £1m move to Leicester City. A Premier League title and a plethora of England caps followed.

Fleetwood went on to win the Conference title that season with a whopping 103 points, and so secure promotion to the Football League for the first time in their history.

Two seasons later they were in League One, hence my return visit with Colchester on the penultimate weekend of the 2014/15 season for what proved to be a highly dramatic 3-2 away win.

Stadium-wise, a frenzy of activity between 2007 and 2011 had left the venue – named after the nearby street of Highbury Avenue rather than a reference to Arsenal's old ground – looking modern and compact. The South Stand, a covered terrace accommodating away fans, was the first to be unveiled, strangely running just two thirds of the way along one end of the pitch. The Highbury Stand followed in 2008, built in front of the old main stand, which can still be glimpsed in its derelict state from certain vantage points. This west side of the ground, incorporating the main stand and the adjacent 'Scratching Shed' standing area, had both been set back from the pitch to accommodate a speedway track which had been a home to Fleetwood Flyers of the National League Division Two between 1948 and 1952.

The North Stand, referred to as the Memorial Stand, was opened in the same year, stretching the full length of one end, but it is the bigger, state-of-the-art Parkside Stand on the east side which is the main feature of the stadium, incorporating 2,000 seats, several executive boxes, a hospitality suite and (most importantly of all!) 20 press seats, all topped off by a pleasing semi-circular roof. Built at a cost of about £4.5m, and boosting the ground's capacity to over 5,000, the Parkside Stand was opened just over a year before my arrival with Braintree, and four years before my return with Colchester, the scene of some late away delight.

'What a rollercoaster of emotions beside the seaside' – so read the opening paragraph of my match report in the following Monday's newspaper.

The U's were actually staring relegation full in the face when trailing 2-1 to the red-and-white-clad hosts. If that scoreline had stayed the same, and lowly rivals Crawley and Crewe had held on to their respective leads, then Tony Humes's men would have been officially relegated. In short, the U's seemed doomed. George Moncur had guided a low shot beyond keeper Chris Maxwell to put the visitors 1-0 up inside two minutes of the second period, only for two goals in a 12-minute spell from Jamie Proctor and substitute David Ball to leave the U's League One existence hanging on a knife-edge.

However, a slice of luck is what is often needed in such desperate circumstances, and it duly arrived on 85 minutes when Gavin Massey's intended cross took a deflection off a defender to deceive Maxwell and fly into the net. Two minutes later, 2-2 became 2-3 as Chris Porter rammed home a penalty after substitute Dion Sembie-Ferris had been chopped down in the box by defender Nathan Pond.

'It was up and down, but we never gave up. A draw was no good for us today. We are all battling for our lives, and we've got a belief that we can get out of it,' insisted Humes, whose side did take four points from their final two fixtures to stay up. Fleetwood were safe in mid-table.

It was an afternoon of raw emotion. I recall a few angry U's supporters invading the pitch at one point, when their team looked down and out. Match-winner Porter, always very tactful, explained, 'Fans are entitled to their opinions. But it's times like this when we need the fans to be behind us.'

Many U's supporters might have lost their voices after such a frenetic afternoon, though they were in the right place for a remedy. The Fisherman's Friend, that rather potent menthol lozenge, can cure any degree of sore throat, and the manufacturer (Lofthouse Fleetwood) is fortuitously based close to Highbury Stadium. The lozenge has reliably been curing respiratory problems since the 1860s, originally with deep-sea fishermen as its target audience, although football fans could do worse than suck on one of their liquorice lozenges after a raucous afternoon.

I was back at Highbury Stadium with Colchester just four months later for another League One clash on 22 August 2015. This time there was no happy ending, just a 4-0 drubbing, the U's slipping to second-from-bottom of the table, which is where they were destined to finish the season.

I didn't need a Fisherman's Friend that evening, and neither did any of the subdued U's fans, who officially numbered 142. The throat was still sound, it was just the head that was throbbing.

117 PIRELLI STADIUM

Club: Burton Albion
Founded: 1950
Ground: Pirelli Stadium (since 2005)
First visit: 28 November 2015; Burton 5 Colchester 1

Two League One visits; the first a horribly one-sided affair, the second a slender opening day away victory. The small, simple Pirelli Stadium, functional but very welcoming, has hosted the most successful period of Burton Albion's history since the Staffordshire club moved 200 yards along the road from their previous Eton Park home in 1950.

The pride of Burton upon Trent was certainly on an upward trend when I visited with managerless Colchester United in late November, 2015, although I was not expecting a 5-1 thrashing.

The caretakers, John McGreal, left, interim manager, and Wayne Brown, soon-to-be caretaker boss, before the U's 5-1 defeat at Burton Albion in 2015.

The Brewers, a nickname celebrating the town's brewing heritage, had moved to their new stadium ten years previously, during the summer of 2005. Fans at the old Eton Park could see the new stadium gradually take shape over an 18-month period further along

Princess Way, on the former site of the Pirelli Sports and Social Club. The land had been donated to the club by Pirelli in return for the naming rights to the stadium, a happy partnership, and the result was a compact venue of four separate stands, built at a cost of £7.2m and currently boasting a capacity of 6,912.

The modest media lounge and press box are in the main South Stand, the only all-seater stand, the other three all being small covered terraces with rather stark back walls, including the Popside opposite and the away fans in the East Stand, below a roof from which hangs a scoreboard. All are straight-edged and rather clinical. The South Stand, however, is attractive from the outside, with its glass frontage and 'Burton Albion' emblazoned in bright yellow lettering, and the interior has a row of windows above the dark blue and yellow seats, topped by a wide band of white panelling. It looks the part.

The whole place was buzzing on my first visit, the Brewers going great guns under ex-Leeds and Chelsea front-man Jimmy Floyd Hasselbaink. They had been crowned League Two champions the previous season to reach League One for the first time in their history, and were destined to complete back-to-back promotions at the end of the season to soar into the Championship as runners-up to Wigan Athletic. This was achieved even though Hasselbaink had left for QPR in December, to be replaced by the returning Nigel Clough, who had laid the foundations for the club's elevation to the Football League in 2009. By contrast, Colchester were on course for relegation back to the fourth tier.

I think it's fair to say that the U's were in turmoil for this third-tier fixture. Tony Humes had departed just two days earlier after 15 months at the helm, leaving his assistant Richard Hall and under-21 development coach John McGreal to take the reins on a joint interim basis for a big test at the Pirelli Stadium. It was a test that the players failed, yet again.

Ipswich Town fans celebrate behind the goal at the Pirelli Stadium. (WP)

Burton were riding high in third spot, and had only conceded 14 goals in their first 18 fixtures, but the U's made it too easy for them. Despite their lofty position, the Brewers had only mustered 17 goals from their first 18 games. Yet they managed to bang home five against the all-at-sea U's, which was particularly painful for Hall and McGreal, who had both been solid centre-halves during their playing days.

Charlton loanee winger Callum Harriott did put the U's ahead after just four minutes, but they were soon buried under an avalanche of goals with Nasser El Khayati, Mark Duffy, Tom Naylor, Lucas Akins and Timmy Thiele all on target.

Caretaker Hall was visibly upset by the departure of Humes, a sentiment he expressed during his post-match interview at the Pirelli, 'I felt every jeer [from the fans]. I felt every stab and I felt everything for him. We were a partnership. Ultimately it was his decision. On the pitch, today was the same old story. Individual errors have cost us.'

Hasselbaink had sympathy for his opponents. The Dutchman said, 'I don't think it was a 5-1 game. I don't think that we deserved five goals.' All in all, it was not a happy first visit to the Pirelli Stadium.

But my second trip was a happier experience, a 1-0 opening-day win for Ipswich Town at the start of the 2019/20 campaign, Town's first down in the third tier for 62 years following relegation the previous season. Regular *East Anglian Daily Times* Town correspondent Stuart Watson had chosen to attend a family wedding, on the opening day of the season, so I was summoned off the bench to preside over a narrow win with colleague Andy Warren.

A familiar face, Luke Garbutt, marked his Ipswich debut with the winning goal via a deflected shot on 11 minutes, as Paul Lambert's men survived a feisty encounter and one injury-time scare when giant keeper Tomas Holy, another debutant, dithered too long and had his kick charged down by Liam Boyce, the ball taking an age to drop, fortunately the wrong side of the post. Burton had ended the game with ten men due to Stephen Quinn's 78th-minute dismissal, so it would have been a real kick in the teeth to concede such a late equaliser.

Having known left-footer Garbutt well from his days as a loanee at Colchester, it was no hardship to interview him after the game, in front of the away dugout. 'It was a special moment and it was nice to get off the mark so early on, and show the fans what I can do. That's the first time I have scored a goal on my debut for a club,' enthused Garbutt, who had enjoyed previous loan spells at Cheltenham, Colchester, Fulham, Wigan and Oxford, but had only ever made five league appearances for his parent club Everton.

The days of banging out a report, and grabbing a few quotes from the press lounge or in front of the away coach, before making a quick return to the car to hit the road before 6pm on a Saturday evening were long gone, unfortunately. The demands of social media, extra stories on the website and especially the need for a post-match video delay the departure until nearer 7pm these days. In fact, the Pirelli Stadium was deserted by the time that Andy Warren and I sat down to muse over the match in front of the video camera handled so expertly by our younger and more technically-savvy colleague, Ross Halls.

Andy began by wrongly introducing me as Stuart Watson. I explained that a follically challenged Stuart had undergone a hair transplant over the summer, aiming for the Jimmy Bullard look. To be honest, the content didn't get much better for the rest of the five-minute clip.

Good old Burton. A graveyard for visiting interim managers, and a home for dodgy post-match videos.

118 THE HIVE STADIUM

Club: Barnet
Founded: 1888
Ground: The Hive Stadium (from 2013)
First visit: 17 September 2016; Barnet 1 Colchester 1

It's not a bad way to spend a Saturday afternoon, watching the trains rumble past on the Jubilee Line of the London underground between Canons Park and Queensbury, on a raised embankment behind the West Stand at the Hive Stadium, home to Barnet since 2013. To be honest, it's often preferable to what is being served up on the pitch.

Although the press box area is located opposite in the Hive Stand, at the back of which are the main club offices and banqueting facilities, this is not really the main focal point of the ground. Only a 'privileged few' get to seat here, with a mere six rows of seats

A train trundles past between two stands at The Hive during a visit by Colchester United. (CM)

Colchester United players celebrate a winning goal by Sammie Szmodics at The Hive in 2017.

numbering about 750 in total spread across the bottom in front of an office-type back wall, bland and grey. The press, directors, corporate guests, a few injured or out-of-favour players and other officials tend to frequent this stand, which was extended in 2015, a year before my first visit with Colchester United.

It is the much bigger and taller Legends Stand, behind which the trains emerge and disappear, where the main action takes place, with its 2,700 seats, most of them bright orange with an additional band of black seats. The away fans take over the north end, where an equally high new seated stand was opened in the summer of 2016, just a few months before my first visit, while home fans can stand and watch the game from the Bees Terrace at the smaller south end.

It is a world away from Underhill, the Bees' former ground for 106 years between 1907 and 2013. Geographically, the Hive is in Edgware, in the borough of Harrow, six miles away from Barnet. Aesthetically, the Hive's modern look, surrounded by all-weather pitches and playing fields, is a bit different to Underhill, which was hemmed in by residential streets, narrow lanes and back gardens. In fact, it's quite a pleasant walk from Canons Park underground station to the Hive, across green playing fields with Barnet's new ground plus the arch of Wembley Stadium in the distance – Wembley is only three miles away.

Up closer, my first impression was that I was heading for a sports centre, rather than a football ground, not really surprising when considered that the Hive was Barnet's training complex from 2009, four years before their final move from Underhill. The entrance is quite well hidden off Camrose Avenue, with a couple of distinctive orange welcome signs, and there's a wide expanse of playing fields and enclosed all-weather floodlit pitches surrounding the main stadium and car park. I felt ready to play a relaxed five-a-side, not report on a League Two fixture in mid-September, 2016.

The match was intriguing. I managed to find an upstairs press lounge before kick-off, which resembled a boardroom with tea-making facilities, and lost count of the number of trains that trundled past the Legends Stand during a nervy 90 minutes of football, a game featuring contrasting styles. Barnet, promoted back into the Football League as National League champions in 2014/15, were a good old-fashioned fourth tier team packed with experienced journeymen and powerhouse players. They were a handful for Colchester's much younger, less streetwise brigade, who had slipped down from League One just a few months earlier.

The black and amber Bees proved tough, physical opposition, and deserved their point from a 1-1 draw after Reading loanee Tarique Fosu had put the visitors ahead inside six minutes with his first goal for the club. Martin Allen, in his 14th year as a club manager, saw his side blow chance after chance until Curtis Weston swept home an 82nd-minute equaliser.

I'm not saying the contest was drab, or the train-spotting a bit humdrum, but I did find time to calculate the age differences of the two teams, which proved revealing. Ten of Barnet's 18-man squad were aged 27 or over, spearheaded by 36-year-old centre-half Michael Nelson, while just two of the U's 18-man squad were older than 24 – skipper Luke Prosser and striker Chris Porter. Further calculations were made: Barnet's average age was 26.4; the U's average just 22.6. I know, fascinating.

I was back at the Hive, counting trains from the press area, for another U's away day in November 2017 when a wonderful late strike from Sammie Szmodics clinched a 1-0 win for the visitors. On as a substitute, Szmodics curled home a long-range pearler within ten minutes of his introduction. The defeat saw the Bees drop into the relegation zone, and they duly went down on the final day of the season on goal difference below Morecambe, despite winning their last three matches and taking 13 points from 15 in their last five, with Martin Allen back as manager from mid-March. The escape act was thwarted by Morecambe securing a point in a goalless draw at Coventry on the final day.

I have yet to return, although I did get to within three miles of the Hive when taking part in the Sunny Hill parkrun in nearby Hendon, ironically in the borough of Barnet. The sun didn't shine at Sunny Hill Park – it was wet and windy that Saturday morning – and although I could see Wembley from the top of the hill to the south, I couldn't make out the Hive to the west. A hidden gem.

119 RODNEY PARADE

Club: Newport County
Founded: 1912 (as Newport & Monmouth County AFC), reformed in 1989
Ground: Rodney Parade (opened 1877, Newport County's home since 2012)
First league visit: 14 January 2017; Newport 1 Colchester 1

While the majority of my more recent 'first' visits to football venues have been to new purpose-built stadiums, perhaps understandably, Rodney Parade bucks that trend. Not only is Newport County's current home one of the oldest sports venues in the Football League, but it was also designed without football in mind. Instead, the land was first acquired by Newport Athletic Club in 1877, two years after that club's foundation, and was used as a venue for cricket, athletics, tennis and rugby union. In fact, association football was not played at Rodney Parade until as late as 2012, with the arrival of Newport County.

My first visit was just a year later, in 2013, although that was for an FA Cup tie featuring non-league Braintree Town. A return trip with Colchester United in mid-January 2017 saw my first league encounter in this corner of South Wales, by which time I knew what to expect. Namely, a wonderfully sprawling ground, with a hotchpotch of different stands, a big playing surface and an unusual layout.

And while many of the new, smaller, out-of-town stadiums all look very similar and are bereft of personality, that accusation cannot be aimed at Rodney Parade, which is instantly recognisable and deliciously unique, conveniently sited close to the city centre on the east bank of the River Usk.

Football remains the poor cousin to rugby union in these parts, and Rodney Parade does still feel more like a rugby venue than a haven for footy, which in fact it is. The ground is owned and operated by the Welsh Rugby Union, and is home to Newport RFC and the Dragons (formerly Newport Gwent Dragons). The extra line markings on the pitch, for rugby purposes, plus the well-worn state of the playing surface, are tell-tale signs that football does not rule the roost there.

My first visit with Braintree for an FA Cup first round replay on a Tuesday evening in November 2013 was a bit of a blur under the lights. Alan Devonshire's Braintree team, who only narrowly missed out on the National League play-offs that season, were knocked out by a slender 1-0 scoreline, undone by Robbie Wilmott's 45th-minute free kick. Newport had just returned to the Football League via the play-offs the previous season and had the best home record in League Two with six wins from eight. 'We had a few chances,' remarked Devonshire, the former England and West Ham midfielder, a man of few words. 'But Newport are a good side, so I wouldn't say this was a wasted opportunity.' The crowd was a sparse 1,406, and I recall rattling around in a relatively empty, antiquated West Stand, with just the odd reporter in the large press area. The whole place had an odd feel to it.

I appreciated this more on my return with Colchester United for a Saturday afternoon League Two tussle on 14 January 2017. I had time to appreciate all the nooks and crannies of Rodney Parade.

The ground is well hidden behind houses, and a warren of alleyways, despite being so close to the River Usk, and it can be a stern test of navigational skills to find the entrance to the stadium and locate the appropriate stand, via a large grass area beyond the main gates. The old two-tiered Hazells Stand, complete with its 40 press seats, is a throwback to olden times with its supporting pillars spread across the middle of the stand, topped by a chunky roof which does not stretch all the way along. There is a terrace paddock section in front of the seats, made up of shallow, crumbling steps, with open areas at both ends. Opposite, and looking out of place surrounded by old, quirky structures, is the Bisley Stand, all shiny and modern having been opened in 2011. The multi-coloured seats, principally reds, ambers and blacks, are eye-catching, as are the four rather neat little floodlights which poke out across the top of a very high roof.

What gives Rodney Parade its rather peculiar personality are the two open ends. The uncovered Town Terrace seems to be miles from the pitch – well, several yards away at least – while the far end is a mishmash of temporary seats with a strange building squeezed in at one corner, housing the changing rooms, with a pyramid-shaped roof.

Such is Rodney Parade. There is nowhere else quite like it. Ugly, but strangely appealing. Odd, but rather endearing.

And so to that visit with Colchester United, newcomers to Rodney Parade, in early 2017. This was proper lower-league football. A pudding of a pitch and a real scrap between a home team fighting for their lives, and a visiting team dreaming of promotion. Newport were rock-bottom of the Football League and were on the back of eight straight defeats, having won just four games from 24 all season. The U's, by contrast, were on a five-game winning streak. The outcome was a 1-1 draw, which strangely suited the U's more than the Exiles.

Josh Sheehan's deflected low drive on 23 minutes was matched by Chris Porter's super-cool penalty just 12 minutes later. Porter's equaliser came after Darren Jones had needlessly fouled U's striker Kurtis Guthrie, whose main claim to fame was that he had begun his

Rodney Parade, the home of Newport County. (CM)

footballing career on the island of Jersey. The draw may have ended Newport's rotten run, but new boss Graham Westley still faced a daunting task with his side marooned at the bottom by five points.

'When my defenders were asked to stand tall, they did just that. We knew that Newport would be up and around us, having brought in a lot of new personnel recently,' explained U's boss John McGreal, with reference to Westley's feverish activity during the January transfer window which numbered 14 new players.

There was a happy ending for the Exiles, a nickname harking back to the early days of the club's reformation in 1989, when they led a nomadic existence, starting with a first season 80 miles away at Moreton-in-Marsh. Manager Westley, who had been appointed the previous October, was unable to halt the slide, and by the time that he departed in March the Welsh club were 11 points adrift of safety with just 12 games left. Newport-born Mike Flynn, who had been recruited by Westley as a player, took caretaker charge and the transformation was immediate. The deficit was wiped out and in the end it came down to the final game of the season, and in fact the final few minutes. Defender Mark O'Brien netted an 89th-minute winner in a 2-1 home victory over Notts County, the drama unfolding in front of a record league crowd for the ground of 7,326, so completing the 'great escape' at the expense of Hartlepool, who were relegated out of the Football League.

An unconventional but exciting end to a campaign. A bit like Rodney Parade, where anything goes, and where everything is not always as it seems.

120 GLOBE ARENA

Club: Morecambe
Founded: 1920
Ground: Globe Arena (since 2010)
First visit: 17 April 2017; Morecambe 1 Colchester 1

The Globe Arena, the neat little home of Morecambe since 2010, after 89 years at Christie Park, has a dubious claim to fame among my personal recollections – it was the backdrop for the dullest of all goalless stalemates, as part of a 510-mile round trip to the distant Lancashire coast on a cold midweek evening in mid-March 2018.

I questioned my sanity that night, or at least my enthusiasm for reporting on League Two football, and my capacity to take the rough with the smooth. And yet I also had to take my hat off to the small pocket of Colchester United supporters who braved the trip without any need for writing post-match reports for a local newspaper. The U's official following was 52, and I managed to count most of them, from an overall crowd of just 893.

In fact, I think this was the first time I had covered a Football League match featuring an attendance of below 1,000. A low-key, dour affair, bereft of entertainment, ending in a predictable point apiece to bring closure to a forgettable night.

The view from the press box at the Globe Arena during the warm-up. (CM)

Yet this was not my first visit to the Globe Arena. There have been brighter more colourful clashes, with more talking points and even a few goals. And believe it or not, I am a big fan of the place.

There is nothing overbearing about the Globe Arena. In fact, the opposite is the case. The surrounding area is dominated by a sprawling caravan site, with a Marstons pub (alas, despite my surname I have no connection with Marstons Brewery), The Hurley Flyer, conveniently located just outside the ground. The first impressions of the stadium are favourable, with a smart, chunky frontage sporting the red and white club crest of a shrimp above the entrance to the Main Stand.

The stand is on three floors, and outside accommodates just over 2,000 seats, the central section all-red and the rest all white, with a corporate glassed area at the rear. The views are excellent, and the press well catered for, although the rest of the stadium is far more modest, especially the open North Terrace opposite which amounts to nothing more than a few steps in front of a formidable perimeter brick wall, split into two halves by a service entrance. Only the die-hards tend to stand there in all weathers, braving the wind and rain that sweeps in from the coast. There are covered terraces at both ends, the home fans in the bigger West Terrace and the away supporters housed in the smaller East Terrace. Conditions in the latter are cramped, to say the least, with fans often referring to the incredibly tight turnstile blocks which are very unforgiving for the 'larger' supporter, and the lack of space behind the stand to queue for refreshments.

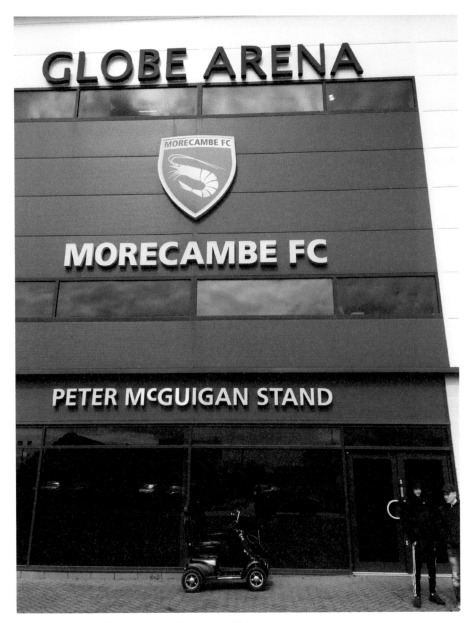

The grand frontage of Morecambe's Globe Arena. (CM)

Still this is Morecambe, not Manchester United, and the club can feel proud of their home, named after Globe Construction, the company that built the ground. The official capacity is 6,476, and it fulfils the main aim of aping the club's former Christie Park, with its one main stand and three terraces. A modern version of an old home.

My first visit was an Easter Monday clash on 17 April 2017 when Colchester's play-off hopes took a big hit following a 1-1 draw. U's old boy Michael Rose, as so often happens with former players, managed to score against his ex-employers via a late penalty. For a long time it looked as though right-back Richard Brindley was going to be the unlikely match-winner for the U's. Brindley put John McGreal's side ahead with a curling free kick on 22 minutes, so notching his first goal of the season in his 40th appearance, and his first goal for more than a year. An away win for the U's would have seen them move level on points with the play-off places, but instead substitute Alex Wynter upended Antony Evans in the box, enabling Rose to dispatch an 87th-minute spot-kick for a share of the spoils.

Boss McGreal was seething. He admitted, 'It's a sore one for us to accept, especially as the games are running out. We just needed to take responsibility and manage the game. We had it won, so I'm gutted and devastated.' It ended up being a costly dropped two points, because after the final three games of the campaign the U's found themselves one point and one place outside the play-offs.

A year later came another U's disappointment at the Globe Arena, which was fast becoming a graveyard for their play-off hopes. The 52 hardy visiting fans didn't have much to talk about on the long journey home to Essex through the early hours of a Wednesday morning. A 0-0 draw with hardly any goalmouth action, and the fourth lowest gate (893) that the U's have ever played in front of in the Football League (before the arrival of Covid-19 and the need to play league games behind closed doors). The lowest remains the 804 who watched the U's match at Hartlepool in May 1983.

'It's been the story of our season,' rued McGreal. 'It wasn't wet and it wasn't windy, so there are no excuses.'

Indeed, I enjoyed some rare luxury on this trip, with a pre-match run in the spring sunshine on the promenade around Morecambe Bay, and then an overnight stay in a bed-and-breakfast, with a hearty full English to follow the next morning.

Shame about the game.

121 THE NEW LAWN

Club: Forest Green Rovers
Founded: 1889
Ground: The New Lawn (since 2006)
First league visit: 2 April 2018; Forest Green Rovers 1 Colchester 2

My two step-sons, Jack and Harry, are very different characters, but they share certain similarities. Here are two quick examples: they are both strictly vegan; and neither of them have attended a football match at the New Lawn.

However, I guarantee that if they were to roll up to the home of Forest Green Rovers, on the western edge of the small town of Nailsworth, in the delightful Cotswolds – which I admit is unlikely – then they would both love the catering, if not the footy.

A side view of the main stand at the New Lawn, the home of Forest Green Rovers. (CM)

All-vegan menus, solar panels, cow manure, recycled rainwater, robotic lawn mowers. The New Lawn, home to Forest Green Rovers since 2006, is like no other football ground in the country, if not the world. Inspired by chairman Dale Vince, a former New Age Traveller turned millionaire businessman who owns the green energy company Ecotricity, based at nearby Stroud, the club has been a beacon for eco-friendly innovations while also enjoying unprecedented success on the pitch over the last decade.

I visited during the club's first season in the Football League in 2017/18, following their promotion through the play-offs with a 3-1 win over Tranmere Rovers in the final at Wembley, although it was not my first appearance at the often-dubbed 'Little Club on the Hill'. Like with Fleetwood Town's Highbury Stadium, I had undertaken a recce with my laptop and reporter's cap while accompanying Braintree Town during their days in the National League, so I had prior knowledge of the scenic approach along twisting country lanes, and the lofty, rural setting of the miniature stadium with a capacity of just over 5,000.

Forest Green were already making waves in the footballing world when I covered the Iron's 2-0 away win in March 2014, although at the time it was still a vegetarian football club (one of Vince's first acts was to ban red meat from the club menu), not officially a vegan one. That change came when Rovers became the first club to host a 'vegan football match' in 2015. Two years later they were officially recognised as the 'world's first vegan football club' on receiving the trademark from the Vegan Society. Fajitas, sweet potato fries, veggie burgers and Quorn and leek pies were all on offer in the club restaurant when I turned up with Colchester United for a League Two tussle on Easter Monday 2018. It was a culinary delight, without a meat burger, cup of Bovril or chocolate Mars bar in sight.

Having spent nearly the first 100 years of their life pottering around in the lower leagues of Stroud and then Gloucestershire, Rovers were promoted to the Southern League as Hellenic League Premier Division champions in 1982, and then reached the Conference in 1998. But it was only after Vince took over as a major shareholder and chairman in 2010 that financially-troubled Rovers underwent a revolution, both on and off the pitch. By the time of the club's elevation to the Football League in 2017, following three successive play-off campaigns, Rovers' non-footballing innovations had already captured the imagination and taken root.

Over the years, the New Lawn has become a home to the world's first organic football pitch, fertilised with cow manure, and also the first solar-powered, GPS-directed robot lawn mower, affectionately called the 'mow bot'. Solar panels have been installed in the stadium roof and surrounding area, and rainwater is collected to use for irrigating the pitch, to avoid a dependence on water mains. And so the list goes on.

On the organic pitch, the U's coped well in the eco-friendly environment. I watched from the press box in the main East Stand, looking out over the shallow open terracing of the west side opposite to rolling fields beyond, as goals from Drey Wright and Ben

The view from the press box at the New Lawn, situated in the Cotswolds. (CM)

Stevenson secured a 2-1 win for the Essex visitors. Perched on top of a hill on the site of old school playing fields, only about 200 yards away from its former long-term home (The Lawn), I imagine this can be a wickedly cold place to watch football on a deep mid-winter afternoon, especially for the away fans exposed to the elements on the uncovered far side. Fortunately, it was a mild early April afternoon when the U's first came to town.

I was still digesting my vegan fajita and sweet potato fries when Wright broke the deadlock inside the first 20 seconds, bundling home from close range from Sammie Szmodics's low cross. Rovers levelled through striker Reuben Reid's 37th-minute penalty, but the U's started the second half just as impressively as they had the first with midfielder Stevenson netting what proved to be the winner just 85 seconds after the restart. The Wolves loanee arrowed a glorious 20-yard drive into the far corner of the net. The result left John McGreal's men four points adrift of the play-offs, with five games remaining, while Mark Cooper's Forest Green were six points and two places clear of the relegation zone.

The U's only picked up one more point from their last five games, to drift into mid-table, but Rovers picked up a vital seven more points, which proved crucial, because they finished their inaugural season in the Football League just a point clear of the relegation zone and second-from-bottom Barnet.

I resisted the temptation to stop for a chicken burger on my long 200-mile journey home from Gloucestershire to Suffolk that Easter evening. In fact, I already felt a little fitter, and a little healthier, perhaps helped by the steep walk up from the town centre to The New Lawn before kick-off, as well as the plant-based diet. From now on, it would be vegan eateries rather than greasy spoon cafes for me, with just the odd lapse here and there.

At least that's what I told myself.

122 KASSAM STADIUM

Club: Oxford United
Founded: 1893 (as Headington United)
Ground: Kassam Stadium (since 2001)
First visit: 14 January 2020; Oxford 0 Ipswich 0

A wild night in Oxford. You can't beat it.

The Kassam Stadium, the home of Oxford United since 2001, played host to one of the most weather-beaten games of football I have seen in many a year, in mid-January 2020.

With the exception of Ipswich Town's home clash with Leicester City the week before Christmas in 2010, staged in a glorious winter wonderland during the Roy Keane era – when the pitch was covered in snow, the lines had to keep being cleared, and Portman Road was home to a blizzard – this Town trip to Oxford featured the most extreme weather conditions I can remember while cowering in a press box.

The torrential rain falling during Town's League One stalemate at the Kassam Stadium, as viewed from the press box in early 2020. (CM)

Wind and rain; rain and wind.

The heavens opened that evening. Would the match start? Would the match finish?

The shrewd money would have been on an abandonment, especially when referee Tom Nield took off the players for an 18-minute period during the worst of the weather, when the ball had difficulty rolling across the sodden surface. But the players did come back on to play out a fairly predictable goalless draw.

Keane's men were already 3-0 up against visiting Leicester when referee Stuart Attwell called for a 17-minute halt in play early in the second half to clear the pitch. Play then resumed and Town ran out comfortable 3-0 winners in that Championship duel. But there was no such luck for Paul Lambert's troops at the blue-seated Kassam. The match escaped an abandonment but neither side really looked like scoring. Town had appeals for a penalty turned down on the stroke of half-time when striker James Norwood appeared to be upended in the box, while Karl Robinson's Oxford side threatened late on through a long-range shot by Josh Ruffels, which was smothered by keeper Will Norris. But that was just about it.

The wind and rain had won the day, or rather the night. Town missed a chance to burst back into the League One automatic promotion zone, while Oxford consolidated themselves in the play-off slots. The highlight, for me, was munching on a pie while watching the rain lashing down from the warmth of the press lounge, a welcome haven which affords a great view of the pitch through big glass windows at the rear of the resplendent South Stand.

I found the whole experience quite apt on this, my first visit, given the 'stormy' start to life for the Kassam Stadium. Oxford's proposed new home, after 76 years at their beloved Manor Ground from 1926 to 2001, was plagued by problems long before a ball was kicked in anger. Even now it looks strange and eerie, with its one completely open West End overlooking a car park, a stark contrast to the three big stands that otherwise skirt the pitch.

And no, for once I didn't have that reassuring ability to see my car from the press box (unlike past visits to the likes of Blackpool and Exeter, when their stadiums were being upgraded and stands demolished). Instead, my car was parked half a mile up Grenoble Road as a result of me having lingered a bit too long in the city centre earlier in the day, watching the rowers on the River Thames and sizing up a few of the 45 university colleges and private halls, wondering which one I would have attended if I had studied just that bit harder at school. Christ Church probably, or maybe Magdalen College.

The Kassam Stadium is situated about four miles south of the city centre and its array of university colleges, in the Blackbird Leys area. And despite only having three sides, it still looks an impressive stadium. The three stands are all substantial and the entrance is very striking with its reflective glass panelling, especially when the rain is hammering down. But there was a time when it looked like the place would remain a skeleton, no more than an expensive white elephant. Indeed, the early days of the Kassam were rocky, very rocky.

Construction started in 1996 but was suspended before Christmas 1997, blighted by financial problems. It was a long suspension. In fact, tools were downed and no further work was done until February 2000, following Firoz Kassam's purchase of the club in early 1999. Oxford's uncertainty off the pitch was mirrored by the uncertainty on it. The club's best players were sold to ease the financial difficulties, so that although construction had started around the time that the U's had won promotion to the second tier, two relegations soon followed, with the club finally beginning life at their new ground in the fourth tier.

Worse was to follow, before things got any better. Home form at the Kassam was pretty dreadful during the early months, and the unthinkable happened in 2005/06 with relegation out of the Football League. Oxford fans could have been excused for starting to pine for life back at the Manor Ground.

But the good times did return to Oxford. They were back in the Football League after a four-year absence in 2010, and regained League One status six years later as runners-up to Northampton, on the back of former Colchester United loanee Kemar Roofe's 26-goal spree across all competitions.

The Kassam Stadium is a happier place to be, even on a wild night in January.

123 KINGSMEADOW

Club: AFC Wimbledon
Founded: 2002
Ground: Kingsmeadow (opened 1989, AFC Wimbledon 2002–2020)
First visit: 11 February 2020; AFC Wimbledon 0 Ipswich 0

Ipswich Town, with me in tow, paid both their first and last visit to Kingsmeadow, in Norbiton, Kingston upon Thames, on a cold February Tuesday evening.

I, for that matter, had actually been to Kingsmeadow once before, or rather next door at the Kingston Athletics Centre behind the aptly named Athletics End, back in 2009. The sporting competition was a Southern Inter-Counties athletics meeting for under-13s (boys and girls), a rather specialist event, I know, but then my youngest step-son Harry was representing Suffolk over the 100m and 200m sprints, so I had a good reason to be in attendance. We were holidaying in a caravan in the New Forest at the time, so it was not too far to travel to leafy Surrey.

There was not too much excitement that day but, in truth, it was probably still more riveting than the fare served up on Town's visit for a League One contest, just a few metres away, for a goalless 'cracker' in early 2020.

There are 0-0s, and then there are 0-0s. Some are rip-roaring, incident-packed affairs, the deadlock unbroken but the supporters still treated to a performance of flair, passion and aggression. Others are dull in the extreme. And 'dull' summed up my only Kingsmeadow footballing experience, during the Wombles' 18th and last year at the stadium.

Still, when I was watching young Harry charge around the Kingston track in the summer of 2009, neighbouring AFC Wimbledon had only just secured promotion to the Conference Premier after being crowned Conference South champions. It was their fourth promotion in a magical spell which saw them clinch six promotions in just 13 seasons to be propelled from the Combined Counties League Premier to League One. Not bad for a club that had only been formed in 2002, in response to Wimbledon FC's move to Milton Keynes the following year.

Kingsmeadow, originally the home of Kingstonian FC, who built the complex in 1989, has been much-changed since my earlier track and field experience next door. It has been extended and redeveloped over the years, while still retaining its small, non-league identity, tucked away behind houses just off the busy Kingston Road. In fact, it is easy to miss, albeit for the smart entrance with its arched 'Kingsmeadow' sign on top, and some slender floodlights behind.

Inside, the place is a little cramped and even claustrophobic, especially if you happen to be one of a big gathering of away supporters packed tightly on the partially covered shallow terrace along the side of the pitch in the East Stand. It pays to be tall in such an environment. I was lucky to be shoehorned into the overspill area of the press box, in

The teams emerge from the tunnel at Kingsmeadow, with the press box behind, with the author sitting low to the left, in 2020. (WP)

the Paul Strank Stand opposite, which doubled up as the away directors' section. It was like a double booking. Town owner Marcus Evans, renowned for being a bit of a recluse, especially when it comes to the media spotlight, was sitting just behind and was therefore ironically in the press overspill, certainly a first. He did not look particularly comfortable.

The whole stadium doesn't hold more than 5,000 – the official capacity is just 4,850, with 2,265 seats in the Paul Strank Stand and Kingston Road End combined – but the fans have the advantage of being very close to the action, and within touching distance of the players, especially at the Athletics End. The banter between supporters and officials smacks of non-league, usually ending in wry smiles all round.

And although we didn't know it at the time, this was to be the third-last AFC Wimbledon home match held at Kingsmeadow, before they moved in to a new stadium at their old Plough Lane site in November 2020, via a brief stay as tenants at Loftus Road for a few fixtures. Two more goalless draws followed, against Blackpool and Bolton, before the season was cut short by the coronavirus pandemic in mid-March.

On the pitch that night, Town blew several chances to score in the second half but, as happened for so much of the truncated 2019/20 season, they came up short. For me, the two highlights were Town striker James Norwood rattling the underside of the bar, and the media rep asking me whether I wanted tea or coffee for the half-time interval. Small pleasures.

Otherwise, nothing much happened, just as 11 years earlier that under-13 inter-counties athletics meeting was largely uneventful. For the record, Harry did not win, or medal, but, as we all know, it's the taking part that counts.

And again, for the record, 11 years later during the half-time interval, I chose tea, not coffee.

124 MOOR LANE

Club: Salford City
Founded: 1940 (as Salford Central)
Ground: Moor Lane (since 1978)
First visit: 22 February 2020; Salford 1 Colchester 2

The rise of Salford City, in the same vein as Fleetwood Town and Forest Green Rovers, has been rapid. On the pitch, the Greater Manchester club celebrated promotion four times in just five seasons, between 2014 and 2019, to leapfrog from the Northern Premier League Division One to the EFL League Two; and off the pitch, Moor Lane has been completely transformed, with the old stadium demolished to make way for four new stands during 2017.

Sure, there is a Meccano-look and a non-league whiff to Moor Lane, with its red-painted metal structures and its temporary containers and cabins dotted around, housing the toilets, club shop, food outlets and alike. The perimeter fence can also give the impression of a prison rather than a football stadium, but really Salford City's revamped new home is more than adequate. In fact, it does a fine job, helped by the surrounding leafy lanes, framed by tall trees.

This was the last of my 'first visits' before the coronavirus lockdown, Colchester United marking their first appearance at a rain-soaked and windswept Moor Lane with a 2-1 away win in February 2020. Just as at Oxford United's Kassam Stadium from a month earlier, the match was dogged by heavy rain storms which threatened to turn Salford's sloping pitch – it slopes from one side to the other, down from the Moor Lane Stand towards the Nevile Road Stand – into an unplayable quagmire. Fortunately, the rain did ease and, after the muddy surface had passed a couple of pitch inspections, a half-decent League Two tussle ensued.

I had left Suffolk well before the crack of dawn, on the stroke of 5am, to reach south Manchester in time to take part in a local parkrun with my nephew Matt Le Poidevin, a medical student at the university. Like all good medical students, he was rather the worse for wear after a big night out, and was nursing a sore hip after a fall during the early hours. In fact, he was still in bed when I rang the front door bell of his student house, at 8.30am, but a quick turnaround saw us both on the start line of the Fletcher Moss parkrun, close to the River Mersey in nearby Didsbury, in time for the 9am start.

The cobwebs were blown away by a swift 5k around Fletcher Moss Park, though both of us finished way behind a first-placed young Dutchman whom we surmised was wearing a pair of Nike Vaporfly shoes, a brand famed for their world record-breaking feats. Our respective pairs of trainers, shoddy by comparison, had four different coloured laces between them, testimony to the impoverished lifestyles of a regional sports hack and a fourth-year medical student.

The view from the press box at Moor Lane, with the spire of St Paul's Church in the background. (CM)

Back on the League Two football trail, we agreed to meet before kick-off at Moor Lane, nine miles to the north on the other side of Manchester. I was bound for the press box in the Neville Road Stand, which had replaced the former Main Stand, while my nephew Matt had planned to join the Colchester United away fans on the East Terrace. However, true to form, Matt and his student friends rather misjudged the timing of the taxi journey from south Manchester to Salford, and arrived just as referee Andy Haines blew his whistle to start the match. They nipped in to the West Terrace on the other side of the ground, just as another squally shower struck to further saturate a sticky playing surface.

The West Terrace had been the first of the four stands to be constructed in a frenzy of building activity, from when the planned renovations were given the go-ahead in October 2016 to when the whole new stadium was finished and officially opened by former Manchester United boss Sir Alex Ferguson in October 2017. The transformation had been completed inside just a ten-month period, with four bright red stands enclosed around one roof, with a capacity of just over 5,000. The whole place was unrecognisable from its former look.

It was tight but compact in the South Stand. There were just six rows of seats along this side of the pitch, and the press section was towards one end, closest to the West Terrace, with the rain sweeping across to dampen team sheets and give laptops a quick soaking. I met up with Matt and his fellow medics at half-time, jostling for position in the queues for burgers behind the West Terrace, by which time Colchester had already established a good 2-1 lead.

Teenager Kwame Poku broke the deadlock with a terrific solo goal, his curling 20-yarder zooming past Salford keeper Kyle Letheren, and Guayan international Callum Harriott doubled the U's lead with an equally clinical low drive in the 41st minute. The hosts, safely in mid-table, scored before half-time through Fleetwood loanee Ash Hunter's close-range finish. Graham Alexander's side went on to dominate the second half, bossing possession and territory, but John McGreal's visitors held on to cement their play-off berth.

McGreal revealed, 'We were at the ground at 8am this morning [three hours after I had left Suffolk!] because we knew that there was a pitch inspection, so we asked the groundsman to get to work on the pitch. When we got there the pitch was unplayable, but there were four or five hours to work on it. I know it's a new stadium, and so the fans want to come here, but they turned up in their numbers and really backed us.'

As for Salford, they are still heading on an upward trajectory.

When five of Manchester United's famous Class of '92 joined forces with businessman Peter Lim to take over the club in 2014, one of the group, Ryan Giggs, revealed that the new consortium's target was to bring Championship football to Salford City within 15 years. And they were well ahead of schedule when securing promotion to the Football League just five years in by beating AFC Fylde in the 2018/19 National League play-off final. Another member of the Class of '92, David Beckham, bought a ten per cent share in the club in early 2019, so Moor Lane is a good place for celebrity spotting.

In fact, the new-look stadium was to my liking. The floodlights are eye-catching, modelled in the shape of the club badge with a six-sided red frame, and the view from the press box, while low-down near pitch level, was dominated by the spire of St Paul's Church to the north-east, a rather satisfying sight. I find it's always comforting to have a church spire in the background, when looking out from a Football League press box, certainly preferable to a motorway service station or a sprawling car park.

Industrial it might look, with all its containers, cabins and metal framework, but Salford's Moor Lane, with its sloping pitch, temporary toilets and surrounding trees, is a fine place to spend a Saturday afternoon, even if the driving rain is sweeping through the press box, and your nephew is nursing sore legs and a sore head in the packed West Terrace.

SECTION SEVEN – BEST AND WORST: MANAGERS AND PLAYERS HAVE THEIR SAY

Here's where the experts take over.

A selection of former Ipswich Town and Colchester United players and managers, from the 1970s through to the current day, reveal their choices for 'best' and 'worst' away grounds.

Below are the fruits of these individual interrogations.

RICHARD WILKINS

(Colchester United 1986–1990 and 1996–2000, 325 appearances; Cambridge United 1990–'94, 105 appearances)

Favourite away ground: Highbury

'I was lucky enough to play at Wembley twice during my career, but as a one-off Highbury was a bit special for an FA Cup quarter-final tie with Cambridge United [March 1991]. The ground was packed, and there were about 8,000 Cambridge fans in the crowd. The ground was all enclosed, and the fans were almost on top of you, a bit like Colchester United's old Layer Road ground in that respect. There was also such a camber that you couldn't see the lines on the opposite side of the pitch. We gave Arsenal a real good test that afternoon, and at 1-1 John Taylor went through on goal twice, trying to round keeper David Seaman. On both occasions, Seaman was the winner. Arsenal went on to win the league that season [1990/91], so it showed how well we did to push them, and the winner was very fortuitous with Tony Adams kneeing it over the line.'

Worst away ground: The Shay

'I had the misfortune to play at Halifax's The Shay a few times, usually night games, so we would have to travel up during the day [from Colchester]. It was always so cold and so miserable, and the pitch was not great either. They didn't have the greatest support, it always seemed to be blowing a gale and the changing rooms were not the best.'

JOHN WARK

(Ipswich Town 1975–1984, 1988–1990 and 1991–'97, 679 appearances)

Favourite away ground: Anfield

'Although I ended up playing for Liverpool [from 1984–'88], I always loved playing at Anfield as a member of the visiting team. Not that we [Ipswich Town] ever did that well. We won just once [in 1995] during my time, but the atmosphere was always unique. The home fans always have fun. I remember playing in one match, when I got struck in the nether regions. It was very painful, prompting the home fans to start singing "Johnny Wark, Johnny Wark" in very high-pitched voices!'

Worst away ground: Old Trafford

'Ironically, although I often got some good results with Ipswich at Old Trafford, especially during the early 1980s, this ground will forever be scarred for me by our 9-0 defeat [March 1995]. I have nothing against Old Trafford, and never feared playing there, but that 9-0 still hurts to this day.'

GEORGE BURLEY

(Ipswich Town 1973–1985, 500 appearances; Ipswich manager 1994–2002; Colchester United player-manager June to December 1994)

Favourite away ground: Old Trafford

'It didn't get any better than making my debut away at Manchester United as a 17-year-old. It was a dream come true being up against a player like George Best in my very first game, and in such a superb stadium as Old Trafford, with its terrific atmosphere.'

Worst away ground: Deepdale

'I can never remember getting a good result from visits to Preston North End. I also lost in the play-offs there, so I don't have any good memories. Every player has a ground such as this.'

GERAINT WILLIAMS

(Ipswich Town 1992–98, 264 appearances; Colchester United 1998–2000, 43 appearances; Colchester manager 2006–08)

Favourite away ground: Anfield

'My first visit to Anfield was like a dream come true. I wasn't that young at the time, aged about 25 and playing for Derby County. About an hour before kick off, the manager Arthur Cox got up and left the dressing room to go pitchside. Even by that time the whole of the Kop was packed, with the fans singing and swaying. I had a massive big smile on my face when I saw that scene. Arthur had been concerned that some of the players would be scared, playing in such an atmosphere, and some of them did keep their heads down and

Geraint Williams, as Colchester United boss, talking to George Burley, manager of Southampton. (WP)

could not look up when they went down the tunnel, but he needn't have worried about me. He saw the smile on my face and knew that I would be all right. The Liverpool fans did not let me down that day. It made a massive impression on me. I never got to play for Liverpool, but the next best thing was playing against them.'

Worst away ground: Springfield Park

'I remember going to Wigan's old ground on a Tuesday night in winter when the pitch was terrible. We were ankle-deep in mud, it was tipping down with rain and there were only about 1,500 fans inside the stadium. Alan Ball was playing for us [Bristol Rovers] and he chose to wear rubber boots, not studs, despite the awful playing surface. Yet he completely ran the show. He managed to play one-touch football that night, a touch of class, helping us to a 5-0 victory. Alan showed that you shouldn't blame any pitch, however bad. He could play on any surface, a proper footballer.'

KEM IZZET

(Colchester United 2001–2013, 473 appearances)

Favourite away ground: Elland Road

'The atmosphere was always excellent away at Leeds, and the place oozed history. However, being half-Turkish lined me up for some serious abuse from the Leeds fans!'

Worst away ground: Victoria Park

'I've chosen Hartlepool's home ground, purely down to how cold it always was whenever I played there with Colchester United. It would take an eternity to get up there, and then it would be disgustingly cold. But I must also mention Millwall's The Den. That was just a

Kem Izzet, in action scoring at Portsmouth in 2001. (WP)

horrible place to play football because of the amount of abuse I always received whenever I got close to the home fans.'

MICK MILLS

(Ipswich Town 1966–1982, club record 741 appearances; Colchester United manager January to May 1990)

Favourite away ground: White Hart Lane

'Ipswich supporters might not like this, but I couldn't wait to play at White Hart Lane because I was a Tottenham fan as a kid. So that made it very personal for me, playing at that ground. There was also no better atmosphere in the country. Outside England, Real Madrid's Bernabéu was my favourite place to play. In general, the football stadiums are better now than back in my day. They are more impressive structures with excellent facilities. However, the atmosphere was far better back in those days [1970s and '80s] There was great energy from the supporters, standing on the terraces, which translated on to the pitch and into the players.'

Worst away ground: Ayresome Park

'I never liked playing at Middlesbrough's old ground. The pitch was too wide open, and it was always freezing cold and usually blowing a gale whenever we visited. Ayresome Park was also where we finally failed in our bid to win the title [the First Division, on 2 May 1981], even though we were leading 1-0 that day.'

JOE KEITH

(Colchester United 1999–2005, 246 games)

Favourite away ground: Hillsborough

'Scoring two goals in two matches there, within a few months of each other, must mean Hillsborough is top of my list. I scored with a shot into the top corner in a 1-0 win towards the end of one season [April 2004], and then scored with a free kick in a 3-0 win at the start of the next season [August 2004]. So two goals, two wins, two clean sheets, and the fact Hillsborough has so much history with such big crowds seals it for me. However, Tranmere's Prenton Park is also up there among my favourites, even though it wasn't a particularly nice place to go. The fans were hostile, but I scored a couple of headers up there. It was a good stadium in which to play football, there was a big main stand, and on one of my first visits [in 2002] Jason Koumas was playing for Tranmere. We just couldn't get near him!'

Worst away ground: The Den

'As soon as the Millwall fans read in the matchday programme that I used to be on West Ham's books, that guaranteed I would be in for a lot of abuse. It was always so hostile at The Den, and I don't think I ever won there. I didn't play the day that Colchester lost 6-1 on Boxing Day [2000)], but I was there watching from the stands. I used to take most of the corners, so I got a lot of abuse from the home fans.'

TOM LAPSLIE

(Colchester United 2014 onwards, 160 appearances going into 2021)

Favourite away ground: Brisbane Road

'It's a close call between Leyton Orient and Cambridge United, because we take a big following to both venues. I think that always helps, to have a big away support, and we always seem to have good results whenever we go to either club as well. But I would edge towards Leyton Orient's Brisbane Road, as I was born just down the road from the stadium and so therefore friends and family who supported Leyton Orient would be at the game.'

Worst away ground: Crown Ground

'The changing rooms at Accrington Stanley are tiny, and we never seem to get a good result up there, so the away changing room is always a deflating place to be after the game. Usually there's only one shower that "works", and by that I mean it drips cold water. After a bad result it's a very sombre atmosphere in the dressing room, at the best of times, and its made doubly worse when you have to queue up for half-an-hour for a cold shower!'

TERRY BUTCHER

(Ipswich Town 1976–86, 351 appearances)

Favourite away ground: Bernabéu

'There's nothing quite like the home of Real Madrid. As soon as you arrive, you can tell that the place lives and breathes football. That feeling is everywhere. It's a great amphitheatre, and a daunting place to play football.'

Worst away ground: Carrow Road

'My worst experience was losing a League Cup semi-final at arch rivals Norwich in 1985, and it was made worse by the fact that the dressing rooms were temporary because of work to a new stand following a fire the previous year. That meant the two temporary dressing rooms were stacked on top of each other, which meant we could hear Norwich celebrating. It was a terrible night.'

PAUL GIBBS

(Colchester United 1995–'97, 56 appearances)

Favourite away ground: Victoria Park

I found Hartlepool's ground to be very intimidating, and actually hated it. In fact, I could even put it second on my list of worst grounds, and yet perversely it was where I made my professional league debut, with Colchester United. So it is a bittersweet place for me. I would love to include Wembley as well, because I class that as an away ground and I was lucky enough to play there three times, with two defeats and one victory, while also scoring. So Victoria Park and Wembley, chalk and cheese.'

Worst away ground: Brunton Park

'Carlisle United tops the list, because that's where I broke my leg. I have no happy memories of that place.'

CRAIG FORREST

(Ipswich Town 1985–1997, 304 appearances; Colchester United on loan 1987–88, 11 appearances)

Favourite away ground: Anfield

'Bruce Grobbelaar was my idol when I was growing up, as he was a Vancouver Whitecap. Also we saw a lot of Liverpool on TV in Canada. Winning at Anfield was a special moment in my career.'

Worst away ground: The Den

'It was intimidating even just driving to Millwall's old Den. The tunnel leading on to the pitch was tight, and the fans would absolutely abuse you from the start of the match to the finish.'

PAUL ABRAHAMS

(Colchester United 1991–95 and 1996–99, 178 appearances)

Favourite away ground: Wembley

'I was spoilt being able to call Layer Road and Griffin Park as football homes, both steeped in history and tight to the pitch, which generated noise and atmosphere no matter what the size of the crowd. But I have to settle for one of the most iconic stadiums of all-time, Wembley Stadium, which I visited with Colchester United on no less than three occasions during the 1990s. Very few get that opportunity once, let alone three times, and being part of a play-off winning squad [1997/98], and the year before at the final of the Auto Windscreens Shield [Football League Trophy] when almost 50,000 fans turned up, the majority of whom came from my home town of Colchester, one fifth of the 150,000 population, gives me fond memories to this day.'

Worst away ground: The Shay

'My career was in an era when all grounds were creaking at the seams, and stands were randomly being removed, improved or erected. Grounds I vividly remember include Northampton Town's County Ground, where we used to fetch balls off the cricket pitch, and Belle Vue on the day that Donny [Doncaster Rovers] were relegated from the Football League and the fans kept invading the pitch. Other memories are of getting bitten by the River Severn midges at Shrewsbury's Gay Meadow, and the famous slope at Underhill where you could be 4-0 up against Barnet at half-time and still lose 5-4!

'However, The Shay at Halifax was an experience that left a lasting impression. I recall cars behind the goal, a former speedway track and at least four stands down the side of the cow-field pitch, all of different shapes and sizes, one of which would have done well to accommodate more than 20 fans. I spent 90 minutes taking in the scenery and being intrigued by Jimmy Case's hearing aids while trying not to be kicked by him. Fortunately, Jimmy must have been nearly 50 by then, and I was a little more mobile and still in my teens. Yet somehow he still managed to leave one or two on me!'

SIMON MILTON

(Ipswich Town 1987–98, 338 appearances)

Favourite away ground: Craven Cottage

'I was born in Fulham, so always wanted to play at Craven Cottage, but during all my years at Ipswich the two clubs were never in the same division. However, we did draw them in the League Cup. I was not the first in the Milton family to play at Fulham. My cousin Steve played for them, as did an uncle before the war. In fact, there is quite a family history attached to the club, and there were about 20 members of my family watching that day [17 September 1996]. I ended up scoring a wonder goal, in about the 78th minute, so it's a brilliant memory for me. It's a great club, approached along proper London streets down by the River Thames, even though it lives in the shadow of Stamford Bridge. I had the good fortune to play at all the top grounds in the country, but Craven Cottage was my favourite.'

Worst away ground: Boundary Park

'I used to hate playing at Oldham, back in the days when they played on the dreaded plastic pitch. Joe Royle was the manager and they had a very good team, including the likes of Ian Marshall, Mike Milligan, Andy Ritchie and Denis Irwin. We never got anything out of our visits. Oldham were magnificent on that surface, and it was always freezing cold.'

GAVIN JOHNSON

(Ipswich Town 1989–95, 158 appearances; Colchester United 1999–2005, 167 appearances)

Favourite away ground: White Hart Lane

'I was a big Tottenham fan as a lad, growing up watching the likes of Glenn Hoddle on the TV, so it was a dream come true to play at the old White Hart Lane. I played there a couple of times, but the one that made the biggest impression was when Frank Yallop fired a long-range screamer into the roof of the net [a 2-0 win for Ipswich in January 1993]. Funny enough, I would also include Springfield Park as one of my favourites, having played there for Wigan Athletic just before the club moved to their new stadium. There was usually a good atmosphere, especially when we were going for promotion and we had

Gavin Johnson, nursing a broken leg at Port Vale in September, 2002. (WP)

crowds of three or four thousand. It reminded me a bit of Layer Road on a Friday night under the lights, with the fans so close to the pitch and almost on top of you.'

Worst away ground: Vale Park

'From a personal point of view, Port Vale sticks out because it was where I broke my leg while playing for Colchester during Steve Whitton's era.'

SCOTT MCGLEISH

(Colchester United 1996 and 2001–04, 184 appearances)

Favourite away ground: Emirates Stadium

'This is an easy choice for me to make. I played there for Leyton Orient in an FA Cup fifth round replay tie [2 March 2011], after we had drawn 1-1 with Arsenal at home.'

Worst away ground: Crown Ground

'Accrington was probably the worst. The changing rooms were so tiny, and you then had to walk down some concrete steps to get to the pitch, which always seemed to be very boggy every time I played there.'

THE FINAL WORD

JUST A few weeks after my visit to Salford's Moor Lane, for ground number 124, the COVID-19 pandemic took hold.

Journalists were still permitted to attend matches, a real privilege, though I must confess I have not enjoyed sitting in press boxes while all around is soulless and empty.

To all intents and purposes, most games I have witnessed inside empty stadiums have felt nothing more than training exercises, more low-key than even an early-summer pre-season friendly.

Football needs fans. Even football journalists need fans!

Post-pandemic, there is naturally no end to the total number of Football League clubs and grounds you can visit, either in the press box or in the away end. That final whistle never blows.

Carl Marston interviewing John-Joe O'Toole at a Colchester United press day in 2012.

Clubs occasionally move homes, like Brentford's switch from Griffin Park to the Brentford Community Stadium in 2020, while others join the 92 club via promotion from the National League, like Harrogate Town and Barrow both achieved in 2020.

Hence there is always another prized destination just around the corner for you to conquer.

Personally, I arrived on the journalistic scene just a little too late to frequent the press boxes of the Old Show Ground, Fellows Park and Loakes Park, the former homes of Scunthorpe (until 1988), Walsall and Wycombe (both until 1990) respectively.

And as yet I have never had the pleasure of reporting on a team at the Tottenham Hotspur Stadium or Manchester City's Etihad Stadium.

But I live in hope.

My flask is always at the ready, and my laptop is always fully charged. All I need is a nod and a wink, and the right kind of fixture, perhaps a surprise cup draw or an appropriate friendly, and I will be at the club's main reception uttering the immortal words, 'Press pass, please!'

Carl Marston working in the press box at Rochdale's Spotland during his 1,000th U's match.

BS - #0003 - 050721 - C0 - 234/156/20 - PB - 9781780916224